THE FORBIDDEN BODY

The Forbidden Body

Sex, Horror, and the Religious Imagination

Douglas E. Cowan

NEW YORK UNIVERSITY PRESS

New York

NEW YORK UNIVERSITY PRESS
New York
www.nyupress.org

References to Internet websites (URLs) were accurate at the time of writing. Neither the author nor New York University Press is responsible for URLs that may have expired or changed since the manuscript was prepared.

Library of Congress Cataloging-in-Publication Data
Names: Cowan, Douglas E., author.
Title: The forbidden body : sex, horror, and the religious imagination / Douglas E. Cowan.
Description: New York : New York University Press, [2022] | Includes bibliographical references and index.
Identifiers: LCCN 2021034899 | ISBN 9781479803101 (hardback) | ISBN 9781479803118 (paperback) | ISBN 9781479803125 (ebook) | ISBN 9781479803132 (ebook other)
Subjects: LCSH: Sex--Religious aspects. | Human body--Religious aspects. | Horror. | Popular culture--Religious aspects.
Classification: LCC BL65.S4 C69 2022 | DDC 791.43/6820212--dc23
LC record available at https://lccn.loc.gov/2021034899

New York University Press books are printed on acid-free paper, and their binding materials are chosen for strength and durability. We strive to use environmentally responsible suppliers and materials to the greatest extent possible in publishing our books.

Manufactured in the United States of America

10 9 8 7 6 5 4 3 2 1

Also available as an ebook

Some people prefer their sex and horror separate,
others not so much.
This is for them.

CONTENTS

PREFACE

"To a new world of gods and monsters!" So says Dr. Pretorius in James Whale's classic *Bride of Frankenstein*. The Pretorian proclamation notwithstanding, gods and monsters have been with us for as long as we can remember, and central to the religious imagination since time immemorial. Serious attention to "religion and the monstrous," however, is relatively recent. Timothy Beal's *Religion and Its Monsters* has become something of a classic in its own right, concerned principally with what we might call "a biblical genealogy of religious monstrosity." Or, put differently, "the Bible and things that have scared the shit out of us." Scott Poole's masterful *Monsters in America*, on the other hand, eschews a biblical approach, considering the monstrous in more historical perspective. Both, however, avoid including sex, sexuality, and sexual monstrosity in their discussions. Indeed, most of the many other scholars, writers, and critics who could be mentioned here do the same.

Let's talk about sex, baby.

This book explores some of the dark, disturbing places where sexual behavior, erotic and sexual representation, and the sexualized body come together with religion and horror. If horror is one axis of transgression across the cultural domains of religious belief and practice, when scary stories are sexualized (or eroticized) in the context of the religious imagination, their transgressive effects are intensified. That is, when our sexual bodies are located at the spiritual heart of horror, our most regressive attitudes toward that which is most basic to our nature are often revealed and reinforced.

Before we begin, though, a couple of caveats.

First and foremost, books such as this should always be considered as invitations rather than exhortations or interpretive foreclosures. Ways of looking at horror, rather than *the* way of looking. In this context, stories of any kind are only useful as exemplars for exploring larger theoretical constructs, methodological approaches, and landscapes of the religious imagination. That is, they are less important in themselves, in what we learn about *them*, than in what they disclose, discover, or discomfort about *us*. This point is often missed both by those who adopt a "complete guide to everything" approach, as well as by those who criticize writers for not dealing with their favorite novel, movie, television series, video-game franchise, or what have you. The former assume too much, believing that the "complete guide to insert-pop-culture-product-here" is not only possible but desirable, while the latter assume too little, implying that if their favorites are not discussed, then the topic has not been considered in sufficient depth.

Rather, the choices we make are only and always pathways into a greater understanding of the religious imagination, but they do not, nor could they ever, represent the sum of its contents. There is simply no way to catalogue, let alone consider in any depth, the entirety of the horror mode. So, the particular details of a short story such as Caitlín Kiernan's "Houses Under the Sea," for example, or John Guillermin's 1976 remake of *King Kong*, are less important in themselves than for what they can tell us about the ways in which we configure both the unseen order and our varied responses to it, as well as the power that myth and religion still wield, especially when plied in terms of the sexual body.

Second, a word about spoilers: they are an unavoidable reality in any book like this. Readers will learn things about stories and movies that, if they have not read or seen them, they would not otherwise know—including, sometimes, how things end, who the villain really is, or what happens to Little Nell when the train comes 'round the mountain. Narrative context is essential. Too little detail, and those who are not familiar with the story can feel left out. Too much, and you risk assembling a collection of plot synopses strung together with an occasional nod toward an interpretative thread. No choice will satisfy everyone, but that, too, is a reality. To quote Jonathan Z. Smith's *Imagining Religion*, however, I hope that the choices I have made will serve as "exempli gratia of some fundamental issue in the imagination of religion."

My thanks to all those who have challenged and encouraged me in our shared passion for the monstrous, just a few of whom include Rebecca Booth, Valeska Griffiths, and Erin Thompson at House of Leaves Publishing (for permission to build on ideas I first explored in the introduction to *Scared Sacred: Idolatry, Religion, and Worship in the Hor-*

ror Film); Brandon Grafius and John Morehead, editors of *Theology and Horror: Explorations in the Dark Religious Imagination* (for permission to use material from "Consider the Yattering"). In addition to John, with whom I've enjoyed a "horrific" friendship for two decades, I'd like to thank Joe Laycock, James McGrath, Natasha Mikles, Steve Wiggins, and especially my colleague Jeff Wilson. I'm sure that to anyone watching from the outside, our many fruitful conversations about horror, fantasy, and science fiction look like nothing more than full-on nerd sessions, and the both of us, monster nerds. All of you continue to inspire me.

Introduction

It's a scene that plays out every year all over the world. As Hallowe'en approaches, friends gather around a television set, the modern equivalent of a campfire in the woods, and huddle together for a horror movie marathon. Passing around beer and popcorn, they egg each other on as fan favorites unreel on the screen. Some crack jokes, covering their discomfort with bluster and bravado, while others clutch blankets, taking paradoxical delight in the electric *frisson* of their shared startle response. In Wes Craven's *Scream*, a dozen or so such friends giggle, shudder, and flinch at the jump scares in John Carpenter's 1978 classic, *Halloween*. As the dread Michael Myers, wearing an expressionless white mask and wielding an enormous chef's knife, gradually kills off young people who look remarkably like those watching the film, one of them takes a swallow of beer, and asks boozily, "How can you watch this shit over and over?"[1]

Indeed, it's a good question.

And, whenever I am interviewed about horror—usually around Hallowe'en—it inevitably arises: What is it about *horror*? Why do so many of us like to be scared, whether it's in the theater or on the couch, whether reading spooky books or playing games based on events that, if we encountered them in real life, would leave us gibbering in terror? What is the appeal of the ghost story and the monster movie, principal actors in arguably the most durable mode of human storytelling?[2] Because, among other things, *haven't* we seen all these movies, read all these stories, and played all these games before? As one character in the 2016 horror short *Vexed* points out, "I knew the entire plot of the film just by reading the title." When his girlfriend demurs, he shows her the DVD case and deadpans, "*Blood Summer Four: Beach Vacation Massacre?*"[3]

And he's not wrong. Except that that isn't really the point.

Certainly, some horror authors—Stephen King is a good example— kindle the fear response by signaling from the outset what is going to happen, and then daring readers to follow them into the fire. Rather than bad things happening gradually, as in Peter Straub's debut novella, "Blue Rose," or his classic, *Ghost Story*, instead of the creeping anxiety of Shirley Jackson's *Haunting of Hill House* or Mariko Koike's *Graveyard Apartment*, many of King's stories tell us all but explicitly what is going to happen.[4] We know from the opening scenes of *Pet Sematary*, for instance, that little Gage Creed will likely not survive the novel's first act. More than that, we know exactly how he will die, and what will happen after.[5] All that remains is to see how bad things get. In this case, our horror is the slow-motion product of something we know is coming and cannot avoid. It's like an accident we see from a distance, but from which we cannot turn away as we draw ever closer.

Philosopher Noël Carroll, on the other hand, argues that our love of horror is due in large part to a built-in desire to unravel the mystery, to unmask the villain, to find out what happens in the end. In short, we are pattern-seeking creatures, and solving the puzzle contributes to the process by which we bring order to chaos, meaning to a world that in many cases makes no sense. Stories that unfold slowly but surely keep us watching the shadows, peeking around corners, and scanning the tree line to see what, if anything, is there. Is it really a ghost, and, if so, *who* is the ghost? (Think M. Night Shyamalan's *Sixth Sense*, or the first season of *American Horror Story*.) What is the monster really like, and is there really a monster at all? (Think every episode of *Scooby-Doo* you've ever seen, or many of the most famous Victorian ghost stories.) Is the central conflict psychological, supernatural, or some nonexclusive marriage of both? (Think the different ways of reading *Rosemary's Baby* as opposed to the more restricted possibilities available for *The Exorcist*.)[6] And, if there really *is* a monster, who will survive to tell the tale once it steps from the shadows and into the light? (Think Ridley Scott's master class, *Alien*. Full stop.) And Carroll is not wrong either. It is not that some kind of horrific reveal is not a necessary condition of the successful horror experience; it is just that by itself it is not sufficient to explain the encounter as a whole.

Conversely, relying on current academic fashion for evolutionary psychology as an overarching explanation for an astonishingly diverse range of human behaviors—not least of which is our almost universal impulse to religious belief and practice—Mathias Clasen insists that "horror fiction is crucially dependent on evolved properties of the human central nervous system."[7] More than that, he continues, horror "achieves its peculiar affective goal by targeting an evolved defence system, the fear system."[8] Or, put differently, horror succeeds when it tells us scary stories about things that we have evolved to fear. Which is all well and good, I suppose, except that this doesn't tell us very much. And, while not technically incorrect, Clasen's post hoc argument could be made for many different aspects of human evolution: the development of sex-specific arousal cues and mating preferences; our ability to enjoy the taste of things that will not kill us, while generally turning up our noses at things that will at least make us gravely ill; the pleasure we take in music over, say, the sound of an avalanche. Indeed, our ability to associate certain types of sound with the potential for danger is no less "crucially dependent on evolved properties of the human central nervous system" than our ongoing fascination with scary stories or devotion to horror cinema. None of which, however, explains the spectrum of human sexuality, the fact that we have folded food preparation into everything from religious ritual to reality television, or, most importantly, why we continue to fear certain things and not others.

Because, call them the creeps, the jitters, or even the heebie-jeebies, think for a moment about all the different ways we name our fear, the different qualities that mark our widely varied anxieties. We are not talking about synonyms here, as though describing minor variants of the same thing, but different species on the phylogenetic tree of human fearing. *Phobias*, for example, we often label "irrational," though they seem eminently rational to those of us who suffer from them. They may even have provided us some measure of evolutionary advantage: fear of heights keeps us from falling to our deaths, while fear of dark, confined spaces ensures we will not generally venture too far into labyrinthine cave systems. Fear of spiders, well, just makes good sense. *Panic* is different from *dread*—the one triggering our fight-or-flight response, the other burning more slowly in imagined reaction to a danger that may or may not be present. Both of these, however, can differ significantly from *stark terror* and *cosmic horror*, where the former is a function of the potential for our imminent destruction, the latter, certainty of our existential insignificance. Even *despair* is a distinct species of fear, a way of being afraid that is deeply rooted in an inability to see beyond the problems of the present moment.[9]

Regardless of how we catalog the motley crew of human fearing, neither Carroll nor Clasen considers in any real depth why we fear the particular things we do, and why we continue to fear them—especially those things in which both writers insist we no longer believe. Giant sharks, serial killers, and natural disasters may be far less common than horror cinema would have us think, but all of these at least exist somewhere in the real world. Demons, ghosts, and wicked witches, on the other hand, otherworldly beings such as *pontianak* and *kuntilanak*, *yurei* and *yokei*, succubi, incubi, and myriad others besides—all these are different, relying for their chilling power less on the certainty that they do exist than on a lingering uncertainty that they do not.[10] This problem becomes even more enticing when we introduce sex into the horrific equation, that aspect of human behavior and imagination that religion in particular has fought to control more than any other.

And this is precisely where things get interesting.

The Problem of "Religious Questions"

In a number of works, and continuing in this book, I suggest that our species-wide addiction to the fear response, and particularly the range of supernatural horror-worlds it both engenders and perpetuates, has less to do with conviction and assurance than with ambiguity and insecurity. Principally, horror enchants because, even when things turn out "all right" in the end, scary stories consistently challenge our lack of durable answers to what I have taken to calling "properly human questions," the ones we cannot help but ask, and that all but define us as a species: Who are we? Where do we come from? Why do we suffer, what can we do about it, and does it serve any purpose? What happens to us when we die, and is it something we should look forward to—or dread? Is there something or someone else out there, and, if so, does it care about us? And, beating at the heart of all these, arguably the most basic question of all: Do we matter?

While these are colloquially known as "religious questions," they are only idiomatically so. That is, they are often coopted by religion, and relegated to religious professionals as the near-exclusive arbiters of these fundamental aspects of the human experience. But this is not and should not be the case, if for no other reason than that questions of origin and destiny, of purpose and meaning, of suffering and salvation, of divine investment or cosmic indifference belong to us all by virtue of our human being, not the simple fact of our participation in this or that community of faith. Certainly, religious believers seem at times the most concerned to answer these questions and thus to declare propriety over them, but that does not mean that their claims to ownership have any de facto merit. Indeed, perhaps the most terrifying thing about the prospect of a supernatural *demimonde*, a spectral half-world that we sense exists all around us and continue to make real through the stories we tell about it, is that the universe is not only *not* made with us in mind but could very well be populated by vastly powerful beings that have anything but our best interests at heart.[11]

So, we may make it out of the theater alive, survive till the end of the book, beat the boss monster in the final room of the game, and that's fine. But the questions that continually prompt these various storyworld journeys do not go away, regardless of our religious faith and the promises of our gods. And that is the point. The desperate inquiries that drive horrific narratives are not settled, despite those who contend that getting out alive at the end is horror's principal pleasure—and, arguably, religion's single greatest failure to launch in the face of suffering. That is, contrary to so many religious traditions, horror rarely tries to convince us that it has an enduring answer, that there isn't another monster lurking in the shadows, another demon standing in the narthex, another *something* waiting out there somewhere. Hansel and Gretel may have dispatched the wicked witch, but it's still a big, dark, spooky forest. That much hasn't changed in tens of thousands of years, and the delicious problem of horror is that, though the monsters may be defeated for the moment, they have not been destroyed. Our insatiable appetite for sequels, reboots, retellings, and reimaginings—even when we have heard them all before and recognize that remakes rarely hold a candle to the original—means, if nothing else, that the myriad things haunting our night terrors and waking dreams are not gone for good. Monsters come back. Monsters always come back, and the answers that are sufficient for the moment rarely satisfy in all the moments to come.[12]

Religion, on the other hand—not the *religious imagination*, which we will discuss a bit later, but *religion*—is often predicated on the power of exclusivities and the implicit fear of exclusion, on claims to have not only an answer but *the* answer. For those who believe correctly, we are told, who direct their prayers appropriately, perform rituals faithfully, and, for the purposes of this book, keep their bodies in their proper place, things will turn out alright in the cosmic end. In this sense, "religion" could not be more different from "horror." And, because of this, I suspect that many believers agree with theologian Bryan Stone, who contends that "horror is the film genre least amenable to religious sensibilities" and that "rarely have films [in general, though horror specifically] treated religious faith on its own terms or explored religious values and motivations with much complexity."[13]

Contrary to what Stone and similar critics assert, however, religion and horror are not competitors in the arena of the human imagination, the one a scruffy relation rooting for scraps below the high table of the other. Rather, they are cultural siblings, modes of storytelling and world building that share an intimate and paradoxical concern for the same questions that lie at the fluctuating, often terrifying core of what it means to be human. True, not all horror culture is either implicitly or explicitly religious, as religion is popularly understood, but a significant amount is, and much of the rest concerns itself with exploring precisely these properly human questions. In this fashion, "horror stories are popular existentialism," wrote Bram Stoker Award winner Dennis Etchison, which is to say, horror, especially supernatural horror, shows us aspects of the religious imagination at work in popular culture and, not infrequently, in real time.[14] Bryan Stone may believe that in the horror genre "religious symbols [are] splattered together with no rhyme or reason—a little Buddhism here, a little Christianity there, maybe an ancient book, or a crucifix thrown in for good measure," but simply because he is unconvinced by the storyworld rationale does not mean that it is not there.[15] Nor does it mean that millions of other people will not find its presence meaningful, however frightening they might also find its implications. Just because "an ancient book" may mean H. P. Lovecraft's *Necronomicon* or *Warhammer 40K*'s *Codicium Aeternum* (also known as the *Grimoire of True Names*) instead of the Bible or the Qu'ran deprives it of none of the power we have come to lodge in sacred texts. The reality is that, even in their least artfully realized instances, horror movies and scary stories often take religion far more at its word than do many of this faith or that's most ardent followers. By refusing to reduce religious belief or experience to allegory, to diminish any horrific potential by resorting either to psychological metaphor or cinematic veneer, what Stone calls "a pseudo-religious feel," horror culture continually both confronts us with the questions that religion insists it has already answered and questions the substance and limitations of those answers.[16]

In *Sacred Terror*, I explored the religious dimensions of horror, the supposedly sacred things that scare us witless in the dead of night. Building on that, this book asks, Of all the scary things out there, where do we find sex and religion in horrific juxtaposition, and what happens when we do? Whether it is a half-naked woman offered as a sacrifice to some malevolent deity or brutally sexualized *giallo* films such as Sergio Martino's *Mountain of the Cannibal God*, whether it is low-budget movie franchises of soft-core nunsploitation or witchcraft, or simply the erotic difference between the British and Spanish versions of the 1931 *Dracula*, why are sex and horror so often intimately bound together on religion's altar?

For that, grab some popcorn, and let's return for a moment to *Halloween*.

Don't You Know the Rules?

"When do we see breasts?" demands Stuart (Matthew Lillard), leering at his friends and moving closer to the center of *Scream*'s frame. "I want to see Jamie Lee's breasts. When do we *see* Jamie Lee's breasts?"[17]

Randy (Jamie Kennedy), the uber-fan and authority on all things *Halloween*, replies that break-out star Jamie Lee Curtis "was always the virgin in the horror movies. She never showed her tits." According to Randy, this all-but-singular trait allowed Curtis to survive her various horror outings.[18] "Only virgins can do that. Don't you know the rules?" When someone asks, "What rules?" he is shocked and appalled, pausing the tape just as Michael Myers raises his trademark blade. "Jesus Christ!" he explodes, looking at the group in disbelief. "You don't know the rules?"[19]

Taking his place in front of the television, Randy lectures them on the "*rules* that one must abide by in order to successfully survive a horror movie. For instance," he says as they lean in, "number one: you can *never* have sex." Tension bursts in a chorus of jeers from his friends, many of whom are hoping for precisely that later in the evening. Randy shakes his head. "Big no-no! *Big* no-no!" he continues through a shower of popcorn and the occasional beer can. "Sex equals death, ok?"[20]

While it may not always equal death, per se—though it does often enough, and virginity is not always sufficient protection against it—sex is rarely the solution to any problem in a horror movie or scary story. Arguably our most primal urge, sex is the one impulse over which we have least control. Time, money, relationships, careers, occasionally even our lives—all of these we will sacrifice to follow a siren call bred so deep in our bones that everything else fades to insignificance. To speak in the language of Ridley Scott's *Alien*, sex is our species' "Special Order 937," before which "all other priorities are [all too often] rescinded."[21] Devoting enormous amounts of energy to the biological, emotional, and mental enigma Freud called our "polymorphous perversity," human history demonstrates a web of desire spun from bewildering strands of erotic attraction, sexual arousal, and libidinal performance—as well as an equally diverse range of attempts to contain and control them.

"A disposition to perversions," Freud wrote in the summary to *Three Essays on the Theory of Sexuality* (by which he meant behaviors outside prevailing social convention, what we would call today "paraphilias"), "is an original and universal disposition of the human sexual instinct."[22] More than that, what arouses and excites us, what determines the direction, vigor, and contours of our sexual selves, develops early in life and remains relatively stable throughout. Whether we are able to realize it fully or not, as writer Sallie Tisdale warns us, we "forget the bell curve of human desire" to our peril, if for no other reason than that "few of us have much say about where on the curve we land."[23] Whatever our sexual orientation, whatever our particular proclivity or paraphilia, whatever it is on the rainbow palette of arousal that gets us off, we are all excited by something. And whether we are willing to admit it or not, whether we act on our impulses or don't, whether society condones or suppresses our sexual choice, and whether we ourselves are horrified or repelled by what so many consider our "baser" instincts, the brute fact is that we cannot escape our reality as sexual beings.[24] For billions of people, this is the monster that always comes . . . back, and, therefore, must be regulated, restrained, or repressed.

"Among the forces restricting the direction taken by the sexual instinct," Freud continues, almost a century before the Internet was born and exposed for all to see our "billion wicked thoughts," as sociologists Ogi Ogas and Sai Gaddam put it, "we laid emphasis upon shame, disgust, pity and the structures of morality and authority erected by society."[25] Whatever else we may think about Freud's theories in general, he wasn't wrong about that. And each of these—shame, disgust, pity, morality, and authority—is but one of the myriad stones laid in the foundation of religion's ongoing attempts to keep our bodies in their proper place, to curb the fear our sexual selves expose.

On the other hand, "the potential for vileness, depravity, brutality, and unspeakable despair stemming from matters sexual," writes Michele Slung in the introduction to *I Shudder at Your Touch*, her collected *Tales of Sex and Horror*, "is nearly limitless, and so too, is the vulnerability."[26] Here, we could easily substitute "religious" for "sexual," and Slung's comments would lose none of their emotional potency, cultural resonance, or historical accuracy. After all, is there a single activity over which religion has sought to exercise such extraordinary control as sexuality, upon which it has placed such limits and conditions in terms of the propriety of sexual relations, and for which it has pronounced such dire consequences in the all-but-inevitable event of transgression?

To take just one example, consider the curious case of Ms. Rebecca Paulson.

Sex, Horror, and "The Revelations of 'Becka Paulson"

"Let's get down to brass tacks, in the Christian grammar, we have no *right* to sex. The place where the church confers that privilege on you is the wedding; weddings grant us license to have sex with one person. Chastity, in other words, is a fact of gospel life."[27] Contrary to what you might think, this is not Augustine, retrospectively agonizing over "the lust that excites the indecent parts of the body" and results "in a pleasure surpassing all physical delights"; neither is it Tertullian, raging against women as "the devil's gateway," nor even someone like feminist "thealogian" Mary Daly, convinced to her dying breath of the ontological evil of male lust.[28] Rather, Lauren Winner is an associate professor of Christian spirituality at Duke University, the "gothic wonderland" briefly famous in 2014 for the Belle Knox porn panic, and a former senior editor at *Christianity Today*. In *Real Sex: The Naked Truth about Chastity*, a title that fairly drips with double entendres, she stipulates that "in the New Testament, sex beyond the boundaries of marriage—the boundaries of communally granted sanction of sex—is simply off limits. To have sex outside those bounds is to commit an offense against the Body. Abstinence before marriage, and fidelity within marriage; any other kind of sex is embodied apostasy."[29]

Take a moment to read that last bit again and consider its implications: *any other kind of sex is embodied apostasy.* For a believer, especially one whose cosmic circumstances depend on the exclusive nature of their beliefs, being labeled an apostate can be one of the worst fates imaginable.[30] At the very least, it means being cut off from one's family and community, but it often entails considerably more. Many Muslim-majority countries still criminalize apostasy, and some invoke the death penalty for it—though, it is important to point out that Islam is hardly the only religious tradition to have taken this rather draconian position. For more than three centuries, the medieval Christian inquisitions sought out apostates with ruthless determination. Even today, though with less-lethal consequences, tens of thousands of fundamentalist Protestants devote their waking hours to rooting out even the barest hint of what they consider heresy—which tends to be any version of Christian belief that differs from their own.[31] At worst, though, apostates are denied whatever eternal comforts their traditions teach them await us after death. They are excluded forever from their vision of reward in the afterlife.

This is the power both of religion—as a social and cultural institution that often leverages ignorance, preys on fear, and presumes to tell not only the truth but The Truth—and of the diverse vagaries of the religious imagination that have held humankind in thrall for thousands of generations. It's difficult not to imagine the multitude of sexual tripwires laid throughout Winner's manifesto in favor of marital monogamy and premarital chastity. Is masturbation apostasy?[32] (If so, then how few of us remain within the fold?) Or, à la Bill Clinton's famous impeachment defense—"I did not have sexual relations with that woman, Miss Lewinsky"—what does Winner actually consider "sex"?[33] And what about Jesus' infamous thought-control provision in Matthew 5:28, about looking at a woman with lust in your heart—a caveat that makes George Orwell's Anti-Sex League seem benign by comparison?[34] No other basic human need, no other "vexing matter of bodily desire," is subject to this kind of surveillance, scrutiny, constraint, and reproach.[35]

Although he does not write about sex very often, at least not explicitly and certainly not in the same way as, say, Clive Barker, Caitlín Kiernan, Edward Lee, Alan Moore, or Wrath James White, Stephen King often examines ways in which we suffer at the hands of our own religious imagination—including in his contribution to *I Shudder at Your Touch*. As with so many of his stories, "The Revelations of 'Becka Paulson" begins with a disturbingly mundane, almost blasé statement of fact: "What happened was simple enough—at least at the start. What happened was that Rebecca Paulson shot herself in the head with her husband Joe's .22-calibre pistol."[36] There are no moral implications here, no questions of legal jeopardy or eternal destiny. She shot herself, so it's not murder. It was an accident, so it's not suicide. And, anyway, she survived. This is, after all, Stephen King. In the days following her near-fatal mishap, though, 'Becka's life becomes more complicated when Jesus himself begins to tell her "the most amazing, terrible, distressing things imaginable."[37]

And what her Lord and Savior wants to talk about more than anything else, it seems, is sex. Like the humiliating fact that Joe is cheating on her with the new postmistress, the loathsome Nancy Voss, who just transferred in from Falmouth. Or that, long ago, but not so far away, "Abel Harlingen slathered lard on his cock and then slid it up his son's back door with a grunt and a sigh."[38] Or that "Alice Kimball, who taught at the Haven Grammar School, was a lesbian."[39] Or that "Darla Gaines, the pretty seventeen-year-old girl who brought the Sunday paper," likes to smoke "the reefer" with her boyfriend "after doing what they called 'the horizontal bop.'"[40] Indeed, "it seemed that Jesus knew something unpleasant or upsetting about everyone" in Derry, Maine, the dark, ambiguous heart of King's voluminous storyworld. In one way or another, at least as far as 'Becka Paulson's religious imagination was concerned, everyone's bodies were out of place but hers.

In one sense, she suffers the same fear of divine surveillance that constantly judges *Carrie*'s Margaret White, King's archetypal sinner caught in the hands of an angry, implacable god.[41] But, à la *The Dead Zone*'s

Vera Smith, this is also the god whose attention places 'Becka at the center of the divine plan, ensuring her a leading role in the cosmic passion play.[42] After all, Jesus was talking to *her*, not Nancy Voss or Alice Kimball or Darla Gaines. And certainly not Abel Harlingen. These things, however, "sickened her," and knowing them "destroyed her sleep."[43] In fact, on the one hand, what Jesus revealed to 'Becka was "destroying her sanity."[44] On the other, though, in what amounts to the chicken-or-the-egg problem of the religious imagination, 'Becka felt "a grisly sort of compulsion in knowing the things that Jesus told her."[45] They offered a salacious tincture distilled from her own piety, self-righteousness, moral outrage, and sexual repression. None of this should surprise us, given that for Rebecca Paulson, who is far more Margaret White's storyworld-sister than Vera Smith's, "sex was just as her mother told her it would be, nasty and brutish, sometimes painful, and always humiliating."[46] It represented nothing more than the "animalism of sexual congress, with its grunting and thrusting and that final squirt of sticky stuff that smelled faintly like codfish and looked like cheap dish detergent."[47]

Given her antisexual upbringing and relentlessly fundamentalist religious socialization, it should come as no surprise that "'Becka did not connect the onset of these divine communications with the hole in her head at all," the hole that allowed her to push an eyebrow pencil five inches straight into her head.[48] Indeed, in many ways, this prodigious failure of Occam's Razor represents the sine qua non of the religious experience, the power of the religious imagination to offer compelling explanations that are almost entirely at odds with reality. Something so strange occurs that we have no way to fit it into any normal category of experience, so we seek a framework of extraordinary explanation for this particular set of exceptional facts. The burning bush, the voice in the cave, the talking donkey, and now "The Revelations of 'Becka Paulson"—all examples of what we might call the "Katz Model of Contextual Interpretation."

In his classic essay on the nature of mystical experience—for which we could easily substitute "the religious imagination"—philosopher Steven Katz insists that expectation structures experience: What we presume we will see conditions what we do see. Indeed, Katz's "single epistemological assumption" is that *"there are NO pure (i.e., unmediated) experiences."*[49] That is, "The experience itself as well as the form in which it is reported is shaped by concepts which the mystic"—insert the unfortunate 'Becka Paulson—"brings to, and which shape, [her] experience."[50] When the extraordinary appears in our living room, we interpret it through the dominant filters that our (sub)culture provides, the codes and symbols that are most readily available to us. Which is to say, no matter where we come from, "our social worlds shape our religious visions," and we cannot escape their influence.[51] If 'Becka Paulson had been receiving her revelations from the "big brindle tom named Ozzie Nelson," for example, or the bedframe, or the garbage disposal, or a carton of Grade A eggs (Extra Large), she would quite reasonably conclude that something was seriously wrong—perhaps the catastrophic injury that resulted when "a .22 Winchester short entered her brain just above the left eye."[52]

But she didn't. And that's important.

It was Jesus who spoke to her.

Because 'Becka was used to watching "Jimmy Swaggart and Rex Humbard and Jerry Falwell" every Sunday, the televangelism culture of the 1980s had already primed the pump on her religious imagination. Add to Katz's insight the "availability heuristic," the social-psychological principle that the more easily we can draw to mind an example of something, the more likely we are to think that thing true or significant, and 'Becka's socialization has replaced the strop for Occam's Razor with a sturdy belt of ready-made truth. Indeed, had the cat talked, the bedframe moved, or eggs cooked themselves on her cracked Formica countertop, the same fundamentalist subculture to which she was devoted would have warned her explicitly of demonic activity. But this was different; this was Jesus, and "He was the Savior."[53]

"Jesus was on top of the Paulson's Zenith television and He had been in that same spot for just about twenty years," the "beautiful 3-D picture" depicting him just as she had always imagined.[54] "Dressed in a simple white robe," he was "holding a shepherd's staff. . . . His hair was not too long, and perfectly neat . . . and His eyes were brown and mild and kind. Behind him, in perfect perspective, sheep as white as linens in a TV soap commercial trailed away into the distance."[55] She felt as though she could reach into his picture and touch his hand.

Between the image, which she thought of as "created" because "*made* [was] much too mundane a word for a likeness which seemed so real," and the decades of reality maintenance received from her coterie of televised Sunday visitors, we begin to see more of the religious imagination at work.[56] Like Vera Smith, Rebecca Paulson berates her husband for "the Devil's work," particularly Joe's monthly card game, when he has "his dirty-talking, beer-swilling friends in to play poker."[57] Like *Needful Things*' Myrtle Keeton, she is not having any truck with the Church of Rome either.[58] With her newfound religious insight, the secret power of her "revelations," 'Becka suddenly realizes why Joe had wanted to get rid of Jesus' picture all these years. "He must have had that idea all along," she imagined, "that that picture was a *magic* picture. Oh . . . she supposed *sacred* was a better word, *magic* was for pagans—headhunters and Catholics and people like that—but they came almost to one and the same, didn't they?"[59]

'Becka Paulson "knows" the reason for her revelations. There is a logic to her suffering servanthood that goes far beyond the .22-calibre bullet lodged somewhere between her frontal and parietal lobes, and it comes down to the troubled, tormented relationship between our religious faith and our sexual desires, both domains replete with "potential for vileness, depravity, brutality, and unspeakable despair."[60] But that is not to say that the whole thing still didn't come as something of a shock. "Joe's granddad was a whoremaster of the purest ray serene, as you well know, 'Becka," the 3-D Jesus says when he speaks to her for the first time. "Spent his whole life pecker-led. And when he came up here, do you know what we said? 'No room!' That's what we said. . . . 'Go see Mr. Splitfoot down below,' we said.'"[61]

Not surprisingly, "'Becka fled, shrieking, from the house."[62]

A generation ago, Stephen King suggested in *Danse Macabre* that horror acts principally as "an agent of the status quo."[63] While much of his fiction since then, especially novels such as *Desperation*, *Duma Key*, *Revival*, and *Under the Dome*, suggest that he is not nearly so sanguine about that as he once was, much of horror culture remains a fundamentally conservative art form.[64] "We go to [horror movies]," he continues, "to reestablish our feelings of essential normality."[65] And, in this, horror shares the stage with nothing so much as religion, which throughout history has shown itself an essentially conformist cultural medium. While religion as patently obvious prop, readily identifiable character, and explicit set dressing takes center stage in a great many horror stories, in many more it lurks in the background, scratching under the floorboards, whispering in the dark, or pulling strings from behind the curtain. And, whether we claim a particular religious allegiance or not, we all carry a duffel bag full of religiously inspired stories around with us, stories that reinforce conventional moralities, and feature in the end the world as many of us believe it should be.

Ambiguity, Belief, and the Enigma of Horror

Neither Noël Carroll nor Mathias Clasen would suggest that Jesus was actually talking to 'Becka Paulson, or that her putative revelations were anything other than the result of traumatic brain injury filtered through her fundamentalist Christian faith. Except, perhaps, for one thing—she is not wrong. As far as King's storyworld is concerned, as far as we know, Joe *is* sleeping with Nancy, Alice *is* a lesbian, and Abel Harlingen's son *has* lived his entire life as the victim of childhood sexual abuse. Put differently, in the context of the horror mode, neither the drive to unravel the mystery nor the "evolved properties of the human nervous system" account for the persistence of ambiguity or the power of belief.

Understood as resistance to a particularity of reading, *ambiguity* challenges the exclusivity of any one interpretation, and asks, instead, *Are you sure? Really? Are you sure it couldn't be something else?* While it is a bit of a cliché to suggest that we fear the unknown, that does not mean it is not true. In many cases, our most deeply embedded fears are animated by things we are least capable of putting into words, least able to understand and explain—and, thus, explain away. That is, the horror mode often haunts the shifting ground created by ambivalence and uncertainty. James Van Hollander's Lovecraftian short story "Susie," for example, locates this insecurity in the context of a potentially demonic breeding program, and poses one of the principal questions of supernatural horror: Is it real? Is this really happening? Are the boundaries of the "half-world between what we know and what we fear" really so very thin?[66]

Susie is an elderly woman, confined in her final days to "Butler Sanatorium," a "Gothic Revival Place of Moan" where she lies "anguished with the burden of a Thousand Unborn."[67] Already, we are in unfamiliar territory as she "curses the frailty of human life as Doctor Farnell clamps cool fingers under her tongue," and an "alkaloid bitterness spirals down her gullet."[68] Rather than the question of what *is* happening to Susie, though, is the problem of what she *thinks* is happening, what she is *convinced* others are doing to her, and how that fear locates her experience in uncanny and unnatural circumstances—another common marker of the religious imagination at work. On the one hand, she has little control over her body or what is being done to it—not by doctors like Farnell, nor by the nursing staff, nor by the "crowd-sized tangle" of otherworldly entities that she believes flood into her room late at night.[69] On the other hand, she gains control over what remains of her life by alternately accusing a nurse of sexual abuse and placing herself at the center of cosmic significance. At the end of her own life, Susie becomes the bearer of an unholy savior through whom she will, paradoxically, alleviate "the plight of the Thousand Unborn, whose fate must devolve on her beloved, sublimely gifted, weakling invalid useless child."[70]

"You touched me," Susie says simply. "Your hands lingered." Startled and affronted, the other woman protests that "all I did was perform my duty as a nurse." "You kept staring at my nakedness," Susie insists. But the nurse will not be dissuaded and provides the singular tilt on the axis of ambiguity. "Your belly-skin has tattoos," she tells her patient, "symbols in strange colors, scurrying around like beetles. Especially near the sutures. And someone had put furry boots on your legs. They looked like goat-feet."[71]

"By the time the ether wore off," the shaken nurse continues, "by the time you stopped vomiting, the tattoos vanished. I don't know how you got rid of the boots."[72] In that first clause, so brief that in the rush to find out what happens we miss what might be happening, we glimpse the shadow of a thumb on the scales of reality, this story's .22 Winchester short, the potential for naturalizing the unnatural narrative and explaining it away. Administering ether as an anesthetic was tricky business at the best of times, and, though heavier than air, the fumes presented more than a little danger to medical personnel. That is, the possibility exists that the moving, wriggling tattoos and scurrying symbols, the furred boots that mysteriously disappear, were all part of the nurse's own ether-induced hallucination, informed at least in part by the old woman's dementia. "When you washed the host-body, your hand lingered," the "pluralized Susie" insists. "You caressed the host-body." Once again, the nurse indignantly protests her innocence, seeking solace in her own religious convictions. "Lookie, missus, I don't ever touch the Host except when the priest places it on my tongue."[73] "'You touched *this* flesh,' Susie, unable to move, gestures with her chin. 'The flesh of *this* body.'"[74]

Later, we are given a few more paltry grains of rationality, slender hints that this is all in Susie's mind, a byproduct of fever, a brain sliding into the dark, and the "delirium [that] convinces her that the pad and the length of her body form a human-skinned flying carpet."[75] Though we are told, mercifully perhaps, that this is nothing but a "carpet of dreams," how terrifying must they be for the dreamer, for the one consumed by this new reality? "In the midnight hospital room the dying entity jolts awake. The plight of her Unborn Brood knifes into her. Her helplessness is unbearable. To open time she summons a tangible ideation of her consort and bleats *Iä! Iä! Iä!* without uttering its truest name. . . . Fully aroused, the avatar mounts her, thrusts, groans, boasts, its mind maggoty with spirochetes. *Iä!* Between her thighs Susie feels the potent fecundating seed of death."[76]

Unlike 'Becka Paulson's living room, beyond the nurse's brief appeal to Catholic mass, there is no recognizable religion here in Butler's palliative care ward. But there are resonances of stories told throughout history. An imprisoned young princess is visited by the king of the gods, who appears as a shower of gold and cuts "the knot of intact virginity," leaving her pregnant with the hero, Perseus.[77] A young queen carried away in her dreams by a group of spirits is magically impregnated by an elephant, and later gives birth to the Buddha. A young girl engaged to a carpenter is confronted by an angel who tells her, "Do not be afraid, for you have found favor with God. You will conceive and give birth to a son" (Lk. 1:30–31). Now, this is *not* to suggest that Van Hollander is simply mapping the rich cartography of these stories onto his own narrative, and that by identifying this we have somehow solved the story's puzzle. No. Rather, the ambivalence of both 'Becka and Susie's experiences forces us to consider the difference between a *riddle* and an *enigma*.

This is a particularly useful distinction when considering ways in which the vast array of scary stories, the complex nature of human sexuality, and the byzantine landscape of the religious imagination intersect. While riddles and enigmas are often colloquially used as synonyms, they differ in significant ways, principally through control of the answer. Put simply, someone who poses a riddle gatekeeps the response because she has the correct answer in mind already. The question presupposes an answer. The so-called riddle of the Sphinx is one of the most famous classical examples, while Monty Python's "Bridge of Death" is one of the funniest.[78] With enigmas, however, this is not always the case. A person proposing an enigma may not have a particular answer in mind. She may not even know that there is *an* answer.[79]

Metanarrative approaches to horror, whether psychological, sociological, or grounded in one's preferred ideological commitment, often make what is, essentially, a category error: mistaking the horror story for a riddle (i.e., something to be solved, confident of an answer), when it is frequently an enigma (i.e., something to be explored, though with no a priori assurance of resolution). No matter how many explanations we offer, enigmas always leave us with more questions than answers. Indeed, enigma, enduring mystery, the cryptic and tenebrous unknown—these are fundamental engines of horror-world storymaking.

"Solving the riddle" of a film, novel, or short story, however, is an attempt to bring meaning under control, often by restricting its interpretation within the bounds of a particular worldview. Since Lovecraftian "Elder Gods" do not exist, then Susie's experience cannot be divine possession and impregnation, and her experience must point to deeper traumas associated with senility, narcotics, and the inevitable approach of the eternal dark. If the possibility of divine revelation is ruled out a priori, then 'Becka Paulson's experience is some as-yet-unknown side effect of catastrophic brain injury. Interpretations such as this, though, often require us to read a text eisegetically, injecting our assumptions into it and rejecting much of what is happening in front of us in favor of an analysis more suited to those presuppositions. These approaches often refuse to take the storyworld for what it is and ask what it means to explore *that* world: a place where the Elder Gods do exist, and messages from a 3-D picture of Jesus are possible. For metanarrative approaches, *elusiveness of meaning* is a problem that demands confinement and constraint. Commitment to a particular disciplinary or ideological framework—Freudian psychoanalysis, feminist criticism, Marxist materialism, evolutionary biology, name your passion—often exacerbates this, and the reason seems relatively straightforward. Riddles reinforce the boundaries of one's worldview, since the answers—whatever they may be—are already contained within those boundaries, and the gatekeepers of the answer determine the correctness of the response. Because enigmas advance the possibility that there is no fixed meaning, no binding answer to the puzzle, they challenge not only the boundaries of this or that consensus reality but the possibility that consensus reality exists at all.

Reiterating the relatively uncontroversial "reality simulation model" of human addiction to stories, Mathias Clasen points out that we "find pleasure in make-believe" because it "allows [us] to experience negative emotions at high levels of intensity within a safe context. And this is what horror offers."[80] While this is certainly true in some instances, Clasen pointedly ignores horror stories that are structured on worldviews in which hundreds of millions of people *do* believe and that deeply inform their lives, worldviews that for them are anything but "make-believe." Since we are "tripwired for agency detection," Clasen insists that "belief in supernatural agents is a predictable and natural byproduct of ordinary human cognition."[81] He declines to explain *why* this should be the case, offering instead a retrospective observation masquerading as analytic insight. Blending religious myopia and Western bias, he concludes that "most of us don't believe that we have had firsthand experience with demons or ghosts, yet we can easily mentally simulate such experience and entertain as rich concepts such agents"—again providing no evidence why any of this should be so.[82] Despite his offhand conflation of supernatural categories, the reality is that myriad cultures around the world do live as closely with ghosts, demons, and an unseen host of other entities as they do their own family and friends.

Indonesian horror culture, for example, is "considered one of the least adulterated conductors of traditional customs, history and fears indigenous to the Indonesian people."[83] There, no matter how they appear initially or what their origin, monsters are most often revealed to be ghosts, and the story's supernatural context is almost always a battle between good and bad magic. Despite the overwhelming predominance of both Christianity and Islam in Nigeria, enduring local beliefs are intimately bound up with relations between the seen and unseen orders of reality.[84] Eight thousand miles away in Japan, *mizuko kuyo*, literally "water babies," is one of the most common religious rituals, and practiced by men and women of a wide variety of faiths. Intended to appease the spirits of aborted fetuses, stillborn babies, and children who die in infancy, the rite prevents them from returning to our world as hungry ghosts.[85] We could easily stack up countless other non-Western examples of such phenomena—not to mention the prominence of spiritualist practices in the West. From the reality of possession experiences that lie at the heart of religious convention to haunting spirits and a deep-seated belief in a demonic order that constantly threatens our own, Clasen makes no attempt to account for belief in these and innumerable other terrifying products of the religious imagination—other than to imply that they amount to little more than cultural delusions.

Grand unified theories of horror such as this are not wrong, per se, though some may seem less insightful or more inflexible than others. Rather, they are incomplete. At the most basic level, metanarrative theories of horror fall short by virtue of overreach. The constraints of their own ideological commitments force them to treat scary stories as puzzles to be solved or riddles to be answered, rather than as enigmas to be explored. No single perspective can encompass or explain the complex phenomena of human fearing, especially when those fears are refracted through the kaleidoscope of the religious imagination and confront the often messy realities of our sexual nature.

Indeed, in some sense, we are all still children in need of assurance that there are no monsters under the bed or in the closet, and yet, for all that, we are still unsure that there aren't. And, as we will see, there *are* significant psychological investments in horror culture, and horror *is* arguably the premier genre through which sociological fears are represented in, paradoxically, nonthreatening ways.[86] Similarly, religious believers *will* almost inevitably interpret scary stories through the lens of their own faith, either spinning them as cautionary tales or mapping the horror landscape to suit their theological worldview. We *have* evolved to fear some things over others, and, in many cases, those fears have kept us alive. But why these fears and not others? And why do those fears simply refuse to die, regardless of how we evolve?

Exploring the Dark, Disturbing Spaces Ahead

As any number of psychologists, sociologists, and anthropologists have pointed out, pollution is a function of both hygiene and convention.[87] Dirt is soil where we do not want it; a flood is water where it is not supposed to be. Rich black topsoil may be ideal for growing vegetables, and one's garden might desperately need the rain, but bring either into the house and the former becomes dirt, the latter a leak. Each becomes a problem because context is key. Muddy footprints appearing on the kitchen floor (*The Haunting of Bly Manor*) or a growing pool in the basement (*Dark Water*) become all the more disturbing when we cannot locate the source. The religious imagination is little different, aggressively separating the world into varieties of the sacred, the profane, and the liminal spaces in between, then appealing to an array of doctrines and beliefs, practices and rituals to both understand and negotiate among them. Nowhere, though, is the power of the unseen order invoked more readily and more harshly than when it comes to our bodies—and what we do with them. A brutal murder is a simple, if gory, homicide in one instance, the centerpiece of religious ritual in another. Virginity is prized above all physical attributes in one setting; in another it is a spiritual resource to be ceremonially deployed in the service of one's gods. Once again, context is key.

Laying aside questions of one's eternal destination, the religious imagination has policed no other aspect of human being so rigidly, nor done so in as many different ways, as the human body.[88] No other part of what it means to *be* human has been so cruelly bent in service to our various gods and, not infrequently, those who claim to serve them. As long as the body remains in its proper place, the stories tell us, everything is fine. Step out of that place, though, present the body in a different way, a forbidden style, a tainted or polluted form, make a ritual misstep, leave an ablution undone, dress inappropriately, or find a body where it is not supposed to be—then soil becomes dirt, acceptance turns to abjection, the holy turns horrifying.

This is where our enigmatic journey begins.

Starting with one of the iconic moments in twentieth-century horror cinema, chapter 1 explores the central axis of the book: the various ways we find—or create—bodies out of place, and what they reveal about the relationship between the horror mode and the religious imagination. As a function of social dislocation and cultural transgression, "bodies out of place" inevitably invokes the sexual body's (un)holy trinity: sexual development and the spectrum of sexual attraction; sex and gender, the shifting confluence of biology, social construction, and, not infrequently, religious mandate; and sexual behavior itself, especially as it is either regulated or denied by religious tradition, employed and instrumentalized in the context of rite and ritual, or used as a means to identify and marginalize the threatening religious Other. Fear of the power of our own bodies can give way to the uses we make of—or the restrictions we place upon—the bodies of others. In this, horror culture is rarely about transcendence, and far more often about trespass and transgression—both of which, however, remain matters of context and perspective.

Chapter 1 also introduces three essential waypoints for the dark road ahead, specific "movements beyond" that inform the ways in which I approach spooky stories and scary movies throughout this book. Taking us from the constraints of the horror *genre* to thinking in terms of a broader horror *mode* and examining how horror narratives move from *skepticism* to *realization* moves us, finally, beyond the limitations of *religion* to the indefinite horizons of the *religious imagination*.

Through the lens of B-movies, chapter 2 investigates horror culture as a species of morality play that often turns on the balance of licit and illicit sexualities, products both of explicit religious codes and of consensus morality drawn from implicit religious conditioning. Historically, this moral entrepreneurship has been one of the most common ways of interpreting horror culture. It is also the least ambiguous and the least complicated. Put differently, superficial and obvious allegories about social codes and sexual transgressions demand the least of us because we recognize in them that which is most familiar. After all, "sex equals death, OK?" From crab monsters and giant leeches to the most iconic of horror characters, this chapter explores the cultural construction and reinforcement of fear as a function of conventional moralities, traditions that almost inevitably support (and are supported by) dominant religious concerns. Through the use of religious competitors, however, horror culture also often confounds and contests these established wisdoms. Inverted by divergent expectations and subverted by alternative visions, it often presents unorthodox interpretations of what William James called "the unseen order."[89]

Keeping bodies in their proper place, religiously, ritually, socially, sexually, is the framework by which we maintain the illusion of control—which brings us to chapter 3. Most discussions of horror culture (including my own) deal with scary stories, cinema horror, or some hybrid of the two. Few examine the visual culture of horror and ask what "sex, horror, and religion" mean through an artist's eyes. Many readers will be familiar with the Dutch painter Hieronymus Bosch (ca. 1450–1516), particularly his triptychs, *The Last Judgment* and *The Garden of Earthly Delights*. Aspects of both feature numerous bodies wrenched violently out of place as punishment for various sins, but how many people, then or now, considered them in depth? Similarly, five hundred years later, far more people see the cover of a magazine than read its contents, look at a movie poster than buy tickets for the film, or glance at a billboard than investigate the product. Asking what modern visual culture can tell us about sex, horror, and the religious imagination, then, this chapter looks particularly at the work of Margaret Brundage, the most popular cover artist for *Weird Tales* during the golden age of the pulps, and her influence on fantasy horror artists ranging from Alessandro Biffignandi to Frank Frazetta, and Fernando Carcupino to Rowena Morrill. While in many of these cases "sex" is little more than a synonym for nudity (or the eroticization of partial nudity), this chapter explores the sexualized body as ritual resource, something that, once again, illustrates how limited and provincial are the boundaries we often place on the perspectival nature of religion. That is, what seems horrific in one religious context is business as usual in another. And, in this regard, more than any other ritual action, human sacrifice remains religion's dirty little secret, challenging conventional pieties about the nature of the gods, as well as the essential goodness, morality, and decency of the religious imagination. This brings us to the problem of sacred flesh.

Although films ranging from *The Sinful Nuns of St. Valentine* and *Sacred Flesh* to *The Devils* and *The Other Hell* have often placed the horrific, the sexual, and the religious in intense, symbiotic relationship, so-called nunsploitation cinema is hardly the only example of this relationship. Chapter 4 continues the path set in chapter 3 through a historical look at ways in which the horror mode eroticizes the religious body, including fetishizing the imaginal body of the unattainable Other (i.e., the horror of one's own lustful imagination); the flesh as a marker of sacramental acceptance (i.e., the sexualized fear of ritual impurity); the paradox of the wanton virgin (i.e., our ambivalence over the [im]possibility of ritual purity); and the potential for sexual invasion by the demonic Other (i.e., fear of a supernatural evil that we are powerless to resist). As much as anything, this points to the reality that the horror mode is not limited to fiction, to "stories that neither side believes."[90] Rather, horrific notions of the sexualized religious body cross the boundaries from "mere" stories into real life, and vice versa—often with real-world consequences. That devout religious believers could give themselves willingly—and, in terms of their ritual profession, sexually—to the Devil rather than to God, on the other hand, takes us deeper into the forest.

Chapter 5 examines ways in which horror culture leverages fears of witchcraft that remain deeply rooted in our society, fears that are often emphasized through a sexualized portrayal of the witch. Whether this means simple nudity (i.e., "skyclad" in a ceremonial context) or ritual carnality (i.e., the infamous "congress with the Devil"), overt or unconventional sexuality becomes the signifier of women (and, very occasionally, men) who are considered "out of control," whose bodies are out of place, and, most importantly, whose religious choices make them a danger to the community at large. This chapter, however, also considers ways in which our erotic fascination with what is culturally regarded as evil destabilizes that relationship in the real world. Nineteenth-century advertisements for Pears soap, for example, twentieth-century pinup art, and graphic novels such as *Hex Wives* present significantly different visions of what it means to sexualize the witch than low-budget horror films like *Ouija House* or the soft-core horror series *Witchcraft*, a straight-to-DVD franchise that numbers to this point sixteen entries. More than that, what happens when the sexualized representation of modern Witchcraft affects the daily lives of real-world Pagans? And, what happens if we take a classic horror film such as Robin Hardy's *Wicker Man* and subvert the presumed perspective of the film—if we ask what makes it "horror"?

However much horror writers may deny allegiance to organized religion, supernatural horror-worlds only emerge in the context of the religious imagination. They make little sense apart from the religious worldviews in which they come embedded and whose values they reproduce, refract, or resist—even if we do not immediately recognize them as "religious." Chapter 6 opens with Clive Barker's well-known short story "Jacqueline Ess: Her Will and Testament," and invites us to explore the darkness within, stories that appear to happen, as Stephen

King would say, "just because they happen." Because it is easy to reduce stories such as these to riddles, rather than treat them as enigmas, this chapter considers the explicitly enigmatic aspects of sex, horror, and the religious. Particularly, it does so in terms of two ways we often choose to face the enigma of the holy—escape and encounter—but also as a way of exploring what Rudolf Otto famously labeled "the numinous," and what anthropologist Tanya Luhrmann calls "interpretive drift." If this is the darkness within, though, the darkness without leads us into the next chapter: sex, horror, and the Lovecraftian mode.

Drawing less on Lovecraft himself—who was notoriously asexual, if not antisexual—chapter 7 considers examples of "Cthulhu's Spawn"—writers, artists, and filmmakers who either participate in the narrative context of Lovecraft's dark, supernatural storyverse or use what fans have come to call the "Cthulhu Mythos." This does not mean slavish imitation of Lovecraft's often overwrought style (parodied, for example, in Ramsay Campbell's delightful epistolary short story, "The Correspondence of Cameron Thaddeus Nash," and most obviously on display in Lovecraft's own "At the Mountains of Madness"). Nor does it mean simply the introduction of one or another member of Lovecraft's mythic pantheon. Rather, from low-budget video to drug-fueled *lustmord*, these stories explore the various pillars of the Lovecraftian mode: fears of alien invasion, incursion, and interbreeding; archaeology and the primordial challenge to consensus history; and, most prominently, cosmic indifference and the problem of human importance.

This brings us to the final chapter—or at least the one that ends the book. Looking down the road and around the corner, chapter 8 discusses three possible waypoints for continuing the cartography of horror. First, through the work of Edward Lee and Wrath James White, it considers the niche genre of splatter-horror. Whether we admit it or not, our religious behavior is often predicated on fear of the gods, and our desperate attempts to keep bodies in their proper place become the site of unimaginable cruelty. Anti-theist horror, however, often contests this reading, by not only displaying bodies out of place but taking a certain horrific delight in demonstrating contempt for the religious worldviews that box the compass of sexual propriety. Next, again looking at White, the chapter points to the important issue of queer theory in the horror mode. And, finally, comparing Matthew Lewis with his contemporary, the Marquis de Sade, I encourage further exploration of Sade as a classic exercise in sex, horror, and the religious imagination. This is not about Sade, per se, though, but "Sade," what we could call the Sadeian imaginary: the ways in which Sadeian horror revels in bodies out of place, and, in doing so, reflects, refracts, confronts, and ultimately subverts religion's ability to provide order, comfort, and stability.

But, first, *The Exorcist*.

1

Bodies Out of Place

Fearing Flesh in Three Movements

"No, please! Oh, no, please, *no!*"

A child's desperate cry. A young mother's body forced into motion even before her brain is fully engaged. Scrambling up the stairs, driven by nothing more than the primal urge to protect her daughter, Chris Mac-Neil races down the hall and flings open the bedroom door. Figurines fly through the room, a favorite doll caroms off the wall, and records shatter against the window frame—all the sundry moments of a little girl's life caught in the supernatural maelstrom their world has become.

"No, *please!*" the little girl shrieks.

Chris turns to the bed, eyes widening in renewed horror as a rasping, malignant voice issues from her daughter's drawn and cracked lips. And what it says freezes the blood in her veins.

"*Let Jesus fuck you!*"[1]

Director William Friedkin considers this sequence, known colloquially as "the crucifix masturbation scene," to be *The Exorcist*'s "single defining image," the quintessence of one of Western culture's most enduring horror stories.[2] Including the admittedly dated special effect for which the film is still best known—the infamous moment when the demon Pazuzu twists young Regan MacNeil's head completely around—the so-called masturbation scene itself is very short. Consider how screenwriter William Peter Blatty describes it in the novel on which the film is based: "Regan, her legs propped up and spread wide on a bed that was violently bouncing and shaking, clutched the bone-white crucifix in raw-knuckled hands, the bone-white crucifix poised at her vagina, the bone-white crucifix she stared at with terror. . . . Regan's piercing cry of terror turned to a guttural, yelping laugh of malevolent spite and rage triumphant while she thrust down the crucifix into her vagina and began to masturbate furiously."[3]

In Friedkin's film, however, this horrifying moment unreels in significantly less time than it takes just to read Blatty's description. A few quick cuts show us, first, a hand, presumably Regan's, holding aloft a large, bloody crucifix. Then, a single shot from the waist down as the crucifix slams into her "vagina"—in reality, a prop box, positioned off-set and stuffed with "a sponge and red food coloring."[4] We do not actually see then child-actor Linda Blair's face; indeed, even the legs in the shot belonged to Blair's uncredited, much older, body double, Eileen Dietz. Following this is a quick reaction shot of the Regan-thing (to borrow some language from Stephen King) staring in malign fascination at the central icon of the Roman Catholic Church as it raises her arm once again. Then, finally, mercifully, Chris MacNeil leaps toward the bed in an effort to grab her daughter's hand. Over this frenetic action, three times the Regan-thing shouts, "*Let Jesus fuck you!*"

In its 1973 theatrical release, *The Exorcist*'s running time was a little more than two hours. This entire sequence—from the moment we see the "bone-white crucifix" to Chris struggling to wrench it from the thing that has control of her daughter—lasts less than three seconds, about seventy frames. It just seems so much longer. Thanks to Friedkin's directorial sleight-of-hand, tour de force editing done principally to avoid community-standards censorship, audiences never actually see Regan masturbate with a crucifix. They are convinced, however, that they have, and that conviction lends the scene an alarming durability, a lasting effect that far exceeds its minimal screen time. Indeed, now that you know how it was done, that it was all camera tricks and careful editing, ask yourself if it is any less disturbing for all that, any less horrifying.

Then ask yourself why not.

"This scene is still very shocking," writes one YouTube viewer more than four decades after crowds lined up in the cold and the rain, sometimes for hours on end, to see *The Exorcist* when it first opened. "This is the scariest scene in any movie. Period," writes another viewer, while someone else states simply, "I'm not even religious, but there is just something so disturbing/abominable about this scene." In fact, many of the more than three hundred comments posted on just this particular YouTube upload of the scene suggest in one way or another that "even by today's standards this is appalling."[5] "The crucifix and the vagina are things that never appear together," says Friedkin, because

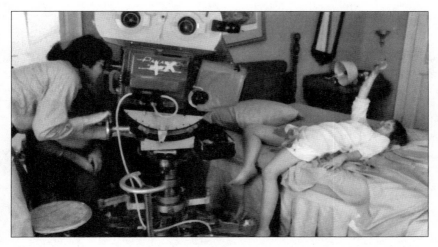

Figure 1.1. William Friedkin directing Linda Blair in *The Exorcist*. Source: Phillippe, *Leap of Faith*.

any relationship between them is regarded as "taboo in most people's consciousness."[6]

"Let Jesus fuck you!"

Just four words, yet it is difficult to imagine capturing the fraught relationship between sex, horror, and the religious imagination in a more visceral way. And in this, Regan MacNeil's is the quintessential body out of place.

Not surprisingly, interpretations of this scene have varied widely, both at the time of the film's release and in the generation since. Carol Clover, for example, considers *The Exorcist* "a very nearly incoherent cinematic text"—not least because of the infamous masturbation scene, which she cannot even bring herself to name.[7] Rather, the possessed Regan "stabs a cross in and out of her vagina."[8] As a plain description of the scene, this is not inaccurate, but, as many critics have pointed out, when it comes to horror texts, the devil—especially in a film such as *The Exorcist*—really *is* in the details. That is, this is a *crucifix*, not a cross, and the difference here is crucial: the scene's connotation is clearly a horrific and religiously specific masturbation, not simply gory self-mutilation.

Writing shortly after the film's release, psychologist Benjamin Beit-Hallahmi declared that, wherever we find it, "the demonic in literature and art is a combination of forbidden aggressive and sexual drives."[9] Nodding explicitly to Freud, he continues that "we may say that the demonic is a projection of the id, by which the forbidden desires of sex and aggression are thrown outward, so that the source of evil is seen outside the self."[10] In this way, Regan's possession and its explicitly sexualized embodiment are rendered symbolic, a terrifying allegory for psychosexual processes we all experience, none of us fully understand, and few of us can control. More than a generation later, Sara Williams follows the same path into the psychoanalytic forest, though in her case, even more explicitly than Beit-Hallahmi and in a manner more closely aligned with orthodox Freudianism. For her, the crucifix scene is an outrageous episode of oedipal hysteria, and Regan's "acts of masturbation become symbolic [of] paternal penetration." Rather than describing a supernatural assault that she cannot comprehend and is powerless to resist, the sequence "confirms Regan's unconscious desire to have sex with her [absent] father, as she uses Christ on the Cross, God's representative on earth, to penetrate herself."[11] Even though Williams's grasp of Christian systematic theology seems a bit thin here and her ability to connect the cinematic dots more than a little tenuous, she doubles down on her psychoanalytic reading. Rather than describing "the demon's desire to corrupt the body of an innocent through a sacrilegious act," she concludes, the crucifix masturbation sequence actually "expresses Regan's wish to have sex with the (Holy) Father, whom Freud identified as interchangeable with the Devil and the biological father."[12] In *Dark Romance*, on the other hand, David Hogan simply damns *The Exorcist* with faint praise. Though "well directed and convincingly acted," he ultimately thinks it "blatant and crude," "a shamelessly manipulative piece of work that arouses audiences with bludgeoning shock rather than true horror"—a judgment, it is worth noting, that depends entirely both on what we mean by "true horror" and on what we consider to be bodies out of place.[13]

Bodies Out of Place

Before it was sanitized, sensationalized, and ultimately commodified for Western participants, Buddhist and Hindu tantra referred to religious practices by which devotees sought enlightenment through the deliberate challenge of social and cultural taboos—particularly proscriptions around death, sexuality, and pollution. Deliberately setting the body out of place, among other things this included the consumption of bodily waste, prolonged physical contact with dead bodies, and, for lower-level practitioners, specialized sexual practices.[14] Tantrikas sought their cosmic answers in transgression, not hours-long orgasm, as some Western enthusiasts would have us believe. One of the most extreme forms of esoteric tantra is the so-called corpse ritual.

On the night of a new moon, writes anthropologist June McDaniel, the devotee "should bring a corpse, young and attractive, low-caste, of a person who died by violence, drowning, or snakebite." After suitable preparations, the tantrika will then "sit on the corpse and contemplate the god or goddess. He or she will experience fearful images and sounds, as well as temptations, but he must remain emotionally detached—or else he may go insane."[15] Some scholars speculate that, at one time, securing a *ritually appropriate corpse* included murder—which is to say, a body violently wrenched from its normal place, and recast in a ceremonially proper, if horrific place.[16]

Here are just a few of the other ways in which the horror mode renders bodies out of place, many of which we will consider in more depth throughout this book, but all of which are deeply invested in the religious imagination. Some have been with us since the emergence of our species as *Homo narrans*, while others are more recent, populating our nightmares and day-terrors as explicit functions of social dislocation, cultural offense, or ritual transgression.

The Disembodied

From campfire tales to the latest Netflix or Shudder catalogue of binge-horror television, ghosts have always been with us. Indeed, from visitations to apparitions, garden-variety poltergeists to "a focused, non-terminal, repeating phantasm or a class five full-roaming vapour," fear of the *disembodied* remains the most common doorway into the horror mode and an enduring connection to the religious imagination.[17] Spooks and haunting spirits, unseen ancestors who live with us still, the restless and the revenant—all these and more are the spectral dramatis personae that shaped our earliest religious imaginings, the moment when we began to wonder, What happens when we die? Where do we go when life here goes on without us? No tradition known to us lacks a ritual process intended both to ensure proper passage to the afterlife for those who have died and to protect those who remain on this side of the dark boundary from the predations of those who have crossed over.[18]

At some point in our lives, we each become aware of our own mortality, the brute fact of a world in which we will be no more, and that will continue, in most cases, as if we had never been. For the hero Gilgamesh, the central character in humankind's earliest known epic narrative, it is the death of his friend Enkidu. So profoundly terrified is he by this that Gilgamesh wanders the land looking for the secret of immortality, eventually calling on Enkidu's ghost for the answer.[19] Thousands of years later, and a generation after a Danish king's ghost trod the battlements of Elsinore, a Qing dynasty tutor named Pu Songling collected dozens of *Strange Tales from a Chinese Studio*—including one about a man who fights off the sexual advances of a female ghost by biting her cheek, and another about a sexually predacious spirit whose "mighty member" was more than most living women could endure.[20] Two hundred years after that and across the Sea of Japan, writer Lafcadio Hearn published his collection of *Kwaidan*—literally, "ghost stories"—and kickstarted a Western fascination with Asian horror that continues to this day.[21]

From *Ju-on* and *Ringu*, both of which have grown into popular J-horror franchises in Japan and internationally, to adolescent ghost-hunting clubs in Goa (*Typewriter*), an Indonesian girl's ability to see the supernatural (*The 3rd Eye*), the revenant spirit of a murdered teenager with a postmortem ability to seduce any man she wants in her paradoxical desire to be killed over and over (*Tomie*), the long-running *American Horror Story*, and a docuseries of *Haunted* reenactments that were originally produced in the Czech Republic, more than any other way of storytelling, the horror stories ask simply, Why are we so afraid of ghosts? Why do friends and loved ones to whom we were devoted in life inspire such fear in death?[22] For some reason, says Norma, the elderly, blind psychic in *The Scarlet Gospels*, Clive Barker's long-awaited sequel to *The Hellbound Heart*, "at a certain point in the evolution of the species a profound superstition was sewn into the human heart that the dead were to be considered sources of terror rather than enlightenment."[23] At the window, in the mirror, or hovering on the edges of our peripheral vision, the faces of the dead reflect forever the fear of our own mortality.

The Reanimated Body

Just as we fear the disembodied, so too are we haunted by horror of the *reanimated body*, dead bodies that have not remained in their proper place. Whatever form reanimation takes—vampires, mummies, zombies, or creatures ranging from Mary Shelley's *Frankenstein* to those who cross the deadfall beyond Stephen King's *Pet Sematary*—rather than the peace that we so ardently hope comes with death, reanimation becomes an undead ordeal.[24] Here the horror mode fluctuates between origin stories and adjustment narratives: Where did they come from? Is it something we did to ourselves, or something that was done to us? Perhaps vampires have always been with us, an alternate species living in the dark places of history, feeding just enough to sustain their relatively small numbers (e.g., the *Underworld* franchise). Maybe we created them through a religious ritual gone horribly wrong (e.g., John Carpenter's *Vampires*, or Ricky Lau's *Mr. Vampire*) or the advent of a mysterious plague (e.g., Richard Matheson's classic novel, *I am Legend*, or the Sperig Brothers' somewhat less-than-classic *Daybreakers*)? Mummies, on the other hand, whether they were created to guard the tombs of the pharaohs (*The Mummy*, 1932) or as punishment for trespassing on the pharaoh's sexual domain (*The Mummy*, 1999), are almost always the undead product of human interference in the unseen order. Fortunately, though, vampires and mummies rarely travel in large groups, and, by themselves, seldom signal the apocalypse.

Cue *The Walking Dead*.

While some stories allude to the origins of the undead—a virus (*28 Days Later*) or a genetic weapons program (*Resident Evil*), the fictional chemical "2-4-5 Trioxin" (*Return of the Living Dead*), an occult ritual (*White Zombie*), or a mad scientist's experiments in "electrobiology" (*Man-Made Monster*)—most focus on living in the midst of (read: surviving) a zombie apocalypse. Nearly a decade after Rick Grimes first stumbled out of the hospital and realized that life (and death) had irrevocably changed, fan-generated theories about how the dead began walking seem almost as difficult to put down as the walkers themselves. Robert Kirkman, who created the original *Walking Dead* graphic novel and cocreated the television series, insists that he knows the zombie origin story, but that he will take it to his grave—no pun intended. "It's dumb," he said in one interview, and "it's really just unimportant to the overall story."[25] The reason people keep coming back to the narrative season after season is not to learn where the zombies came from but to see how we survive them, and (in a show famous for killing off popular characters) who survives in their midst.

The Australian television series *Glitch*, on the other hand, tells the story of a group of people who mysteriously rise from the grave—but express no interest in eating their fellow Aussies. In a much more intelligent way than the "always double-tap" kinetics of its American counterparts, *Glitch* combines the threat of a world extinction event with the search to understand what has happened to these men and women, what it means that their bodies are now so profoundly out of place, and, ultimately, what it means to be human in light of that change.

Bodies in Translation

Whether we are "turned" by an *ur*-vampire or rise from the dead by virtue of design or misadventure, reanimation is always about what happens when we become the monster, when we inhabit *translated bodies*. A particular concern of those who write in the Lovecraftian mode, these are, among many others, bodies translated into grotesque parodies of their individual passions. Like the inhabitants of Innsmouth and their literary descendants, these are bodies that gradually become the object of their obsession or devotion.[26] Like poor Riley Whately, the *Call Girl of Cthulhu* raped and transformed into a vessel for the Old Ones courtesy of the Sleeper of R'lyeh and his earthly acolytes, the Church of Starry Wisdom. Or like the hideously "altered" Adam Grimm, a victim of "fanatical devil-worshippers—the black monks of Erlik who dwell in the forgotten and accursed city of Yaghlan."[27]

In Robert E. Howard's multivalently racist short story "Black Hound of Death," we are initially meant to think that the principal villain of the piece is not Grimm, but the convicted murderer, Tope Braxton. In a manner common to much of the so-called golden age of pulps (roughly the mid-1930s to the mid-1950s), Howard's story did little but reinforce cultural stereotypes and social fear of the racialized Other—especially when there is a perceived sexual threat to a white woman. A black man, Braxton is repeatedly described as "ape-like," and his body "was like a shape from the abyss whence mankind crawled ages ago." He projects a "primitive ferocity," from his "massive, apish arms" and "huge, sloping shoulders" to his "wide, flat nostrils" and "thick lips that writhed back from tusk-like teeth."[28] Indeed, Howard initially portrays Braxton as "unbelievably primitive, atavistic enough to plunge into uninhabited wilderness and live like a blood-mad gorilla."[29]

The real villain of the story—although no one, perhaps save Gloria Brent, the young damsel in distress, is not in some sense villainous—is Adam Grimm. He is so, however, not by virtue of his nature, as Howard depicts Tope Braxton, but as a result of the change wrought in him by "the black devil-monks of Yaghlan," whose dark rituals rendered him "no longer a human being."[30] That is, as a white man he is not inherently dangerous, but becomes so by malevolent, supernatural design. This secretive religious sect Howard places "among the black mountains of Inner Mongolia," another of the story's racist vectors. And, when Grimm finally confronts his erstwhile friends, he anchors the interpretation in his experiences there. That is, he intends to kill Gloria "as I have seen women slain in Mongolia," "skinned alive," and "she shall not die until there is no longer an inch of skin left on her body below her neck!"[31] However gruesome Howard's description, "Black Hound of Death" also points to the culturfactual nature of horror, how pulp fiction, for example, both draws on and contributes to popular real-world fear.[32]

"Americans Escape from Tibet" read the *Washington Post* headline less than a decade before Howard wrote his story, and there faced "inhuman cruelty," while a *Post* special report written two decades earlier called Tibet "a kingdom of filth and depravity."[33] Reporting on the return of Russian symbolist painter Nicholas Roerich's expedition to Asia, the *New York Times* headline screamed, "Black Bon Po Rites Rampant in Tibet," adding the tantalizing possibility of "Druidic influence," while the *Atlanta Constitution* informed readers that "demonology and witchcraft now rule Tibetan Buddhism [*sic*]."[34] Fortunately, heralded the *Daily Boston Globe*, after being detained for several months by Tibetan authorities, Roerich and his group were allowed to leave, and "nine white persons in the party are safe."[35] A few years earlier, a *Times Sunday Magazine* article began by telling readers breathlessly that "sorcery and the black art are now universally practiced throughout Tibet" and that "in these devil dances the Lamas wear wonderful silk robes and highly ornamented headgear. Round the waist they wear an apron made from human bones, while in their hands they carry a cup made from a human skull, and a trumpet fashioned from a human thighbone."[36] While, today, we would interpret this as an expression of Tibetan Buddhist nonattachment—even to the body, a condition of successful transition through the bardo state—the unnamed *Sunday Magazine* writer concludes that "this is probably a survival of the cannibalism that was undoubtedly practiced in Tibet in olden times."[37] From this, it is not difficult to see Howard's description of "fanatical devil-worshippers—the black monks of Erlik who dwell in the forgotten and accursed city of Yahglan." Though he places them "among the black mountains of Inner Mongolia," they resonate at least as much with the dark reaches of his more famous Hyboria, but far more with contemporary media descriptions of Roerich's real-world expedition to the Roof of the World.

Violated Bodies

Depending on how we approach the problem, the concept of bodies out of place almost always invokes in some way the violated body. Stories such as "Black Hound of Death" express the paradox of violation, especially in one of its most common derivatives, the *sexually violated body*.[38] When "private dick Harry Childe is sent a snuff movie of his partner being hideously murdered," reads the back-cover blurb for Philip José Farmer's *Image of the Beast*, for example, tracking the killers takes Childe "into a waking nightmare of sexual brutality and supernatural bestiality, as he becomes entangled with sex-starved she-ghosts, snake-women, a filthy human sow, and a woman who gives birth to a limbless, ectoplasmic simulacrum of satanic child-killer Gilles de Rais."[39] As much as the horror mode reveals our fear of what others may do to us, the ways in which they may violate our bodies, it also shows us the power of our own bodies—either our inability to control them and resist their urges, or our willingness to give in to what many consider their basest desires.

Simon Strantzas's short story "Thistle's Find," which could have been subtitled "Adventures in Interdimensional Sex Trafficking," mixes Lovecraftian horror with a classic rape-revenge story like *I Spit on Your Grave*. Dr. Thistle, an old man with "gray wrinkles," "jaundiced eyes," and "dressed only in an undershirt and boxer shorts," invokes the specter of Crawford Tillinghast, the quintessential "mad scientist" in H. P. Lovecraft's famous short story "From Beyond."[40] Like Tillinghast, Thistle has opened a portal between dimensions and revealed a world "almost nothing like ours."[41] Although he "discovered it many years ago," he tells Owen, the narrator, "over time the barrier between there and here has grown thin."[42] In the sense of pop-science-meets-new-age-metaphysics, observation affects reality at the quantum level, and Thistle's study of this strange other world has rendered the boundary between the seen and the unseen "so thin" that it produced a "quantum hole."[43] What Thistle brought through, though, has little to do with scientific curiosity. Peering into a world populated by what he casually calls "ghouls," creatures with a very specific Lovecraftian resonance, "Thistle's Find" rends the sheer membrane separating horror from eroticism.[44]

"The creature he stole from the other world," Owen tells us, "looked to me like no creature at all, but instead a teenage girl, no more than fifteen. She was tied down spread-eagle. And she was naked."[45] When the old man comments on her beauty and the fact that "she looks almost human," Owen realizes that "the primal side of me was reacting to her nakedness in a way I was trying desperately to stop."[46] Notwithstanding what he styles his "primal urges," evolutionary demands so deeply bred in the bone that his erectile response is all but autonomic, it is not hard to imagine her terror. After all, consider the numberless young women who have found themselves in similar situations: kidnapped and presented for rape at the hands of a colonial power or an invading army, or displayed for the prurient interests of those who consider themselves more highly evolved.

"I walked slowly to the girl," Owen recounts, "forcing my eyes away from her tiny breasts and the allure of her naked mons, I kept my eyes on hers, looking for any sign of humanity in them, but there was nothing there. Only animal ferocity."[47] How many colonial letters home, official and unofficial reports, diary entries, and church communiqués made similar observations about indigenous peoples from the Arctic Circle to the Solomon Islands, and from East Africa to the Americas? Men, women, and children snatched from their homes, herded aboard strange vessels, and taken to places they did not even know existed, there to be exhibited as "savages," beasts that present only the surface appearance of humankind, and appropriate only for the so-called human zoos of nineteenth-century Europe.[48]

While this story might seem little more than a PSA about colonialism, racism, kidnapping, and rape, all told through the lens of "From Beyond"—and, to be sure, it *is* all that—it raises a number of other questions, other issues that keep us firmly mired in ambiguity, refusing to let us off the hook quite so easily as some would prefer.

First, there is the recurring horror that Owen feels, not only at the brutal depravity of Thistle's grimy interdimensional brothel but at his own physical response to the girl, in spite of who or what he thinks she is, and how she came to be there. Despite what he knows of her origins, and notwithstanding the tenuous moral overlays of his own society, the appearance of her strapped to Thistle's table still leaves him painfully aroused—and there appears to be nothing he can do about it. Which is to say, we are so rarely in complete control of our sexual response.

Despite the guardrails set in place by social contract, legal proscription, and religious mandate, this is the oft-terrifying reality of human sexuality. On the one hand, Thistle and those for whom he has procured the young woman—the myriad unnamed men who "might pay for the experience of fucking an animal shaped like a teenage girl"—epitomize the destructive male lust described by radical feminist Mary Daly.[49] "It means 'sexual desire, especially of a violent, self-indulgent character,'" Daly writes in her introduction to *Pure Lust*. "Phallic lust, violent and self-indulgent, [that] levels all life, dismembering spirit/matter. . . . This lust is *pure* in the sense that it is characterized by unmitigated malevolence. It is *pure* in the sense that it is ontologically evil."[50]

On the other hand, suggest psychologist Christopher Ryan and his partner, psychiatrist Cecilda Jethá, the urges Daly detests in men as a group, and Owen abhors about himself in particular, in large measure define what it means to be human. "We have another quality that is *especially human* in addition to our disproportionately large brains and associated capacity for language," they write in *Sex at Dawn*, their challenge to the "standard model" of human sexual evolution. "Pair-bonded 'monogamous' animals are almost always *hyposexual*, having sex as the Vatican recommends: infrequently, quietly, and for reproduction only."[51] Rather, "human beings, regardless of religion, are at the other end of the libidinal spectrum: *hyper*sexuality personified."[52] This is perhaps an uncomfortable commentary on our own sexual nature, but Ryan and Jethá contend that we have evolved to be neither monogamous nor particularly choosy in our mating habits. "Mating" here should be understood in the loosest possible sense, a penchant that both religious tradition and cultural convention have tried desperately to limit, restrict, eliminate, or bend to some other purpose. As with the terrified young girl who may or may not have been a ghoul, as with poor, possibly deluded "Susie," and as with the demonic transformation of Regan MacNeil, when the horror mode takes a Lovecraftian turn, sexual violation by *alien bodies* often challenges our sense of place in a universe that suddenly seems to care very little for us.

Abnormal Bodies

Also dictated by social convention and regulated by the religious imagination, *abnormal bodies* breach a particular culture's biological norms. Those who do not, or cannot, conform to those standards are threatened in a variety of ways precisely because they themselves are seen as a threat. "Any creature that shall seem to be human," declared the "Repentances" in John Wyndham's classic novel, *The Chrysalids*, "but is not formed thus is not human. It is a blasphemy against the true Image of God, and hateful in the sight of God."[53] "Keep pure the stock of the Lord!" "Watch thou for the mutant!" "Blessed is the norm!"—whether preached from the pulpit or hung vigilant over the family dining table, these are the watchwords by which Wyndham's postapocalyptic body is kept in its proper place. "For no one who has a blemish shall draw near," Moses is reputed to have told the nascent people of Israel (Lev. 21:18–20), and similarly, "any who is blind or lame, or one who has a mutilated face or a limb too long, or one who has a broken foot or a broken hand, or a hunchback or a dwarf, or a man with a blemish in his eyes or an itching disease or scabs or crushed testicles."[54] That is, no one with these infirmities—through no fault of their own, it need be said—is permitted to make offerings to Yahweh, to participate fully in their theocratic society. Their abnormal bodies have cast them out, whether literally, figuratively, or ceremonially. And, lest we forget, the religious imagination most often renders fundamentally atypical the bodies of women: shut out entirely from the holy of holies, forbidden from ritual worship during menstruation, denied the right of leadership in any number of traditions by simple virtue of her sex, and, in more

than a few religious fever-dreams, held accountable for the cosmic fall
of humankind.

Rather than the imprimatur of bodies out of place, horror often confronts us with the reality that concepts such as "beauty," "normality," and
"purity" are culturally constructed, socially reinforced, and meaningful only within particular contexts. In "Underneath an Arkham Moon,"
for example, Jessica Salmonson and W. H. Pugmire invoke one of H.
P. Lovecraft's principal fears of the abnormal body: the danger of the
genetically compromised Other, whether contaminated from within or
without.

To most people, Alluna and Mehmeh are little more than "Arkham
devils," "witch-born" and barely human if human at all. Deformed certainly, demented possibly, they have been "tainted [with] witch-blood"
and, through generations of inbreeding, blasphemously endowed with
"arcane senses."[55] Partially fused along the spine, Alluna and Mehmeh
are conjoined twins. While Alluna is fully developed, her sister, a curious hump that lived on Alluna's back, had "barely any legs, and the
tiny feet of an infant," as well as arms that were "long and spindly and
curiously hinged."[56] "Mehmeh could never speak," Alluna tells us, "and
most of my kin assumed her simple, like a child. She was not simple."[57]
While this could be read as little more than commentary on the kind of
social and cultural disparagement used throughout history to reinforce
in-group and out-group boundaries, and prominent among a number of
Lovecraft's friends and literary peers, the lens of the religious imagination reveals far more to the story.

"To outsiders," Alluna continues, "there is both horror and disdain for
our inbred kind, but from within, those among us who are least human
are most divine."[58] Indeed, it is not uncommon in our own history for
those furthest from the cultural norm to be considered closest to revela-
tory power. For her part, in the dank confines of Arkham, drawn by a
"perverse urge" bred deep in the bones of her people, Alluna is bent on
inverting the *heiros gamos*, the sacred marriage between goddess and
god. Summoning "the beast of legend" into her "aphotic marriage chamber," she recounts that "in this creature's pallid luminosity" she recognized "the true and divine spark of angels, inclusive of the fallen. An
egomaniacal pride sprang within me, that I might be the Mother of the
One, the darkly beatific and transcendently inhuman savior."[59] Notwith-

standing the myriad images crowding the arcane cathedrals of our religious imagination, how could the realm of angels and demons, of gods and demigods, be anything *but* frighteningly inhuman?

In all of this, bodies out of place regularly invoke some confluence of the sexual body's (un)holy trinity: *sexuality*, which includes sexual development and the spectrum of sexual attraction, which emerges in us long before we are aware of it and remains relatively stable throughout our lives; *gender*, that is, the ambiguous conjunction of biology, social construction, cultural practice, and, not infrequently, religious mandate in determining who and, more importantly, what we are as sexual beings; and *sex* itself, especially as it is restricted by religious doctrine, expressed through religious ritual, or condemned as a consequence of religious revelation. In addition to the ambiguity of horror, exploring this tripartite enigma requires three additional movements if we hope even to understand the question of fearing flesh.

Fearing Flesh in Three Movements

Shrieking at her erstwhile lover, outraged at being callously cast aside, the young woman vents the full fury of her emotion. After all, he told her she was different. He told her she was special. He told her that he loved her. Now, stripped naked, her suffering stretched taut, she backs up against the dread Pillar of Souls. In pure *Hellraiser* fashion, hooked chains shoot from hidden openings in the massive sculpture, catching her flesh and holding her fast. One hook embeds in her forehead and tugs, flaying the skin from her body in a single, fluid motion. She screams, this time in disbelief and terror, shock shielding her brain for a few precious seconds before what remains of her body is drawn in and consumed by the Pillar itself. She reemerges, finally, as a face embossed on the demonic column's marble surface, her mouth set in an endless silent cry.

Until that moment, the Pillar of Souls had been nothing more than an interesting addition to the hapless thug Monroe's predatory man-cave. Elaborately carved with the bodies of men and women writhing in sexual torment and ecstasy, the Pillar's dangerous eroticism sat quietly in the corner, mute witness to the anguish of the women Monroe uses and discards night after night.

"Jesus Christ!" he gasps.

"Not quite," replies another, far more malevolent face. Also sculpted into the Pillar is the Cenobite, the Hell Priest known as Pinhead, central character in Clive Barker's *Hellraiser* mythos. "What did you see?" he continues amiably. "The same as I? Appetites sated, desires indulged, a miniature of the world and how it will succumb to us? You *enjoyed* the girl?"—pause for dramatic effect—"So did I."[60]

"No!" yells Monroe. "It's not the same. No, what you did, that was fuckin' evil, man!"[61]

"Oh, how uncomfortable that word must feel on your lips," the Cenobite says. "Evil . . . good." He chuckles cruelly, as though recalling humans without number who have squirmed on this particular hook. Then he speaks.

"There is no good, Monroe, there is no evil. There is only flesh."[62]

Scenes such as this, from *Hellraiser III: Hell on Earth, The Exorcist*'s crucifix masturbation sequence, and other examples we will examine going forward, invite, indeed demand, that we move beyond any singular metanarrative, any pretense to knowing in the final analysis what something means. Meaning is not an artifact to be uncovered on the psychologist's couch, through a sociologist's survey, or in the conventional pieties of a particular ideological commitment. Rather, it is a *culturfact* that exists in the gaps and cracks between our perennial questions about the nature of reality, the precarious confidence of our answers, and the stories we tell and retell in those obscure spaces. Stories that embed our prejudices toward and fear of others. Stories that reflect and refract our erratic hope that there is light at the end of life's tunnel. Stories that both challenge and reinforce what we consider consensus reality. Indeed, engaging the enigmatic culturfact of horror in this way requires us to make three particular movements that will guide our explorations into, as Pinhead says in the film for which the *Hellraiser* franchise is named, "the further regions of experience."[63] These are the movements beyond genre, beyond skepticism, and, finally, beyond religion.

Beyond Genre: The Horror Mode

Few *Hellraiser* fans, or even those who catch Pinhead's iconic visage out of the corner of their eye, doubt where you would find the franchise on the shelves. The same would be true for Regan MacNeil's ravaged face and tortured body. Despite *The Exorcist*'s pride of place in twentieth-century horror, however, William Peter Blatty did not believe he was writing a horror novel. "The humiliating God's-honest truth of the matter," he admitted a couple of years before his passing, "is that while I was working on 'The Exorcist,' what I thought I was writing was a novel of faith in the popular dress of a thrilling and suspenseful detective story—in other words, a sermon that no one could sleep through."[64] This points us to the question of the horror *genre* versus the horror *mode*.

By and large, genre is a function of marketing, created to serve the economics of publishing by targeting specific consumer interests. If you want *The Hellbound Heart*, you go to the horror section in your local bookstore; if you want any of the myriad *Hellraiser* films, you turn to the horror category on streaming services or download sites. As I wrote over a decade ago, "non-horror films may frighten the audience to tell their stories, but horror films tell stories to frighten their audiences. In the former, fear is a side effect; in the latter, it is the object of the exercise."[65] Genre helps us to tell the difference, and I stand by that definition in its most basic sense. But as literary critic, editor, and publisher David Hartwell points out, over the last century "genrefication" has severely constrained our ability to recognize larger narrative horizons of human fearing and, thus, to explore the enigma of horror as fully as we might.

For Hartwell, "horror is not in the end either a marketing category or a genre, but a literary mode that has been used in every genre and category."[66] Thus, the horror mode is defined less by its reliance on ghosts or monsters or demons—however often they may play their horrific part—than by "the creation of an atmosphere and emotional environment that sparks a transaction between the reader and the text which yields the horrific response."[67] Indeed, he writes elsewhere, rather than the visceral shock of gore, in terms of the horror mode, this "emotional transaction is paramount and definitive."[68] In books and short stories, cinema and television, visual arts, role-playing and video games, this "emotional transaction" constitutes "the essence of the experience of reading horror fiction, and not any *thing* contained within that text."[69] Call it "weird fiction," "dark fantasy," "splatterpunk," "torture porn," "kwaidan," or just plain "horror," the horrific is always a function of an affective negotiation between what the author, artist, or director presents and what we bring to our experience of that presentation.[70] This triggers the next movement, down the slope from skepticism to realization.

Beyond Skepticism: The New Normal

"To feel the unease aimed at in a ghost story," wrote historian Jacques Barzun, "one must start by being certain that there is no such thing as a ghost"—or a monster or a demon or primeval gods, for that matter.[71] For Monroe, "Jesus Christ!" is not a prayer of supplication but an ejaculation of disbelief. Which is to say, in many cases (though not all), rather than credulity, skepticism is a precondition of horror. Ghosts are not real, monsters do not exist, and demons neither possess little girls nor flay young women alive just to taste their suffering. Except when they do, and that's the point. Thus, the second movement is from Barzun's "confident skepticism" to horrific realization, especially when those who come to dispel the fear of frightening phenomena are themselves converted to belief in it.

Much of the horror mode regularly dresses its sets in claims to reason and appeals to the technology of rationalism, both of which are intended to throw the story's horrific reality into stark relief. In *Bloodline*, the fourth entry in the *Hellraiser* franchise, a Paris physician lectures a young toymaker: "This is the eighteenth century, Phillipe, not the Dark Ages. The world is ruled by reason! We've even gotten rid of God."[72] Enter the Hell Priest, Pinhead. Barely five minutes into Tim Burton's dark and lavish version of *Sleepy Hollow*, Ichabod Crane pleads with his peers to accept the fact that "the millennium is almost upon us, gentlemen. In a few months, we will be living in the nineteenth century!"[73] Enter the revenant spirit of a Hessian mercenary. In Edgar Ulmer's *Daughter of Dr. Jekyll*, George Hastings insists that his fiancée, the eponymous doctor's only child, could not have inherited her father's malevolent condition—presented in this outing as lycanthropy. It's "ridiculous," he tells her. "We're living in the twentieth century. This is an age of reason, not superstition! Everything you've shown me has a reasonable explanation."[74] Enter the werewolf, concealed here in the guise of the young woman's doctor. Even in such a niche genre as Christian apocalyptic fiction, which serves principally as literary comfort food for fundamentalist believers, among the welter of predictable plotting and potted dialogue is the stock character of a journalist left behind in the wake of the Rapture. The cultural icon of skepticism and nonbelief, he or she is convinced there must be a rational explanation for the global horror that has occurred. Enter the Antichrist.[75]

In Nick Murphy's Edwardian ghost story, *The Awakening*, a kind of *Downton Abbey* meets *The Sixth Sense*, arch-skeptic Florence Cathcart devotes her life to debunking the paranormal and the supernatural. Like the *Ghostbusters*, both old and new, like any number of paranormal "reality shows"—only the most ridiculous of which outfits its cast in mock tactical vests—Florence has her collection of ghost-hunting equipment: tripwires and bells; potassium permanganate powder, less for detecting ghosts than for spotting those who pretend to be ghosts; a Marconi magnetic field generator; as well as the usual assortment of sound recorders and cameras.[76] As set-piece props, these are the trappings of rationality, the material culture of skepticism that anchors us to the solid foundation of the seen, the known, the measurable, and, therefore, the explainable. "This is not a feeling," Florence insists. "This is a thesis. It's science."[77]

By the end of the film, though, we are not sure what *The Awakening* actually is: the slow rise to consciousness of one's own death, a caught-dead story masquerading as a hunt for the supernatural, or less the tale of a haunting spirit than of a spirit haunted by loneliness after death? Indeed, in the midst of the ambiguity that marks the horror mode at its best, we are not entirely sure whether Florence Cathcart herself is alive or dead.

Caitlín Kiernan's Lovecraftian short story "Pickman's Other Model (1929)" similarly demonstrates this tenuous relationship between rationalism and realization: confident skepticism bleeding slowly into horrified certainty that anything we *think* we know pales to insignificance before even a hint of what is *really* out there.

"I have never been much for movies," the unnamed narrator tells us initially, "preferring, instead, to take my entertainment in the theater, always favoring living actors over those flickering, garish ghosts magnified and splashed across the walls of dark and smoky rooms at twenty-four frames per second."[78] Unable "to get past the knowledge that the apparent motion is merely an optical illusion," for him films remain, in fact, what they are: a "clever precession of still images."[79] Which is to say, his reaction is precisely the opposite from that of countless millions of moviegoers who do see in "moving pictures" some reflection of real life, and for whom they constitute the "real." Encountering the mysterious Vera Endecott, however, changes all that, and challenges everything he thinks he knows about the world.

Daughter of the "distinctly unsavory" Iscariot Snow, a man accused of "sorcery and witchcraft, incest, and even cannibalism," Vera performs in a variety of underground films that the narrator has been persuaded to view.[80] Rather than the "wood nymphs" who appear first on the screen, though, he watches, fascinated and horrified, as the actors magically transform into "prisoners, or condemned souls bound eternally for their sins." Like Monroe confronted by the Pillar of Souls, he "can only stare in wonder at the confusion of arms and legs, hips and breasts and faces marked by untold ages of the ceaseless agony of this contortion and transformation."[81] The centerpiece sin, however, quickly becomes apparent.

Sitting in a "musty private screening room near Harvard Square," surrounded by "a small circle of aficionados of grotesque cinema," he watches "*The Necrophile*," a "blatantly pornographic pastiche of the widely circulated 1918 publicity stills of Theda Bara lying in various risqué poses with a human skeleton."[82] Vera Endecott, Kiernan's literary stand-in for the woman marketed by Hollywood as "the archetype of the sexual vampire," takes still photography to the next carnal level.[83] Lying with the skeleton on a stone floor, she "caressed all the osseous angles of its arms and legs and lavished kisses upon its lipless mouth, before masturbating, first with the bones of its right hand, and then by rubbing herself against the crest of an ilium." Finally, "her lust apparently satiated, the actress lay down with her skeletal lover."[84]

Shaken to the core, the narrator leaves the theater, entirely at a loss to explain "how the deception has been accomplished." Given the limitations of "the prosaic magic of filmmaking," he cannot reconcile what he is convinced he saw onscreen with what he knows cannot be the case. Whatever had been captured there on those "17,000 or so frames"— whatever it was that he did "not want to see, and [does] not want to know"—must be *something other* than a few moments' cinematic fantasy.[85] The urge to rationalize, however, to explain the inexplicable, is as strong in us as the will to believe the unbelievable—if for no other reason than that the alternative is often too horrifying to imagine.

This is the moment in John Carpenter's *The Thing* when Palmer, see-ing a human head grow legs and skitter out of the room, exclaims, "You *gotta'* be fuckin' kidding!"[86] This is the moment in the pilot episode of Showtime's *Penny Dreadful* when, having fought the cursed denizens of a terrifying demimonde, reluctant gun-for-hire Ethan Chandler con-fronts the mysterious Vanessa Ives and Sir Malcolm Murray and asks, "Who the fuck *are* you people?"[87] This is the moment in *Hellraiser III*, after a kindly, well-meaning priest reassures reporter Joey Summerskill that "demons aren't real. They're parables, metaphors," she points down the aisle as the door creaks open and Pinhead appears: "Then what the fuck is *that?*"[88] This is the moment when we realize how misplaced is our confidence in consensus reality, and a perverse ambiguity takes its place as the new normal. This leads to the third movement, the one that takes us beyond religion as we so often understand it.

Beyond Religion: The Religious Imagination

On the surface, *The Exorcist* and *Hellraiser III* have little in common. The Roman Catholic Church exists in the real world, while the Cenobites stepped through from the imagination of a man Stephen King described as "the future of horror." There is a Rite of Exorcism, whatever liberties Blatty and Friedkin may have taken with it, but the Pillar of Souls is noth-ing more than plywood, paint, and plaster. While *hell* forms the common armature between them, the explicitly religious concept around which their separate stories are shaped, they do not so much share religion in common as they are joined by the religious imagination.

Most of us are confident that we know religion when we see it. A church building, with hard, wooden pews polished smooth by genera-tions of worshipers. A neighborhood mosque, so much a part of the community's life that Mecca itself seems to live within its familiar spaces. A temple, stark against the backdrop of the suburban landscape, an-nouncing for all with eyes to see, Here you will find your gods. For many of us, however, *religion* is limited only to what we recognize as religion, what we know from our own relatively narrow experience. Indeed, some critics insist, rather misguidedly in my view, that "the sacred as depicted in the world religions ought to remain the benchmark for understanding what should count as most genuinely sacred."[89]

The *religious imagination*, on the other hand, the ubiquitous impulse to picture a world beyond our own and to locate ourselves in cosmic circumstances, is a much larger phenomenon, infinitely more varied, and considerably more rewarding analytically. Put differently, while all religions emerge as products of the religious imagination, not all aspects of the religious imagination ultimately take their place in the world as lived religions. Far more of them come to us through myth and legend, fable and fairy tale, short stories and pulp novels, film and television, literary horror, weird fiction, graphic storytelling, visual arts, and participative culture—just to name a few. Which is to say, the myriad narrative experiences in and through which Homo sapiens have sought meaning in their twin guise as *Homo narrans* and *Homo fabulans*.[90] Restricting discussion only to what we can readily identify (or have been socialized to distinguish) as "religion" severely limits our ability to recognize those other culturfacts of the religious imagination—often because what they disclose makes us so profoundly uncomfortable.

Imagining the Religious Imagination

More than a century ago, in the second of his prestigious Gifford Lectures in Natural Theology, psychologist and philosopher William James (no relation to M. R.) defined religion in a couple of different ways. On the one hand, he told Europe's assembled scholarly elite, it is "the feelings, acts, and experiences of individual [persons] in their solitude, so far as they apprehend themselves to stand in relation to whatever they may consider the divine."[91] Keep that in mind: *whatever they may consider the divine*. However, because this is the only definition indexed in *The Varieties of Religious Experience*, it tends to be the one with which people are most familiar. More's the pity, because the second definition, although more difficult to find, is at least as useful for our purposes.

That is, in his third lecture, James suggests that "the life of religion," when conceived in "the broadest and most general terms possible . . . consists of the belief that there is an unseen order, and that our supreme good lies in harmonious adjustment thereto."[92] While the *religious imagination* can be the product of individual belief or solitary pursuit, *religion* is both a social process and a cultural phenomenon. It takes place in the context of a community and extrudes from the religious imagination into consensus reality only and always as a function of community. Taken together, these definitions offer a number of benefits that become especially apparent when we consider the various intersections of religion, the religious imagination, and the horror mode.

First and foremost, "the belief that there is an unseen order" concedes nothing more than that what we see, hear, and feel around us is not the measure of the way things really are, that *something else* exists beyond, above, behind, or beside what we consider reality. Perhaps there is an all-powerful being either running things for our benefit or eyeing us with cold, cosmic indifference. Perhaps a variety of gods, greater and lesser, manage the affairs of the world, or what we imagine as gods are no more than technologically advanced extraterrestrials or interdimensionals.[93] Or, perhaps this unseen order comprises an impersonal array of energies and forces, which we can access for good or ill, but to which we are still ultimately bound whether we wish it or not. It doesn't really matter, because "belief that there is an unseen order" usefully precludes the need for specific gods, let alone *a* god, some form of supreme god, or even the notion of "gods" at all. It simply recognizes that the material universe as we so narrowly apprehend it is not all that there is.

Second, the sense of mystery retained by James's definitions obviates any need to adjudicate religious authenticity, historical or otherwise, ideologically motivated or not. Put differently, we need not engage in fruitless debate over whose invisible super-friends are real and whose are not. Religion is no longer limited either to a particular theological agenda or to what people most readily recognize as religion—which, not surprisingly, is usually their own. Given the astonishing diversity of belief, practice, ritual, and experience encompassed by "whatever they may consider the divine," James proposes that we set aside issues of legitimacy and, given its impracticality, resist "the temptation to establish whether something is 'true' or not."[94]

As much as anything, this encourages explorations of the religious imagination well apart from any dependence on religions as they exist—or are imagined to exist—in the real world. Of course, in many, perhaps even most, cases, the former will either reflect or refract the latter. The horror mode will reveal facets of real-world religion we might not otherwise be willing to face. *The Exorcist* is unimaginable apart from its Roman Catholic underpinning, *The Omen* from its reliance on Protestant dispensationalism and belief in the Antichrist, or *Rosemary's Baby* from the popular fear of shadowy satanic cults hiding in plain sight. *Assassin's Creed*, a 2016 movie based on the popular stealth-combat videogame franchise, is grounded in a particular interpretation of the real-world horrors of the Spanish Inquisition. That said, though, this does not mean that the horror mode must correlate in some way to religion in the real world, as though religious belief and practice as we find them on the street or in the pew provide a necessary limit-case for consideration of the religious imagination. The enduring horror of galactic warfare embodied in the massively popular *Warhammer 40K*, for example, is based explicitly in institutionalized religious conflict, and, thus, the religious imagination.[95] The central narrative driving the equally influential *Halo* franchise is one of resistance to extraterrestrial religious conquest.[96] Once freed from the demands of correlation to religious traditions in the "real" world, we can more easily avoid the superficial "this-kind-of-looks-like-that" comparison that litters so much of the scholarship on religion and popular culture. Because James's definitions oppose any restriction on what is conventionally or doctrinally regarded as "religion," they open up the vistas of the religious imagination to exploration through horror, science fiction, fantasy, and their web of varied hybrids.

Following from this, then, James's definitions expose the false dichotomy between religion and magic, an artificial separation that usually intends to privilege the former at the expense of the latter. Ever since Émile Durkheim pronounced rather dogmatically that "there is no Church of Magic," theologically motivated distinctions between religion and magic have been almost de rigueur, and pursued primarily for the purpose of legitimating the authority of one vision of the unseen order at the expense of others.[97] Real religions pray; false ones cast spells. Real religions worship gods; false ones bow down before idols. In a word, real religions are good; false ones not so much. Once divorced from this misleading duality, however, the unseen order could as reasonably accommodate the hierarchy of spirits with whom an occultist such as Lon Milo DuQuette claims to live as it does the pecking order of saints, angels, and demons catalogued by legions of Catholic dogmatic theologians.[98] It could as reasonably (or certainly no *less* reasonably) be the domain of vast and indifferent cosmic forces that have as much regard for human concerns as we have for the innumerable creatures we exterminate with no more than a passing thought. And, as much as anything, it recognizes that those who cast spells "are neither fools, escapists nor superstitious." As modern Witches Janet and Stewart Farrar remind us, for example, "If witchcraft did not have a coherent rationale, such people could only keep going by a kind of deliberate schizophrenia."[99] Since there is little evidence that this is the case, we are left seeking other explanations.

Finally, James's definitions are sufficiently broad to allow us to disentangle religion from the good, moral, and decent fallacy—arguably its principal benefit for any discussion of the religious imagination and the horror mode. Also known as "approbation bias," this is the somewhat self-serving metanarrative that if evil is perpetrated by religious believers, either through their particular interpretation of the faith or at the alleged behest of their god, it cannot be "real" religion. In this sense, religion becomes, by definition, a desirable aspect of human culture, and works at all times for the good of humankind—both in this life and in the next. It is difficult to imagine a less tenable position from which to view the world around us. Indeed, as physicist and Nobel laureate Steven Weinberg pointed out in an address to the American Association for the Advancement of Science, "With or without religion, good people can behave well and bad people can do evil; but for good people to do evil—that takes religion."[100] Absent the good, moral, and decent fallacy, then, Charles Wesley's "gentle Jesus, meek and mild" has no more intrinsic hold on the religious imagination than, say, the "grinning, vulpine" Christ of Stephen King's "He Who Walks Behind the Rows," and the orthodox god of a small fishing village is no more inherently reasonable than H. P. Lovecraft's "debased quasi-pagan thing imported from the East a century before."[101] In point of fact, throughout history, nothing should be more apparent than that what some "consider the divine" others regard as the quintessence of the unholy. "Angels to some, demons to others," as the Hell Priest would say.[102] One person's monster is another's supreme being. And, what those monstrous beings often require in order to ensure "harmonious adjustment" between our world and theirs can be truly terrifying.

Don't believe me? Ask Vera Endecott.

Not surprisingly, things do not end well for "Pickman's Other Model." Indeed, Vera's body is eventually discovered "dangling from the trunk of an oak tree growing near the center of King's Chapel Burial Ground."[103]

According to newspaper accounts, her corpse was suspended a full seventeen feet off the ground, bound round the waist and chest with interwo-
ven lengths of jute rope and baling wire. . . . Her body had been stripped
of all clothing, disemboweled, her throat cut, and her tongue removed.
Her lips had been sewn shut with cat-gut stitches. About her neck was
a wooden placard, upon which one word had been written in what is
believed to be the dead woman's own blood: *apostate*.[104]

Like heaven and hell, like the soul and the spirit, "apostate" is another of those words that has no meaning apart from the religious
imagination, the devotional or sanctified context in which it comes embedded. From what has she apostatized? To what gods had she pledged
an allegiance now presumably forsaken? Whatever else it is, hers is
not simple murder, and death alone does not seem penalty enough for
whatever she has done. Hung, bound, stripped, and disemboweled—
all these suggest hideous punishment for the most grievous offense.
Throat cut, tongue removed, lips sewn shut—these speak to the revelation of secrets that were not hers to share. Somehow, we can imagine, she made the esoteric exoteric, which means that there is still a
group out there, a religious community to which she belonged—and
for which she now hangs as a mute, horrific warning to any others who
would cross their designs.

Hers is suddenly a body rendered out of place in a number of ways.

To reiterate, contrary to what many critics contend, and notwithstanding any discomfort we may feel, religion and horror are not competitors in the arena of the human imagination, but cultural siblings
concerned with exploring the same perennial questions. In some cases,
these explorations tread familiar territory. James Herbert's *Shrine*, for
example, asks what happens when a small English village become the
site of an apparent Marian visitation. Though he insists that he remains
a staunch Roman Catholic, "the whole point about my books, the same
as the religious bit in *Shrine*, is that it's all nonsense. The moment we,
as men, think we can conceive what is actually happening out there,
that's when we've got to be wrong, because it's too big for us. We don't
understand it. We can't understand it."[105] Put differently, the pale and
provincial confines of "religion" can never pretend to approach, let alone
encompass the limitless horizons of the "religious imagination."

Others use the horror mode to map territories far beyond the familiar. Though raised in the Presbyterian Church, dark fantasist Michael McDowell is antireligious. On the existence of the supernatural, however, he is more of a Lovecraftian, and believes that "there is something out there that is malevolent and there is no way of making whatever it is conform to our petty beliefs in rationality and in things going along as they should. . . . Not only are we small, but we're powerless and insignificant."[106] However far we may insist we have traveled from Plato's cave, "we dwell forever in realms of shadow," writes Donald Burleson. "Strangely complacent, we wander through our weary days as if we understood the texture of the world."[107]

"The whole point about good horror fiction," said Clive Barker in a 1988 interview for the magazine *Graffiti*, "is that it subverts systems without offering up coherent alternative systems. . . . Great fantasy helps you deal with exploration of the problems and ideas which confront you on a day-to-day basis."[108] That is, it leaves reality permanently askew, vertiginously tilted and never returned to square and level. In what we might call "the once seen problem," once you've had your "what the fuck is *that*?" moment, you can't ever go back to the way things were. In order to understand how much has changed, however, we do need some sense of "the way things were," and the ways in which the horror mode reinforces notions of "the way things should be." For this, then, we consider crab monsters and giant leeches.

2

Crab Monsters and Giant Leeches

Exploitation and the Socially Approved Body

Rolling behind the opening credits, the artistic montage resembles nothing so much as a crude tribute to Jules Verne's venerable *20,000 Leagues Under the Sea*. The establishing shot, however, is pure Cecil B. DeMille and the biblical epics he made famous. Reminiscent of a scene from *The Ten Commandments*, released the previous year and still one of Hollywood's highest-grossing films, lowering clouds roil across an angry sky as a booming voice announces, "And the Lord said, I will destroy man whom I have made from the face of the earth; both man and beast, and the creeping things, and the fowls of the air, for it repenteth me that I have made them."[1]

This is not DeMille, however, nor one of his many imitators, but Roger Corman's 1957 creature feature, *Attack of the Crab Monsters*. Written by Charles Griffith specifically for the drive-in and Saturday matinée markets, this classic "bug-eyed monster" movie originally hit theaters on a double bill with *Not of This Earth* (another of the *nine* films Corman both produced and directed that year, six of which Griffith wrote).[2] And, in all ways, *Crab Monsters* followed Corman's low-budget strategy: make every foot of precious film stock count, reuse previously shot footage where you can, and "borrow" it from other films when you can't.[3] More than that, everything in a Corman film had to be about tension, suspense, and, most importantly, action—whether it fit the plot, advanced a story, or even followed the script. In his mind, despite the divine voiceover, no one was paying to see a film with a message.

But that did not mean that there was not a message to be seen.

Cut to a small boat landing on a deserted beach. A group of scientists have come to this remote corner of the Pacific in a desperate search for their missing colleagues. "Strange," one of them says, "we can see only a small part of the island from here, but yet you can feel . . . lack of wel-

54

come, lack of abiding life, huh?"[4] As another skiff lands, a sailor loses his balance, tumbling into the low surf just yards from shore. On the sandy bottom, *something* stirs, wakes, then attacks. A brief swirl at the surface, and a few seconds later the man's now-headless body is hauled back into the boat. Lack of welcome, indeed. Standing on shore, arms akimbo, the junior officer in charge simply grits his teeth and sighs. "Cover him," he says, as though this kind of thing happens every other week, and he is more concerned with looming paperwork than losing a crew member in a few feet of water. Barely three minutes into the film and we are already bound by what Jonathan Gottschall calls "the fat rope of trouble."[5]

B-horror is not known for its subtlety.

In fact, Corman disliked the term "B-movie" intensely. He considered it a relic of the Hollywood studio system, in which "A-movies," featuring high production values and the contract stars of the day, were paired with much-lower-budget fare as a way of giving moviegoers more value for their money. It was not that Corman was under any illusion about the quality of his own cinematic products—creature features such as *Day the World Ended*, *It Conquered the World*, *She Gods of Shark Reef*, *The Undead*, and (quite possibly my favorite title) *The Saga of the Viking Women and Their Voyage to the Waters of the Great Sea Serpent*—but he preferred to call them "exploitation films."[6] According to one of his former story editors, these were "low-cost pictures that rely on showmanship to appeal to a broad popular audience," principally by "'exploiting' hot topics of the day."[7] The question, of course, is, What "hot topics"? And, while the notion of exploitation is hardly limited to B-movies, how are these topics exploited, and what can that tell us about prevailing cultural values, stereotypes, and prejudices?[8]

At first approximation, B-movies exploit the notion of "entertainment as value," a stubborn reality that art historian Helen Searing identifies as the principal "contradiction at the heart of most serious horror film criticism."[9] That is, while countless millions enjoy the frisson of spooky stories and scary movies, that alone does not seem enough to justify ivory-tower attention. Enjoyment, the academic argument implies, may be a necessary condition, but it is not sufficient for us to consider second- and third-tier cinema horror (and such literary counterparts as pulp and genre fiction, men's adventure magazines, comic books, and weekly manga) intellectually important. The reason seems clear, as William Tsutsui muses in his delightful *Godzilla on My Mind*: "Sometimes, all those youthful hours spent watching Godzilla movies may not seem quite so squandered if we can convince ourselves that the films were somehow educational, or edifying, or even indoctrinating, and not just empty cinematic calories, imported sci-fi junk food with no nutritional value for mind, character, or soul."[10] Put bluntly, though, the B-movie has only one goal: "to make money by appealing to the public's taste for crude entertainment—without apology."[11] And, unapologetically, movies such as *Attack of the Crab Monsters* and its numberless cinematic cohort constitute "a primary source of the kind of unsophisticated but essential pleasures human beings have always craved."[12] The two key phrases here are "the public's taste" and "unsophisticated but essential," concepts that cut to the quick of why these kinds of stories appeal to so many, and remain so durable in that appeal. Put simply, they *like* them.

And, after all, is escapism really so bad? I mean, can't it just be about having a good time, even if that entails being scared witless with your friends on the couch or in a movie theater? Indeed, "the *fun* of playing," writes Johan Huizinga at the beginning of his classic text, *Homo Ludens*, "resists all analysis, all logical interpretation. As a concept, it cannot be reduced to any other mental category."[13] Calling onto the carpet the scholarly rush to find Something Important to Say, both Searing and Tsutsui implicitly indict academics who routinely dismiss the notion of enjoyment as value, fun as social and cultural benefit, and entertainment as something worthwhile in its own right. Because, regardless of where we find it or how we come by it, enjoyment *is* an essential ingredient in human flourishing, especially when it supports our species' prosocial nature and contributes to processes of intragroup bonding and intergroup cooperation. That said, though, this kind of erudite prejudice has plagued the scholarly study of popular culture for decades, despite the cold, hard facts that Roger Corman boasts of never making a creature feature that lost money, that Stephen King moves more books in one day than most scholars will sell in their entire careers, and that there is such a constant reinvention and reinvestment in popular culture that it positively dwarfs all other contributors to our cultural stock of knowledge.[14] The problem is thinking that it cannot be both, that acknowledging enjoyment as value—even if it is a laughable B-horror flick like *Attack of the Crab Monsters*—and considering what we find intellectually worthy of study are somehow mutually exclusive.

More than a generation ago, film critic Ado Kyrou proffered a useful conceptual touchstone to help probe, if not necessarily resolve this dilemma, another way of considering pop culture as an enigma rather than a riddle. Defending the experimental and often iconoclastic films being made by surrealists and the French avant-garde, he wrote that, despite whatever pressure we may feel to notice only the highbrow aspects of culture these directors challenged and critiqued, we must "learn to look at 'bad' films"—or what are colloquially considered so.[15] That is, we should not only *watch* "bad films," but precisely because they are so popular, we must *look* at them in order to learn their codes and their grammar, to *listen* for the small narrative details that hint at the possibility of something more. And, however obvious and simplistic these B-movie morphologies may appear initially, we must ask how they relate to the cultures that produce them. Because "bad" movies, Kyrou insisted, "are often sublime," and learning to look means exploring the landscape of B-movie sublimity.[16] For him, this meant opening up the "undiscovered country" lurking beneath the surface of "films the 'aesthetes' disdain and the church reproves."[17] Rather than "the manifest aspects of film," Kyrou suggested, "it is their latent content that must be prospected" if we are to "find the most unexpected riches there."[18] As critics ranging from Helen Searing to Stephen King, and from Cyndy Hendershot to David Skal and Marc Jancovich note, the B-movies that were produced in their hundreds and released almost as throwaway cinematic products often function as "oddly sensitive barometers of free-floating social anxieties"—concerns that Corman and his fellow filmmakers could easily exploit.[19]

Chief among these, of course, is sex, and Corman made no secret of his willingness to take advantage of this particular anxiety. Indeed, legendary director and former Corman employee Martin Scorsese recalls his boss telling him, "Read the script, rewrite as much as you want, but remember, Marty, that you must have some nudity at least every fifteen pages."[20] It wasn't that they were making pornography, Corman emphasized, but simply that their films were exploiting our species' natural instinct to pay attention to the sexual. "Not complete nudity," he warned his protégé, though, but "maybe a little off-the-shoulder, or some leg, just to keep the audience interest up."[21]

And, for this, we need look no further than the posters and lobby cards advertising any number of 1950s science fiction and horror movies—many of which bore only passing resemblance to the film's plot, but almost all of which continued the cover-art traditions developed during the golden age of pulp fiction. On *The Day the Earth Stood Still*, for instance, the giant robot Gort lays waste to entire armored divisions with its cyclopean death-ray—while carrying a screaming, lingerie-clad blonde woman in its stout metal arms. When *The Monster That Challenged the World* crawled "from the depths to terrify and torture," the first thing it grabbed was a scantily clad brunette who immediately fainted from terror. As *The Invasion of the Saucer-Men* brought their "creeping horror from the depths of time and space," they made off with a similarly unconscious woman wrapped in a towel—but only just barely. One poster for *Attack of the Crab Monsters* advertises "a tidal wave of terror," as the eponymous leviathan grasps yet another screaming blonde in its giant claw—the image a far cry from lone female star Pamela Duncan's wavy brunette bob. From *Robot Monster* to *Tobor the Great*, from *Revenge of the Creature* and *Forbidden Planet* to *The Mole People* and *From Hell It Came*, the nearly nude woman, who is always either wide-eyed and shrieking in terror, or passed out from fright, was one of the most common tropes of B-movie artwork.[22] And for one very simple reason: "People are hard-wired to notice sexually relevant information."[23]

As media scholar Tom Reichert, who researches sexualization in advertising, points out, the "shapes of buttocks, breasts, and broad shoulders have been hard-wired into our brains and then onto our minds as an evolving grammar of both survival and pleasure."[24] This brief comment exposes the essential sexual differences setting humans apart from virtually every other species. On the one hand, the biological fact that women do not come into heat, and may conceive at any time between the onset of menses and the end of menopause, has served our evolutionary survival in the face of a number of distinct physical disadvantages. On the other, the sociological fact that humans participate in such an astonishing array of sexual activity, both for reasons other than the need for procreation and long after the desire and ability to bear children has ended, means that for hundreds of millions of people sexual activity and sexual representation comprise either a significant form of

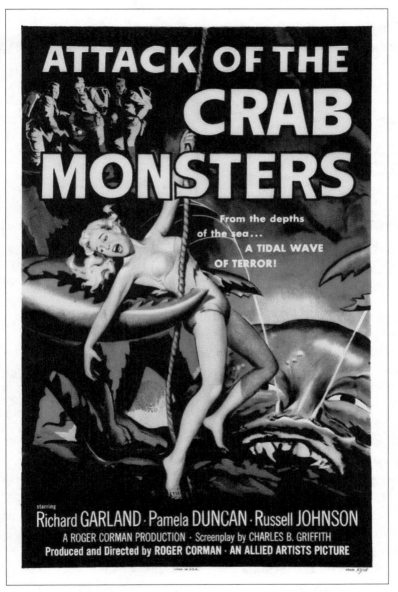

Figure 2.1. Movie poster for Gene Corman's *Attack of the Crab Monsters*.

recreation or an ongoing source of social anxiety—not infrequently both at the same time. In either case, and whether implicit or explicit, sex becomes a near-constant topic of cultural conversation.[25]

Sexual relevance, though, is never without context. Corman may not have been making pornography, but he recognized that it is not only the fact of "sexually relevant information" that B-movies exploit but the cultural milieu that both shapes the particular relevance and suggests how an audience is meant to understand a film's sexual information. That is, it exploits, and in some cases confronts, a culture's "recipe knowledge" about sexual relations and relationships.

According to sociologists Peter Berger and Thomas Luckmann, "recipe knowledge" constitutes "the sum total 'what everybody knows' about a social world, an assemblage of maxims, morals, proverbial nuggets of wisdom, values and beliefs, myths, and so forth."[26] Woven from an interdependent web of family connections, education and social upbringing, religious belief and participation, friendship networks, media consumption, state mandate, and general conversation, this "recipe knowledge" both frames and reinforces culturally "appropriate rules of conduct."[27] Put differently, it creates the sociological well of "normal" from which filmmakers such as Corman draw, which their cinematic products occasionally challenge, and to which they reflexively contribute, whether they intend to or not. In terms of socially approved bodies in much of Western culture, and the intersection of sex, horror, and the religious imagination in particular, B-movies exploit the millennia-long effects of three concepts rooted deep in the cultural soil of "what everybody knows": "Thou shalt not commit adultery" (Ex. 20:14); "Thou shalt not covet thy neighbor's wife" (Ex. 20:17); and "Whosoever looketh on a woman to lust after her hath committed adultery with her already in his heart" (Matt. 5:28).

Consider the sexual state of play during the 1950s heyday of B-horror. However infrequently some of these statutes may have been enforced, most American states at the time criminalized adultery, while many of them also made fornication illegal, and all states had "sodomy" laws on the books. While vibrators in the 1950s were rudimentary at best, even today a number of US states either ban or severely limit the sale of sex toys.[28] Back then, popular magazines ranging from *Collier's* to *Harper's*, and from *Good Housekeeping* and *Reader's Digest* to *Do It Yourself* and the *Saturday Evening Post* relentlessly promoted the so-called nuclear family as the American sexual ideal, and magazines such as the nascent *Playboy* were seen as a major threat to that model. Hyperbolic antipornography crusades such as the Gathings Committee, and Frederic Wertham's campaign to censor popular comic books, were both grounded in the presumed protection of this family model.[29] Divorced Roman Catholics were denied the Eucharist, while in Protestant circles the battle over women's ordination often turned on whether or not the woman in question was willing to give up what many in the church to this day still consider her "natural" function.

In Hollywood, the now-infamous Motion Picture Production Code, colloquially known as the Hays Code (for politician William H. Hays, the first chairman of the Motion Picture Producers and Distributors of America), had gradually enforced a set of restrictions aimed mainly at controlling onscreen representations of sex, violence, and religion.[30] The year 1933 saw the formation of the National Legion of Decency, also known as the Catholic Legion of Decency, the original membership pledge for which read, in part, "I condemn absolutely those salacious motion pictures which, with other degrading agencies, are corrupting public morals and promoting a sex mania in our land." As film historian Gregory Black notes, "At masses all across the nation, Catholics were given no choice by their priests but to stand and take the Legion pledge."[31] Although the Hays Code was originally circulated in 1927, it was not until prominent Catholic layman Joseph Breen took over the office in 1934 that the Code's various provisions began to see more rigorous enforcement. The dreaded "C" rating, for example, meant that a film was condemned for viewing by Roman Catholics. Filmmakers feared this grade for the potential protests and boycotts it heralded, while some bishops even insisted that Catholics who saw forbidden films had committed a sin worthy of confession.

Oriented around the "general principle" that "no picture shall be produced that will lower the moral standards of those who see it," the Hays Code was meant to ensure that "correct standards of life" would always be maintained onscreen.[32] While we should always question who gets to decide what constitute these "correct standards" and on what grounds, underpinning this principle was the fundamental proposition that "evil" must never be "made to appear *attractive* or *alluring*," nor must "the *sympathy* of the audience [ever be] thrown on the side of crime, wrong-doing, evil, [or] sin."[33] Since many of the Code's articles have this distinctly theological timbre, it is no surprise that religious faith must never be held up to ridicule, nor "ministers of religion" portrayed as "villains."[34] Article IX enjoined that "bedrooms must be treated with good taste and delicacy."[35] And, to that end, the Code reserved its longest section for restrictions on sexuality and sexual representation, clearly the central anxieties keeping Hays, Breen, and their fellow movie censors—whether proudly Catholic or putatively secular—up at night. In all cinematic products, even those intended for "maturer minds" and "restricted to a *limited* audience," two assumptions governed everything: upholding "the sanctity of the institution of marriage and the home," and never representing "low forms of sex relationship" as "the accepted or common thing."[36]

Specifically, the Hays Code stipulated that *adultery* must never be "justified or presented attractively," and that any scene featuring "excessive and lustful kissing, lustful embraces, [or] suggestive postures and gestures" was prohibited in case it might "stimulate the lower and baser elements."[37] "*Sex perversion* [i.e., homosexuality] or any inference to it is forbidden," read Article II.4.[38] Similarly proscribed was any exhibition of "*white slavery.*" Nonwhite slavery, apparently, was just fine, given that the next article only reinforced this patent Hollywood racism: "*Miscegenation* (sex relationships between black and white races) is forbidden."[39] "*Complete nudity* is never permitted," the Code warned, and could never be considered "*necessary for the plot.*"[40] This meant either "nudity in fact or in silhouette" and included "any lecherous or licentious notice thereof by other characters."[41] Indeed, those who framed the Code recognized what they regarded as a rather unsavory reality of human sexual arousal, that is, that "*transparent* or *translucent materials* and silhouettes are frequently more suggestive than actual exposure."[42] We are aroused more by anticipation than by fulfillment. Grounded in the rampant antisexualism of the day, the Code justified all of these provisions in terms that had been common among moral crusaders for decades: their fear of "the effect of nudity or semi-nudity upon the normal man or woman, and much more upon the young and upon immature persons," something that they claimed "has been honestly recognized by all lawmakers and moralists."[43]

Exploitation, Context, and Social Convention

B-horror may not always invoke the religious imagination as explicitly as the opening narration from *Attack of the Crab Monsters*, but it both draws on and reinforces established cultural mores that are often religiously grounded. When bodies are somehow sexually out of place, they are either imperiled (the particular *threat* is what sexualizes and must therefore be eliminated) or they are punished in some way (sexualization *is* the threat and must be suppressed). When the religious imagination does put in an explicit appearance, it regularly highlights the problem of evil or the presence of the monstrous as a function of the sexual appetite. But, per Stephen King, "A good horror director must have a clear sense of where the taboo line lies."[44] In this way, by relying on and underpinning prevailing cultural scripts, B-horror contributes to a potent culturfactual process going back generations. Even when placing sexuality only obliquely in the public eye, but condemning illicit sexual behavior and killing off (or terrorizing) inappropriately sexualized participants, it consistently locates anything but conventional sexuality on the wrong side of the cinematic tracks.

Invasion of the Saucer Men (sans the unconscious damsel in distress), for example, leverages both the "based on real events gambit" and the classic campfire ghost story of the "hitchhiker with a hook for a hand"—often an escaped convict with a particular penchant for teenagers parked in a remote lover's lane.[45] In this case, the context is a young couple who are planning to elope, and their rejection of the social propriety that a traditional wedding represents—not to mention skirting her father's obvious disapproval of his daughter's intended. In Roger Corman's 1957 *The Undead*, which was also penned by *Crab Monsters'* Charles Griffith, parapsychologist Quintus Ratcliff wants to use a dangerous form of hypnotic regression—a technique he learned in "the desert huts of the shamans of Khazakh"—to prove the existence of reincarnation. "Where will you find a subject weak and impressionable enough to arrive in the required depth of trance?" asks Dr. Ogilvie, his skeptical former supervisor.[46] Enter street prostitute "Diana Love" (*Crab Monsters'* Pamela Duncan). "What's her full name?" Ogilvie asks. "Who knows?" Ratcliff responds with a shrug. "Where'd you find her?" the older man presses. "What does it matter?" Ratcliff insists, reinforcing the conventional piety not only of the expendable female but of the disposable sex worker—the one who is disposable precisely because she has made sex her profession.[47] "Her type is the most easily influenced of basic character groups," the obsessed Ratcliff continues. "It's almost devoid of will power. That's why I chose one of her kind."[48]

Her kind. Just sit with that for a second.

Even a generation later, with the Hays Code firmly in filmmaking's rear-view mirror, we still find its footprints on film. In Larry Cohen's low-budget classic *Q: The Winged Serpent*, a shadowy religious group believes that through a series of bizarre blood rituals it has prayed a modern incarnation of the Mesoamerican god Quetzalcoatl into existence. A "gritty Sam Fuller enthusiast who turned to Cormanesque splat," writes film critic Tom Huddleston, even in what could be a straight-up monster movie, "Cohen just couldn't let go of his pet themes—male insecurity, racial tension, religious short-sightedness, and social inequity."[49] Not to mention creature-feature sexual transgression. Presenting the initial attacks of its titular antagonist as a form of "just desserts" for sexual wrongdoing, *Q*'s opening scenes are standard, low-budget, tension-building fare: the irritating squeal of a window washer's squeegee masks the off-screen approach of the creature. "Oh, hello again, you little creep," an attractive young woman in a high-rise office says to herself, as the worker outside taps on the window and waves. "Here again today? How many times can you wash that same dumb window?"[50] "I know you love me, baby," he mutters, continuing to knock on the window as he washes it far more times than strictly necessary. "I wish he'd just take a walk," she says, exasperated.[51] Cue Q. The window washer looks up suddenly, and we hear the sound of an enormous bite. Turning back, the woman screams in horror as the man's now-headless body hangs from its harness, gouts of blood pulsing against the soapy windowpane.

Presaging the next attack, we have a (monstrous) bird's-eye view of lower Manhattan as *something* soars over the city. On an apartment rooftop, a young woman removes her top to sunbathe. Cohen cuts to a building across the street and a different instance of illicit sexual surveillance: a man with a telescope, another voyeur fantasizing about a relationship he will never have. Back on the roof, the camera pushes in as the woman rubs suntan lotion into her bare breasts, while across the street, eye glued to his spyglass, the man claps his hands with glee. His arousal turns to horror as, just barely onscreen now, the creature stoops to attack and the woman screams in terror. As the creature carries its prey to an aerie atop the iconic Chrysler Building, New Yorkers look up, some screaming, others covering their mouths in mute terror, as blood and pieces of torn flesh rain from the skies.

In the first instance, Q took the one who is tempted by lust, in the second, the object of lustful temptation. Here we have the two sides of Western ambivalence toward sexuality: the men who have lusted after women in their hearts (to use the biblical metaphor) and the presumed problem of female sexual display that tempts men toward moral transgression (to speak, at least inferentially, with Tertullian). From "appropriate" gender roles to punishment for forbidden sexuality to the importance of cultural context in the eroticization of the dangerous Other, let's consider a few other B-horror gems.

Or, to paraphrase *Scream*'s Randy, "Inappropriate sex causes death, ok?"

Crab Monsters and Correct Standards of Life

Returning to our remote Pacific island, we watch the "fat rope of trouble" Corman demanded further entangle the dwindling group of marine scientists. As biologist Martha Hunter (Pamela Duncan) scuba dives in the shallows off the beach where the team landed the day before—though no mention is made of what might have decapitated the unfortunate sailor, and no apparent precautions taken to ensure it doesn't happen again—we catch another fleeting glimpse of the crab monster. The sudden movement frightens Martha, disorienting her underwater. Out of nowhere, though, and in the nick of time, her love interest, Dale Drewer (Richard Garland), appears. After a few tense moments hiding in a sunken wreck, he guides his damsel-in-distress to the surface and the presumed safety of the beach. That night, even though Martha and Dale are clearly a couple, 1950s cinematic propriety provides them separate bedrooms at the island's tiny research facility.

Things only get worse from there.

When the navy lieutenant attempts to leave the island to get help, his seaplane mysteriously explodes. An overnight earthquake opens an enormous pit outside the research center, and as the scientists prepare to investigate, another tremor pitches one of them unceremoniously into the hole. In good 1950s B-horror fashion, Martha screams and faints when she sees him fall, presumably to his death. That evening, the unmistakable sound of a Hammond organ and the skittering of violins ratchets up the tension as an unknown *something* begins tearing its way through the walls of the research station bungalow. While most of the other men race out into the night in what seems like a vain attempt to prove they are not afraid, Dale remains inside with Martha. Even when he is attacked by a giant telepathic crab, however, he, too, shows little fear and no obvious surprise. A violent storm rages throughout the night, as tremors and quakes wrack the island, and massive landslides slowly sink it into the sea. And as was ever his lot onscreen, Hank Chapman (played by *Gilligan's Island*'s beloved Professor, Russell Johnson) struggles to fix their broken radio.

Even in the face of monstrous killer crustaceans, extinction-level meteorological and geological phenomena, and all-around imminent destruction, Martha turns to Hank as he works, and says casually, "Well, I guess it's about time I fixed us some food."[52] With this one line, apropos of nothing in the scene and serving no purpose in the larger *Crab Monsters* narrative, Martha reiterates the "correct standards" approach endorsed by the Hays Code: men fix things, women fix lunch. Martha Hunter may be a scientist and a valued colleague of those who have been lost on the island, but she is still bound by the cinematic gender norms the Hays Code demands, and films such as this reinforce. What happens, though, when leading ladies flaunt those norms?

Giant Leeches and the Sanctity of Marriage

Produced in 1959 by Roger Corman's younger brother, Gene, and directed by Bernard Kowalski, who was known mainly for helming television series (which may explain this film's distinctly episodic structure), *Attack of the Giant Leeches* is a "ludicrous hybrid of white trash and monster genres," at least according to acclaimed film critic Leonard Maltin.[53] As with so many others films, the premise is B-horror simple: A mysterious creature haunts the depths of the Florida Everglades, and bad things are happening. When local alligator poacher and town drunk Lem Sawyer tells his friends at the general store that it was "like one o' them, uh, like one o' them 'octy-pusses' things," everyone just laughs.

"Lem," chuckles resident roué Cal Moulton, "you sure that critter wasn't pink?"[54]

Most of this scene, however, is stolen by the marital discord between Liz Walker (Yvette Vickers) and her husband, Dave, the store owner, played by Bruno VeSota, one of Corman's stable of supporting actors. Recalling Helen Searing's general appraisal of B-horror, nothing about this scene is subtle. As the menfolk rib Lem about whatever he thinks he saw in the swamp, honky-tonk music blares from a back room. Dave yells to turn it down, and Liz sashays out, wearing nothing but a push-up bra and a short, sheer nightie. Lounging against the door frame and clearly enjoying the effect she has on the rest of the men, she brushes her teeth in an unmistakable allusion to fellatio. Though only six years younger, but more than a head shorter than the very heavy-set VeSota, petite, blonde Vickers seems more like Dave's rebellious teenage daughter than his wife—a distinction that is not lost on his so-called friends. Indeed, Vickers looks far more the *Playboy* centerfold that she was just a few months prior to the film's release than the wife of a backwoods shopkeeper, and their relationship is best summed up by *Mystery Science Theater 3000*'s Tom Servo, who simply breathes, "Lolitaaa . . ." as Liz flounces into the back.[55]

Returning to their bedroom, she changes the record, and crooning clarinets replace the honky-tonk piano. She retouches her makeup, puts on perfume, then slowly rubs moisturizer into her legs. The tension is palpable as her husband sits in a corner, occasionally mopping his face with a bandana. Even the forced perspective of the frame diminishes Dave, who looks like a nervous patron at a low-rent strip club. And, despite the fact that she has just performed the equivalent of a burlesque show, Liz's first words to him are, "Stop lookin' at me like that."[56] It is obvious that Dave loves his wife, but the worst-kept secret in their small town is that she is a tireless sexual temptress, and he the pathetic cuckold.

A few days later, when Dave leaves to deliver some groceries, his wife's current paramour slips in through the back. "You want somethin', Cal?" Liz asks coquettishly. "I sure do, honey," he replies, and they leave on a clandestine drive through the Everglades. Not content to play the dupe forever, Dave follows, eventually confronting the lovers at gunpoint. Firing an occasional shotgun blast to spur them on, he forces them deeper

Figure 2.2. Liz (Yvette Vickers) taunts her husband, Dave (Bruno VeSota), in *Attack of the Giant Leeches*.

and deeper into the swamp, though it is not clear whether he intends to kill them or simply scare them straight. Before long, exhausted and terrified, the illicit lovers turn on each other, Cal accusing Liz of starting the affair. "It wasn't my fault, honest," he pleads, his excuses sounding as hollow as Adam's in the face of Yahweh's Edenic condemnation (Gen. 3:10–12). "She kept playin' up to me every time you turned your back. It wasn't my fault!" Stunned, Liz spits derisively, "And you call yourself a 'man,' you and your muscles?" "Shut up, you *tramp!*" Cal shouts, lashing out at her. "If it wasn't for you, I wouldn't be in this fix. It's all your fault!"[57] As they beg for their lives, Dave forces them down into the swamp itself. For the first time, the camera focuses solely on Liz as the dank water rises to her chin, and she implores Dave to forgive her.

"You think you've learned enough to stay away from my woman, Cal?" Dave asks, his face softening ever so slightly. Surprise and relief wash over Cal and Liz, but as they scramble to get out of the water the film's titular monsters attack. Human-sized, intelligent "leeches" that store their victims in a submerged larder erupt from the swamp and drag the erstwhile lovers under. The last thing we hear is Liz's scream—cut short, then . . . crickets.[58]

No, literally, crickets.

Despite their marquee billing, the giant leeches are actually second-ary to the narrative, serving principally as monstrous subtext for the two main plot lines that structure the film (it is too much to call them "character arcs"): one of these, the love triangle between Liz, Dave, and Cal, the other the Hays-appropriate relationship between local game warden Steve Benton, his properly chaste fiancée, Nan Greyson, and her father, the kindly town doctor. When we first meet Nan and Steve, the difference between the two couples could not be more apparent. Played by tall, blonde, lantern-jawed Ken Clark, Steve bemoans the fact that all he could do for a small animal caught in a poacher's cruel trap is put it out of its misery.

Sitting in his truck—for no reason the film makes clear—Nan, played by Jan Shepard, is demurely dressed, including a cardigan that she but-tons close around her shoulders. Though, throughout the film, they argue about the best way to track down whatever is killing people in the swamp, Steve and Nan's relationship assures the audience of the nuclear family bond enshrined in the Hays Code. Indeed, the juxtaposi-tion of these two relational triads is so sharply defined—the film ends as Liz's dead body is pulled from the water just before Steve blows up the leeches' lair, while Nan hugs her man as they both walk out of the frame ahead of the end credits—it begs the question where we should look for even the rudiments of Kyrou's B-movie "sublimity." Two places: the un-certainty of narrative outcome, and a potential of sympathy for the devil.

The uncertainty of narrative outcome pivots on the potential for resolu-tion, both of the personal relationships between the two principal couples and in terms of their connection to the film's monstrous Other. For Steve and Nan, neither outcome is ever really in doubt. No matter how much they may disagree—even when Steve threatens to arrest Nan's father for meddling in the hunt for the creatures—nothing in the film suggests any-thing other than that they will be together at the end. And, despite the fact that they spend a good portion of the film's run time fruitlessly searching the 'glades, neither is there any doubt that Steve will eventually hunt down and destroy the giant leeches—though the soundtrack over the final shot leaves open the unfortunate possibility of a sequel.[59]

With Dave and Liz, however, the situation is more complicated than it first appears. In spite of the way she treats him, Dave undoubtedly loves Liz. He can even tolerate being the object of town gossip and ridicule if he thinks there is a chance that she might return his love at some point. As he chases Liz and Cal through the swamp, we watch him waver between the profound sense of betrayal fueling his desire for revenge and a genuine hope that, on the one hand, Cal will have "learned enough to stay away from" Liz and, on the other, sparing them will demonstrate the depth of love he actually feels for her.[60]

The second- and third-reel monster hunt is cut together with scenes of the leeches' underwater lair, in reality a dry cave where victims are stored alive and gradually bled to death. In addition to Liz and Cal, the leeches' pantry is currently stocked with all but one of the men originally shown leering at Liz and sharing the sexual joke at Dave's expense. As Steve and the other monster hunters close in from above, Liz alone remains alive—the "last girl standing," as it were. And, for a moment, as she rolls into the water in a desperate attempt to escape, it seems that she might actually survive. But only for a moment, because by this point in the film there is no relationship for her to reclaim. Pleading for his life until the bitter end, Cal is dead at the "hands" of the giant leeches. But, more importantly, Dave is gone as well. Overwhelmed by grief and horror, he knows only that something immensely terrifying has happened to Liz, and that he was as unable to protect her from that as he was to prevent her sexual indiscretions. In shock and despair after being arrested for Cal and Liz's "murder," Dave hangs himself in his jail cell. For him, hope vanished into the water just as certainly as his beloved, unfaithful Liz. In this way, not only could adultery not be presented less attractively, but it positively poisons everything it touches. Where, then, to find sympathy for the devil? Because, at the end of the day, for all her outward beauty there is nothing attractive about Liz at all.

When Kyrou advises us to seek the sublime in "bad" films through the latent rather than the overt, he means those aspects of a story that demand more of us as interpreters than simply attending to the onscreen action, a "beauty otherwise unnoticed," as anime legend Hayao Miyazaki would say.[61] As Dave follows the lovers to their swampy tryst, Kowalski edits the film to keep us guessing whether Dave will simply shoot them when his suspicions are confirmed, or find some path toward clemency, if not necessarily forgiveness. And, watching this, it is easy to miss the one fleeting moment that gives Liz's character a suggestion of complexity and nuance, a hint that she might be something more than simply a Hays Code cipher.

Lying in each other's arms beside the water, engaging in textbook examples of "excessive and lustful kissing," accompanied by plenty of "lustful embraces," Cal marvels how "a real woman like you [could be] tied in with a tub of lard like him."[62] She lays her head on his chest, and her voice softens for the only time in the film.

LIZ

My first husband was a no-good bum. Couldn't keep a job more'n a week. Used to get lushed up, come home an' beat up on me. One night he tried to hold up a gas station. He's so drunk, he couldn't even run. They caught him less than a mile away. Got sent up. I got a divorce. After three years workin' in a lousy beanery, I was ready for the first guy who said a nice word to me. It was Dave.

Once again, however much her initial fondness for Dave has eroded, nothing in the film suggests that his feelings for her were anything but genuine—nor that they continue to be so right up until the moment she disappears beneath the surface of the water. In the film's "mirror, mirror" moment, how many women (and men, it need be said) will see their own experiences either reflected or refracted in Liz's brief story of spousal abuse, social abandonment, and grinding poverty and, if even for a moment, look at her as something other than simply the town tramp? As I have noted elsewhere, "Regardless of the medium, running in the background of all popular culture is a stealth program we might call WYBIWYG. *What you bring is what you get.* Our biases and prejudices, the various elements of our socialization, the culturally constructed and reinforced filters through which we view the world— all these inevitably lend shape and texture to what we see and how we see it."[63] The story unfolding onscreen holds up a mirror to our own lives, often reflecting in discomfiting fashion how few of us can claim to be anything close to the "fairest in the land." "Film," wrote David Hogan nearly a generation after *Giant Leeches*, "particularly popular film, is *us*," and "the horror film, as the most basic and primal of all movie genres, has always been in a unique position as ideal chronicler of contemporary mores."[64]

And, in that vein, we travel from the backwoods of the Florida Everglades to a castle deep in "the horseshoe of the Carpathians."[65]

The Spanish Count and the Eroticization of Evil

Dracula. All over the world, just the name is enough to evoke at least a bit of a shiver, and it is difficult to estimate how many imitators Bram Stoker's most (in)famous character has inspired, nor how many versions of his story have been told. From musical theater to graphic novels, from sugary breakfast cereal to a child's first math teacher, and from blockbuster movies with A-list casting and cutting-edge special effects to Hallowe'en costumes with homemade fangs and ketchup for blood, Stoker's enigmatic Count is arguably the most famous creature to feature as fully in our dreams as in our nightmares.

Whatever else vampires in general—or Dracula in particular—represent, their narrative presence signals a contested vision of the unseen order. They too are a product of the religious imagination, insofar as they propose a different answer to the question that very likely started it all: What happens when we die? Call it heaven or hell, call it the Otherworld or the Summerland, call it the Bardo, the Celestial Kingdom, or any number of other theological metaphors we have used to describe what lies beyond what we see here and fear for the future—all are aspects of the religious imagination. Or, as it is with vampires, mummies, and zombies, call it what happens when we die badly but don't remain dead.[66] Because "gentlemen," intones Professor van Helsing, gravely summing up the problem in Tod Browning's 1931 Universal classic, "we are dealing with the *un*dead."[67] Thus, as much as anything, they represent a religious threat—or at least an implied risk to the storyworld's established religious order. Which means that any notion we had about consensus reality, whether informed by the rationalism of nineteenth-century Western medicine or the supernaturalism of the dominant religious worldview, has flown out the window.

Although, along with witches, zombies, and the occasional werewolf, vampires of all kinds populate a carousel of revolving horror fads, they have always been among the most highly sexualized of Universal Pictures' golden-age stable of B-horror monsters.[68] In a 2020 iteration, for example, Netflix's eponymous three-part miniseries, one of the first questions the highly unorthodox Sister Agatha (van Helsing) asks the nearly catatonic Jonathan Harker is, "Did you have sexual relations with Count Dracula?"[69] Not "Did he bite you?" Not "Did you drink anything that he poured for you?" But "Did you sleep with him?" Far from being a novel or innovative way of treating the question of vampirism, and the narrative problem of Dracula, this is a standard trope drawing on Victorian fear of "tainted" blood, whether through miscegenation, sexually transmitted disease, or the latter as a consequence of the former.[70] Indeed, no creature feature so reeks of sexuality, repressed or otherwise, as the vampire story.[71] If mummy movies are essentially stories about lovers separated by time and tragedy, vampire films are often barely concealed erotica—and, sometimes, not even that barely concealed.

From the magnetic menace of Bela Lugosi to Frank Langella's charming urbanity, and from Jamie Gillis's pornographic bloodlust to the brooding elegance of Gloria Holden, described in *Dracula's Daughter* as "a dangerous-looking brunette," much of the commentary has focused on the ur-vampire him- or herself.[72] Very often, however, Dracula's sexual predation is revealed far more clearly in the effect he has on those around him, those he bends to the dark side of his will, rather than on the Master himself. Thus, not only does the existence of such a creature challenge consensus reality; his (or her) effects reshape social decorum.

They eroticize evil.

"There was something about them that made me uneasy," writes Bram Stoker's Jonathan Harker, describing the sudden appearance of Dracula's beautiful "wives," "some longing and at the same time some deadly fear. I felt in my heart a wicked, burning desire that they would kiss me with those red lips."[73] As they drift over toward his bed, whispering among themselves, he feels "an agony of delightful anticipation," aroused by "a deliberate voluptuousness which was both thrilling and repulsive."[74] Feeling "the soft, shivering touch of [her] lips on the supersensitive skin of my throat," he continues, already anxious that his beloved Mina would somehow find this journal, "I closed my eyes in a languorous ecstasy and waited—waited with a beating heart."[75] Stoker's prose leaves very little to the imagination, but how to represent this profound shift in social convention and sexual propriety onscreen? While we could survey tens of thousands of vampire stories, hoping to find some measure of comparability, rarely does pop culture provide close examples that demonstrate in few uncertain terms the difference between the cultures for which they were produced. Takashi Shimizu's 2002 J-horror classic, *Ju-on*, which he remade the following year and released in North America as *The Grudge*, is one, and to a lesser degree Hideo Nakata's *Ringu* and its Western counterpart, *The Ring*.[76]

Universal Pictures' 1931 *Dracula* is another.

It is well-known Hollywood lore that, in late 1930, Tod Browning shot his *Dracula* on the Universal Studios lot during the daytime, while George Melford filmed the Spanish-language version, *Drácula*, during the nighttime hours. In *Hollywood Gothic*, the definitive work on the development of *Dracula* from fin-de-siècle nail biter to cinematic legend, film historian David Skal disputes the widespread belief that the two productions shared stock footage. Skal insists they did not, but since both companies used the same sets, backdrops, and studio lots, and worked from the same shooting script with often identical camera placements, it is not hard to get this impression.[77] Indeed, despite the fact that the Spanish version is nearly half-again as long as its English counterpart, just the similarity of blocking and lighting makes many sequences in one film (choose your language preference) look like a shot-for-shot remake of the other.

While similarly costumed and employing many of the same general movements to convey vampiric menace, Melford's Drácula (Carlos Villarías) is not nearly so suavely seductive as Bela Lugosi in the role he made iconic, but he is more overtly monstrous. Likewise, although Dracula's "wives" are dressed almost identically in both versions, so much so that viewers might be forgiven for thinking the Spanish and English actors wore the same costumes, the English version teases out their menace, while the Spanish one tenders it more openly. Not so the principal human women at the heart of Dracula's desire: Lucy/Lucía Weston and Mina/Éva Seward.[78]

"I remember when I saw the English version later," recounts Lupita Tovar, who played Éva as a breakout role in the Spanish *Drácula*, "the wardrobe was different. The dresses that [her English-version counterpart] Helen Chandler wore were all covered up. What they gave me were big décolletage, you know, what you would call 'sexy.'"[79] In one of the first things she comments on in this interview, Tovar recalls being surprised by the difference, because it simply never occurred to her that she or Carmen Guerrero (Lucía) would be costumed in any way other than they were. "We Latins have a different way of expressing ourselves, you know?" she continues. "Emotional. And I think the American people were kind of subdued . . . more reserved."[80] The evening gowns in which Éva and Lucía attend the symphony the night they meet Drácula, for example, are considerably more daring than those given to Mina and Lucy in Browning's production. Indeed, the costuming for the four women in this scene spans the modesty spectrum from almost prim (Mina) to swank flapper (Lucía).

For historian of religion Jonathan Z. Smith, the intellectual act of comparison has become, unfortunately, "chiefly an affair of the recollection of similarity," its main goal to discern some measure of "contiguity" between cultural products and practices.[81] Smith saw this as a mistake, principally because "the issue of difference has been all but forgotten."[82] To counter this, his essay "In Comparison a Magic Dwells" encouraged a critical path that takes *difference* as the linchpin of analytic utility. That is, as I have put it, "The significance of comparison lies in *explaining* the difference between versions of something, not simply in pointing out their similarities."[83] While comparison certainly requires some basic similitude, it is "at base, never identity."[84] Rather, comparison "requires the *postulation of difference* as the ground of its being interesting."[85] In this, then, consider the "death" of Lucy/Lucía, and the sexual (d)evolution of Mina/Éva, specifically through the lens of the bedroom and the balcony.

In the English version, Lucy bids goodnight to Mina and prepares for bed, dressed in off-white satin, with a long, matching bed jacket. As she opens the window, the set lighting reflects off the fabric, virtually blowing out the image and allowing not even a suggestion of what might lie underneath. From the gathering fog below, Dracula watches, and we see, as though through his eyes, Lucy slip the bedjacket from her shoulder. Her image, however, occupies only a very small portion of the screen in the lower right corner, a tiny movement of white against a field of inky black. Lucía's lingerie, on the other hand, is itself black, sheerer and far more suggestive than the opaque costume provided for the English version. Rather than from the street, we view Lucía from within her bedroom as she slips off the see-through bedjacket, the only intimation of vampiric threat a couple of cutaways to Drácula's wide, glowing eyes. If the English version locates the Count as a stalker watching from the bushes, the Spanish version invites us into the scene itself.

As Lucía reads in bed, her lace décolletage is clearly revealed, whereas in the English version Lucy has snuggled down beneath a heavy quilted comforter, drawing it up almost to her chin. The camera placement in the English shot locates us across the room, as though we are looking at Lucy from the vantage point of, say, her dressing table. In the Spanish version, our point of view is much closer, more intimate, as though we are standing above and a bit behind, gazing down at her. Suddenly, we become the vampiric voyeur, the sexual predator—something the blocking, camera setup, and lighting never permit in the English version. Indeed, the overall aesthetic of Melford's film is far more erotic than Browning's, and highlights the fact that this is as much a story of sexual seduction as it is a tale of supernatural taint and contagion.

Dracula takes Lucy fully that night, but his sexual corruption of Mina is played out more gradually. Once again, though, comparison reveals significant differences between the two productions. As Mina begins to fall under the Count's pernicious spell, we never actually see him make physical contact. The social propriety of bodies must be kept in place, even as the unfolding story throws the human body out of place in the most hideous manner possible. When next we see Mina, she is still dressed demurely, though a scarf wrapped around her throat signals the danger she is in. Costume designers Ed Ware and Vera West, uncredited in Browning's film, marked Mina's decline through changes to her wardrobe. As she falls further and further under Dracula's spell, she is no longer the reserved young woman in virginal white. As her transformation proceeds, her gowns take on more color, the better to highlight Chandler's pale skin. With long, bell sleeves and a neckline plunging to the limits of early–Hays Code discretion, they resemble more the flowing garments of Dracula's three seductive "wives" than those of a genteel young lady in fin-de-siècle London. Later, as her vampiric seduction deepens, her gown darkens even further, its bright satin sheen now reflecting the moonlight on the balcony.

After the initial attack on Éva, Tovar's dress is similar to Chandler's: layers of white organdy and tulle, her shoulders covered modestly, the paradigmatic damsel in distress. She too wears a scarf, though draped around her neck rather than wrapped, and the entire effect is the antithesis of that created by Lucía's sheer black lingerie. As with the English version, though, when we see Éva again, her costume is becoming more daring, more risqué. Rather than color, though, the Spanish version marks the change through the cut of her dress. The bodice is tighter, accentuating Tovar's narrow waist and ample bust, the better to follow Melford's directorial advice that she not be afraid to lean forward in the interest of the film. When she meets Juan on the balcony the next night, rather than a marcel wave, her thick, dark hair is now worn loose on her bare shoulders. Instead of a squared bodice, the gown is a sleeveless empire cut with a plunging neckline that exposes far more of Tovar's breasts than would have been acceptable in Hays Code Hollywood. No longer the damsel in distress, she is now the coy seductress.

In both productions, this difference is also reflected in Harker's reaction to the shift in his fiancée. The greater the evil, the more alluring she appears. When his beloved emerges onto the English balcony, John rushes to her. "Mina," he says, with only the barest hint of an up-and-down glance, "you're like a changed girl. Oh, you look *wonderful*." "I feel wonderful," she replies. "I've never felt better in my life."[86] Despite his fleeting once-over, Mina's response clearly signals that John is overjoyed more at her apparent recovery than the shift in her erotic sensibility. The scene plays out very differently on the Spanish terrace.

Rather than meet him on the balcony, Éva takes Juan by the hand and leads him out into the moonlight, almost twirling to show herself off. "Tell me," she asks gaily, "why are you staring at me like that?" "You're so . . . I can hardly believe it!" he replies, leaving the rest to the audience's imagination—which is more than can be said for much of Tovar's gown. "You look like a different woman," he says, taking her by the hands and quite explicitly looking her up and down. The scene embodies two principal aspects of human arousal cuing: men like to look, women like to be looked at.[87] Rather than simple relief that his fiancée is feeling better, Juan is clearly taken with the overt sexuality of Éva's new look—an eroticism that is linked explicitly to the horror of her burgeoning vampirism. "Darling, you look *terrific*," he exclaims.

Éva chuckles, turning to display herself fully to the audience, completing her transformation from modest young lady to the cinematic archetype of woman as sexual vampire. Rather than sitting on the divan in a classic two-shot, as Mina and John do in the English version, Éva lounges back against the balustrade, a posture that could not help but call to mind Theda Bara. She is now the temptress, and clearly enjoying every moment of her newfound sex appeal. But we also know that her increased sexuality and heightened eroticism—her obvious change in sexual awareness—are all functions of her supernatural taint at the hands of Drácula. And this, even more so than the English version, reinforces conventional social boundaries about acceptable sexual behavior. Once again, the supernatural contagion forces bodies out of place, and overt sexuality comes only at the cost of the vampire's (un)deadly gift.

"I have looked for God everywhere in this world," Sister Agatha laments to the traumatized Jonathan Harker, "and never found him."[88] Toward the end of the first part of the Netflix triptych, when Harker has begun his vampiric turn, he faces Dracula on a lonely parapet. As he does so, a crucifix reflects the last rays of the setting sun onto the Count's face in the form of a cross, and the vampire recoils as we have seen him do countless times in endless films. Upon hearing this, Agatha assumes that the cross—not the sunlight—is what Dracula fears, and suddenly believes that this is the evidence of God for which she has searched in vain her entire life. "Count Dracula fears the cross! He fears the symbol of our Lord!" she exults. "Do you understand what this means? *God is real*. God is real, and I have found him at last."[89] In this brief moment, though, Sister Agatha van Helsing, latest incarnation of the most famous vampire hunter of them all, commits the cardinal fallacy of the religious imagination, the one on which so much of horror culture draws.

And to which we turn next.

3

Altared Bodies

Sexuality, Sacrifice, and the Horrific Aesthetic

Faustian bargains rarely turn out well.

Love, Death & Robots is a Netflix anthology series of animated science fiction and horror short films. From postapocalyptic tourism ("Three Robots") and Special Forces werewolves operating in the Afghan mountains ("Shape-Shifters") to super-intelligent breakfast food ("When the Yogurt Takes Over") and what is essentially "a thousand different ways to kill Hitler" ("Alternate Histories"), it ranges across mordant humor, surreal murder mystery, and straight-up supernatural horror. Concluding the series' first volume is István Zorkóczy's "Secret War." Known mostly for cinematic trailer work in such popular videogame franchises as *Assassin's Creed* and *Halo*, Zorkóczy brings to this story the same cut-scene aesthetic that turns these games into vast and complex story-worlds, rather than just brightly colored episodes of run-and-gun, pick-the-lock, and defeat-the-Boss.

It is winter 1943. Deep in the endless tracts of Siberian forest, a squad of Soviet soldiers hunts an enemy that leaves only panic, gore, and devastation in its wake. This is not the aftermath of the German blitzkrieg, however, nor the terrifying passage of SS Panzer divisions. This is something else. Something much worse. Something they have been fighting since long before the savagery of Hitler's armies reached the Motherland. For over two decades, hordes of eldritch creatures have been pouring up from holes in the ground. Little more than teeth, sinew, and long, razor-sharp claws, they hunger only for the kill, immune to their own countless fallen in the endless pursuit of flesh.

"Ghouls," David Amendola, on whose short story the film is based, calls them.[1]

As night falls, weary survivors of the latest skirmish gather around a small campfire. Safe for the moment, they share a bit of scavenged food and savor "the luxury of a smoke, rolling strong, coarse tobacco in newsprint to make crude cigarettes."[2] Their commander, Lieutenant Zakharov, leafs through a small notebook taken from the body of a soldier found frozen in the snow. Arcane symbols and cryptic references to something known as "Operation Hades" clutter its blood-stained pages. "Does it mean anything to you?" asks the hulking machine gunner, Kravchenko. "I've heard rumors of it," Zakharov replies quietly.[3]

What follows is the equivalent of a videogame cut-scene, a brief exposition that stitches one combat sequence to another and provides a narrative underpinning for the gamer. That is, by creating a storyworld, cut-scenes tell us the *how* and the *why* of what is happening onscreen, rather than just how many enemies we need to kill or secrets discover in order to level up.

"'Hades,'" Zakharov explains, "was an operation focused on exploring arcane peasant myths."[4] The scene shifts to flashback and voiceover. During the chaos of the Russian Civil War, as the White Army fell back before the advancing Bolsheviks, an intelligence officer named Grishin "was dispatched on a secret mission. He was an occultist. His assignment was to perform a certain black magic ritual whispered about among the Kolyaks. It was meant to summon unholy creatures who would fight beside the Red Army."[5]

All the popular trappings of occultism and black magic are here. Hidden in the dense forest, a ring of standing stones sits atop a lonely cliff. Hooded figures, their dark robes inscribed with esoteric glyphs, mutter and chant in the flickering torchlight. And there is a woman. As we will see, it is almost always a woman. She is naked, suspended from ropes in the center of the circle, her arms crossed in front of her, her legs spread obscenely in what is obviously intended to have occult significance. Her head lolls, and, at this point, we do not know whether she is alive or dead. The leader, his robe already stained with blood, approaches her and makes a series of small cutting motions. Then, a shot of her torso, blood streaming from between her breasts, a complex symbol inscribed on her chest, her abdomen sliced open as though for an autopsy. The priest anoints Grishin with the dead woman's blood.

The ritual apparently complete, the ground begins to crack around them, and a large ghoul claws its way from the earth. The first of those called forth from its hellish domain, the creature immediately turns on

Figure 3.1. Ritual sacrifice scene from "The Secret War." Source: Netflix.

those who released it. It cannot be contained, and it will not be controlled. As with so many of our attempts to manipulate the unseen order to our advantage, to bargain with powers beyond imagining in pursuit of our own petty agendas, we are the ones who lose in the end. Grishin dies screaming, and the flashback closes. "The operation doesn't seem to have worked out very well for him," Kravchenko observes drily.

Indeed, Faustian bargains rarely turn out well.

On Amazon's Internet Movie Database, one of the most popular online reference sources for all things cinema, television, and videogame, the first two plot keywords for "The Secret War" are "human sacrifice" and "naked female corpse."[6] In Amendola's original story, however, this entire scene is reduced to less than one sentence, that Grishin's "assignment had been to perform black magic rituals in the arctic to summon the ghouls."[7] That's it, that's all. No mention of torchlit menhirs or mysterious, hooded figures, nor of young women bound, mutilated, and offered to unnamed gods by malevolent priests. Yet, in Philip Gellat's *Love, Death & Robots* adaptation, her grisly sacrifice is central to the plot, the independent liturgical variable in pursuit of whatever bleak millennium these terrifying creatures proclaim. Indeed, out of the film's short, fourteen-minute running time, well over a minute is devoted to this cut-scene, through which she exemplifies the horrific aesthetic of sacrifice.

We do not know the young woman's name, nor where she came from, nor whether her family will ever learn what happened in this terrible place. We do not know how she came to be here, and, while we might imagine she was a virgin, we do not even know that for sure. What we do know is that very little of this matters, because, in the context of "arcane peasant myths" and "a certain black magic ritual," her body is the ceremonial focal point. As the ritual resource on which their dark sacrament depends, it is simultaneously in and out of place. Unlike Vera Endecott, ritually desecrated and hung up as a grisly warning to any errant faithful, this woman is a reservoir of supernatural power tapped to herald the unnatural advent of the ghouls.[8]

Call it occultism, call it black magic, call it arcane peasant mythology, call it whatever you want—make no mistake, this is still the religious imagination at work. And this is that imagination's dirty little secret. "Any religion that required sacrifice," wrote R. H. Sales more than a generation ago, "would practice human sacrifice, if the theory behind the system were driven to its logical conclusion. The more valuable the sacrifice, the more 'power' it would have for the one who offered it."[9] Indeed, this is the sine qua non of sacrifice itself, the scale of ritual efficacy that culminates in a human life—the "altared" body.

Sex, Horror, and the Religious Imagination's Dirty Little Secret

"It is something of a scandal in religious studies and anthropology," writes David Carrasco, however, that, rather than the "fulsome record of real, historical human sacrifices from Mesoamerica," not to mention North America and Europe, the vast majority of "significant theories of ritual sacrifice" based their analyses on "animal sacrifice or literary accounts of human sacrifices from Western classics."[10] Which is to say, despite its relatively widespread historical reality, we tend to sweep this more distasteful aspect of our religious past under a rug woven from convenient strands of progressive revelation (*we* understand the gods better than *they* did!), the good, moral, and decent fallacy (that's not *real* religion!), and the merciful shroud of time (wait, they did *what* to people?).

The horror mode, however, will not let us forget and, when used as a lens to interrogate the tenebrous spaces of our religious imagination, this is one of its principal virtues. Indeed, more than any other popular genre, cultural tradition, or aesthetic practice, horror consistently confronts us with the worst that that imagination has to offer, while only inconsistently taking refuge in the promises made by our various religions. That things always turn out alright in the end is a common misconception among critics of the horror mode.[11] Rather, spooky tales and scary movies take seriously what Stephen King considers "the primary duty of literature" (which we might creatively misread as storyworld creation in general), which is "to tell us the truth about ourselves by telling us lies about people who never existed."[12] Especially lies about things we least want to face. Lies about things we cannot bring ourselves to remember on our own. And there is arguably no place where the horror mode takes religion more at its word than the sacrificial altar. Because, more than any other ritual practice, human sacrifice in the name of one's god(s) acutely confronts our commitment to two things: the principle of religious freedom, and the problem of approbation bias.

When human sacrifice is ruled illegal, for example (because, however ritually conceived, it is murder, after all), should those whose gods demand it in return for divine benevolence be themselves considered victims of religious persecution? This is certainly the subtext of Jonathan Thomas's short story "The King of Cat Swamp," as the mysterious Mr. Castro tells Dwight and Edith Nickerson how his people dwelt on their land long before these two terrified yuppies built their "upper-crust Colonial Revival" McMansion and filled it with lifestyle accoutrements ranging "from Japanese woodblock prints on wall to Erté bust on Corinthian pedestal to bronze figurines on mantel from Benin."[13] Escaping rampant religious persecution in Europe, Castro's ancestors fled to this part of the Americas, eventually retreating to "territory shunned as worthless and unlucky"—the eponymous Cat Swamp—but where "they could practice their rituals and libations in privacy, to curry the favour of divine powers sovereign over the earth and sea and stars."[14]

While the old man laments that the gods of his people did eventually come to accept small, furry creatures as sacrifice, the seriousness of their own situation gradually dawns on Dwight and Edith, a terrifying reality for which neither that "liter of Edmundo Dantes" rum they kept "locked in the bottom drawer of Second Empire china cabinet," nor the "McCoy bowl full of Lindt chocolates" had prepared them.[15] "Much more pleasing to those powers," Castro tells them calmly, as any hope that their erstwhile guest is simply mad slips away, "was the blood of living men, which the fishermen also supplied when drunkenness made them easy marks, or when the furious kinfolk of a ravished native woman delivered them bound and naked."[16] Like all good horror, however, "The King of Cat Swamp" is as much about the questions it prompts us to ask as it is about the story it purports to tell.

Put differently, whether they know it or not, and however they seek to mitigate or explain it away, when it comes to the often tenuous relationships we have with our gods, the scholars David Carrasco critiques remain committed to some form of the good, moral, and decent fallacy. As though writing with "The Secret War" firmly in view, for example, James Booth notes that "human sacrifice lies at the heart of European perceptions of the primitive" and frequently "evokes horror tinged with prurient fascination."[17] An example of horror-mode orientalization that both distances the viewer and domesticates that which is viewed, these perceptions allow us the frisson of fear, while keeping us safe behind conceptual enclaves of the "primitive."

In addition to Eurocentric reliance on literary references, which are more easily dismissed as hyperbole and propaganda designed as the ultimate form of religious Othering, scholars account for the widespread practice of human sacrifice in various ways. Whether understood as an occasional ritual within a larger symbolic universe or as a regular constituent in negotiations with the unseen order, these explanatory strategies generally reject any religious context as "mere mystification."[18] They "postulate practical, though unintentional functions," which when combined with cannibalism, for instance, constitute "a means of population control . . . or a way of adding amino acids to the stewpot."[19] Not surprisingly, human sacrifice was well known as "an instrument of political repression." According to anthropologist John Ingham, "Whatever else it may have been, human sacrifice was a symbolic expression of political domination and economic appropriation, as well as a means to their social production and reproduction."[20]

Taking a rather different approach, based in what he regards as the fundamental "irrationality" of human sacrifice, economist Peter Leeson argues that it functions as a social "technology for protecting property rights," a practice that when framed as "religious obligation" intends principally "to incentivize community members to contribute wealth for destruction."[21] In this, though, like Mathias Clasen, Leeson ignores the fact that for those who live within that symbolic universe, the practice of human sacrifice is entirely rational. Indeed, for them, to believe otherwise would be sheer folly. Classicist Ruth Scodel generally concurs with Leeson, though pointing to the long history of sexualized display of the sacrificial object—particularly virginal women—going back at least to Euripedes and Aeschylus. That is, in addition to their ritual potency, "virgins were a decorative presence at sacrifices."[22] "This excessive exposure of the virgin," she continues, "is an important part of the horror of human sacrifice"—something of which, as we will see, modern horror culture takes full advantage.[23] In this context, sacrificial display "is based on the virgin's value as a precious object," essentially as sexualized chattel "analogous to luxury goods whose proper use is dedication to the gods" through "a wasteful form of overconspicuous consumption."[24]

Anthropologist Michael Harner, on the other hand, who left the academy to establish his own form of neo-shamanic practice, largely dismissed religious explanations for human sacrifice in Mesoamerican cultures, promoting instead an "ecological hypothesis" based on population pressure and unreliable food sources.[25] Others disagree. Reluctant to accept Harner's specific thesis, for instance, Michael Winkelman acknowledges that among the Aztecs human sacrifice took place because they believed "the gods required it," but he concludes nonetheless that the "cosmological hypothesis is true but uninformative. Religious justifications for human sacrifice and cannibalism do not alone explain such beliefs and behavior."[26]

To which we might reply, given the range and depth of atrocity committed throughout history at the behest of this god or that, and notwithstanding what it says both about the gods and the men and women willing to follow them, Why not? Recalling Steven Weinberg's observation, could we imagine this level of self-righteous violence without some form of divine imprimatur? And, if we could, then why bother with heavenly sanction at all? To suggest the "insufficiency" of "religious justification"—that is, our relationship with the gods upon whom we are convinced our entire existence depends—is to willfully ignore not only the clear evidence of history but the cultural power of the most significant meaning-making process our species has ever known.

Crucial to remember at all points, declared Jonathan Z. Smith bluntly, is that "religion is not nice."[27] In addition to the hope and purpose and sense of place in the world it has provided for billions of people, "it has been responsible for more death and suffering than any other human activity."[28] This does not mean that it cannot ever *be* nice, or that believers don't ever *do* nice things (especially for their own coreligionists) but simply that, as the horror mode so consistently reminds us, "nice" has no useful place in defining what we mean by religion.

It is also worth noting that, strictly speaking, we are not talking about ritual murder here. However monstrous her death may be, the mere fact that someone like Vera Endecott is murdered in ritual fashion does not mean that her death is sacrificial in nature. Form must follow function. Put differently, all human sacrifice is ritual murder, but not all ritual murder is human sacrifice.[29] As Michael Newton points out, human sacrifice is "any ritualistic homicide *impelled by metaphysical considerations*."[30] Or, to speak once again with William James, to maintain or bring about "harmonious adjustment" with the "unseen order" in pursuit of one's "supreme good"—however we conceptualize that order, whatever its demands are understood to be, and no matter what we consider our summum bonum. "It matters not if blood is shed for Yahweh, Lucifer, or Ba'al," Newton continues, "to sanctify construction projects, bless a harvest, or protect a drug deal in the making."[31] Or, in the context of the horror mode, to usher in the return of Lovecraftian primal gods (as in Michael Shea's short story, "Nemo me impune lacessit"), to peer behind the veil separating life from death (Caitlín Kiernan's "Houndwife"), to raise a ghoul army to fight in a bloody civil war, or any of the other myriad reasons for which we have offered our fellow humans on the sacrificial altar.[32] "If the killers view their act as necessary to effect some metaphysical result, it is sacrifice, whatever uninvolved bystanders may decide after the fact."[33]

Stepping back from the altar for a moment, it is important to remember that all religion shares three cardinal presumptions, few of which believers readily acknowledge, and all of which many vehemently deny. That is, regardless of tradition, lineage, or dogma, religion is fundamentally conjectural, nonfalsifiable, and theoretical. First, any particular religious worldview is based on unproved assumptions that (a) the gods actually exist, (b) we have correctly identified those gods, and (c) we properly understand both our place in their plans and the mechanisms that allow our participation in them. While different species of evidence—from sacred texts to miraculous healing, from prophetic speech to the power of prayer—lead billions of people to accept as true an astonishing range of religious claims, the brute fact remains that all religious worldviews are socially constructed in this manner. As a result, they are by definition precarious and unstable, subject at all times to the corrosive effect of the question we whisper in the shadow of our devotions: "How do I know I'm right?"[34] We may believe profoundly in the reality of our gods, but depth of belief does not correlate to proof of existence.[35]

Next, while it seems obvious in the abstract, the nonfalsifiable character of religious belief is epitomized by the intuitively correct, but logically fallacious claim, "You can't prove my gods *don't* exist." Leveraging our evolution as both pattern-seeking and meaning-making creatures, this nonfalsifiability privileges the ambiguity and elasticity of evidence we are willing to consider in support of the patterns we find and the meanings we make. In what is sometimes known as "confirmation bias," other times the "sharpshooter fallacy," this means that we tend to lend more significance to things that support our beliefs than we do those that challenge or disprove them—especially when those beliefs are staked to cosmic consequences.[36]

Finally, and notwithstanding religion's speculative and nonfalsifiable dispositions, all religious worldviews are theoretical. That is, they provide "a framework of explanation for a set of observed facts," from which proceeds a grounding for action in the world.[37] If the religious imagination provides a way of understanding "what if" (the world worked like this?), it also supplies the rationale for acting "as if" (the world does work this way). Put differently, theology both recapitulates cosmology and animates praxis. It *describes* the way the world is and *prescribes* behavior in that world. Of course, this is not meant to imply that any particular framework is accurate or reliable—or that its impulses and imperatives are even remotely reasonable when viewed from the outside. But that's not the point. Whether true or not, it fulfills the evolutionary mandate of the religious imagination to the extent that it provides

believers with a sense of meaning, purpose, and cosmic significance—
believers who subsequently act as if what they believe is true. More than
that, and especially in terms of the intersection between horror and the
religious imagination, it means that no one pantheon—Lovecraft's hideous "elder gods," for example, or the yōkai-infested world of *mangaka*
Junji Ito—is inherently less reasonable than any other.

In this sense, then, and to explore the horror mode's landscape of
sacrifice more deeply, come with me to Skull Island.

Ritual, Rarity, and the God of Skull Island

The *Los Angeles Times* called it "a spectacular picture, a sensational
thriller," while Atlanta film critic Mollie Merrick hailed it as a "mas-
terpiece," telling readers that "from a purely technical standpoint 'King
Kong' is the most difficult translation of an idea into a motion picture
structure ever attempted."[38] "Say 'There ain't no such animal' all you
will," exclaimed the *Chicago Daily Tribune*'s Mae Tinee (i.e., "matinee,"
a pseudonym used by various *Tribune* reviewers), but "on the Palace
screen there APPEARS to be JUST such an animal. And the faking is
so marvelous that it seems real!"[39] Watching the stop-motion Kong
rampage wild-eyed through the native village in search of Ann Darrow
(Fay Wray, in the role for which she is still best known), smashing huts,
crushing some villagers underfoot while eating others whole, modern
viewers might find it difficult to appreciate the mindscape of audiences
for whom this level and complexity of creature-feature special effects
were entirely new.[40] Barely five years had passed since "talkies" began
to supplant silent films, and *King Kong* director Merien Cooper insisted
that making such a film would have been impossible even a few years
earlier.[41] One fight sequence alone, the battle on the ledge between a
pterodactyl and Kong (who is protecting Ann from becoming a take-
away meal), took seven weeks to film—all for a scene that lasted less
than a minute onscreen.

While the technical aspects of creature-feature puppetry and stop-
motion animation are important and set the tone for generations of special effects artists ranging from the legendary Ray Harryhausen to Tim
Burton, Henry Selick, and Travis Knight, at least as difficult here was
translating the terrifying *idea* of Kong as something distinct and apart

from the shocking reality of his onscreen presence.[42] That is, conveying what Kong *meant* to the people for whom he was a god.

King Kong hit theaters in March 1933, with John Guillermin's remake following over forty years later. Peter Jackson's 2005 version hews more closely to Cooper's original, but weaves together aspects of cinematic homage, play-within-a-play, and the lengthy (if occasionally tedious) CGI action sequences for which Jackson and his team are best known. In each film, though, four waypoints mark the narrative journey to and from Skull Island, four iconic scenes around which the story of Kong is woven. The *sacrifice scene* introduces the beautiful blonde victim as the putative "bride of Kong" offered in place of the indigenous woman initially meant for the ritual, while the *log-bridge scene* separates this "victim" from the main body of her rescue party. This both solidifies the relationship between the male and female protagonists and establishes Kong as a curious protector rather than a predatory monster. By parodying the Skull Island sacrifice, the *exhibition scene* reinforces our perception of Western hubris through the cruelty of Kong's capture and display as "the eighth wonder of the world." And, finally, the *death of Kong* raises the perennial, and always perspectival, question of who is the real monster.[43] For our purposes, we will concentrate on the first of these scenes, which highlights the altared body in terms of three intervailing concepts: "ritual as if your life depended on it," "the quid pro quo problem," and the "horrific aesthetic of human sacrifice."

Although our species has imagined its various "deities and modes of interaction with them" for as long as we have had records, and millennia before that, Jonathan Z. Smith argues that we have "had only the last few centuries to imagine religion."[44] In a passage that never fails to confound my students, he writes that "while there is a staggering amount of data" for what, by whatever criteria, we would characterize as "religious" (part of what I am calling "the religious imagination"), "*there is no data for religion*."[45] Rather, for Smith, "religion is solely the creation of the scholar's study," a concept "created solely for the scholar's analytic purposes by [their] imaginative acts of comparison and generalization. Religion has no independent existence apart from the academy."[46] Since this seems so deeply counterintuitive, if not entirely wrong-headed, what could he possibly mean? *No such thing as religion?* How absurd. He answers this, if obliquely, by pointing out that "for the self-conscious student of religion, no datum possesses intrinsic interest. It is of value only insofar as it can serve as exempli gratia of some fundamental issue in the imagination of religion."[47]

No datum possesses intrinsic interest. Or, put in the context of a sociology of religion, *nothing is inherently sacred*, but is so only by the consent of and ongoing agreement among those who regard it as sacred. That is, religion is not something sui generis. This is particularly significant for scholars who "[accept] neither the boundaries of canon nor of community in constituting [their] intellectual domain."[48] It is difficult to overstate the importance of Smith's comment here, especially in terms of religion and popular culture, an intellectual domain that many critics consider so far below the salt of acceptable academic canon that it is frivolous at best, at worst hazardous to the "real" work of scholarship. Yet, consider the power of popular culture, a force we ignore only to our detriment, and which is expressed most succinctly in the simple question, "How do you know what you know?"

Setting aside those who make specific efforts to learn about the global spectrum of religious belief and practice, arguably almost everything people do know about religions other than their own—and a good deal about their own faith as well—comes to them through popular culture, which includes movies and television, genre and literary fiction, comic books and graphic novels, as well as cosplay and gameplay. Consider just these few examples.

When asked what witches do to little children, how many people would not respond, whether tongue-in-cheek or no, "Why, they eat them, of course"? After all, isn't that what stories ranging from "Hansel and Gretel" to *Hocus Pocus* to *The Witch* tell us, in one way or another? While many Christians may have heard of the Gospel of Thomas, millions more were exposed to it through Rupert Wainwright's 1999 film, *Stigmata*. Knowing nothing else, then, this becomes "what they know" about that text. Rather than rely on their sacred book itself, tens of millions of Bible-believing Christians found the eschatological aspects of their worldview far more palatably explained through the *Left Behind* series written by Tim LaHaye and Jerry Jenkins.[49] And for countless more people who came across these novels in Costco or Walmart, rather than niche Christian bookshops, this image contributed to "what they know" about evangelical Christianity. Finally, but for the fact that Dan Brown included the word **"Fact"** in boldface at the top of his brief prefatory note to *The Da Vinci Code*, we might have been spared the welter of books, articles, sermons, and blog posts "cracking," "breaking," or otherwise exposing the book's flaws.[50] None of it would have been deemed necessary had those who were horrified by the mere thought that Jesus might have had sex with Mary Magdalene simply recognized Brown's book as the tepid boarding-lounge read that it is. The fact that *The Da Vinci Code* is a fictionalized account based loosely on popular nonfiction works of Christian conspiracism only confused the point.[51]

And that is the point.

Two social-psychological principles in particular help explain the significance of these examples and, thus, the power of popular culture to shape our various cultural stocks of knowledge: the availability heuristic and source dissociation. Rather than discrete mechanisms, these are two elements in a suite of conceptual tools that humans have evolved to aid in the processes of pattern seeking and meaning making.[52] Put briefly, the availability heuristic tells us that the more easily we can draw an example of something to mind, the more likely we are to think that thing either true or significant. That is, whatever is most "available" to us becomes "what we know" about that thing. If all someone knows about the Holy Grail is what they learned from Ron Howard's adaptation of *The Da Vinci Code* or Steven Speilberg's *Indiana Jones and the Last Crusade*, then those films become the stock of knowledge on which they draw when the so-called cup of Christ comes up in conversation. Source dissociation, on the other hand, describes our tendency to forget where we learned things that we consider true or significant. Thus, what we know about the Grail becomes less the product of a couple of action/suspense movies than "something we saw somewhere." It constitutes our "recipe knowledge" about that thing. When different aspects of religious belief and practice are depicted, while we may recognize something as belonging to this religion or that, most people do not know enough to distinguish where religious reality ends and fantasy religion begins—especially in the horror mode, where reality is often just as horrific as fantasy.

Ritual as if Your Life Depended on It

A generation ago, although not speaking to Jonathan Z. Smith directly, Roman Catholic theologian Ernst Feil suggested another way of understanding his somewhat perplexing comments. Feil argued that, prior to the sixteenth century, the dominant cosmological sense in the West was constituted by *religio* as opposed to *religion*—a distinction that very likely applied to the rest of the world, and in many places continues to this day. Although this may seem like a distinction without much of a difference, for Feil, "*religio* means the careful and even fearful fulfilment of all that man owes to God or to the gods."[53] Whether our supreme good entails a bountiful harvest and food for the winter, or simply surviving the next battle with a neighboring tribe, what we owe to the gods "means something very necessary."[54] It is not, however, the kind of nebulous *something* that is so often implicated in the beliefs of those who claim to be "spiritual but not religious." Rather, for most of the time since the evolutionary emergence of the religious imagination, this has been "something very concrete."[55] Put simply, this is ritual action as if your life depended on it, because as far as you were concerned . . . it did.

This meant, for example, "the careful enacting of rituals before political or military action, as well as, in fear and trembling, attending to every sacrifice and to other demands, handed down from the past to be passed on to future generations."[56] Thus, contra writers like Michael Winkelman, in the context of *religio*, a prayer before combat is not simply something that we *do*, but something that we *must* do if we are to expect any kind of success on the battlefield. A baptism is not a social ritual done just to appease convention or family obligation but an eternal-life-or-death moment, particularly in circumstances of high infant mortality. A sacrifice, especially a human sacrifice, is not something we perform because of some abstract concept of the relationship between our world and the unseen order but precisely because of a compulsory connection between them that we ignore both to our immediate peril and to our cosmic destiny. For many people raised in late-modern secular societies, where religious participation is often as much a matter of fashion, choice, or inertia as anything else, it is difficult to imagine what this kind of terrifying divine imperative must have been like.

Fortunately, the horror mode is there to remind us.

"Holy mackerel, what a show!" exclaims filmmaker Carl Denham, peering through the bushes as he and his production crew catch their first glimpse of the Skull Island villagers preparing for the "bride of Kong" ritual. Other than the festively ominous visual of a young woman being readied for the giant ape who lives beyond the massive village walls, Cooper's *King Kong* offers no larger context than this for the sacrifice that animates the first act. Through Denham's eyes, though, at the intersection of racism and religious prejudice, it is just the kind of "savage" ritual that his well-to-do Western audiences would expect from "people like that." Exotic ceremonies carried out by primitive tribes, all intended to appease some choleric local deity.

In this case, a young girl kneels in the midst of sweating drummers, chanting villagers, and ceremonial dancers dressed as stylized gorillas. Older women adorn her with flowers and lei, as she fidgets and looks around, her eyes wide. Clearly terrified, she sees the ceremony for what it is, for what she has always been taught that it is. All Denham sees, though, is the potential footage that could put him back on top in Hollywood. "Boy, if I could only get a picture before they see us," he says, motioning his camera operator forward. Catching sight of the intruders, the village chief halts the ceremony abruptly. The ritual is "spoiled because we've seen it," the boat captain explains.[57]

Although bits of dialogue such as this are easily missed in the rush to find out what *happens* in a film, it's worth hitting "Pause" because they often contribute to a deeper understanding of what's actually *going on*. They reveal what's at stake for the characters. In this case, what seems like a throwaway comment from the captain actually points directly to the power of what Feil means by "*religio*." That is, this is not a show for tourists. This is not something meant for outsiders. As far as the islanders are concerned, this *is* life or death. By occasionally offering a young woman as the "bride of Kong," they placate the creature they revere as a god. They ritually recruit their deity for the protection of the village from the terrors of the island.[58] And, in doing so, they place themselves in service to the unseen order they believe Kong represents. It does not matter how "irrational" any of this appears to us, nor even whether it conforms to our understanding of "religion." However unwilling interlopers may be to appreciate it, the "bride of Kong" ritual *is* an act of worship, with its own internal logic, and entailing beliefs and practices no less sacred to the Skull Island villagers than the Eucharist is to Roman Catholics, *jumu'ah* (Friday prayer service) is to Muslims, or *matsuri* (ritual festivals) are to Shinto believers. Simply because strangers cannot recognize the sacrality of the ritual moment does not mean that it is not there.[59]

The Quid Pro Quo Problem

When the chief sees Ann Darrow for the first time, this sense of devotional importance becomes even more apparent. "He says, 'Look at the golden woman,'" the captain translates, glancing around uneasily. "Yeah," replies Denham, "blondes are scarce around here."[60] Immediately, the chief offers to trade a number of local women for Ann. This could be read as a statement about racialized inferiority, and Merien Cooper certainly frames it that way—despite the ugly subtext of Denham's own purposes on Skull Island, and his later willingness to use Ann as bait in his bid to capture Kong. Conversely, it could be read as a comment on women both as male property and the preferred currency in a divine transaction—hardly unheard of in any number of off-screen religious traditions. Indeed, this represents simply one mythologized instance of what many anthropologists suggest is a dominant evolutionary pattern in reproductive competition; that is, in terms of "the male psyche," "women [are] always a resource and always in short supply."[61]

In terms of *religio*, however, this brief interchange demonstrates the importance of rarity in the ritual process, the sacramental merit of scarcity. That is, with her pale skin and blonde hair, Ann is regarded as a far more valuable, indeed singular, ritual commodity for the islanders to offer up to their god. She has greater exchange value at the altar. Because the transactional nature of any sacrifice is quid pro quo, literally "this for that," offering someone who by virtue of her uniqueness is presumably of increased ceremonial worth adds to the presumed potency of the sacrifice itself.

Whether a specific ritual is intended to ensure that the sun will rise or the lambs will ewe, whether sacrifice is offered to pay for the sins of the tribe or to usher the dead into a fruitful afterlife, all such acts of devotion rely, among other things, on three factors: the correlation fallacy; fear of a ritual misstep; and the power of ambiguity. Seeing in one thing the cause of another is the essence of the correlation fallacy. We dutifully repeat the sacred words, and the orchards fill with fruit. We make that ritual atonement, and the gods' punishment passes us by. We offer this sacrifice, and we no longer need fear the monsters that lurk in the jungle. This illusion of control becomes the engine of significance for the religious imagination, the balance point keeping us afloat on Lovecraft's "black seas of infinity."[62] No matter how grotesque or benign the rite, nor for which species of god it is performed, no matter how its priests have cloaked it in ritual and ceremony, every sacrifice ever offered has been made upon this conceptual altar.

Actively colluding with this is the fear of a ritual misstep, the fear of *not* paying attention to something when we should, of *not* doing something when required. For the Skull Islanders, this is the fear of *not* offering to Kong the most valuable sacrificial object available. Indeed, the fear that we might anger the gods through some small ceremonial oversight, a prayer incorrectly uttered, or an offering inappropriately made still drives us with a species-wide devotion that positively approaches mania. Over time, maintained through cultural convention and the support of our fellow believers, our illusions and our fears coalesce in the form of convictions. "We have always done" becomes "We must always do."

It is worth remembering, though, what Nietzsche wrote in the last sane year of his life: "Convictions might be more dangerous enemies of truth than lies."[63] That is, while we often hold on to our convictions—especially our religious convictions—in the face of skepticism, contradiction, even conclusive disconfirmation, their hold on us is always tempered by doubt. After all, we don't *know* the gods aren't there, we can't *prove* they don't exist, and so, much of our religious belief and practice turns on our ongoing unwillingness to bet against the cosmic house. On Skull Island, this means, What happens if we let "the golden woman" go, and this angers Kong because we have not honored the "bride" ritual in the fullest possible measure?

When Denham refuses to surrender Ann, and the film crew beats a hasty retreat to the ship, the islanders' response reinforces this conviction of ritual value. That night, while basking in the afterglow of her first shared kiss with the handsome first mate, Ann is hauled over the side by a small raiding party and returned to the island. Many Depression-era audiences would have seen in this another example of the exotic "native captivity" narrative by which millions of Western readers of the period were both titillated and fascinated.[64] But it is also the essence of sacrifice. As far as those who live in the shadow of Kong are concerned, the god of Skull Island will not be denied, and demands the most valuable sacrifice available. After all, their lives depend on it.

This time, torchlit dancing and wild chanting accompany the frightened young woman as she is dragged through the frenzied crowd. The enormous village gates open to reveal a squat, stepped pyramid in the Mesoamerican style—another dimension of religious Othering that relies on the relative ignorance people have about traditions even moderately different from their own.[65] Ann is tied between two posts at its top, the position normally reserved for the sacrificial altar. As the gates close, the camera pulls back, creating a tableau that renders the significance of the scene's ritual nature unmistakable to Western audiences. Against the dark backdrop of the forest, framed by the massive log walls, "the golden woman" hangs for a few seconds almost spotlit between the ritual pillars, head down and looking to the left, legs together and bent at the knees: the classic cruciform pose.

Although spotting "Christ figures" on film has become something of an academic drinking game in recent decades, it has been taken to questionable extremes. In an oft-cited, if ill-considered essay, for example, Anton Kozlovic proffers a set of twenty-five so-called "Structural Characteristics of the Christ-Figure," including that such a person is often simple and poor; almost always male; accompanied by twelve associates; usually human, but could also be either animal or extraterrestrial; about thirty years of age; accompanied by a "sexually identified woman"; and, oddly enough, "frequently depicted with blue eyes."[66] This usually (but not always) male, usually (but not always) human will (usually but not always) offer himself up as "a willing sacrifice," and, as the linchpin characteristic on which many interpreters rely, at some point is found in a cruciform pose.[67] The problem here is that almost any character— including the most villainous, and those whose arms simply pinwheel out as they fall—could be made to fit Kozlovic's pattern if one looks sufficiently hard. Moreover, as I have written elsewhere, "Elements of the Christian story are broad enough in the context of ordinary human experience—release from oppression, the nobility of self-sacrifice, a 'Golden Rule' of ethical behavior—that *not* to find something to interpret in this fashion would be surprising."[68] However, this is not to say that, knowing how it will resonate with target audiences, filmmakers do not occasionally make the image explicit.[69] So it is on Skull Island. The villagers may not recognize the significance of Ann's posture as the gates shut and the enormous bolt is shot, but few in Cooper's Western audiences would be able to miss the horrific aesthetic of human sacrifice beating at the sacred heart of their own faith.

The Horrific Aesthetic of Human Sacrifice

John Guillermin's version of *King Kong* can be compared to Cooper's film in a number of ways. In 1933, Denham's New York exhibition of Kong is meant as a spectacle for the well-heeled, a bread-and-circuses marvel to take their minds off the problems of the nation. Apart from out-of-work actor Ann Darrow, however, we see very little of the abject poverty that still held much of the country in its grip.[70] More than a generation later, rather than a film crew's search for their next big picture, a manufactured oil crisis has led to petroleum exploration on Skull Island. And, if 1933's *Kong* is without doubt ruled by the Beast, the 1976 film is governed by the beauty, "Dwan" (Jessica Lange, in her debut role).[71] In the original, the female lead is a rescued waif, while the remake presents her as the hedonistic temptress.

Although the Hays Code was introduced in 1927, Cooper's *King Kong* initially appeared just before the most rigorous period of film censorship began, leading some critics to mislabel it "pre-Code." When the film was re-released in 1938, however, several scenes, including one where a curious Kong undresses Ann with his colossal finger, were sacrificed on the altar of Hays-era censorship. By 1976, however, the Hays Code had lost its hold on the American public, and Guillermin presents a more highly sexualized, occasionally ribald telling of the story. Indeed, if Cooper's film is a Depression-era "Beauty and the Beast," much of Guillermin's version is more akin to "Gidget Meets the Gorilla."

Rather than Ann Darrow hired off the street in New York minutes before Denham's boat sails for Skull Island, for example, Dwan is rescued at sea in the aftermath of a yacht explosion. Inexplicably perky after what must have been a harrowing ordeal, she cheerfully and more than a little flirtatiously asks her rescuers, "Did you ever meet anyone whose life was saved by *Deep Throat*?"[72] Apparently, she alone declined to take part in movie night aboard the boat, to watch what is now one of the most (in)famous adult films of all time.[73] And, when the boat mysteriously explodes during the screening, she alone survives. In what could be a rather unsubtle nod to the emergent antiporn feminism of the day, everyone caught below decks watching porn dies a horrible death.[74] *Res ipsa loquitur*, it seems. As they arrive at Skull Island, all the men on the ship are fully dressed, while Dwan has deliberately cut down whatever clothing was available and created an outfit that would make Ellie May Clampett blush. Indeed, the moment they step ashore, she begins vamping for hunky photographer and environmental activist Jack Prescott (Jeff Daniels) in a fashion-shoot-cum-*Playboy*-pictorial riff.

While the same basic elements constitute the sacrifice scene in both the 1933 and the 1976 versions, the latter presents the ritual itself in a more highly eroticized fashion. Carried in on a litter, the "bride of Kong" is adorned with a grass headpiece woven to resemble long, blonde hair—one of the few overt call-backs to "the golden woman" more than a generation earlier. Villagers stamp and shout; dancers wearing costumes that resemble Dogon masks perform their ceremonial duty. "Hey, Jack," says Dwan, delighted at the unexpected possibility of a party, "maybe it's a wedding." "Good guess," he replies, snapping away with his Nikon.[75] As she asks about the groom, a muscular young man, partially naked though dressed once again as a stylized gorilla, approaches the young woman. Dancing suggestively, even obscenely before her, he explicitly sexualizes the "marriage rite." "The one in the ape mask," Jack says, appearing to know far more about the ritual than he has let on, "you might say, uh, that's the groom's stand-in. The actual groom's on the other side of the wall."[76] When the ceremony is stopped—this time by the "groom"—Jack translates from the islander's tone, "He's probably telling us we've contaminated their magic."[77] The intersection of Western prejudice and ignorance is no less in evidence here, though, than in Cooper's original. "It's just some nutty religion," says Fred Wilson (the Carl Denham character). "A priest gets dressed up like an ape and gets laid."[78]

When Dwan is captured by the islanders that night, rather than being simply dragged toward the place of sacrifice, as was Ann, she is ornately costumed for the ritual, adorned with shell garlands, and treated as the honored guest at a village féte. In this case, the ceremonial value of the sacrifice is measured in the preparation of the sacrificial victim. More-over, unlike Ann, who approaches the altar in stark, open-mouthed ter-ror, Dwan is drugged and, in a languorous stupor, borne on an ornate litter toward the massive village gates. Paradoxically, although the sac-rifice has been scripted as a "marriage," and the groom's dance explicitly sexualized, the clothing given Dwan for the ritual is far less revealing, in-deed far more discreet than the "beach blanket bingo" look she affected on the ship. Her demeanor has changed as well, going from over-the-top flirtation and borderline exhibitionism to a languid nonchalance, an almost protective modesty gifted her by the narcotic. Tied between the ritual pillars, she is not in an explicitly cruciform pose, but the sexu-alized image of a woman in mortal danger as a result of the religious imagination is still fully in view, an aesthetic we owe in large measure to a six-foot-tall, chain-smoking fashion illustrator from Chicago.

Imag(in)ing the Sacrificial Aesthetic

Unlike filmmaking, "illustrating horror fiction is a challenge," wrote author and editor Robert Weinberg, "for the very nature of the subject matter makes the creation of visual images difficult."[79] Indeed, visual horror is always an artistic balancing act: show enough to interest poten-tial readers, but not so much that they don't feel the need to read the story. When does pulp cover art for a story such as G. G. Pendarves's 1932 "Altar of Melek Taos," for example, or Seabury Quinn's 1933 "Hand of Glory" turn a mere "penny dreadful" into a set piece from the Grand Guignol?[80] Described as "a vivid narrative of the devil-worshipping Yezidees," the Pendarves cover art shows a turbaned figure dragging a scantily clad blonde woman toward a winged, golden idol. Perched like a gargoyle on a pillar of fire, the dread "Melek Taos" gazes down las-civiously, talons clutched as though anticipating the rapture of her pale flesh. Another short story at the intersection of weird fiction, religious intolerance, and straight-up racism, "Altar of Melek Taos" capitalizes on centuries of Muslim and Christian accusations of devil worship against the Yazidi people of northern Iraq, principally in terms of "Melek Taus," first among the seven divine beings at the heart of the Yazidi religion. The sacrificial aesthetic here is, once again, the explicitly sexualized "damsel in distress" motif.

Figure 3.2. Cover art for *Weird Tales*, September 1932, by Margaret Brundage.

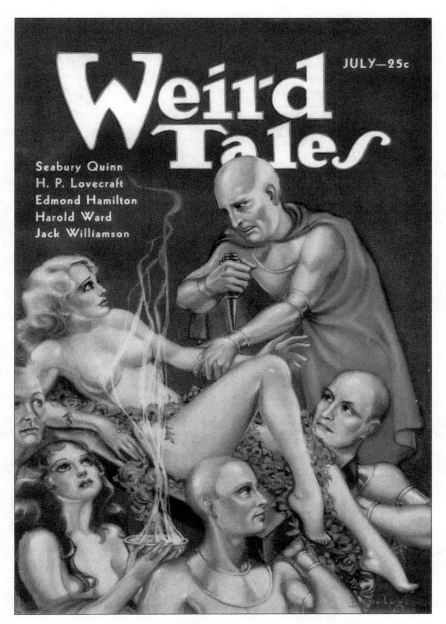

Figure 3.3. Cover art for *Weird Tales*, July 1933, by Margaret Brundage.

Likewise, the cover art for "The Hand of Glory," labeled simply as "a stirring tale of ['occult detective'] Jules de Grandin," features a very similar-looking blonde woman, nude once again and carried on a rose-strewn sedan chair. As a shaven-headed priest approaches holding a ritual dagger, delicate tendrils of incense from a brazier carried by one of the nearly nude worshipers lend the woman what little modesty she has. While cover paintings for pulp magazines, as well as the pen-and-ink artwork inside, were meant to enhance a story's "mood and atmosphere," to "[create] a sense of terror," Weinberg notes that the line that keeps "a frightening illustration" from becoming little more than "an object of revulsion" is often very thin. And, for much of the 1930s, that line was drawn by Margaret Brundage, the "Queen of the Pulps" who produced the cover art for both stories.[81]

Educated at the Art Institute of Chicago in fashion design and illustration, Brundage had difficulty finding work in that industry during the Depression. A single mother with a young child to support, she let her fingers do the walking one day, and came across a Yellow Pages ad for something called "Weird Tales." She had never heard of Farnsworth Wright's horror pulp, but since it was the only magazine with offices in Chicago, she brought in her portfolio. Immediately taken with both the technical skill of her work and its dreamy eroticism, Wright commissioned a cover for one of his other magazines, *Oriental Stories*.[82] The result was artwork for Dorothy Quick's story "Scented Gardens": a nearly nude, generically Asian belly dancer performing before the idol of a multi-armed Hindu god. Within a few months, Wright had moved Brundage over to his flagship publication, *Weird Tales*, beginning with her cover painting for "The Altar of Melek Taos."

From 1933 to 1938, Brundage produced sixty-six *Weird Tales* covers, more than any other single artist, and more than many others combined. Paid the modern equivalent of just over eighteen hundred dollars for each piece, she worked mainly in pastel chalks, and her colorful, often gauzy cover art showcased her fashion background. Most important for Wright, however, was that each cover "[featured] a prominent female figure, usually just partially clothed, with a vague menace in the background."[83] While only a few of her covers made the sacrificial aesthetic quite as explicit as for "The Hand of Glory," a great many of her works clothed the "vague menace in the background" in explicitly religious terms—that is, the sexualized woman in religiously oriented danger.

After reading the story that Wright had selected for the cover art and using nude magazines for reference, Brundage drew a number of sketches highlighting "scenes that stood out as the most dramatic in the story."[84] It quickly became clear, though, she recalled in an interview shortly before her death in 1976, "that they would always pick the one that showed a girl with the least amount of clothing."[85] Indeed, as her *Weird Tales* work progressed, "Brundage's women lost more and more of their clothing and her paintings became more and more erotic."[86] Wright knew his market, and the simple fact was that cover art featuring nude or semi-nude women in all manner of danger sold more issues than those that did not. Moreover, as Weinberg points out, "Brundage covers were the only competition that *Weird Tales* could offer" in the face of the skyrocketing number of pulp magazines suddenly crowding the newsstands of the day.[87] This was not lost on those who contributed their penny-a-word short stories and novellas to the magazine. According to Weinberg, "seeing the slant that Wright had given his cover art" through Brundage and her imitators, *Weird Tales* authors quickly "made sure that their stories always featured at least one scene with a naked woman in jeopardy."[88] The so-called pillar of *Weird Tales*, Seabury Quinn, editor of a mortician's journal turned pulp fiction writer, particularly knew how to grab the cover for his work. In the more than ninety stories starring his occult detective Jules de Grandin—the *Weird Tales* version of Agatha Christie's wildly popular Hercule Poirot, who debuted only five years before de Grandin—Quinn "was careful to always feature a scene that could translate to appropriately salacious artwork."[89]

This is an important point, if for no other reason than that it illustrates the influence of artwork on storytelling and narrative, when the relationship is often assumed to be the other way around. While "you can't judge a book by its cover" is something of a cliché, pulp publishers such as Farnsworth Wright and his countless competitors were banking on the fact that potential customers would do precisely that. Indeed, it is not difficult to imagine the chagrin of readers who, enticed by the cover art for the July 1936 issue of *Weird Tales*, for example, found no narrative reference to the painting at all—despite the issue's table of contents noting that Brundage's cover art was "illustrating a scene in 'Red Nails.'"

In this case, the Robert E. Howard novella, one of his last "Conan" adventures, was serialized across three issues, and readers had to wait until the last few pages of the third installment for the scene Brundage's cover depicted. Given that the bulk of the story is given over to sword-and-sorcery combat scenes, when Brundage read it to get ideas for potential cover art, it is not difficult to see why she chose the passage she did, although altering it just slightly to suit Wright's cover specifications.

"On that altar lay Valeria," Howard wrote, "stark naked, her white flesh gleaming in shocking contrast to the glistening ebon stone. She was not bound. She lay at full length, her arms stretched out above her head to their fullest extent. At the head of the altar knelt a young *man*, holding her wrists firmly. A young woman knelt at the other end of the altar, grasping her ankles."[90] Brundage replaced the male character with another young woman.

One thing that the popularity of pulp cover art such as this indicated in no uncertain terms was that the Hays Code did not have nearly so strong a grip on the public imagination as its creators might have hoped. Sex and horror in all its myriad forms, especially when mixed with the more risqué elements of the religious imagination, still sold extremely well. Indeed, many of Brundage's most erotically charged artworks appeared at precisely the same time that movie producers were struggling with the Code's increasingly stringent enforcement under Joseph Breen. Recall, for example, the Code's warnings about "nudity in fact or in silhouette," or its injunction that "brutality and possible gruesomeness" should be "treated within the careful limits of good taste."[91] Similar deference should be shown the "ceremonies of any definite religion," nor should aspersions be cast "on any religious faith" or religious leaders mocked or turned into "villains."[92] Even the most cursory review of Brundage's cover paintings for *Weird Tales*, however, reveals not only that the Code had no effect on pulp artwork whatsoever but that, for Margaret Brundage and her fellow cover artists at least, their work was fairly defined by all those things forbidden moviegoers. On the one hand, this startling difference indicates a culture trying to come to grips with a new form of entertainment, struggling to understand the effects and implications of the new medium of film, just as it had the advent of popular fiction not so many decades before and as it would the "problem" of

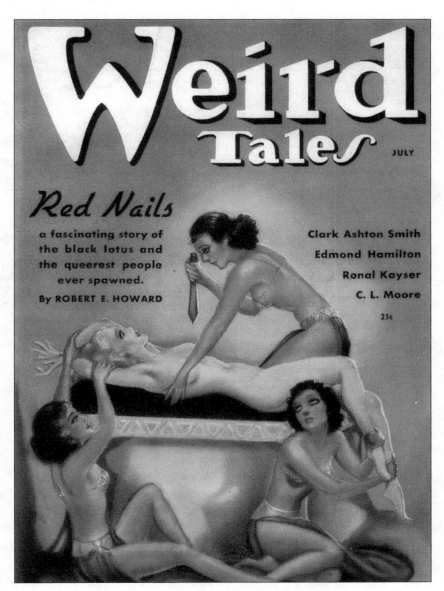

Figure 3.4. Cover art for *Weird Tales*, July 1937, by Margaret Brundage.

comic books in decades to come. On the other, it contributed to the prominence of the sacrificial aesthetic in popular culture.

More than any other social institution, religion has set the boundaries on sexual behavior, both practically and theoretically, just as it has determined the consequences for transgressing those boundaries. "Historically speaking," write Christopher Ryan and Cacilda Jethá, "Judaism, Christianity, Islam, and Hinduism"—religious traditions that account for a significant majority of the global population—"each share a fundamental concern over the punishment for a woman's sexual freedom."[93] That is, a woman's "sexual freedom" is regarded as a resource, as something to be hoarded and, in terms of the sacrificial aesthetic, to be spent in the service of one's god(s). And, by providing the legitimation and infrastructure to support this sexual resource accumulation, the religious imagination has established itself as the quintessential arbiter of all things human. The control and hoarding of sexuality—whether through enforced pair bonding or the imagined restraints of one's gods—renders the sexual body (with all its cultural taboos, behavioral preconditions, and various accoutrements) as ritual capital, the more powerful by virtue of its scarcity and desirability. That which is available in abundance is rarely valued as a resource, and is often squandered without a second thought. Sexuality as a resource explains, at least in part, both the sexualized aspects of human sacrifice—the aesthetic as exempli gratia of the *sacrificial imaginary*—and the central place of the woman within that imaginary.

From horror offerings such as *Weird Tales*, *Uncanny Tales*, and *Terror Tales* (you get the idea) to such science fiction and fantasy shelf-mates as the *Avon Fantasy Reader*, *Fantastic Science Fiction*, and *Thrilling Wonder Stories* (which often replaced the "sacrificial aesthetic" with the more "sciency" "women in test tubes" trope), the pulps constituted the literary equivalent of B-horror movies. And their impact has continued. In so-called men's adventure magazines of the 1950s and 1960s, from *All Man* and *Man's Exploits* to *Big Adventure* and *Men Today*, the sacrificial aesthetic (though, in its Nazisploitation mode, now featuring men in dire straits, and threatened by inevitably buxom, barely clad Nazi women) remained firmly entrenched.[94] From poster art for Italian *giallo* horror of the 1960s and 1970s (e.g., *La Bambola di Satana*; *Il Maligno*; *La Morte Scende Leggera*; *La Tredicesima Vergine*), especially the work of Alessandro Biffignandi and Emanuele Taglietti, to cover art for the horror novels of the 1970s and 1980s (e.g., *The Devil Finds Work*; *The Night Church*; *The Sacrifice*), a clear line can be drawn to the sacrificial aesthetic of Margaret Brundage and her fellow pulp artists.[95]

If the horrific aesthetic of sacrifice often sexualizes women (and occasionally men) on the altar, building on a particular set of fears going back centuries, the horror mode just as often fetishizes the men and women (though principally the women) who prostrate themselves in front of it, the ones who have consecrated themselves to their gods and whose sexuality is both saved and spent in different ways. It is to these fetishes we now turn.

4

Sacred Flesh

Fetishizing the Forbidden Body

A secret room, hidden for centuries in the lowest level of a remote Spanish convent. Its massive, wooden-planked door, banded with steel bars and secured by complex locks, does not appear on any building plan in the church archives. An architectural metaphor for everything we struggle to keep hidden away. What could possibly go wrong?

Welcome to *The Convent of Hell*.[1]

Our story opens with the mortification of young Sister Inés, who has been discovered masturbating in a bathtub. As an act of enforced penance, she now lies bound to a rude cot in a cluttered storeroom. "Was this what you were looking for?" asks the Mother Superior, cradling an enormous wooden dildo, the handle of which resembles nothing so much as the crank on a medieval torture rack.[2] "What's the matter?" she says, smiling cruelly. "Afraid it'll be too *big* for you? That it won't fit in your itty bitty pussy?" Holding the young woman in place, two other nuns leer at her as the abbess continues, "Don't worry. With a little axle grease it'll slide all the way in."[3]

Pleading for mercy and shrieking hysterically, Sister Inés begs them to stop. "Look how it slides in," whispers the head of the convent as a final scream tears itself from her young charge's lips. "Take her to the infirmary," she orders, wiping fresh hymenal blood from the vile sex toy.[4] Later, secure in her own cell, Mother Superior—who, in stockings and garters, balcony bra, and beauty mark, is the very image of the fetishized nun—masturbates furiously to her fantasy of the young woman's suffering.

Suspicion of the cloister and its residents (both literal and metaphorical), and especially such hypersexualized imaginings of what goes on there, has a long history in Western art and literature. Indeed, caricaturing nuns, monks, priests, and pastors as a way of critiquing religious hypocrisy goes back at least to the *Canterbury Tales* (particularly Chaucer's less-than-charitable description of the monk and the Prioress) and to the *Decameron* of his Italian contemporary, Giovanni Boccaccio (especially the story of Masetto, who "pretends to be dumb and becomes a gardener at a convent where all the nuns vie to lie with him").[5] From Chaucer and Boccaccio to Diderot's *The Nun* and Sade's depiction of the clergy in such novels as *Juliette*, *Justine*, and *The 120 Days of Sodom*, from Matthew Lewis's *The Monk* to Aldous Huxley's historical novel, *The Devils of Loudun*, caricature gave way to fetishization, and light-hearted satire to Grand Guignol horror. During the nineteenth century, sexualized fear of Catholic religious in particular grew to something of a cottage industry among North American Protestants anxious about the encroaching power of Rome. And, by the 1970s, this popular sexualization emerged full blown as "nunsploitation," a niche staple of horror cinema, pornography, fetish culture, and even haute couture.[6] In this way, and not unlike B-horror's "last girl standing," the fetishized nun has become as much historical trope as it is theological burlesque.

The novelty of any particular story is only one aspect of what makes popular culture *popular*, one facet of what draws audiences to the theater, the bookshop, or the art gallery. At least as important is the trope, the combination of a subject's familiarity and aspects of what media scholar Henry Jenkins labels "transmedia storytelling" and I have called elsewhere pop culture's "relentless intertextuality."[7] If, as we saw, explaining difference yields the significance of comparison, then the importance of familiarity is that it allows for some form of "interpretive purchase" on a particular cultural product. Otherwise, it's like trying to read a book with only the barest knowledge of the language and idiom, or watch a film with nothing but the onscreen action to guide one's understanding of the story. Obviously, this can work in certain cases, but rarely in works with any narrative nuance. Despite its rampant popularity in Japan, for example, many Western J-horror fans were baffled by Takashi Shimizu's *Ju-on*. Confused and frustrated by the film's episodic, nonchronological structure, its unfamiliar cultural norms, even the basic Japanese notion of a curse, they were unable to gain sufficient interpretive purchase to understand, let alone enjoy it. It simply didn't "make a lot of sense," wrote one reviewer, while another complained that this "fragmented tale is a tangled mess, and the actors have no characterization to play, apart from shrieking cowardice."[8] When Shimizu remade *Ju-on* for Western audiences as *The Grudge*, he not only edited the story into a more recognizable plot structure but added a number of brief expository scenes specifically intended to allow for this interpretive purchase.[9]

Although the concept of a trope is often so taken for granted now that it has become something of a cliché itself, like seemingly throwaway lines in a B-horror creature feature, we ignore these recurring themes and images to our peril. Rather, by calling out to familiar motifs or narrative elements, stories that provide for this kind of tropic interpretive support encourage ongoing audience investment. And, whether these references are classical or contemporary, drawn from pop-culture genres or contemporary events, and hidden in plain sight or as "easter eggs" for the diehard fan, they all contribute in their way to the stock of "recipe knowledge" that we have about those things.[10] Consider the many millions of moviegoers whose only knowledge of the Norse god of thunder comes from the Marvel cinematic universe, or whose attraction to horror storyworlds blurs the lines between fantasy and reality when it comes to characters such as Creepypasta's "Slenderman" or "Jeff the Killer."[11] We may dismiss pop-culture products as "just a movie" or "only a comic book," and we may argue over what constitutes canon and what doesn't, but the themes and motifs they regularly employ are drawn from mimetic wells of cultural experience in which we are deeply invested. Thus, we should not overlook their importance when we see them, because this kind of trope-driven intertextuality "reinforces storylines, cements fan loyalty and appreciation, and encourages participants to explore connections between different storyworlds."[12] Indeed, Cuban horror auteur Jorge Molina insists that this is one of genre cinema's principal attractions, and he describes his own films, such as *Molina's Culpa* and *Ferozz*, as "an accumulation of shots that I've liked in other films" because "cinema for me is totally referential."[13]

And, in terms of this, Argentinian artists Ignacio Noé and Ricardo Barreiro's 2015 graphic novella, *The Convent of Hell*, does not disappoint. Consider just a few such moments of horrific intertextuality at the "Convent of the Cloistered Barefoot Marionite Sisters."[14]

Following the mortification of Sister Inés and the subsequent discovery of the mysterious door in the cellar, a highly sexualized dream possesses the abbess. A young nun—perhaps a dream-world doppelgänger or an image of herself as a novice—prays before a wall roughly painted with occult symbols. As her supplications reach their climax, she tears her habit open, exposing her breasts. "Shub-niggurath," her dream-self cries out ecstatically, "Yog-Sothoth, Azathoth!! Cthulhu!"[15] Despite explicit reference to the Lovecraft mythos, however, what comes through the eldritch gate is not a nightmare from the dark prophet of Providence. That comes later, when Noé and Barreiro explicitly write the convent into the *Necronomicon*, Lovecraft's infamous fictional grimoire, as one of "the few and very secret entrances to the world of the Elder Gods."[16] Rather, in this instance, a huge, anthropomorphic goat, the quintessential Baphomet, crashes into the improvised ceremonial space. "My God!!" the young woman exclaims, suddenly terrified as the horny monstrosity advances toward her. "What have I done?"[17] When he throws her to the floor, she holds up a hand, protesting, "Please, I'm a virgin."[18] Rudely turning her around, the demon is nothing if not accommodating. "Don't worry," he whispers in the terrified nun's ear, "you'll stay a virgin . . . for now."[19]

Mounting her from the rear, Noé and Barreiro's Satanic avatar graphically refracts the famous *Pan and the She-Goat*, a marble sculpture discovered in the ruins of Herculaneum, a Greek city destroyed along with Pompeii by the eruption of Mount Vesuvius in 79 CE, and known for a similar level of sexual openness.[20] Wearing the cloak of the archetypal Christian adversary, the old gods, it seems, still wield power in the sacred precincts of the new, and we are left with an uncomfortable ambiguity over whether "My God!!" is the nun's panic-stricken cry of greeting, or a plea for help from the deity who no longer watches over that place. Waking from her nightmare, the abbess is astonished to find herself aroused by the ordeal. This time when she masturbates, though, she orgasms with a large candle inserted in her anus.

The next day, determined to learn the secret of the convent, she orders the mysterious cellar door opened. When the locks are broken, though, the nuns shrink back in fear as this time a true Lovecraftian horror bursts into the room. A flurry of tentacles, each rubbery arm tipped with a sinister phallus, emerges from whatever unearthly space lies beyond the door. Seizing the first available Marionite sister, it quickly envelops and strips the screaming woman. Fondling her ever more intimately, the tentacled abomination progresses to vaginal, anal, and oral rape—physical manifestations of everything she has sworn to abjure as a consecrated virgin. Although the other nuns are frozen in terror, with every new invasion of the young nun's body a cut-away panel shows the effect on the Mother Superior, who grows increasingly turned on with each grotesque violation. Finally, the abbess orgasms as the Great Old One lifts the other woman high into the air, sexually impaled, every tentacular phallus ejaculating at once. A rain of eldritch sperm covers her body, and unable to withstand the supernatural assault, she dies naked on the rude stone floor.[21]

We are never told her name.[21]

The barrier between the worlds breached at last, the demonic presence in the convent increases in the days that follow. And, as the power of flesh overwhelms the nuns' celibate profession, a diabolical orgy convenes in earnest. "We are all yours, Master!" cries one Marionite, throwing her arms wide toward the life-sized corpus on a wall-mounted crucifix. "Yours for your pleasure and enjoyment!" she shrieks as the Christ transmutes into an ithyphallic Baphomet.[22] The worship of Christ, supposedly embodied in the sacred continence of their own flesh, has transmuted into a sacrament of lust, an erotic flood of forbidden sensuality. The next panel—Noé and Barreiro's satanic goat lolling on the cross, his enormous phallus suspended above the cruciform Sister Agatha—explicitly calls to mind *Le Calvaire* (*Calvary*) by Belgian symbolist Félicien Rops, a nineteenth-century printmaker and engraver whose thoughts on the nature of humanity elevated blasphemy to high art.

One in a series of five engravings entitled *Les Sataniques*, which a contemporary reviewer dismissed as "an idiotic mixture of bar-room mysticism and boulevard pornography," but which proved to be extraordinarily popular nonetheless, *Le Calvaire* is also considered one of the most theologically disturbing.[23] Few descriptions of the image, however, can match that of Rops's contemporary Joris-Karl Huysmans, whose own novel, *La-bàs* (*Down There*), described the dark, occult underworld of fin-de-siècle Paris. "The unspeakable Beast," Huysman wrote in his 1889 volume of art criticism, *Certains*, "hangs there with his money-box

Figure 4.1. *The Convent of Hell*, by Ignacio Noé and Ricardo Barreiro.

Figure 4.2. *Le Calvaire*, by Félicien Rops (1882;
heliogravure etching, 12 x 18.5 inches).

mouth and his walrus teeth. Smiling, his chin in the air, he reaches out
with his unnailed feet, grips the main of a naked woman standing before
him, and slowly strangles her with the locks of her own hair, while she,
terrified, her arms outstretched dies in a spasm of atrocious pleasure."[24]

One of the few exterior panels in Noé and Barreiro's graphic novella
both invokes and inverts Nahum Tate's traditional Christmas hymn, as
a shepherd and his small family watch their flocks by night as light-
ning crashes down and sulphurous smoke engulfs the Marionite cloister.
"My God!" cries the woman. "What's going on at the convent?" "I don't
know," replies the man, his arm around her shoulder, his face stoic, "but
it looks like something evil."[25]

The question, though, is how does he know? How do any of us know?
By virtue of the good, moral, and decent fallacy, we assume that we
know, but how? Simply lifting the veil on a particular trope's source material is rarely enough to tell us much about the importance of an image

or a theme. Instead, we must ask why something *is* a trope, why it carries cultural weight *as* a trope. And, in the context of the horror mode, for that we turn to sociophobics.

Sociophobics and Sacred Flesh

"What does it take to create a successful horror film?" ask psychologists Hank Davis and Andrea Javor.[26] Claiming to find "some striking evolutionary parallels" between "religion, death, and horror movies" (and presaging Mathias Clasen's argument by more than a decade), they contend that these films "are most successful when their content adheres to the evolved structures of the human mind."[27] Even creatively misreading this once again to include all aspects of horror culture, their approach still tells us little more than that we tend to fear things we have evolved to fear, and that scary movies work when they show us things that scare us. But, however anemic the basic reasoning, they're not wrong. Some things we do fear by virtue of who we are as human beings, our adaptation to an environment that can turn hostile in a moment, or as links in a food chain of which we are not always the apex predator.

Other things, though, we learn to fear. We are taught to fear them. Other things we fear because our culture warns us that too much is at stake for us *not* to fear them.

This is *sociophobics*.

For more than a generation now, scholars from a variety of disciplines have recognized that the problem of fearing—what we fear, why we fear it, and how we manage that fear—is at least as much an anthropological and sociological phenomenon as it is psychological. That is, while certain fears have kept us alive long enough to evolve, others have evolved through a process of social construction, and often serve far different agendas than mere survival. "Fearing is an event that takes place in a social setting," writes anthropologist David Scruton in his introduction to the concept of sociophobics.[28] Some cultures fear ghosts and haunting spirits, while others either do not or do so with a wink and a nod. Fear of the reanimated dead is binge television in one part of the world, but a real-world anxiety in places where it is bound explicitly to the religious imagination.[29] Put differently, "It is impossible to understand what human fearing is," Scruton continues, "unless we treat fearing as a function of cultural experience, which people participate in because they are members of specific societies at particular times."[30]

To speak once again with Nietzsche, this sociological process of fearing manifests as a consequence of conviction, and, because "every conviction has its history," specific fears become the ongoing product of social convention, ritual maintenance, and cultural reinforcement.[31] Every conviction had "its preliminary forms, its tentative shapes, its blunders," Nietzsche wrote, and "it *becomes* a conviction after *not* being one for a long time, after *hardly* being one for an even longer time."[32] That is, convictions have a story, a past from which they emerge and evolve, advance and retreat, shift, change, and adapt to circumstance. Once established, though, convictions are amazingly resilient. Resistant to criticism and challenge alike, they underpin the development and decay of social relationships. They shape the criteria by which cultural groups determine acceptance or exclusion, gauge conformity or deviance, extract compliance and exact retribution. Convictions structure institutions as they rise, then watch over them as they gradually (or precipitously) fall into ruin, inevitably to be replaced by institutions grounded in the power of other convictions. And, throughout history, we find that our convictions have been built on changing understandings of what we fear and what it means to fear those things.

Consider, for example, that from the eighth to the twelfth centuries, because it presumed upon the sovereignty of almighty God, the Roman Catholic Church regarded belief in witchcraft as a sin. By the late Middle Ages, however, during the long, dark decades of the Inquisition (which was principally a hunt for heresy, of which pacts with the Devil were but one unholy species), as well as the witch hunts themselves (which were based on a theory of spiritual contagion originating in these infernal compacts), *not* believing in witches was considered a sin.

Few cultural domains disclose the shifting social construction of human fearing more than our supposed interactions with the supernatural, and especially as these relationships are embodied in those supposedly consecrated to divine service. Our brief visit to *The Convent of Hell* lays bare two overarching sociophobics particular to consecrated religious, two layers of fearing and sacred flesh: suspicion and anxiety, and anathema and atrocity.

Suspicion and Anxiety: Fetishizing the Unattainable Other

Fetishizing dedicated religious, especially in terms of dress, deportment, and, most significantly, debauchery has a lengthy history in Western art, and ranges from parody and political satire to censure and open condemnation in the name of competing social and evangelistic agendas. Two of the most vigorous artistic critics were Thomas Rowlandson and Clovis Trouille.

Rowlandson and the Clerical Caricature

Thomas Rowlandson (1756–1827) was a prolific satirist and caricaturist whose work consistently lampooned the pretensions and presumptions of Georgian society, especially when those involved its more salacious aspects. The clergy were in no way exempt from this, and a number of Rowlandson's works depict religious leaders either frequenting prostitutes (e.g., *Quaker in Love*) or attempting to seduce their parishioners (e.g., *The Crowe and the Pigeon*, as well as various denominational iterations of *The Man of Feeling*). Sometimes these attempted seductions succeed. An obvious double entendre, in *The Unwelcome Visitor* (ca. 1800) an elderly Quaker stands pale and quaking as a heavily pregnant young woman appears before him, head bowed, but her eyes raised in silent, almost mocking accusation. Watching from the doorway, finger to his nose, a younger man is clearly enjoying the other's fall from grace. Is he a prankster, a confederate in on a swindle with the young woman, or is this the artist's exposure of a situation so common that it had itself become a trope by Rowlandson's time? Commenting on the difference in artistic development the work displays—the two main figures are carefully drawn, inked, and painted, while the man in the doorway is hastily sketched in—curators of the Rowlandson exhibit at Britain's Royal Collection Trust suggest that the younger man might have been added later, perhaps to suggest an alternate reading of the painting.[33] However Rowlandson intended it, though, the old Quaker is clearly terrified at the possibility of his clerical error.

No such ambiguity is possible with Rowlandson's undated lithograph, *Sexual Habits*. A ribald portrait of a male imposter uncovered in a convent, it was included as an illustration for an edition of Jean de la Fontaine's *Les lunettes*, a classic of seventeenth-century erotic fiction. A bevy of nuns lounges half-dressed, their habits raised above their waists, having just submitted to an intimate inspection by their Mother Superior. Although Rowlandson's painting offers no direct evidence, from de la Fontaine's story we know the alleged crime: the sudden and decidedly unmiraculous appearance of a baby in the cloister. While the other sisters gossip and twitter behind their hands, one young nun lies sprawled in a chair, her legs open, vagina exposed, a languid smile on her face. Determined to get to the root of the problem, the elderly abbess has lifted the veil, as it were, on each of them—until a young man's jauntily erect penis almost hits her in the nose. Her brows shoot up in alarm, her mouth drops open, her pince-nez (the titular *les lunettes*) fly up above her head—all while a portrait of the Virgin Mary at prayer presides over the scene from above the fireplace. For readers of early modern French erotica, as well as those encountering Rowlandson's work in reprint, this epitomizes the popular imagination at work, filling in blanks to the anxious question, What *really* happens behind convent walls?

Symptoms of Sanctity (ca. 1801) presents a far less delicate, though not-uncommon imagining of life in the cloister, one that approaches the horror mode, making apprehension and anxiety about the conventual experience far more explicit. Beneath soaring gothic arches, a young woman kneels at a prie-dieu—chalice, crucifix, and rosary laid out before her. In fancy dress and wedding veil, hands clasped and eyes lifted heavenward, she appears to be pronouncing her vows as a novice. Through consecration as a nun, another virgin bride of Christ, her body moves from one social place to another, from the carnal to the spiritual, the sexual to the sanctified. The scene, however, is dominated by the looming presence of an ugly, obese monk. Rather than joining in prayer for the success of her novitiate, he nestles up to the young woman, staring down her ample décolletage. One hand is draped around her shoulder, the other poised to slip inside her bodice.

Rowlandson inspired a number of similar works, including a pseudonymous, untitled print that could easily be read as a version of "what happened next" in *Symptoms of Sanctity*. An elderly priest, not so corpulent as the other, but naked except for his *zucchetto* (skullcap) and vulpine leer, grasps the metal grillwork separating a small chapel from the central nave of a convent church. A full eucharistic table, complete with chalices, candles, and altar crucifix, stands in the background. Kneeling under the lowermost bar, he thrusts his erect member into a young woman, who looks remarkably like Rowlandson's newly professed novice and who has obligingly presented herself to him. She smiles coyly over her shoulder, as another nun, this one in full habit, holds her gently, perhaps whispering words of less-than-pious encouragement.

Trouille and the Lingerie Aesthetic

By the twentieth century, the tropic image of the fetishized nun had found its most explicit Continental expression in the work of artists such as Clovis Trouille (1889–1975), Suzanne Ballivet (1904–1985), and Paul-Émile Bécat (1885–1960), the latter two of whom also illustrated popular editions of *Les lunettes*. All three shared a conventual lingerie aesthetic that has influenced artists ranging from Milo Manara, Ignacio Noé, and Ricardo Barreiro to photographers, painters, and digital artists who contribute their work to social media sites like DeviantArt, Tumblr, and Flickr, and from Western nunsploitation cinema to the nun-fetish subgenre of Japanese *hentai* (anime and manga pornography).

Trouille's trenchant anticlericalism, however, led him to push this aesthetic further than either Ballivet or Bécat, combining in no uncertain terms a celebration of lust, the horror of death, and condemnation of the Catholic religious imagination as hypocritical slave of the former and hackneyed augur of the latter. Indeed, explicitly echoing such writers as Georges Bataille, many of Trouille's paintings erotically question everything the Roman Catholic Church claims to stand for—particularly its vaunted notion of consecrated virginity.[34]

Although classically trained at the École des Beaux Arts in Amiens, and occasionally claimed by the surrealists as one of their own, Trouille made his living in Paris restoring and decorating department store mannequins. As with his Chicago contemporary, Margaret Brundage, this lengthy experience in the fashion industry expressed itself through his artwork. *Italian Nun Smoking a Cigarette* (1944), for example, resembles the kind of erotic postcard that outraged contemporary moralists because of their supposed availability at newsstands and train stations. A beautiful young nun, complete with smoky eyeshadow and beauty mark, lounges in a cloister porch, holding a cigarette. A tendril of smoke drifts from her bright red lips like incense rising from a brazier. Possibly, she is a Redemptorist, since that order originated in Italy and she is wearing their signature red habit. Her skirts are lifted and one knee drawn up to reveal the kind of sheer stockings and garters that undoubtedly adorned many of Trouille's mannequins. Hardly the soul of conventual modesty, she gazes out at the viewer so brazenly that, rather than a display in Paris's Le Bon Marché, she could as easily grace a shop window in Amsterdam's famous De Wallen district.

Dialogue au Carmel (1944) and *Claustral Dream* (1952), on the other hand, consider both the nature of relationships within the cloister and what is at stake there, particularly in terms of the ubiquity of surveillance and the potential for divine punishment. In the latter, two nuns sit in a cloister bench, which looks out on an interior convent courtyard. Trouille captures them locked in a passionate embrace, their prayer books cast aside. Dressed in the full red habit of a Redemptorist, the nun on the left appears to be older. Cradling the other woman virtually in her lap, her hands are clasped not in prayer but around her lover's waist. The "younger" nun wears a light blue habit, a color often associated in Catholic iconography with the Virgin Mary. Exemplifying Trouille's stocking-garter-and-beauty-mark motif, however, as with the *Italian Nun*, her skirts are hiked up to expose her shapely legs. Holding the other woman behind the head, she pulls her into their kiss. Below and to the left of both women, another nun peeks up through the stone balustrade. Whether she is jealous and angry (cast aside, perhaps, for younger, prettier rival?), or surprised and aroused (what is she doing with her own hand?) is difficult to tell. On the far side of the courtyard, thick garlands of roses—the signature flower of romantic love in French literature—climb up and entwine a large cross, thoroughly obscuring any view of the Christ figure.

Dialogue au Carmel tells a different story, though, again, perhaps a version of "what happened next." Two nuns are in a chapel, one enjoying a postcoital cigarette, the other adjusting her nylons and exposing her shadowy "delta of Venus." Unlike *Claustral Dream*, however, *Dialogue au Carmel* is filled with mordant symbolism.[35] The two pillar candles framing the picture are shaped like erect penises, their wax drippings resembling spent semen or vaginal fluid. No roses adorn this scene, for this is not about love, but lust. An open pulpit Bible faces away, while

Figure 4.3. *Italian Nun Smoking a Cigarette*, by Clovis Trouille (1944; oil on canvas).

a rosary-and-crucifix sits discarded on the bench. Wearing a crown of thorns like some rakish beret, a skull stares sightlessly at the one woman's open legs, and neither nun pays any of these ritual items the slightest attention. Trouille's message seems clear: Whatever the Church has told you is a lie. There is no salvation here; there is no resurrection. Christ's body lies moldering in its forgotten grave, so you might as well enjoy yourselves. There is only flesh.

Finally, *The Immaculate Conception*, for which no precise date is recorded, renders Trouille's anticlericalism most explicit. Unlike the previous examples, rather than a particular scene, this is a tableau, a series of images conjoined by a theme common since the Marquis de Sade and his contemporary, Matthew Lewis: a rampant carnality the Church tries desperately to hide from those who look to it for spiritual guidance, but on whose continuing devotion it depends for its power. Which is to say, for Trouille, this is the base horror of Roman Catholicism in particular, and religion in general: that no matter how it pretends to keep bodies in their continent place, the demands of the flesh will always make themselves known, and often in the most hideous and hypocritical manner imaginable.

Reading the painting from left to right, we watch as a grinning, vulpine pope, complete with papal tiara and ermine-trimmed robe, pleasures a smiling young nun who supports herself on his elaborate crozier. Rather than looking back at her lover, however, she gazes out at the viewer, the heel of her fashionable pump resting on a discarded eucharistic wafer. Beside them, a priest wearing the brimmed *capello Romano* defecates into an altar chalice, while a nun sits in his lap, smiling lasciviously, skirts raised and stockinged legs hooked over his shoulders. In the background, a cardinal and a nun fornicate on the papal altar. On the floor lie two severed heads, staring blankly at a scene out of *Hellraiser*: three sets of bloody female buttocks suspended from hooks and chains. Finally, in the foreground, one breast exposed, another of Trouille's beauty-marked nuns gazes up as she fellates the quintessential Christ figure—an erotic sacrament of adoration. Complete with crown of thorns and sacred heart, her Savior looks down with approval as he places his hand on her veil. Once again, the message is plain: The power of the flesh is simply too strong to resist, and, despite the supposed consequences, no one is safe from its power.

While it is easy to take artworks such as these as hyperbolic anticlerical commentary on the presumed failures of the Catholic Church, they disclose two particular aspects of the social construction of religious fear. In terms of Feil's concept of *religio*, they cast an explicit pall over the character of those on whom hundreds of millions of Catholics depend as signal representatives of the faith. That is, if this is what "religion as if your life depended on it" really looks like, then on what can salvation ultimately depend? Conversely, they highlight a significant cultural ambivalence over the (im)possibility of ritual purity as a pathway to salvation. If men and women consecrated to a life of prayer and divine service can be so egregiously corrupted, what hope have the rest of us to any semblance of sanctity? From Rowlandson's none-too-gentle satire to Trouille's quasi-Sadeian nightmare, this leads us down to *The Convent of Hell's* second metaphorical level: the paradox of the wanton virgin.

Anathema and Atrocity: The Paradox of the Wanton Virgin

In Rowlandson's time, "the basic ideas of what constituted human sexuality were in conflict."[36] Indeed, sexual double standards were no less in evidence then than they are now. On the one hand, women embodied the paradox of the wanton virgin: "sexually insatiable" by nature, but socially "valuable" only so long as their virginity remained intact, that is, "at least until a firm contract of marriage had been made."[37] "The ideal woman," continues historian Vic Gammon, who studies the evolution of desire and attitudes toward death through the medium of the folk song, another classic example of popular culture, "was the virgin spinster and the chaste wife, but because of her ascribed nature, she could easily be transformed into the lusty wench or adulteress."[38] Men, on the other hand, were judged by the bawdy prowess of their "sexual adventuring," the more so the further afield they could boast their so-called wild oats were sown.[39] But, like their Edenic forebear, men could be easily seduced by the female temptress, whom the dour Tertullian originally condemned as "the devil's gateway," "the first deserter of the divine law," and the one "who persuaded him whom the devil was not valiant enough to attack."[40] Two hundred years later, Augustine "took the contempt for sex that saturates the work of the Church Fathers . . . and to it he added a new factor: A personal and theological sexual anxiety."[41]

Indeed, writes Ute Ranke-Heinemann, the first woman to hold a doctorate in Catholic theology, "at the root of the defamation of women in the Church lies the notion that women are unclean and, as such, stand in opposition to the holy."[42]

If we accept David Hartwell's concept of the horror mode as an emotional transaction between the author and the reader—or the filmmaker and the audience, the artist and the viewer, and so forth—then not only are we not confined to the horror genre, per se; we are not limited to fiction at all, given that so many convergences of sex, horror, and the religious imagination are lodged elsewhere. At its most fundamental level, what constitutes the horror mode is what horrifies, or is intended to horrify, a particular audience, whether we find that in fiction or nonfiction, bawdy vernacular ballads or satirical newspaper artwork, thundering homilies delivered from cathedral pulpits or dark mutterings in coffee shop shadows. Sometimes, though, the horror mode is a function of the ambiguous, propagandistic spaces between all of these.

While different colloquial understandings circulate in society about what constitutes "propaganda," most fall under three general rubrics. First is that propaganda is, by definition, a lie, something patently untrue. Of course, sometimes this is the case, but in many (arguably most) instances, propaganda is less often the invention of outright falsehoods than it is the careful management of truths and half-truths toward a particular end. Deceit, then, is less the objective of propaganda than one of the many tools by which a propagandist's real objectives are achieved. Next, there is the belief that "propaganda" is simply the word used to label in some pejorative or dismissive way information of which one disapproves. "Oh, that's just propaganda," we say, as though that settles the issue, without having to investigate the matter further or consider any potentially discomfiting implications. Finally, propaganda is what other people do. That is, we (whoever "we" are) tell the "truth" (whatever that is), while "propaganda" is what they do (because, seriously, what would you expect from people like that?). Theorists ranging from Jacques Ellul to Garth Jowett and Victoria O'Donnell, however, have usefully parsed this understanding, distinguishing between "white" propaganda (in which correctly identified sources "communicate accurate information"), "gray" propaganda ("which is often used to embarrass an enemy or competitor"), and "black" propaganda (where "a false source is given and lies, fabrications, and deceptions are spread").[43] However it is defined, though, Ellul correctly highlights one of propaganda's key traits: that "a prejudice or stereotype is hardly ever changed."[44] Which is to say, propaganda is most successful when it leverages the biases, preconceptions, and conventional pieties of a particular group, rather than trying to change them. Instead of shifting that group's worldview, propaganda manipulates information to reinforce and entrench its existing beliefs, myths, symbol sets, and, most importantly, its sociophobics, the things that group has been taught to fear. Because of its emotional potency, intuitive reliability, and nonfalsifiable character, one of the most effective tools in the propagandist's kit is apostate testimony, the "true story" told by one who was there but who managed to escape.

Consider nearly a century's worth of such affidavits.

"It is to be hoped," wrote the woman known as Maria Monk, arguably the most (in)famous of nineteenth-century former nuns, "that the reader of the ensuing narrative will not suppose that it is a fiction, or that the scenes and persons that I have delineated had not a real existence."[45] Although conflicted about the experiences she wants desperately to recount, she insists that "I have given the world the truth, so far as I have gone, on subjects of which, I am told, it is generally ignorant."[46] And, despite concern that she might not be believed, "I feel perfect confidence, that any facts which may yet be discovered will confirm my words."[47] Likewise, a generation later, former Sister of Charity Edith O'Gorman declared that in publishing *Convent Life Unveiled* she was solely "guided by truth" and did "not make a single statement that can be refuted."[48] More than that, though, she penned her conventual memoir "knowing that the *truth* will never be given to the public except by those who can write as I can, from personal experience and positive knowledge."[49] Insisting that she did not want "the attention of the public for the purpose of exciting sympathy," she claims that her only wish was that her story might "be the means of saving one immortal soul from the slavery of Romanism and the living tomb of convents!"[50]

Lest we think that only those confined to the cloister took issue with their supposed captivity, former Catholic priest Charles Chiniquy promised readers of *Fifty Years in the Church of Rome* that "the superstitious, the ridiculous and humiliating practices, the secret and mental agonies of the monks, the nuns, and the priests, will be shown to you as they were never shown before"—and that by dint of "evidence which my twenty-five years of priesthood only could teach me."[51] For those who know no better, "I was there and you weren't" can be a very compelling argument, especially if you are already inclined to believe the worst the writer has to offer. Lifting the skirts on "the monster Church of Rome," Chiniquy begged "faithful ministers of the Gospel" to read his nearly-nine-hundred-page book and "see the inside life of Popery with the exactness of Photography."[52] Finally, wrote Bernard Fresenborg, in the introduction to his fin-de-siècle diatribe, *"Thirty Years in Hell,"* "What I will now relate is not hear-say, nor something that I have read about, but it is something that *I know about*, and which I have witnessed."[53] "Like a Meteor From God's Throne" reads the frontispiece like a carnival barker's tent placard, "This great book has stirred America from center to circumference. About 400 Large Pages, And each page a stinging rebuke to Roman Catholicism."[54] In fact, so confident was Fresenborg, a Roman Catholic priest who converted to Protestantism less than a year before the book's publication in 1904, that he offered to donate five thousand dollars to charity "if any Catholic priest, bishop or cardinal" could prove "that I have misstated or misrepresented the teachings of Catholicism."[55]

By the time Fresenborg escaped his *"Thirty Years in Hell,"* the conception of women had changed considerably since Rowlandson. From the sexually insatiable temptress of the Georgian period, she had become by the late Victorian era the repository of virtue in whose bosom lay the inestimable power of self-sacrifice for husband and family. Outside the confines of conventual religious life, women across Western Europe and the Americas had been unwittingly registered in what literature scholar Bram Dijkstra labels "the cult of the household nun."[56] Both groups of women, however, were vulnerable to the sexual threat represented by the Roman Catholic Church, and the nineteenth century saw a brisk trade in anti-Catholic literature. Among the encomium of atrocities such writers as Chiniquy, Fresenborg, et al. laid bare, two in particular were meant to horrify readers, both of which turned on the most salacious imaginings of what went on within the confessional box and behind the walls of the convent.

The Confessional

"Imagine the power that a Catholic priest has over a young girl in her teens," Fresenborg wrote, especially since "from infancy these girls and women have been taught that it is almost an impossibility for a priest to commit a sin."[57] This priestly infallibility had a number of advantages, chief among them that they could demand of congregants whatever they liked, and "accomplish any devilish deed they may wish."[58] Even "piously and morally-inclined priests," however, could be tempted to "the plains of immorality" by "one of the most damnable institutions that was ever permitted to exist"—the confessional.[59] "Forced to compel women penitents to pour into his ears their every thought, feeling, desire, emotion and act," Fresenborg continues, assuring his readers in good moral crusader fashion that he takes no pleasure in sharing even these bare hints of the horrors he could relate, "it kindles the fires of unholy thought upon the altars of his better ambitions and before he knows it he has committed adultery and not only ruined his own soul, but has been the implement in the hands of the devil to destroy the virtue of innocent womanhood."[60] Conversely, because parishioners are required to recite chapter-and-verse of their sexual lives, both real and imagined, for "the immorally inclined and licentious priest" the confessional serves as something of a daily peep show leading "both the penitent and the confessor to the lowlands of immorality."[61]

Although Charles Chiniquy's imposing *Fifty Years in the Church of Rome* was one of Canada's best-selling books in the late nineteenth century, his earlier volume, *The Priest, The Woman, and The Confessional*, went through over forty printings by the turn of the twentieth century.[62] "There are two women," he begins, "who ought to be constant objects of the compassion of disciples of Christ": "the Brahmin woman, who, deceived by her priests, burns herself on the corpse of her husband to appease the wrath of her wooden gods" and, even more to be pitied, "the Roman Catholic woman, who, not less deceived by her priest, suffers a torture far more ignominious and cruel in the confessional-box, to appease the wrath of her wafer-god."[63] In a ritual apparently worse than the self-sacrifice of sati, the devout Catholic is forced to reveal "all the most sacred mysteries of their single or married life," to answer "questions which the most depraved woman would never consent to hear from her

Figure 4.4. Illustration from Charles Chiniquy's *50 Years in the Church of Rome* (1886).

vilest seducer."[64] Chiniquy solemnly warns his reader that untold thousands of otherwise virtuous women, their sexual sins still hidden, leave the confessional every year unshriven and believing themselves damned because of it.

The Cloister

Putative conventual memoirs such as *Awful Disclosures of Maria Monk, The Convent and the Manse*, and *Six Months in a Convent*, as well as anti-Catholic novels such as Helen Dhu's *Stanhope Burleigh*, which was rather unsubtly subtitled *The Jesuits in Our Homes*, were written as much to titillate and horrify properly God-fearing Protestants as they were to reassure them of their moral and theological superiority.[65] According to Edith O'Gorman, the vow of chastity meant that nuns were permitted no outward show of affection, that the professed religious "must not raise her eyes when speaking to one of the opposite sex," nor may she "touch a sister's hand, or habit, or allow herself to be touched by another."[66] Daily, they were read injunctions from such moralistic venerables as Alphonse de Ligouri, who warned them that their bodies were continually in danger of being thrown out of place, that any "deliberate glance at a person of a different sex, enkindles an infernal spark which damns the soul."[67]

Should any such impropriety occur, even among the schoolchildren she taught as Sister Teresa de Chantal, O'Gorman writes that she was "forced to recoil from their innocent demonstrations of love as from a serpent's touch"; if she did not, she "would be reported by the spies of the community who were ever on the alert."[68] More than that, "A sister is bound to accuse herself of all things relating to chastity."[69] From errant glances to erotic dreams, haunted by the Matthian thought-crime of lust, any "vision against purity must be minutely detailed to her confessor."[70] As with her secular sisters, this placed the cloistered nun at considerable risk. Such was "the infamous craft of these regulations" that "the priest thus informed can take advantage of her as he may feel inclined."[71] Perhaps he will self-righteously curl his lip in "holy horror," especially if he does not particularly like the penitent, or does not find her suitably attractive.[72] "On the other hand," O'Gorman warns, "should his evil heart suggest to him the moral destruction of this sister, how great the facility he possesses for this accomplishment."[73] Facility, indeed, since as far as she knew her immortal soul hung in the balance of his willingness to grant sometimes daily absolution. And, for writers like O'Gorman, Chiniquy, and Maria Monk, that balance always tipped toward sin.

"The priests who read this book," which was titled in good nineteenth-century fashion, *Awful Disclosures of Maria Monk, As Exhibited in a Narrative of Her Sufferings During Her Residence of Five Years as a Novice and Two Years as a Black Nun in the Hotel Dieu Nunnery, at Montreal, Ont.*, "will acknowledge to themselves the truth of my description, but will, of course, deny it to the world."[74] Cataloguing the precincts of Montreal's so-called Black Nunnery, for example, Maria notes that she has been "credibly informed that masons have been employed at the nunnery since I left it."[75] What could they possibly be covering up? Some unmarked door in a forgotten cellar, perhaps? Or something more sinister? In dry, flat prose, she describes the nuns' daily living quarters, their dining hall and various communal rooms, the private chapels for prayer and adoration. Sleeping quarters were on the second floor, apparently, with a number of other shared living spaces, including storerooms, sitting rooms, which included provision for physicians to enter the convent, and various sick rooms in which the nuns were treated. It's all very plain—mundane, really—and many readers would likely have skipped over this early part of the story, in order to get to the spicier bits they had come to expect. Doing so, however, they would have missed Maria's brief, almost passing description of a few small sick rooms off the convent's main convalescent ward.

"Appropriated to nuns suffering with the most loathsome disease," one such room was stocked with straw mattresses and serviced by a single examination room. "Another door," she writes, "opens into a passage, in which is a staircase leading down."[76] While Maria initially leaves the nature of "the most loathsome disease" vague, her description of what happens next left little to the imagination.

> 11 and 12. Beyond this are two more sick-rooms, in one of which those nuns stay who are waiting their accouchement, and in the other those who have passed it. 13. The next is a small sitting room, where a priest waits to baptize the infants previous to their murder. A passage leads from this room on left, by the doors of two succeeding apartments, neither of which I have ever entered. 14. The first of them is the "holy re-

treat," or room occupied by the priests while suffering the penalty of their licentiousness. 15. The other is a sitting-room, to which they have access. Beyond these the passage leads to two rooms, containing closets for the storage of various articles; and two others, where persons are received who come on business.[77]

A priest waits to baptize the infants previous to their murder.

Only eleven words, but terrifying in the context of the anti-Catholic conjunction of sex, horror, and the religious imagination. Two things in particular are worthy of note. First is the grim banality of Maria's description, the matter-of-fact manner in which she itemizes the convent's grisly architecture. This is significantly at odds with some of the more sensationalist prose later in the book, and presenting it as business as usual at the Hôtel Dieu only increases its gruesomeness. Indeed, it's not difficult to imagine her speaking to a church hall full of credulous, scandalized Protestants, especially during the "several months [she] was fêted in New York society," perhaps using a pointer to indicate the different rooms.[78] Here is "a large community-room for Sundays." *Tap.* Here is what we "call the wax-room, as it contains many figures in wax." *Tap.* And here "is a small sitting room, where a priest waits to baptize the infants previous to their murder."[79] *Tap. Tap.* Moving on, here are some "closets for the storage of various articles."[80] *Tap.* Rather than jump-scares in a slasher movie like *Scream* or *Halloween*, where the price of sex is also death, but which we laugh off when the house lights come up or the video is paused, the horror that crept through the audience at the young woman's chilling words only confirmed the worst of what many of them already believed about Catholics in general and convents in particular.

Lest anyone miss the point, though, Maria makes the tragic circumstances explicit. Tendering the quintessence of anti-Catholic propaganda in the nineteenth century, she states simply that infants fathered by priests and born to the nuns were ritually murdered immediately following their birth. These "little bodies were then taken into the cellar, thrown into the pit I have mentioned"—in which, apparently, the bodies of recalcitrant sisters were also discarded—"and covered with a quantity of lime."[81] More than that, no one at the convent is safe from indictment.

So far as I know, there were no pains taken to preserve secrecy on the subject; that is, I saw no attempt made to keep any inmate of the convent in ignorance of the murder of the children. On the contrary, others were told as well as myself, on their first admission as veiled nuns, that all infants born in the place were baptized and killed without loss of time; and I had been called to witness the murder of the three just mentioned only because I happened to be in the room at the time. That others were killed in the same manner, during my stay at the nunnery, I am well assured.[82]

Although she "cannot speak with precision" just how many innocent victims of their parents' lust died in this wanton and unutterably cruel fashion, she learned "that at least eighteen or twenty infants were smothered and secretly buried in the cellar while I was a nun."[83] If we take her at her word about the veil, that would mean one baby every three months during her time there, mass infanticide on an almost industrial scale.

Second, buried within these short passages are the ways in which bodies move in and out of horrific place at the Hôtel Dieu, and by implication all other Roman Catholic convents. Nuns who survived "their accouchement" were separated from the community, both physically and ritually. Unconfessed and unshriven, spiritually adrift, as long as they lay on those hard, straw mattresses—which made disposing of the gouts of birth-blood easier, as well as hid the inconvenient fact of the birth itself—they were outside a state of grace. Should they die during or in the immediate aftermath of childbirth, a not-unimportant consideration given the high maternal mortality rate at the time, they could look forward to nothing other than eternal damnation. "A nun of our convent," writes Maria, "who had hidden some sin from her confessor, died suddenly, and without anyone to confess her."[84] When the other nuns "assembled to pray for the peace of her soul," however, "she appeared and informed them that it would be of no use, but rather troublesome to her, as her pardon was impossible."[85] This may sound counterintuitive given the popularity of Catholic prayers for the dead, but Maria assured her readers that "the doctrine is that prayers made for the souls guilty of unconfessed sin do not but sink them deeper into hell."[86] Perhaps looking out over her audience at this point, she added that "this is the reason I have heard given for not praying for Protestants."[87]

Cue pearl clutching, general outrage, and angry villagers with torches.[88]

Guilty priests, on the other hand, were ushered into a small "holy retreat," where they "[suffered] the penalty of their licentiousness."[89] No mention is made of how this happened or what the specific penance—perhaps an appropriate performance of contrition and a period of mortification—but the difference in description is startling, and reinforces the fundamental difference in value between male and female bodies. Cold straw mats for one, a "holy retreat" for the other. Each having quite obviously broken their respective vows of chastity, though, the only mechanism that could restore either to sanctity was the very thing that allegedly got them into trouble in the first place. Running throughout anti-Catholic conventual and priestly memoirs is the common thread of the confessional, the only means by which sinful bodies could be returned to their proper ritual place in both the communal structure and the divine order. Otherwise, quite simply, Hell awaits.

A year after *Awful Disclosures* was published, Maria and her supporters released *Further Disclosures by Maria Monk*, once again effusively subtitled *Concerning the Hotel Dieu Nunnery of Montreal; also, Her Visit to Nun's Island and Disclosures Concerning That Secret Retreat*. This volume included a book by Presbyterian minister, publisher, and prominent anti-Catholic activist John Jay Slocum purporting to answer the many criticisms leveled at Maria's story.[90] Quoting the *New York Observer*, Slocum asks rhetorically, "Need I pursue the details of the degenerating process, to show the easy steps by which passion thus restrained, descends to crime?"[91] Given the *Observer*'s overtly anti-Catholic (not to mention antisemitic) stance, of course the gory details need pursuing. In depth, please, and at length, sir! After all, with the "voluntarily incurred temptations" of "this most unnatural intercourse," how could anything but the natural variety result?[92] "Both priests and nuns are kept from its commission by no *human* restraint," Slocum continued, "and certainly by no promise of *divine* assistance, but are left weak and unaided to contend with, and to be vanquished by, this strongest of human passions. Love is thus perverted to lust, and everyone knows that the secret servant of lust, is Murder."[93]

In the case of the Hôtel Dieu, rather than human sacrifice, this meant ritual murder, and here the theological calculus for infanticide is horrific in its expediency. Although common sense tells us that the babies themselves could not possibly have sinned—none lived long enough— they were, in fact, born both in and into sin. Their tiny, squalling bodies were doubly out of place, and doubly damned if something was not done. On the one hand, they were the obvious product of sinful lust, the very issue of that Matthian thought-crime against which professed religious had to be so on guard, but which they were also required to relate in exquisite detail to their confessors. So long as these infants lived, they remained living proof of the wanton virginity of both father and mother—as well as a stain on the religious community unwilling to suffer such little children.

On the other hand, despite coming into the world through no fault of their own, and committing no obvious sin in their brief time here, simply by virtue of being born they fell under the anathema of original sin. As such, and notwithstanding various Catholic attempts to ameliorate the horrifying concept of "babies in hell," they lay condemned to everlasting torment by God the Father—save the ritual intervention of Holy Mother Church. Augustine, to whom much of Catholicism has looked for nearly two millennia for its doctrine of original sin, actually "[rejected] the moral innocence of infants" and regarded "the rage, weeping, and jealousy of which infants are capable proof of original sin."[94] He insisted that through sexual intercourse, the bred-in-the-bone urge that was all but impossible for us to control, and which damned us even if our arousal was involuntary and unwanted, the original burden of sin was inexorably passed on.[95] In place of absolution through confession, baptism conferred the ritual remission of sin on infants born at Hôtel Dieu. Murdered immediately after, their souls were now, presumably, safe from the eternal inferno.

The Horror Mode in Real Time

After nearly three decades on the anti-Catholic sawdust trail, Bernard Fresenborg, "who, for thirty long years tread the slippery and deceitful path of abhorrent Catholicism," retracted his accusations and sought reconciliation with the Church through the Bishop of Amarillo.[96] In his formal letter of recantation, he wrote that "I abjure all my errors against the Roman Catholic Church, including every suspicion of heresy as well as all that I may have written or spoken of a defamatory nature."[97] Conversely, both Chiniquy and O'Gorman maintained their Protestant anti-Catholicism for the rest of their lives. Chiniquy took holy orders as a Presbyterian minister and became famous as the "Apostle of Temperance in Canada." Both *Fifty Years in the Church of Rome* and *The Priest, The Woman, and The Confessional* were bestsellers in their day, and remain in print to this day thanks to fundamentalist Protestant organizations such as Chick Publications. For nearly twenty years, Edith O'Gorman made a living as "the escaped nun," lecturing on the evils of the Roman Catholic Church throughout the United States and Great Britain.

Maria Monk, on the other hand, is a horror story, literally.

Whether the kind of harrowing conditions she relates ever existed at the Hôtel Dieu or not, "Maria Monk" herself did not. Although her name quite likely was Maria, and her father was William Monk, "Maria Monk" was the invention of virulent anti-Catholic nativism in the early nineteenth century. A mentally unstable young woman, Maria was born in 1816, in what is now Saint-Jean-sur-Richelieu, Quebec. By all accounts, she was a difficult child, and by the time she was in her late teens, her mother, Isabella, despaired of controlling her. Having for a number of years already "led the life of a stroller and prostitute," Maria was committed to the Charitable Institution for Female Penitents, also known as the Magdalen Asylum, a Catholic home for prostitutes in Montreal.[98] Less than four months later, however, she was found to be pregnant, and expelled.[99] Making her way to New York, Maria spun lurid tales of her alleged time as a nun at Hôtel Dieu. These first-person atrocity stories fit precisely into the virulent anti-Catholic narrative of preachers and publishers such as J. J. Slocum, George Bourne, and William Hoyt, who together concocted the *Awful Disclosures of Maria Monk*. Indeed, according to Agathe-Henriette Huguet dite Latour, the Montreal philanthropist who operated the home for "nonrespectable women," Maria's architectural description of "the Hôtel Dieu Convent is alone applicable to the Magdalen Asylum."[100]

The literal truth of these events, however, actually matters little in terms of the religious imagination and the propagandistic effect of popular culture. Rather, Maria's story, aided and abetted by her Protestant sponsors and, paradoxically, reinforced through the various exposés that appeared within months of *Awful Disclosures*, demonstrated the workings of the horror mode in real time.

Awful Disclosures was an immediate success, reviewed in newspapers, magazines, and broadsheets throughout North America, and Maria found herself for a time the darling of American anti-Catholic nativism. One contributor to *Zion's Herald* praised Maria for her courage in exposing these "unparalleled sinks of polluting corruption," while "One Who Knows" argued in the *New York Evangelist* that only the complete dissolution of the conventual system would prevent further atrocities in "that abominable prison, blasphemously denominated the Hotel Dieu Nunnery."[101] Numerous other newspapers and broadsheets popularized the anti-Catholic cause. From the *American Protestant Vindicator*, which, in case that was too subtle, changed its name in the late 1830s to *American Protestant Vindicator in Defence of Civil and Religious Liberty Against the Inroads of Popery*, then simply to *The Menace*, and which in the early twentieth century claimed a million and a half subscribers, and from the *Vermont Telegraph*, whose masthead read "I am set for the defense of the gospel," to the *New York Observer*, which may seem an innocuous title today, but was originally published as the *New-York Observer and Religious Chronicle* and later as *Christian Work and Evangelist*—all these and many more popularized the anti-Catholic cause by burnishing the sense of looming dread with a fine patina of imminent threat.

Not everyone believed the stories, though, and many were just as horrified that anyone could credence what journalist and publisher William Leete Stone called quite simply "a humbug."[102] Despite his own strong anti-Catholic leanings, Stone published three books refuting the charges made in *Awful Disclosures*, while the Unitarians could "conceive of nothing more infamous than pandering to the prurient curiosity of low and vulgar minds."[103] Alarmed at the book's implications for the honor of their fair city, Montrealers put up posters denouncing it as "the fabrications of a notorious harlot, the inventions of combined lunacy and profligacy."[104]

Two other items, however, separated by sixty years, demonstrate in no uncertain terms the propagandistic power of such first-person atrocity narratives. Shortly after its publication in 1836, *Awful Disclosures* was reviewed in the *New York Observer*, an article subsequently picked up and reprinted in a number of other journals, magazines, and newspapers.

Whether Maria's claims "are true or false," the reviewer declared, "our opinion of convents and the confessional will remain the same. They undoubtedly afford great facilities for the commission of the crimes here alleged to have been perpetrated."[105] Put differently, We believe it, whether it is true or not, the actual facts be damned. Nearly six decades later, and more than a generation after Maria "died at the almshouse on Blackwell's Island," one man asked the logically fallacious, though emotionally compelling question, "If Miss Monk is not an escaped nun, why did the priests stir up Romish mobs to recapture her?"[106] Following a lecture by Charles Chiniquy, he wrote to *The American*, a weekly nativist broadsheet published in Omaha, Nebraska, wanting to know, "If those convents are not places of lewdness and wickedness, why did Pope Innocent VIII publish a bull demanding reformation in monasteries and other religious places, and declare that 'members of monasteries and other religious houses lead a lascivious and truly dissolute life'?"[107] Finally, in a rhetorical appeal common to conspiracy theories ranging from ghost stories to alien abductions, "Why is it that all escaped nuns tell the same story of those prisons?"[108]

From the fictional convent to the cloister fictionalized, this is the valance of the emotional transaction: horror at the demands of one's own flesh, and the cosmic consequences of giving in to those demands. If, within the cloister, abstinence is the physical telltale of consecration, and sexualization its greatest threat, what happens outside, when the situation is reversed, when celebrating the human sexual urge functions as the hallmark of sacrality? Out from the cloister and over the convent walls, then, we enter next the deep, dark forest.

5

Skyclad

Sexualizing the Dangerous Other

"I am that very witch," the young woman in her late teens says ominously, the eyes of her two small siblings widening in terror. "When I sleep, my spirit slips away from my body and dances naked with the Devil."[1]

In Robert Eggers's relentlessly depressing film, *The Witch*, a seventeenth-century Puritan family embraces banishment from the relative safety of their small New England colony, striking out for a homestead in the wilderness. Appalled at what he regards as the lack of faith shown by his fellow colonists, the family patriarch insists that they move to a place where they can worship God in their own, much stricter way. Leaving "civilization" behind, both literally and metaphorically, they stop on the verge of the quintessential "deep, dark forest."[2]

With a couple of important exceptions, throughout the film the Puritans are shown armored, as it were, in their clothing. Believing that "Satan attacked the soul by assaulting the body," in physically protecting the one, they symbolically safeguard the other.[3] Multiple layers of rough wool and linen shield them from the harshness of land and climate, as well as from the lure of the flesh, a principal sin against which their faith consistently preaches, and by implication the predations of the Devil, who they believe is ever on the prowl.[4] Throughout the film, we see the Puritans clothed except when they have been in contact with "that very witch," whether implicitly or explicitly. And, when we do see them either unclothed or semi-clothed, it is always in one of two ways.

First, when young Caleb catches sight of his older sister's bosom swelling at the top of her bodice, it signals both the pervasive temptation to inappropriate sexuality and the restrictions placed upon it by his religion. Later, when he himself is taken by the witch, and his father returns to the farm after searching for him in vain, the man's semi-nakedness as he washes off the grime of the forest lays bare their collective weakness in the face of the spiritual threat the witch represents. Regardless of their faith, they are powerless against the malign force that lurks beyond the tree line. When the boy is returned, he lies naked and close to death, a proximal effect of what they regard as a preeminent supernatural menace they only barely comprehend, but that they fear to the very core of their being. Although, as historian Elizabeth Reis points out, Puritans believed that because "women's bodies were weaker, the devil could reach women's souls more easily and breach these 'weaker vessels' with greater frequency," it is the menfolk in this particular telling whose flesh most consistently demonstrates this fragility.[5]

The forest witch herself, on the other hand, appears initially as a fairytale character, a furtive Red Riding Hood flitting through the trees. This, of course, reverses the familiar trope, where Red is the victim in the story, not the putative villain. More than a bit flirtatious as she darts among the gloomy pines and cedars, she represents "an almost blameless evil," as critic Jess Joho puts it, "a fact of living on earth that's as material as rain or food poisoning."[6] Which is to say, this may not be so much supernatural as a different kind of natural order, an unfamiliar perspective on consensus reality that respects neither Christian god nor Puritan creed, and recasts notions of good, evil, and the spaces in between with a terrifying ambiguity.

When we do first see the witch fully naked—"skyclad," in modern Pagan terminology—the image is anything but sexualized, as she pulverizes the unfortunate infant Sam for the bloody witches' salve used to anoint her body.[7] In this scene, her lumpy and misshapen physical appearance calls to mind such images as Albrecht Dürer's famous engravings *The Four Witches* (1497) and *Witch Riding Backwards on a Goat* (1500), and, even more explicitly, *The Witches*, a woodcut produced in 1510 by Dürer's most gifted apprentice, Hans Baldung Grien.[8] Indeed, much of the film's early imagery seems to draw on Dürer's and Baldung Grien's work. In addition to the common theme that witches require the bodies and/or the life essence of children as the price of whatever beauty or longevity they have, this points to the difference between nudity and sexuality, that one does not necessarily connote the other, however often both are conflated and confused. That is, the boundaries between bodies and what they mean are once again blurred, the conditions by which they are considered in or out of place becoming vague and ill defined.

This is especially the case in the film's final scene. Led by the massive he-goat, "Black Philip," the implicit Satanic signifier throughout the story, the young woman, Thomasin, sheds her clothes and walks naked through the moonlit forest toward a clearing where a group of witches chant wildly and dance around a bonfire. As she enters what the women have transformed into a sacred grove, they begin to rise up in ecstatic flight, one of them astride a long stick, another seeming to dance in midair, one more observing from the sidelines beside Black Philip—a closing image that mimics nothing so much as Francisco Goya's 1798 paintings *The Witches' Flight* and *The Witches' Sabbath*.[9]

To this point in the film, the forest witch has been a solitary threat, a single woman who happens to dwell within reach of the Puritan farmstead. In this, she fits much more readily into the "Hansel and Gretel" model, especially given the film's original subtitle, "A New-England Folktale," a rhetorical touch that lends the story a certain traditional, based-on-real-events cachet.[10] As Thomasin approaches the firelight, however, we realize that the danger now comprises an entire magic circle—a significantly greater threat, not only in the immediate context of the Puritan family but to the efficacy of the larger Christian faith they represent. Here, we are confronted by the horror-mode problem of *deus absconditus* and the insignificance of faith.[11] That is, the God whose will they left the colony to follow more faithfully is nowhere to be found. He could protect neither Sam nor Caleb—nor, we should imagine, the numberless others who have fallen victim to the coven over the years. And now Thomasin is lost to this absent deity, suffering what many believers today would still call a fate worse than death. At least Sam is dead, presumably safe in the arms of Jesus. His sister, on the other hand, so far as the Puritans are concerned, has abandoned both their god and his proffer of eternal salvation.

One of *The Witch*'s principal marketing images depicts Thomasin from the back, naked and silhouetted by cold, blue moonlight, as she walks through the forest to join the witches in their preternatural revels. And, in this, nakedness marks her change of place, the embodied shift from one consensus reality to another. As with so many other aspects of the religious imagination, the significance of emplacement is always perspectival. Buckaroo Banzai may have opined sagely that "no matter where you go, there you are," but what "there you are" means in terms of the horror mode depends entirely on your frame of reference.[12] But if, as Jonathan Z. Smith wrote, "place directs attention," then emplacement tells us the importance of where we are, what we are looking at while we're there, and what that place expects of us.[13] In slipping away to dance naked in the forest, Thomasin has indeed become "that very witch."[14] Even her hands appear less the instruments of prayer and hard work on the farm than as claws eager to be about the Devil's business.[15] And the viewer is left with the implicit question, Whose squalling infant will *she* grind to gory paste in her witch's mortar-and-pestle? Whose innocent death will coat her flesh with eldritch life? Whose body will she render out of place in pursuit of the religious visions that embody her newfound place in the unseen order?

This shift in emplacement is embodied in three ways, each of which reinforces the essential ambiguity lying at the heart of the horror mode. First, by stripping herself of her Puritan "armor," the material expression of her erstwhile faith, Thomasin explicitly casts off its theological trappings, demands, and covenants. Approaching the bonfire as the forest witches drift up into the air, she exchanges one relationship with the unseen order for another, this one, though, predicated on everything she has been warned about her entire life. She replaces one set of harmonious adjustments for their ritual opposite, and one set of convictions about her supreme good for their cultural antithesis. From the time she was a small child, as word of witch trials and executions throughout colonial Massachusetts undoubtedly reached their small corner of "the new world," she likely heard her father read the dour injunction of Exodus, "Thou shalt not suffer a witch to live" (22:18), as he led prayers at the family table. Yet, the film's final scene suggests that she has rejected her upbringing and its religious socialization neither in fear nor in weakness, as was the common Puritan interpretation of the female body.[16] Rather, her nakedness is portrayed as the bodily marker of newly discovered strength. She does not shiver or cringe, nor creep through the woods afraid either of being discovered by the forest witches or of what she might find when she encounters them. Instead, she comes to the circle with her head held high, her footsteps sure, knowing not only who is there, but what—as well as what they represent, what they have done, and what they expect of her.

Second, her nakedness places her explicitly at odds with her former faith's interpretation of their biblical heritage, and embodies a rejection of the moral and cosmological claims of its central sacred narrative. The Edenic story she has heard all her life told her gravely that "the eyes of them both were opened, and they knew that they were naked; and they sewed fig leaves together, and made themselves aprons." And when her quondam god came looking about the garden one evening, both man and woman hid, one of them calling out from the bushes, "I was afraid, because I was naked" (Gen. 3:7, 10). Thus, to be naked was to know shame, to recall the first weakness, the serpent's lie and the original sin—and that particularly as a woman. In rejecting the naked body as the physical marker of female deficiency, Thomasin exits Eden of her own accord. Rather than the flaming sword at her back, there is only the darkness of the Puritan farmstead and its grim theology, while, ahead, the flickering light of the witches' bonfire and the promise of a new family calling her forward.

And third, providing an envelope structure based on Caleb's first awkward glance at her bosom, the film's last moments implicitly sexualize this double rejection. Unlike earlier images of the forest witch as a grotesque crone, Thomasin's image here reflects late modern Western social constructions of female beauty and desirability, indeed, as do a number of the other witches gathered in the forest. She has transformed from the bundled Puritan into the witch as sultry temptress. Similar to Margaret Brundage's pulp horror cover art, promotional materials such as movie posters, trailers, and thumbnails are important paratexts that put paid to the popular notion that you can't judge a book by its cover.[17] Certainly, on one level, this is the case, but for decades the advertising industry has bet their gingerbread house on precisely the opposite: not only that consumers *will* judge a book (or a movie, videogame, or any other product) by its cover but that they will *only* judge it by that. At least until they have paid for their ticket or broken the security seal. For films such as *The Witch* and its numberless progenitors, however, it is axiomatic that orders of magnitude more people will see something like a movie poster, a lobby card, or a streaming service thumbnail than will actually see the film. Yet, these imagistic glancing blows still both draw on and reflexively contribute to the cultural stock of knowledge on which popular understanding of such things as witches and witchcraft—and whatever threat we think they represent—depends.

Whether through film, literature, or a wide variety of graphic arts, horror culture continues to leverage ambivalent fears of witchcraft that remain deeply rooted in our society, fears that are often signaled as much through sexualized portrayals of the witch herself as they are by our allegedly helpless attraction to her. Whether this means simple nudity (i.e., skyclad in a ritual or ceremonial context) or carnal behavior (i.e., either interpersonal or the fabled congress with the Devil), sexuality becomes the signifier of women (and, only very occasionally, men) who are considered out of control, whose bodies are out of place, and, most importantly, whose religious choices make them a danger to the community at large. As historian Ronald Hutton points out, correlations between nudity and witchcraft are culturally pervasive, if not necessarily universal, and "not merely because [nudity] transgressed social norms but because it stripped away [the witches'] everyday identities."[18] They become something else, something monstrously Other. "Children among the Lala of Zambia," for instance, "were told not to go out naked lest they be mistaken for witches," while "Zulu witches were said to ride naked on baboons at night, facing backwards."[19] Even a thousand years before the Common Era, the early followers of Zoroaster believed that those who worshiped the demonic entities of the destructive principle, *aingra mainyu*, worked their rites and rituals "at night, while naked."[20]

In addition to nudity as a rejection of social convention and acceptance of a form of marginalized power, more than any other figure the sexualized witch illustrates our erotic fascination with what for centuries has been culturally regarded as evil, a figure, as Hutton concludes, "whom it was not only proper but necessary to hate actively and openly."[21] It also highlights the fact that our relationship to this sexualized religious Other is often as ambiguous and enigmatic as it is for traditions that insist on the existential threat the witch represents.

Imag(in)ing the Witch: From Dürer to Delicate Skin

Arguably, and again more than any other literary character, the witch blurs the boundaries between fiction and reality, in terms of both belief in her existence and fear of the sexualized power she allegedly wields. Millions of 'tweens may have been caught up in the angst-ridden romance of Stephanie Meyer's *Twilight* saga, but few of them grew into adults believing that vampires and werewolves are real. Tales of lost or ill-fated lovers separated by time and tragic circumstance may ground most of the classic *Mummy* movies, but in their monstrous form mummified corpses are rarely, if ever, the object of erotic attention—just as we likewise reject their actual off-screen reality. Ditto the walking dead. Witches, on the other hand, are in a different category entirely. Depending on which poll one reads, and although the pollster's language is often maddeningly inexact, somewhere between 20 and 30 percent of Americans continue to believe in the existence of witches who are capable of casting evil spells.[22] Among religiously conservative populations, especially Christians who accept a literal interpretation of the Bible, this number rises dramatically, often with very real real-world consequences.

With a number of notable nonhorror exceptions—Angela Lansbury in *Bedknobs and Broomsticks* comes to mind, as do *Bewitched*'s beloved Samantha Stephens, the eponymous *Sabrina the Teenage Witch*, and *Buffy the Vampire Slayer*'s Willow Rosenberg—the horror-mode witch has generally been portrayed in one of two ways: the crone and the vixen. She is either an ugly old woman (whose preferred diet often includes children) or a young woman who is both beautiful and sexually vital, if not voracious (though the blood of children is just as often the unnatural catalyst for her vitality). *The Witch* combines these two representations in the forest witch, while Anna Biller's campy 2016 film, *The Love Witch*, leverages the latter, and Disney's *Hocus Pocus* places them onscreen together in the characters portrayed by Bette Midler and Sarah Jessica Parker (with Kathy Najimy rounding out the middle). Looking further back, however, and farther afield than popular film and television, we find a more complicated story of the ways in which we have imag(in)ed witches and witchcraft.

Art historian Margaret Sullivan argues that Dürer's and Baldung Grien's engravings do *not*, in fact, reflect the popular witch paranoia of the fifteenth century but are better understood in terms of "an earlier era" and "testify to a different sensibility and were produced by artists who could not have foreseen the terrible times to come."[23] Here, we see an effort to reread history as the search for an ur-text, an approach in which the true significance of a story (or in this case, a set of images) lies in the recovered original and the artists' presumed intent. Rather than drawing on, and thus contributing to, the witchcraft imaginary in contemporary local culture, Sullivan argues that Dürer's and Baldung Grien's images "are more plausible as poetic constructions motivated by artistic goals and a fascination with the underside of the ancient world rather than an interest in witch manuals or a compelling concern with witchcraft as a punishable offense."[24] That is, not unlike the work of artists who painted the Virgin and Child with Jesus suckling at Mary's breast as a way of circumventing Church interdiction on the merely naked human form, Dürer's and Baldung Grien's engravings should be considered examples of the ways in which artists developed their skills at what is widely acknowledged as the most challenging artistic subject, the human form.[25]

In terms of the horror mode and the popular imagination on which it relies for its emotional frisson, however, there are a number of problems with this approach. Attempting to divorce Dürer's and Balding Grien's work from institutional conceptions of witchcraft, Sullivan assumes that works such as *The Four Witches* and *The Witches* could not have had multiple sources, various streams of influence and inspiration, including conceptions of witchcraft that were popular at the time. After all, the fairy tales that were collected two centuries later by the Grimm brothers in Germany and Charles Perrault in France were all circulating in oral form while Dürer and Baldung Grien were working as artists.[26]

A fundamental principle of the sociology of knowledge as it was formulated by Karl Mannheim is that not all modes of thought are equally available in all eras.[27] The social worldview in which we participate, and which presents itself to us as objective reality, inevitably constrains not only what we *do* think about particular phenomena but what we *can* think. For Albrecht Dürer and Hans Baldung Grien, both of whom were born near the end of the fifteenth century—the former sixteen years before the publication of the infamous witch-hunting manual, *Malleus Maleficarum*, the latter just a few years before—only a limited number of ways in which one could think about witches were available. Recall that by the fifteenth century, the Roman Catholic Church had declared it a sin to deny the existence of witchcraft. Indeed, the first question asked by the *Malleus* seeks to determine "whether people who hold that witches do not exist are to be regarded as notorious heretics" or just "gravely suspect of holding heretical opinions."[28] As Mannheim continues, "The multiplicity of ways of thinking cannot become a problem in periods when social stability underlies and guarantees the internal unity of a world-view."[29] In declaring nonbelief in witchcraft heretical, the Church highlights the social instability that witches represent. While their engravings may have served to advance Dürer's and Baldung Grien's "artistic goals," and they may very well reflect a "fascination with the underside of the ancient world," that they cannot be seen apart from the social construction of witchcraft available to them at the time seems equally clear.

In these terms, Sullivan also seems to ignore the fact that popular culture, folk beliefs, and oral tradition all circulated together, and contributed to the sociological power of *conversation*, which, as Peter Berger and Thomas Luckmann point out, "is the most important vehicle of reality-maintenance."[30] In this sense, Berger and Luckmann mean ordinary conversation, mundane banter, the kind of routine social interchange that lies at the heart of daily life. A family talking around the dinner table, stall neighbors sharing gossip at the local village market, parishioners whispering among themselves as they wait for the weekly service to begin—all these and more "[take] place against the backdrop of a world that is silently taken for granted."[31] The ability to carry out such everyday conversation "implies an entire world *within which* these apparently simple propositions"—such as the belief that witches are real, that they are capable of casting spells, and that they represent a credible threat to family and faith—"make sense."[32] And, more to the point, they continue, "By virtue of this implication, the exchange confirms the subjective reality of the world."[33]

Witch-hunting manuals such as the *Malleus Maleficarum* and the *Compendium Maleficarum*, which was compiled more than a century later by an Ambrosian monk, emerged as institutionally authorized articulations of beliefs that already existed in oral tradition, and that were well established in local custom and folklore. That is, in conversation. In point of fact, by the time these were published, European society was already deeply imbued with a fear of witches and witchcraft, and had been so for hundreds of years. Whether witchcraft was considered heresy, as it had been in the centuries before Dürer, or a common compact with the Devil, as it was during his lifetime and in the two centuries following, was a technicality, a matter of ecclesiastical nuance and canonical jurisprudence. For the vast majority of the population, the message was much simpler: However the Church decided to label them, witches and witchcraft, as represented by Dürer, his protegé, and their numerous imitators, were a clear and present danger.

Centuries later, however, the art of witchcraft, as it were, had changed dramatically. "Wither! Oh wither! Fair maiden so high?" reads the text for an 1895 soap advertisement in the enormously popular *Punch* magazine. "To write the name of PEARS on the sky. Why go so far from the land of your birth? Because it is written all over the Earth."[34] Above the text, a nude witch rides a broomstick, pointing up to the sky. Wearing nothing but her iconic pointed hat, a diaphanous shawl, and a fetching smile, she beckons women to follow for softer skin, and men, presumably, for something else. Unlike pulp cover art a generation later, in this instance no wisp of smoke or errant fold of cloth hides her pert breasts and erect nipples.[35]

Thirty-five miles north of Boston, one of the early New England colonies played on both its name and its dubious heritage in marketing one of the most popular brands of stockings in America. Indeed, by the mid-1920s, with their Hallowe'en-themed "Flapper Witches," Ipswich Hosiery made the dichotomy between the crone and the maiden explicit in its advertising. Ipswich Hosiery was marketed as the most durable and luxurious of machine-washable stockings, and the Ipswich Witch had been the company's logo since the nineteenth century. Lighted from below, one such Flapper Witch dangles a spider in front of a black cat, while the shadow cast on the wall depicts a more iconic wicked witch pointing to the Ipswich logo. A similar ad shows another Flapper Witch gazing into a crystal ball, her shadowy crone-self holding aloft the company trademark.

In yet another advertisement, a fashionable young witch is secured in a set of wooden stocks, carved with the words, "Behold, Ye People, a Witch." Seemingly unconcerned about her dire circumstances, she looks conspicuously down at her shapely, stockinged legs, while the advertising copy proclaims, "There's modern witchcraft in the flawless knitting of Ipswich stockings. There's witchery in the sheer silken web of them."

From boot polish to apple cider and pain reliever, from beauty cream and specialty rum to nose art on World War II aircraft, the sexy witch was pulled from the broom closet and pressed into service marketing any number of consumer products. Like their cloistered

Figure 5.1. Pears soap advertisement from *Punch* magazine (1895).

Figure 5.2. Ipswich Hosiery advertisement (ca. 1920).

cousins, the fetishized nun, for more than a century sexualized witches have become a regular part of adult Hallowe'en culture and erotic entertainment. Their lusty temptation was celebrated rather than condemned, and such condemnation as there was gradually found itself confined to conservative religious enclaves. She went from the very image of evil to cartoon character, and with a changing sexual culture, the need for a supernaturally erotic temptress became just a fantasy.

Or did it?

Bewitching Culture: The Continuum of Magical Horror

We tend to think of "popular horror" as the particular product of the horror genre: movies such as *The Witch* or *The Blair Witch Project*, graphic novels such as *Wytches*, *Hex Wives*, and *Harrow County*, or pulp fiction ranging from H. P. Lovecraft's "Dreams in the Witch House" to Carter Brown's *Coven*.[36] Accompanied by an appropriately lurid illustration, for instance, *The Coven*'s front cover tells us that private investigator "Rick Holman joins a coven of swinging Hollywood Satanists and finds himself in a witches' brew that leads from magic to orgies to murder!"[37] Laughter, however, is often the antidote to fear, or at least the bandage that keeps the worst of it contained. Thus, Disney highlighted the comedic witch in *Bedknobs and Broomsticks* and *Hocus Pocus*, one sympathetically, the other somewhat less so. Portrayals such as Margaret Hamilton's Wicked Witch of the West in *The Wizard of Oz* have become so iconic that time has rendered them almost a caricature. Even dark fantasies like Roald Dahl's *Witches*, John Updike's *Witches of Eastwick*, and Roberto Aguirre-Sacasa's *Chilling Adventures of Sabrina* have only limited purchase on the emotional transaction of the horror mode. *Bell, Book, and Candle*'s Gillian Holroyd gives up her immortal life as a witch when she falls in love with the entirely human Shep Henderson (James Stewart). Although the reverse of what we see when Thomasin joins the forest witches, this shift in emplacement is also most clearly marked in the way director Richard Quine and art director Cary Odell dress Kim Novak as Gillian. "Throughout most of the film," as I have pointed out elsewhere, "wardrobe and make-up take full advantage of Novak's smoldering beauty: ultra-chic hairstyling and tight-fitting clothes drawn straight from the cover of Paris *Vogue*."[38] Once she falls in love, though, like Thomasin trading one place in the unseen order for another, "rather than turtlenecks, capri pants, and sheath dresses" by celebrity designer Jean Louis, Gillian is almost prim by the end of the film, her body's new emplacement marked by "a white, belted dress, the hem falling demurely below the knee—both color and cut heralding the newfound purity of her mortal life."[39]

Once they become the object of mockery, a way to sell skin cleanser, pantyhose, and Hallowe'en candy, once witches become the butt of sexual jokes and pornographic cartoons, their power over us diminishes significantly. It is difficult to fear what inspires only laughter. Like any number of other mythical creatures that frightened us in our developmental past, they have been controlled and contained. In a word, domesticated.[40] As with many aspects of the horror mode, it's easy to breathe a sigh of relief when the credits roll, the last page turned, or the wicked witch defeated—that is, when the things that scare us have been put back into their proper place. Once again, though, witches and witchcraft prove more difficult to control, especially in terms of the ways in which popular culture continues to reinforce real fears of witchcraft and, as a result, escalates the anxieties of real-life witches.

Popular Culture and the Fear of Witchcraft

"An estimated 9 million women and girls met death by fire between the years of 1300 and 1700 for practising witchcraft," writes fundamentalist Christian and freelance exorcist Bob Larson—although it's difficult to tell whether he thinks this is a bad thing or not.[41] He cites no references, perhaps unaware that the source of this entirely spurious figure is the nineteenth-century suffragette, Matilda Joslyn Gage, and his use of her "statistic" comes less than a year before its popularization in Canadian director Donna Read's putative documentary, The Burning Times.[42] In the latter, two of the three so-called historians Read puts on camera have no online profile whatsoever beyond their appearance in this film. This suggests strongly that they are hired actors merely playing television experts, though this is not something of which many in the audience would be aware. Because, in terms of popular culture and the social construction of fear, whether these "experts" actually exist or not matters little more than the actual existence of wicked witches and flying monkeys. Like Protestant anti-Catholic propaganda, anti-Pagan agit-prop is not meant to change anyone's mind, but to reinforce prejudices and preconceptions held by people already inclined to believe the worst.

"Witches have come a long way in their effects [sic] to glamorize the occult," Larson wrote a decade later in Larson's Book of Spiritual Warfare. "The image of creepy crones has been replaced with the concept of an attractive spell caster who is the envy of ordinary women. Witches today are younger and cuter."[43] And he's not wrong. Of the wildly popular Charmed, he writes that Shannen Doherty "and her fashionable friends fight evil warlocks with supernatural powers."[44] In 1996, "Hollywood cast a spell on young women with 'The Craft,'" while two years later, once Nicole Kidman saw the success of Griffin Dunne's Practical Magic, she apparently "made plans with her husband Tom Cruise on a remake of the 1942 classic 'I Married a Witch,' thus defining herself as the ultimate witch babe."[45] Larson also complains that Sabrina the Teenage Witch, the television adaptation of an early-1960s Archie comics spin-off, was "considered the number one show for children ages 2–11. The executive producer of the show attributed its success to kids' interest in magic"—which is not quite the same as attributing its success to magic. He's not incorrect here, either, insofar as "these more likeable witches appeal to larger audiences of women and children, especially teenage girls."[46] The enormous success of films such as Practical Magic, The Witches of Eastwick, and The Craft, as well as such television series as Charmed, Sabrina the Teenage Witch, and Buffy the Vampire Slayer (on which one of the most popular characters is Willow, the young Wiccan), drove a transmedia popularity in all things modern Pagan—to the point where claims were being made that it was the "fastest growing religion in America," if not the world.[47] For writers such as Larson and his coreligionists, the deep, dark forest is still all around us, and their work provides the only beacon of hope in its depths.

As the fundamentalist Christian readers for whom he writes nod their heads in agreement, perhaps remembering the films, thinking back to the goings-on at Halliwell Manor or supernatural shenanigans at the Spellman household, Larson reminds them of the clear and present danger represented by modern Pagans of all types. "Despite its newfound appeal," he writes, "those lured to the occult should never forget the reality of witchcraft's evil aspect. In Bridgeport, Connecticut, a witch was convicted of statutory rape for seducing a 14-year-old boy and putting a spell on him, hardly the image invoked by Hollywood and network television."[48] And, again, in one sense, he is not wrong. He is not simply lying. Kerry Lynn Patavino, a practicing Wiccan, was found guilty of statutory rape, and there is some evidence that this factored into her case, including attempting to pass off child sexual abuse as participation in the modern Pagan "Great Rite."

In terms of the horror mode, two things are important to note if Larson intends this as a categorical indictment of Paganism per se—which he quite obviously does. First, this was happening at precisely the same time as the massive sex abuse scandal in the Roman Catholic Church was coming to light, a transnational tragedy in which the perpetrators deliberately and repeatedly used their positions as religious leaders to commit, justify, and conceal the ongoing horror of child rape. He is writing more than ten years after the sexual abuse scandals that rocked the evangelical world in the forms of Jim Bakker and Jimmy Swaggart, and a full decade after Jessica Hahn made her own attempt at sexual healing in the pages of *Playboy*.[49] Yet he makes no mention of these. In this, his ideological calculus is clear: Christians good, Pagans not so much.

"One of the things that bothered me a lot," complained one Connecticut Pagan at the time, "was that they had declared [Patavino] in the headlines here as an alleged witch. Because you never hear of an alleged Catholic or an alleged Lutheran."[50] Yet, for Larson the relationship is stark and unassailable: "The reality of witchcraft's evil" leads to child sexual predation, regardless of how much more culturally entrenched or theologically rationalized it might be elsewhere. The point is that sexual abuse of any kind is reprehensible. Full stop. And no religious communities are exempt from indictment, if for no other reason than that they are comprised of human beings, and we have a long and storied history of doing the most heinous things to each other either in the name of or under the cover of our various gods. "Whatever religion somebody is," lamented another Connecticut witch when Patavino finally admitted her guilt in return for a reduction in her sentence, "doesn't change the fact that you have folks who do rotten things."[51]

Second, for Larson and many of his coreligionists, witchcraft *is* the independent theological variable in the abusive equation. Whenever something negative happens, critics of modern Paganism "emphasize the witch part all the time, which hurts any positive accomplishments that others have made."[52] Larson's message is clear, though. In a chapter entitled "That Old Black Magic," witchcraft is not as it is presented "by Hollywood and network television" but is something far darker and, for all its lightsome portrayal, far more insidious.[53] "Modern Witchcraft is indeed a 'made-up' religion," writes Brooks Alexander, founder of the Spiritual Counterfeits Project, one of the large Christian counter-cult organizations in North America. "Modern Witchcraft is spiritually wrong, socially subversive, and psychologically dangerous"—though, to be fair, he thinks this about any religion other than his particular brand of fundamentalist Protestantism.[54] Writing in the *Christian Research Journal*, apologist Richard Howe points out that Christians and Wiccans can share a number of common social concerns, but they remain "mortal foes in what ultimately counts." Indeed, while "there are similarities between flour and ricin," he concludes, "one is a food and the other is a poison."[55] Likewise, in *Dewitched* youth pastor Tim Baker debunks a number of what he considers common misconceptions about Wicca and modern Witchcraft: that they "ride brooms and float"; that they "wear black capes and tall, pointed hats"; that they "hide in the woods"; that they "cast spells on people"; and that they "are evil" and "worship Satan."[56] So far, so good. Except that, "ultimately, all religions" that do not fit Baker's fundamentalist Protestant version of Christianity "are wrong. Every belief that doesn't align itself with Scripture is wrong. Every belief."[57] More to the point, Baker continues, "with Satanism being the oldest non-Christian religion existing in society, Wicca has to be its sibling."[58]

It should be relatively simple to dismiss comments of this sort—especially since, elsewhere, Baker argues with complete sincerity that the *Necronomicon* is an actual magical text "brought to prominence" by "a Satanist and writer" named Howard Phillips Lovecraft—except for the fact that writers such as these contribute to a sociophobic threat of witchcraft that is no less real than for the New England Puritans and no less tangible in its effects.

Popular Culture and the Anxieties of Witches

"Witchcraft is, of course, an old, old chestnut of historical interest and study," wrote historian John Demos in the original preface to his celebrated *Entertaining Satan*.[59] It is, however, a chestnut still roasted openly on modern fires. When the *Daily Mirror*, one of Britain's most popular tabloids, publishes a pre-Hallowe'en article in its "Parenting" section entitled "Witch performs Pagan rituals while NAKED with her children—and claims stripping off helps them bond with nature,"[60] in a manner distinctly reminiscent of nineteenth-century anti-Catholic paranoia, this fuels the fire of anti-Pagan propaganda and sows the seeds of real-world fear for real-life Witches, Wiccans, and Druids. Demos points out that communities constitute the "social matrix of witchcraft," which, not unlike popular anxieties about convents and monasteries, is a function of the stories that circulate within communities about witchcraft.[61] If you doubt how profound the fear of witchcraft remains in our culture, consider the following.

In the summer of 2010, a young Salem, Missouri, woman went to her local library to research her newfound Wiccan beliefs. Logging on, she was astonished to find that a number of sites she wanted to visit were blocked by the library's filter software, which had been originally designed to prevent access to sexually explicit material on publicly accessible computers. When she complained, she was told that the sites could only be unblocked if the librarian "felt patrons had a legitimate reason to view the content."[62] More chilling even than that, she was informed that not only would the sites not be made available but the librarian felt "an obligation" to report people attempting to access blocked sites such as these to the authorities.[63] According to the brief filed by the American Civil Liberties Union, the library's filter software categorized the sites the young woman wanted as "occult," and included the official website for the Wiccan Church, the Wikipedia entry on Wicca, and *The Witches Voice*, then the largest repository of modern Pagan information on the Internet.[64] Three years later, a federal judge prohibited the library from using this kind of filter software. A somewhat Pyrrhic victory given the state of fear in which the young woman lived for that period of time, not insignificantly about what might happen to her children and her presumed fitness as a parent. Indeed, as political scientist Carol Barner-

Barry notes, such incidents are part of a pattern of anti-Pagan incitement that only serves to reinforce a culture of fear for those who belong to "minority religions in a majoritarian America."[65]

Barner-Barry discusses a number of similar instances of religious discrimination against modern Pagans. Crystal Siefferley, a straight-A student with a spotless disciplinary record, was forced to sue her school district when her high school enacted a so-called gang/cult policy, which "prohibited students from belonging to a list of groups that included Pagans and Witches."[66] In another case, a Baltimore student received a daylong suspension for spellcasting. An Oklahoma high school student was suspended for more than two weeks "when school officials accused her of hexing a teacher who fell ill."[67] Despite being an outstanding student, the same young woman had been suspended for nearly three weeks a year earlier when Wiccan literature was found in her bookbag. "The interesting thing about such cases," Barner-Barry concludes drily, "is the readiness of school authorities to take seriously the ability of a student to cast effective spells or hex others."[68]

In terms of the sociophobic threat of witchcraft—that is, what witches do, or are at least believed to do in the fever-dreams of their most ardent opponents—the potential for curses and hexes continues to play a part, but fear of overt sexuality still renders the Pagan body most surely out of place. As it turns out, though, Christians are not the only religious believers who have vastly differing views on appropriate, and by definition inappropriate, sexualities. Even in spiritual communities that pride themselves on attitudes toward the sexual body that are far more open and accepting than Christianity has ever been, unexpected nudity can still generate a firestorm of controversy.

As part of a 2004 article on "Mother Ocean," *newWitch*, a quarterly Pagan magazine, included a black-and-white photograph of a young, pregnant woman reclining in a bed of sea foam.[69] Her head is tilted back, her eyes closed as though enjoying the warmth of the sun on her face. Her legs together and one knee drawn up modestly, there is nothing overtly sexual about the image—beyond the fact that she is naked. Since much of modern Paganism considers itself body positive and nudity friendly, not to mention the explicitly sexualized aspects of Pagan rituals such as the Great Rite, who could possibly object?

As it happens, more than a few people.

The subsequent issue included a lengthy reader complaint from a witch who wrote that her own little witchlings (aged twelve and fourteen) love *newWitch* magazine, often taking it to school to share with their friends, some of whom, she contends, resonate with Paganism. "I couldn't let my kids take issue #7 to school," however, "because of the nudity." She did not go so far as to call the image "pornography," but the message was clear: "Please omit nudity from *newWitch* in the future," or cancel my subscription!⁷⁰ Editor Anna Newkirk Niven, however, is no stranger to controversy in her lengthy career publishing a variety of modern Pagan magazines. Responding not unreasonably that *newWitch* was not intended for adolescent Pagans but for young adults, she replied that her readers were "people old enough to be out on their own and making up their own minds about things."⁷¹ While she recognized that sexuality in all its aspects is an issue that has to be handled with great care in the Pagan community—and that this has not always been the case—*newWitch* covers "topics *explicitly* for people over the age of consent."⁷²

Like so many other religious communities, which are nothing if not diverse, complicated, and contradictory—in a word, messy—some readers applauded Niven's stand on the issue, others not so much. Indeed, sounding suspiciously like builder-generation Protestants grumbling about the mess the youth group made or why the new pastor won't sing their favorite hymns, the next *newWitch* issue featured one "Deeply Disturbed Old Witch" who complained that the magazine was now "too Goth," that the "cartoon art is quite juvenile," and that one of the magazine's regular columnists is "truly pathetic and immature."⁷³ As if that weren't enough, she was "stunned at [Niven's] response to the issue of nudity," vehemently disagreeing with the editor's assessment of her target audience. "Raven," a southern California Pagan, concurred, accusing Niven of "trying way too hard to be 'cutting edge'" and urging her in the end to "do me a favor and stop trying to win an audience by using the same tactics seen in Hollywood."⁷⁴ In what many readers consider the ultimate threat, Raven warns that she is going to give Niven "just one more chance" before she quits *newWitch* for good. If any of these readers commented on the next article in the issue, "Sex, Magic, and Healing," or on such subsequent articles as "A Pagan Look at Sex Toys" or "The Magical, Mystical Phallus," written by gender-nonconforming Pagan Kenaz Filan, it is not recorded.⁷⁵

Trying to push back in the face of a socially constructed fear of witchcraft, sorcery, and nonsanctioned religious practices going back millennia, and which is constantly and consistently reinforced through popular culture, what happens if we switch places? In an episode of the latest televised version of the *Father Brown* mysteries, G. K. Chesterton's eponymous sleuth-priest is taking tea with parish secretary Mrs. McCarthy and Lady Felicia Montague. Conversation turns to *The Mask of the Demon*, a low-budget horror film being shot in their tiny Cotswold village, and Mrs. McCarthy points out that she would never be seen at such a thing, that this kind of "rubbish is just an excuse for blasphemy, and—and scantily clad women. Isn't that right, Father?" "Actually," replies Lady Felicia, ever the free-spirited foil to the other's heavy woolen moralism, "we rather enjoyed *Virgin Vampires* at the Odeon last month. Isn't *that* right, Father?" Caught, as always, between his own personal Scylla and Charybdis, Father Brown sips his tea, and demurs, "It raised some interesting theological questions."[76] Indeed, such films do, and to explore just some of them, come with me to Summerisle.

Summerisle: Switching Places in the Pagan Grove

How do we know we're watching a horror movie? Because we picked it out from the horror section of a video store or streaming service? Because someone told us that it's a horror movie? Perhaps because we have *always* been told that it's a horror movie, and it never occurred to us to question that or wonder why?

Robin Hardy's classic film, *The Wicker Man*, opens as staid, devout police sergeant Neil Howie (Edward Woodward) arrives at the remote Hebridean skerry known as Summerisle to investigate the purported disappearance of a young girl.[77] Summerisle is home to a community of modern Pagans led by the eponymous Lord Summerisle (Christopher Lee), and its inhabitants seek to live according to the "old ways" and worship the pre-Christian gods of their ancestors. Moreover, to everyone's surprise, somehow this rocky islet off the west coast of Scotland has managed to yield abundant apple harvests where common sense says no such fruit should grow. Here, the question of horror turns precisely on that word, "somehow."

At first simply wary of the taciturn islanders as he makes his inquiries, before long Howie is actively appalled by what he discovers there. He threatens the local teacher, Miss Rose (Diane Cilento), with criminal prosecution when he hears her lecturing to a class of young children on the phallic symbolism of the Maypole. He is shocked by the nudity of Pagan girls "at their lessons," as they create a sacred circle together, then one by one leap the Beltaine fires.[78] Mortified when he inadvertently walks in on the librarian (Hammer scream queen Ingrid Pitt) in her bath, he is equally startled when she is not embarrassed at all by his intrusion—indeed, quite the opposite. He is outraged by the candid fertility rites taking place throughout the village at night, and barely resists seduction at the hands of the innkeeper's daughter, Willow (Britt Ekland). Howie is a strict Christian (demonstrated repeatedly through brief flashbacks to his participation in church services), and his anxiety over sex and the sexualized body is clearly cast in the context of his religious commitment.

When Lord Summerisle initially tries to allay the sergeant's fears, telling him that they, too, are "a deeply religious people," Howie fairly explodes. "Religious!" he shouts. "With ruined churches, no ministers, no priests, and children dancing naked?" Summerisle smiles indulgently, looking out the window as young women leap the fire set in the midst of a standing stone circle. "They do love their divinity lessons," he agrees. "But," Howie sputters, unable to believe what he is seeing and hearing, "they are—are naked!" "Naturally," Summerisle replies with puckish double entendre. "It's much too dangerous to jump through fire with your clothes on."[79] More than anything, *The Wicker Man's* narrative pivots on the socially constructed nature of the "aberrant," the uncomfortable reality that the fulcrum of deviance is always balanced by positionality. "What religion can they possibly be learning jumping over bonfires?" Howie demands. "I mean, you—you've got fake—fake—fake biology, fake religion. Sir, have these children never heard of Jesus?"[80] In fact, they have, as Miss Rose tells him pointedly, the Summerisle children learn about Christianity "as a comparative religion."[81] And, in comparison, while for one man the young women's bodies are blasphemously out of place, for the other they are right where they ought to be.

Indeed, from the islanders' point of view, Howie's dogmatic abstinence—which he links in no uncertain terms to the salvation of his immortal soul—seems as bizarre and nonsensical as their more sexually liberated rites and beliefs appear to him. To return to the question before the court, though, What makes *The Wicker Man* a horror movie? After all, with the exception of the final scene, there is nothing particularly horrific about the story. In those last few minutes, we watch as Howie dies in physical agony and spiritual terror, trapped in the enormous sacrificial pyre of the Wicker Man. All around him, the Summerisle pagans sing, dance, and chant in hopes that their offering to "Nuada, our most sacred god of the sun, and to Avellenau, the beloved goddess to our orchards" will portend a bountiful apple harvest.[82] Apart from that scene, it is a straightforward murder mystery that is almost anthropological in the way it explores the difference between the dueling theologies on the island.

According to media scholar Brigid Cherry, *The Wicker Man* "is neither a morality tale which might be said to gender socialise its teen audience, as the slasher film is, for example, nor does it share the concern of body horror and vampire cinema with aberrant sexual practice rendered through metaphors of disease and contagion."[83] That is, she begins with fairly standard attempts to naturalize the unnatural narrative, to make the text conform to particular interpretations and reveal its meaning only to those who possess the proper hermeneutic keys. The significance, however, especially in terms of human experiences that are as complex, confused, and contradictory as sex, horror, and the religious imagination, lies not in finding definitive answers to the questions posed by the film but in trying to understand on some deeper level just what those questions might be. Put differently, *are* slasher films intended as exercises in gender socialization? *Are* "body horror and vampire cinema" concerned with "aberrant sexual practice rendered through metaphors of disease and contagion"? However dated and unproductive these explanations are as grand unified theories of horror, there are elements of them in both categories, and such cinematic texts have certainly been seen in these ways. But these are not the only ways in which they can be interpreted, nor are they even the dominant ways. And, given this, in what then does *The Wicker Man*'s horror inhere? As we have seen in other aspects of the horror mode, the problem is that once critics identify their chosen theoretical underlays, they often believe that they have solved the problem of this film, that book, or whatever pop culture product is under consideration. Rather than answer the questions, though, as often as not this approach merely forecloses asking anything further. Once again, in Cherry, we are faced with a reading that treats the text as though it is a riddle to be answered, rather than an enigma to be explored.

"The Pagan culture as depicted here," Cherry contends, "is both coded as feminine and highly eroticized," and the central "themes of sex and death . . . are presented within the framework of an oppositional Pagan culture at odds with established Christianity."[84] She is not incorrect, except that this is less an analysis of what is happening onscreen than it is a synopsis of the plot. More to the point, though, she argues that *The Wicker Man* "codes the predatory sexuality of the Paganised belief system as a form of monstrosity in general and monstrous-feminine in particular."[85] While she may feel some sympathy for the way Hardy chose to portray the Summerisle pagans, her ideological commitment actually prevents her from taking what is unreeling onscreen seriously. Reiterating that the film's "main female characters" are "sexually active, even predatory"—as if this was somehow a problem—she interprets the film through the psychoanalytic lens ground by Barbara Creed and Julia Kristeva, concluding that if a monster exists on Summerisle, "it is in the figurations of feminine sexuality through landscape and religion, and the inherent link with the Earth Mother archetype which Howie's point of view codes as the monstrous-feminine."[86] Which is certainly one way of looking at it—as long as we accept Neil Howie as the point-of-view character from whom the audience is expected to take its reaction cues, and the one with whom we are expected to identify in the emotional transaction of the horror mode. But why should this be the case? What could we learn if, rather than trying to solve the puzzle that way, we complicate reading the film instead, first by switching religious perspectives, then by abandoning the artificial dichotomy that is implicit in both Howie's perspective and Cherry's interpretation?

Rather than see Willow's attempted seduction of the uncompromising Christian police sergeant as "predatory," why not consider the scene from her point of view? Quite correctly, Cherry writes that "female roles in the [horror] genre often divide along lines of passive and active sexuality," and in so doing they reinforce culturally acceptable norms of sexual behavior that are often rooted in religious doctrine, belief, and socialization.[87]

Which is to say, active female sexuality is predatory—the female body out of place—while passive sexuality embodies a woman's "appropriate" emplacement. Nowhere is this difference more pronounced than in the attempted seduction scene, and the reading Cherry proposes of the film seems reasonable only so long as we accept her assumptions about *The Wicker Man*'s commitment to female predatory monstrosity. The question posed by *The Wicker Man*, though, is, *Does it have to be this way?*

The Siren's Song

Composed by playwright Paul Giovanni for *The Wicker Man*, "Willow's Song" is the melody most often associated with the film and structures the entire attempted seduction scene.[88] Preparing for bed at the local inn, The Green Man, an indignant Howie kneels in prayer, seeking temporary solace in the only way he knows how. A brief, soft-focus flashback takes us to his small country church somewhere in the West Highlands, where he stands at the lectern, sternly reading the gospel text for the day—Jesus' instructions to his disciples at the Last Supper. His reading is cut together with close-ups of him reverently receiving the Eucharist elements, the mimetic symbols of his salvation. The sound of fiddle and guitar coming from the pub downstairs, however, disturbs his ritual, and the flashback ends as he angrily crawls into the narrow bed. As far as he is concerned, nothing about this place makes sense.

Howie places his hand one last time on the Bible beside him, but no sooner does his head hit the pillow than a rhythmic knocking begins on the shared wall between his room and the next. Thumping gently but insistently in time to the drumming of a small *bodhrán* downstairs, Willow lies naked in her own bed, her eyes turned toward Howie's room. A simple melody floats in, and she begins to sing.

> Heigh ho! Who is there?
> No one but me, my dear
> Please come say, How do?
> The things I'll give to you
> By stroke as gentle as a feather
> I'll catch a rainbow from the sky
> And tie the ends together

Heigh ho! I am here
Am I not young and fair?
Please come say, How do?
The things I'll show to you
Would you have a wondrous sight
The midday sun at midnight?

Fair maid, white and red
Comb you smooth and stroke your head
How a maid can milk a bull
And every stroke a bucketful.[89]

As she croons this patently erotic love song, she rises from the bed and begins to dance around the room, sometimes pressing close to their shared wall, at other times swaying to the music and accenting the beat with slaps to her hips and her breasts. The difference between the two rooms could not be more stark and reinforces the question of whose body is out of place on Summerisle. Whereas Howie's room is dark and wreathed in shadows, the color grading of the film rendering it cold and sterile, Willow's is awash with light, soft, warm, and indirect enough to chase away all but the dancing shadows thrown by the young woman herself. She is filmed in slight soft-focus, an effect that only increases the sense of suggestive welcome, while Howie, on the other hand, is filmed in harsh contrast, desaturated colors, and camera angles that reflect the increasingly tortured state of his soul. The scene itself cuts back and forth between the rooms, cozy and inviting in one as Willow sings and dances, bleak and terrifying in the other as Howie desperately fights the deepest wells of his own nature.

Like dance partners separated by the various walls between them, both move toward and away from each other—Willow playfully erotic, Howie as horrified by his own physical response as by the woman who incites it. Lust papers the wall between them, but for one it is a cardinal sin and the source of soul-crushing shame, for the other, simple enjoyment, an offering both to and from the goddess. Since lust is a Christian failing, the Edenic condemnation holds no terrors for Willow. Hers is not the body out of place. Given what she and her fellow Summerislanders have learned about Christianity, she views sex with her as a potentially liberating experience for Howie. A spiritual, in fact ritual act, sexual intercourse, for Willow, appears no less reasonable in the context of her own religious beliefs than Howie's almost pathological avoidance of it seems to him from the confines of his own. Tormented by his rising lust, Howie moves back and forth in the darkened room, at times trying to shut out the sounds of Willow's song, at others almost pathetically embracing the wall between them. As her song draws to a close, and she casts her energy out the window and into the moonlit night, he slumps on the bed, his posture suggesting that, despite all efforts to resist the Matthian injunction that is no doubt ringing in his ears, he reaches for his penis. Fade to black.

On *The Wicker Man* DVD, rather than "Willow's Song," for some reason the scene is chapter-titled, "The Siren's Song," a not-unimportant distinction for the double meaning it suggests. Found in many cultures, "sirens" are mythical female creatures whose beauty and song lured men to their doom. From Howie's point of view, the reference could not be more apt, for in the temptation to physical intimacy, he is the one who "looketh on a woman to lust after her," and thus "hath committed adultery with her already in his heart" (Matt. 5:28). In this, his religious socialization permits him to see nothing except his own destruction. From the Pagan perspective, the siren inference, although it does reinforce a "predatory" interpretation of Summerisle sexuality, is misleading. On the contrary, and somewhat inconsistently, Brigid Cherry notes that Willow is more accurately "equated with Aphrodite," the Greek goddess of love and beauty, and she infers (probably from the Green Man patrons' bawdy rendition of "The Landlord's Daughter") that she "offers sexual initiation to the young men of the island."[90] In this, she could not be more different from the sirens of Greek mythology, who destroyed the men cast up on their island through "the voluptuous and debauched lives they led" there.[91]

The False Dichotomy

Unfortunately, however, by discriminating between "religion" (what she calls "its signifier, the church") and whatever she thinks is happening on Summerisle, Cherry's commitment to "Creed's model of the monstrous-feminine" reinforces a longstanding but false dichotomy between religion and magic.[92] That is, although she sometimes (and inconsistently) refers to the islanders' "alternative religious doctrine," for the most part, rather than religious believers, the Summerisle pagans become unsophisticated participants in "folklore," "fertility rites," and "the occult." Neil Howie, on the other hand, is not simply the representative of one religion among many, but *The Wicker Man*'s signifier of religion per se.[93] "The standards of religion," Cherry writes, "are thus absent or violated," whereas the Summerislanders represent "pre-Christian western traditions of folklore and eroticised ritual—principally the fertility rites and hedonistic practices associated with these."[94] While we might contest her use of "hedonistic," given its often derogatory connotation, ever since Émile Durkheim declared dogmatically that "there is no Church of Magic," scholars, critics, and pundits alike have attempted to define an essential difference between "real" religion and "mere" folk magic.[95]

More often than not, though, this quest has been pursued to reinforce the social dominance of the very traditions that make the determination. Differentiating "religion," which he considers "an end in itself," from "magic," which he dismisses as little more than "a means to an end," Roman Catholic theologian David Blanchard, for example, insists that "magical training does not include theology."[96] Proper religion, on the other hand, "does not depend on technique but rather on a pre-existing faith and the value of belief."[97] As I have written elsewhere, though, "notwithstanding what Blanchard might mean by 'the value of belief' and religion as 'an end in itself,' his message could not be clearer: religion is 'true' and 'worthy,' while magic is neither. It's difficult, however, to imagine a distinction more fraught with problems, more prone to a fallacy of limited alternatives and confounding examples, and more beholden to the kind of theological provincialism that marks so much of our religious imagination."[98]

As historian Keith Thomas points out in his classic *Religion and the Decline of Magic*, two basic principles underpin much of the Christian Church's attitude toward magic, both of which turn on the curiously oxymoronic senses of the word "sanction." First, writes Thomas, "the legitimacy of any magical ritual depended upon the official view taken of it by the Church. So long as theologians permitted the use of, say, holy water or consecrated bells in order to dispel storms, there was nothing 'superstitious' about such activity."[99] That is, since the Church "had no compunction about licensing its own brand of magical remedies," the socially dominant religion sanctions the use of what might otherwise be considered illegitimate "magic." Second, the question of illegitimacy rested on whether a particular phenomenon or effect could be considered natural or unnatural. "What was at issue here," Thomas continues, "was not any difference of religious principle; it was a view of the natural world."[100] That is, if members of the clergy were unable "to accept that [certain] effects could spring from mere nature," they immediately "fell back on the view that they must have stemmed from the Devil."[101] In the first instance, the Church sanctioned the use of magic and granted it permission; in the second, it sanctioned what it considered the illegitimate use of magic by casting it as Satanic. In both cases, the power of the socially dominant religion determined where on the spectrum particular beliefs or practices fell.

To suggest, however, as Blanchard does, that magical beliefs are devoid of "theology"—which means nothing more or less than a way of conceptualizing and interacting with the gods—or, to put it in Neil Howie's terms, they constitute "fake religion," is to imply that Pagans are either gullible, delusional, or both. Indeed, "there is no religion without magic," wrote anthropologist Claude Lévi-Strauss in his classic text, *The Savage Mind*, "any more than there is magic without at least a trace of religion."[102] Ronald Hutton concurs, insisting that, with Paganism's often complex if culturally appropriated and syncretized pantheons, rituals and ceremonies organized according to its own visions of consensus reality, and its commitment to a supernatural order that explicitly confronts and calls into question those of socially dominant religions, the emergence of modern Paganism quite simply "abolishes the traditional Western distinction between religion and magic."[103]

So, is *The Wicker Man* a horror film? In the end, it depends on whom you ask and whose perspective you take. And, in the end, it is this very ambiguity in the horror mode that renders it impossible for Brigid Cherry to land on a particular interpretation, no matter how strong her ideological commitment. Too many confounding images and conflicting themes present themselves. What, though, when the ambivalence deepens? What about even more ambiguous aspects of the relationships between sex, horror, and the religious imagination, which is to say, the enigmatic darkness within?

6

Darkness Within

Encountering the Enigma

"Be a woman," she thinks.[1]

The psychiatrist her unfaithful husband had found for her—as though the problem were all in her head—leans back in his expensive chair. Fingertips steepled in thought, he seems perfectly correct, indeed "perfectly benign," the modern embodiment of men who have kept women like her in their place for generations. First, it was the church, now it is the doctor's office, a new confessional for the latest crop of uniquely female sins. His "framed qualifications" hang level on tastefully papered walls, pens and notepads laid out just so on the leather blotter. Everything in its place. Everything, that is, except for the young woman seated in front of him.[2]

When she was delivered into his care and "practiced compassion" after her ennui-fueled suicide attempt, Doctor Blandish already knew what she needed.[3] He'd seen it so many times before, this endless parade of "women's problems," the "certain needs" they all seemed to have, but that he assured them could be put right "with a little tinkering," "a little reassurance," and "something to help you sleep at nights."[4] He isn't even looking at her. He doesn't need to. She's just like all the others, all those lonely, desperate, abused women for whom the best thing in the world was not a sympathetic ear or a chance to live their lives free of a man's control but simply "a course of sedatives . . . and a holiday."[5]

Now imagine the woman. *You don't know*, she thinks bitterly, staring at him. You couldn't know what it's like to be a woman, no matter what you say. No man could. It's a simple as that. "What would he know about women's needs?" she wonders, sitting rigid as "he lightly patted her hand" and droned on about what she did and didn't want, what really would be best for her.[6] When her thoughts wander to "the body beneath the veneer of his clothes," though, Jacqueline Ess begins to wonder about the mysteries of *his* flesh.[7]

"Be a woman," she thinks. And that's all it takes.

No enchanted glitter falls on Blandish from above, no Disney twirl-and-transform takes him from one thing to another. This is neither gender reassignment nor "fairy-tale transformation." Indeed, "his flesh resisted such magic," and he fights the sudden, violent change with every fiber of his being.[8] Now, in his immaculately appointed office, there is for him only blood and pain and terror, skin warping and distending, bones splintering, and muscles stretching beyond the point where sinews hold. All the frustrations Jacqueline Ess kept locked inside, the wrath of every woman ever put "back in her place" by a man, reaches out and caresses him. "She willed his manly chest to make breasts of itself and it began to swell most fetchingly, until the skin burst and his sternum flew apart. His pelvis, teased to breaking point, fractured at its centre; unbalanced, he toppled over onto his desk and from there stared up at her, his face yellow with shock."[9]

Although initially horrified "at the absurd monstrosity she had made," Jacqueline Ess recovers quickly, astonished, intrigued, and more than a little aroused by this hitherto unknown ability welling up from "the very deep-water trenches of her nature."[10] She regains her composure as the psychiatrist bleeds out at her feet, whimpering incoherently, learning in his final moments what it is to *be* a woman. In the few endless seconds that lie between one way of being Blandish and the next, Jacqueline Ess finds that "she forgot the nausea, and remembered the power." More-over, "She forgot the guilt that seized her afterwards and longed, longed to do it again. Only better."[11] With her newfound ability comes newly awakened desire, a dread seduction that draws her relentlessly in, just as it draws in those whose bodies she ultimately renders out of place.

Days, perhaps weeks later, her philandering husband at last admits what she has known all along. That is, it's "not an affair, Jackie. I love her," if for no other reason, it seems, than that "she's not like you at all."[12] It wasn't all in her head, then, but somehow it's still all her fault. "She's not moody like you," he continues, refusing to look directly at her. "You know, she's just a normal woman."[13] As much as he knows it hurts her, though, once he starts he has to keep going. "I want it all off my chest," and, presumably, onto hers, because that will make him feel better about his myriad betrayals.[14] And isn't that what's really important? In the end, though, he fares no better than the good doctor, enduring the kind of marital separation perhaps ardently desired by legions of women who have been told the same thing.

You know I love you, darling, but the heart wants what the heart wants. "'Shut up,' she thought."[15] And he did.

His jaws snapped closed and his teeth ground themselves together, "cracking and splitting, nerves, calcium and spit making a pinkish foam on his chin."[16] His eyes fall back into his skull, and, as he comes to look less and less like the man she had married, Jacqueline Ess "began to take pleasure in the changes she was willing upon him."[17] She shuts him up completely, "telescoping flesh and resistant bone into a smaller and yet smaller space."[18] Indeed, "now that she had the knack of it," she "folded" and "plucked" and "stretched," until she finally compresses "his spine into a foot-long column of muck, and that was about the end of it."[19]

"As she came out of her ecstasy," writes Clive Barker in "Jacqueline Ess: Her Will and Testament," a novella from the *Books of Blood* anthology that launched him to prominence in the horror world, "she saw Ben sitting on the floor shut up into a space about the size of one of his fine leather suitcases, while blood, bile and lymphatic fluid pulsed weakly from his hushed body," now finally, as it were, in its proper place.[20] It is as if, paraphrasing Barker's most memorable character, the Hell Priest Pinhead, the very recently widowed Mrs. Ess asks, "Castration? Oh, such a limited imagination."[21] This is neither social dislocation nor debates over sexuality and gender. In Barker's storyworld, this is the brute fact of bodies coming together and tearing apart, the reality of fearing flesh and what it can become, what it can both do to us and make us do, especially in the service of its own needs and desires. For Jacqueline Ess, flesh *is* her will and testament—both her own power over the flesh of others, and their flesh as testament to her will.

Since long before the dawn of the historical horizon, while men without number have terrorized women, women have terrified men, especially women who were considered "out of control," who "stepped out of their place" and "challenged the natural order." Little else explains the extraordinary campaign of restriction, regulation, constraint, and outright annihilation women have been forced to endure from so many different quarters and in so many different ways. Women have fought back, however. From the Maenads, the nymphic handmaidens of Dionysus, to such literary descendants as Arthur Machen's Helen, daughter of "The Great God Pan," or the Ur-locs of Edward Lee's splatter-horror novel, *Succubi*; from H. Rider Haggard's She-who-must-be-obeyed to *Hellraiser: Bloodline*'s demon-queen Angelique; and from witches without number, who were said to bend men to their will, to Jacqueline Ess, who can do so literally—the horror mode teems with examples of female power finding its way out of the darkness and into the light.[22] Jacqueline Ess's story fairly epitomizes the notion of "bodies out of place." And, not surprisingly given their shared literary bloodline, she calls to mind nothing so much as the *Hellraiser* Cenobites, and the various ways they create "bodies out of place" as a function of their explorations "in the further regions of experience," their dark, unseen order in which pain and pleasure exist together on a razor's edge.[23]

Once again, though, in the race to domesticate its horror, we can read Jacqueline's story in various ways. The horror-story-as-sociological-commentary, for example, forges a narrative link between our cultural fears and social nightmares. Stephen King wrote of his breakout novel that "*Carrie* is largely about how women find their own channels of power, and what men fear about women and women's sexuality."[24] In the same vein, we can read "Jacqueline Ess" as Clive Barker's call to pay much closer attention to those particular aspects of everyday life. À la Julia Kristeva and Barbara Creed, on the other hand, reading it as some form of psychological metaphor entirely relieves the story of both narrative tension and internal ambiguity. The possibility that all this might actually be happening and what *that* might mean is simply rendered impossible. Perhaps it is a dream sequence that ends as Jacqueline Ess returns to herself, staring across the desk at Doctor Blandish as she meekly accepts another prescription. Perhaps it's a fugue state she enters on the train home, and in which she imagines everything she *would* do, if only she had that kind of power. But the problem is that as far as Barker's storyworld lets us know, the doctor *is* dead, torn apart in the process of womanizing (as it were), and her womanizing husband *is* dead, (almost) neatly packed for his final journey. Thus, in their deaths, and all those that follow, "Her Will and Testament" resists being reduced to a metaphor. Like the religious imagination writ large, the plain sense of the text rejects attempts to read it as an ideological riddle rather than a metaphysical enigma. Because assume for a moment that it is a riddle, and we solve it . . . so what? How much more do we know?

In what King calls "one of those stories where things happen just because they happen," what Jacqueline's mind can conceive, another's body must become.[25] Just as King declines to explain the source of Carrie White's destructive power, the origin of Jacqueline Ess's eroticized telekinesis remains a mystery.[26] In the horrific manifestations of "her will and testament," which embody the adage that "she had him twisted around her little finger," we encounter a modern-day Circe who, rather than change men into animals based on their underlying natures, transforms them in terms of their particular failings—particularly the ways in which they have failed her.[27] This is what Oliver Vassi, Jacqueline's lawyer turned hopeless devotee, learns: that we have repressed the authority of flesh as anything more than simply the vessel and craft of procreation. Bound by the consequent religious need to contain that authority, he tells us, "We cannot believe, we men, that power will ever reside happily in the body of a woman, unless that power is a male child. Not true power. The power must be in male hands, God-given. That's what our fathers tell us, idiots that they were."[28] The weaker sex, indeed, her story tells us. Jacqueline's power over him, however, is not malignant, not really—at least, that's what he tells himself. "It wasn't that she was feeding on me," Vassi insists. "I want to be clear about that. She was no lamia, no succubus . . . she didn't bewitch me; that's a romantic lie to excuse rape. She was a sea and I had to swim in her"—a black sea in which he finds an infinity of ecstasy and torment, and upon which there is, for him at least, no "placid island of ignorance."[29] He knows what she is doing, just as he knows the part he is cast to play, and he submits willingly, longingly, to both.

The flesh wants what the flesh wants, and this scares us as much as anything.

Thus, once again, whatever the process by which Jacqueline Ess works "her last will and testament" on Dr. Blandish, her husband Ben, Oliver Vassi, and all the others who drop at the foot of her dais, it does not matter whether we recognize it as "religion" in any conventional sense. It is enough that we are confronted with an unseen order at work, and one in which Vassi, at least, finds the essence of what he considers the divine. Because, what if the "unseen order" is *within* us, rather than without— the kind of energetic and evolutionary potential that New Age enthusiasts insist lies dormant inside each one of us, just waiting for release?

In this, as a horror-mode metonym, Jacqueline Ess stands in for every person who has ever marveled either at the power of their own body or at their powerlessness before the body of another. Because it is not explained, however, even at the end her flesh remains as much a mystery to her as to her lovers, and her own horrific agency remains, as it were, enigmatic.

These more inscrutable aspects of sex, horror, and the religious imagination challenge precisely such confident pronouncements as Beit-Hallahmi's that any "protection from evil is protection from sexuality," or Creed's generalized dismissal of horror as "a form of modern defilement rite."[30] Stories such as "Jacqueline Ess" either frustrate these easy explanations or surrender to such threadbare attempts at rationalization that we wonder why we bothered to read them in the first place. Stories that "happen just because they happen," however, can help us explore the more enigmatic aspects of our nature, particularly, like poor horrified Owen in "Thistle's Find," the urges and desires that we try desperately to control—but fail. In the first instance, consider a man who runs headlong from his sexual nature, hiding behind his devotional professions, yet whose fall is all but inevitable. In the second, we meet one whose entire professional life denies the possibility of what he encounters in a remote cave at the behest of a beautiful woman.

Escape: Running from the Monster

S, the anonymous narrator of Noel Scanlon's 1984 novel, *Apparitions*, who at times seems little more than the author's barely suppressed fictional avatar, has come to a remote island off Ireland's west coast. A "defrocked priest" who was "once in holy orders," S has most recently become the disciple of a mysterious Indian guru.[31] Together with a small group of other devotees—"four young Indians, two boys and two girls" and "four European girls from the large number who had wanted to join us"—he has established a religious commune on the rocky island of Inishwrack.[32] There, secluded and presumably undistracted by the inconvenience of mundane concerns, they can give themselves over to meditation and the pursuit of spiritual enlightenment. Joss-sticks burn and incense rises in the derelict church they have consecrated as their nascent ashram's temple, its rough-hewn stone walls covered "with Indian hangings depicting scenes similar to those you can see in Khajuraho."[33]

Given that, for most of his life, S has struggled against the deep currents of his own sexual nature, these hangings seem an odd ornamental choice. Many of the temples of Khajuraho, the architectural pride of central India's Chandela Dynasty (ca. 800–1300 CE), are covered with elaborate carvings depicting in explicit detail all manner of our species' polymorphous perversity. And, despite the fact that explicitly erotic sculpture accounts for only a small portion of the external temple decoration, along with the Kama Sutra, the Khajuraho carvings have become synonymous with the orientalization of sex in the West.[34] "There is a generally-held belief that 'free love' abounded there," writes art historian Devangana Desai.[35] Indeed, a History Channel documentary on Khajuraho begins breathlessly, "They *worshiped* sex." And, more than a thousand years after the temples were built, "What has made them famous is *sex*."[36] The narrator's voice drops slightly at the end, forcing a salacious patina onto that last word. Although Desai insists that "nothing is further from the truth," Western representations of Khajuraho—including the implications in such genre horror as Scanlon's novel—reinforce this skewed sense of sexualized religious history.[37] Kanwar Lal's *Cult of Desire*, for example, which purports to be an "objective" historical interpretation of Khajuraho and "the erotic sculpture of India," illustrates this problem from its outset. Opposite the title page a stark caveat warns potential readers, "The sale of this book is strictly restricted to members of the medical and legal professions, and to scholars and research students of Indology, Psychology and Social Sciences."[38] Like those kept out of some nineteenth-century "secret museum," all others are apparently either too fragile or easily swayed to be trusted with thousand-year-old sculptures that "[depict] the entire range of the sexual act, and all manner of poses . . . vulgar as vulgar can be, unnatural as unnatural can be, obscene as obscene can be, and indecent and shocking, disgusting and repulsive!"[39]

Lions and tigers and bears, oh my![40]

Though not without its critics, the classic statement on the problem of "orientalism" is, of course, Edward Said's eponymous text, *Orientalism*. My use here differentiates a lower-case "orientalization" as "an accepted grid for filtering through the Orient into Western consciousness"

Figure 6.1. Detail from the erotic sculpture on the temples at Khajuraho.

that appears in specific pop-cultural products from Said's larger conceptual project of "Orientalism" as "a system of representations framed
by a whole set of forces that brought the Orient into Western learning,
Western consciousness, and later, Western empire."[41] Put differently, but
still per Said's basic tenets, "orientalization" is "better grasped as a set of
constraints upon and limitations of thought," such that it both generates
and reinforces an "ineradicable distinction between Western superiority
and Oriental inferiority."[42] In the horror mode, however, this "ineradicable distinction" becomes more complex, serving as a means both to
escape the demands of the flesh and to explain the inevitable failure of
those attempts.

   Nowhere is this orientalization of sex—controlling our anxiety over,
fascination with, and often powerlessness before sexual desire by rendering it both forbidden and exotic—displayed more clearly than in the
difference between S(canlon)'s descriptions of the European and Indian
women on the island with him.[43] Ursula, for instance, one of the Euro-
peans, is "disturbingly sexual," perhaps because the detached spirituality

S looks for in his followers "was less apparent in her than in the other girls."[44] Far more likely, though, is that Ursula does not defer to him as do the other women in the ashram. "She was the least compliant of the community," he tells us, and her defiant sexuality both tempts and threatens him, the one as a function of the other.

Barely a few pages into the story, in the wake of an unexplained and seemingly inexplicable death on the island, S struggles to regain control of the group. Seeking to enforce "compliance" (i.e., establish his dominance within the community by subjugating her), he commands Ursula to "prostrate herself on the church floor." As he gazes "down on her slim sensuous figure, clad in a light blue sari that clung to her," "something about Ursula's prostrate body held me," and "I saw her prostrate body as intensely erotic."[45] Any spiritual resistance S has to such overt temptation is short-lived, and though (or perhaps because) he had "practiced total sexual abstinence on the island," bare seconds elapse before the two are "conjoined in the dim candlelight before the statue," and he is aware of nothing but "Ursula's energetic writhing on the church floor."[46]

Hardly lovemaking and, despite his description, barely erotic, this is precisely the kind of physical sexuality S so abhors, but whose pull he cannot withstand. "Intercourse with Ursula was, to me, a defeat," he admits.[47] We are left questioning, though, the nature of the defeat. Is it really the collapse of his rigid ascetic discipline that he so regrets? Or, more likely, the failure of his sexual harassment, his vain attempt to force Ursula into submission, which is demonstrated so clearly by the fact that she was able to exert her sexual will over him during what he calls their "casual coupling"?[48] "Who are you to talk about spirituality?" she later demands angrily, and not unreasonably. "After fucking me in the church at the first opportunity you got?"[49]

Compare this to the way S(canlon) describes Manju and Maya, who for him epitomize "something intrinsically different about the oriental and occidental female body."[50] Rather than Ursula and her insubordination, or the tall, ungainly Chris, who "looked rather ridiculous" in her sari, the two young Indian women are "neat, tidy, and controlled."[51] In addition to glistening "black plaits," fresh *tilak* on their foreheads, "ankle bracelets," and "gold arm bangles," "both wore extremely abbreviated cholies that left exposed the rounded sides of their breasts."[52] Most important for S, though, and what makes these aspects of the novel an extended exercise in Scanlon's colonialist orientalization of the female sexual body, is that they look at S "out of their large brown Indian eyes, passively and incuriously, with that special quality never to be found among European females."[53] It is as though they are not persons in any sense, merely orientalized ciphers that allow him to sublimate his own desires while eulogizing his supposed spiritual elevation.

Weeks later, however, having narrowly escaped one of Inishwrack's increasingly dangerous supernatural manifestations—the novel's name-sake "apparitions," the emergence of which is never really explained—S returns to the cottage he shares with Manju and Maya. Apparently over-come by the "feeling of safety" there, he finds himself "suddenly sexually aroused."[54] Indeed, to survive the horror of whatever is happening on the island, S tells himself (and us), "I had to bury myself in something that was firmly rooted in ordinary humanity and desire."[55] Which is to say, the two young Indian women. "My fingers tripped along to that erogenous zone of young brown flesh that lay between [Maya's] low slung sari and brief choli. The feel of that warm flesh lapped and rippled through me. I saw the Indian girls as goddesses of the flesh and desire as a fine thread drawing me towards their silken cobweb."[56]

Because "their eastern minds were beyond my grasp"—another less-than-subtle orientalism—we learn nothing about how either woman understands the encounter. "They weren't lewd in the way Ursula was lewd," S insists, more than a little tellingly, and despite the obvious danger-signaling at the end of the passage. "They were submissive, their eyes downcast. I was the master; they were eager to do my bidding."[57] It is difficult to know how much of this scene reflects Scanlon's own colonialist sexual fantasy, or whether we are meant to interpret it as the presumed spiritual threat of sexual temptation—once again represented as a function of importunate female power—and the very real danger of sexual abuse in closed religious communities. "They didn't bring to the act the western concept of original sin," he continues, "or any of the western mental paraphernalia."[58] Indeed, "They coupled, these oriental beauties, as athletically as depicted on any piece of ancient erotic sculp-ture that adorns any Indian temple, couplings that embrace men and women and gods and demons and deities who are a little of both."[59]

With Ursula, sex is a lustful failure on his part, while with Manju and Maya, it is actually far more complicated. S recognizes the power "rooted in ordinary humanity and desire," and acknowledges his own need for it, yet the women are still depicted as the sexual aggressors in this scenario and he the (un)willing victim caught in their web of sultry temptation. Following on this, although S(canlon) consistently describes the two women in overtly paternalistic terms, as if they are there simply for his sexual comfort, for him they also become the physical loci of supernatural evil on Inishwrack—the "gods and demons and deities who are a little of both." Not unlike Cal Moulton blaming Eve Vickers in *Attack of the Giant Leeches*, S takes full advantage of their sexual availability, all while both blaming them for it and lamenting his own "weakness." Even as he is horrified that his vaunted spiritual maturity "could be so easily seduced by this blatant but submissive carnality," he surrenders to them, once again "driven mad by sensuality and some element of the forbidden that spiced our foreplay."[60] But, even then, it's not his fault. Not really. Convincing himself that Manju and Maya have become the sexualized incarnations of the island's arcane threat, S casts them as the eroticized manifestation of everything that is tearing their little community apart. And, more than that, it's not really even *their* fault. They "had been taken over. Despite their beautiful, familiar bodies, their perfectly oval faces, these girls were strangers. They were hostile. What looked out from their eyes was evil. It was the more horrible because of their beauty."[61] They become the enigmatic faces of sexual horror, filtered through his fevered religious imagination. "I could not believe what had happened to these slim lithe innocent girls, my household goddesses. These golden girls had once been the mascots that sheltered me from evil. They had once been my protection against whatever apparitions might lurk outside. Now they themselves had become that evil."[62]

While parts of *Apparitions* read like a colonialist set-up for third-rate pornography, it is still a horror novel. Terrifying, inexplicable things do happen on Inishwrack, perhaps connected to its Druid history or some sort of parasympathetic response to S's lust, perhaps the hallucinogenic effect of mushrooms that grow wild on the island, or even some unnamed supernatural defense against the incursion of alien religious traditions. All these are on offer, and we are simply never told. It could be that Scanlon is following M. R. James's sage advice that authors of scary stories and weird fiction should "allow us to be just a little in the dark as to the working of their machinery. We do not want to see the bones of their theory about the supernatural," and we can speculate about the events overtaking the small island, but we are never certain.[63] Or, Scanlon may not, in fact, have an answer, and by the end it's a race just to see who can get off the island alive—and at least reasonably sane.

Through S, though, the story illustrates two principal ways by which religious traditions attempt to keep the sexual body in its proper place, to escape the powerful enigma of sexual desire: *detachment*, which is regarded as the vehicle of spiritual development, and *demonization*, which often functions internally as an explanation for personal failure, and externally as an accusation of religious malfeasance.

For centuries, claims of sexual impropriety, predation, and abuse have been common in the social construction of new religious threats.[64] Whether it is a difference in clothing style, an unconventional attitude toward sexual relations, or the explicit (or imagined) sexualization of religious ritual and practice, new religious movements have often been accused of "gross immorality and licentiousness," behavior that would "disgust and repel all right-thinking and god-fearing citizens."[65] Indeed, this is conduct for which, according to some of the Irish locals, S "should be hung drawn and quartered."[66] This aspect of the novel draws on numerous tropes that have marked out new religious movements as "cults" for at least a couple of generations. In addition to S, the sexually obsessed leader of the ashram, for example, we meet the shabby journalist hoping to break the story of a lifetime on the back of prurient imaginings about life on Inishwrack. We have frightened townsfolk who shelter their fear behind the bravado of self-righteousness and who think "it's nothing short of a sacrilege for those hussies out there to call themselves nuns in holy orders."[67] In fact, one woman writes in the local paper, "We will not now stand idly by while the likes of you and your wanton hussies commit immoralities and sacrileges that offend against man and god and the impurity of which is bound to seep across the sea and pollute the moral atmosphere on the mainland."[68] Whatever the reality, that is, nothing could be more horrifying than what they imagine.

Regardless of what outsiders think, though, for S and the Inishwrack ashram, physical detachment, especially in terms of sexual interaction, is the bride-price of enlightenment. As it is for myriad religious traditions around the world, sex has been cast as the brute hallmark of ego, a principal "obstacle to spiritual progress."[69] S himself has for years "foregone all sexual intercourse as all yogis recommend and as is indeed more or less obligatory for the attainment of real spiritual advancement."[70] And he expects no less from those who join him in this "more or less obligatory" quest. "Even the rawest novice is forbidden sex and follows the most rigid discipline," he reflects as the ashram falls apart around him, something he blames explicitly on the fact that he "had sex first with Ursula then with Manju and Maya."[71] This inability "to impose the disciplines of the order"—most particularly on himself—is both his signal failure and his cardinal arrogance. "I could and should have done better," he prays to his absent guru. And he would have, too, "had not my spiritual defences been sadly depleted."[72]

Even in this moment of introspective desperation, however, S looks for an excuse, a way to do anything other than face the dark, disturbing spaces of his own nature. With Ursula, it wasn't really *his* fault: her wanton unwillingness to accept the dictates of the community and the authority of his leadership compromised his spiritual discipline. Likewise, with Manju and Maya, it wasn't really *his* fault: their possession by whatever nameless evil lurked on the island worked through their sexuality, rendering it all but irresistible. And, months later, this enigma is still firmly in play. Of Maya and Manju, no one can tell him, though most of the others have drifted back to their old lives or on to new religious pursuits. Once again in India, though, S prepares to take "orders to become a monk as the guru considers that I am sufficiently spiritually advanced to take that step."[73] In the end, he still seems not to grasp the difference between escaping and simply running away.

Encounter: Drifting toward the Monster

Mathias Clasen may dismiss any contribution people claim Freud and his followers have made to our understanding of the human psyche. He may even deride "the Freudian framework" as "an illusion of privileged access to a hidden layer of textual reality," the principal benefit of which seems to be that it "allows them to talk endlessly about sexual organs, but with straight-faced gravitas."[74] But he cannot really deny the purchase it retains on popular culture. While, more than once in psychologist Gary Fry's short story "Sealed by the Moon," the narrator makes his own rejection of the Vienna Circle explicit, the story itself is filled with Freudian significance, imagery, and, therefore, ambiguity. Indeed, the popular imagination's ongoing fascination with Freud is not unlike the resilience and durability of religion writ large. There may be little in the way of empirical evidence supporting many of his major theories, but that has not kept millions of people from finding within them a framework of explanation for the set of observed facts that constitute their everyday lives. And just as religious believers often find it difficult to reconcile the existence of those who believe differently, critics who do not accept this or that psychological framework often find it impossible to credence those who do.

"There's a place I want you to see," Lily tells her boyfriend, Glenn.[75] In celebration of her twenty-first birthday, they have gone on a weekend camping trip to something Lily calls Mooncap Cave. A therapist and "general counsellor," Glenn is the story's icon of rationality and skepticism, the one through whom we anticipate the horror mode's quintessential "what the fuck?" moment.[76] In this case, however, what we watch is less the visceral shock of horrific confrontation than an encounter mediated by what anthropologist Tanya Luhrmann calls "interpretive drift."[77] This is "the slow, often unacknowledged shift in someone's manner of interpreting events as they become involved with a particular activity."[78] Rather than a Damascus road conversion or a voice suddenly booming from a burning bush, interpretive drift describes a more gradual, even insidious process, "a shift in what one wants to call belief" or, more precisely, "in the types of assertions about the world which a [person] will defend."[79] For Luhrmann, this means the play of "three loosely connected transformations": interpretation, experience, and rationalization.[80] For Glenn, this process of interpretive drift amounts to a classic ritual journey: separation from the world as he knows it, a passage into some form of liminal space, and a return to the world that can never be as he knew it before.[81] His particular task that weekend is to make his way into Mooncap Cave, which "has a hole in its ceiling that you can see straight through," then come back out and tell Lily what he found at its heart.[82]

Their relationship, however, is also a psychological case study in boundary issues. Not only do Glenn and Lily live together, but she is also his client, referred to him in the aftermath of a suicide attempt. Sharing a joint as they set up camp, a familiar narcotic tilt on the narrative axis of explanation, Lily recounts how her parents brought her to this very spot as a child. While Glenn recognizes that "nothing about Lily had ever been normal," not least their relationship, he still cannot grasp the significance of her story.[83] "'Inside the cave *something* dwells,' she went on, the smile in her tone almost palpable. 'But only those tall enough to see the moon fill the hole in the ceiling will ever observe it.'"[84]

Noting that he and his client/lover's father both stand well over six feet, he suspects that "there was probably something Freudian at work here—an Elektra complex or some such—but Glenn had been trained as a general counsellor and not a dyed-in-the-wool psychoanalyst preaching according to Sigmund's orthodoxy."[85] Years ago, her father had gone into Mooncap Cave, she tells him, "raw emotion impeding her throat," but when he had returned to Lily and her mother, "he was a changed man."[86] According to Lily, he encountered "a god of desire, a master of rage, a spiritual advocate of every furtive taboo you or anyone else has ever considered."[87] Glenn prods her to continue, though Lily knows that his "objective distance" is far more for his own protection than hers. Is she trying to tell him that she had been sexually abused by her father, or that she imagined a sexual relationship that was in some way consensual? Is this what prompted her suicide attempt, the one thing they had never discussed either in session or in bed? Perhaps "the drug in her blood had brought dark treasure to the surface."[88]

Not surprisingly, Glenn's initial attempts to rationalize Lily's account of her father and the cave, his skeptical need to naturalize the unnatural narrative that is her life, carves its path between the Elektra complex (the daughter who desires her father) and the incest taboo that Freud insisted was the basis of family stability. "The past is weird, full of stupid nonsense," she tells Glenn as they continue along the trail, "but in this case the myth seemed to *work*. My dad went into the cave alone and observed the cave being sealed by the moon. And when he came out he was a different man."[89] It was "as if he'd *seen* something in there that had changed everything."[90] He had seen something that her own lack of physical stature would never allow her to see, "an ancient god of the darker realms of human experience."[91] Something that she can only experience dimly and vicariously through men as tall as Glenn, and she now craves the second-hand psychosexual thrill of this "god of desire."

"I want *you* to go inside," she said, her manipulative persona reappearing, teasing and taunting. With one hand she pinched her small breasts and then placed the other in her groin, clutching it and rubbing it. "I want to *know* what my dad saw that day fifteen years ago." . . . Now Lily had placed one hand on his groin, which stirred with irrepressible need. "Go in there for me," she said in a low voice, like a coquettish temptress in full force. "And when you come back out, *tell me what you saw*."[92]

Like a monstrous version of Peter Pan, a lost girl (for why else would she need the endless string of therapists and psychologists), Lily (who could be Fry's literary avatar for Lilith) has become a kind of sexual vampire, unable to cross the threshold on her own, and so she feeds on the stories of those who can.[93] For his part, Glenn immediately moves to explain her behavior away, because, however romantic its name, there cannot be anything in the cave but dark and dank and spiderwebs. After all, "gods of desire" aren't real, are they? Outside of the *Hellraiser* franchise, these "angels to some, demons to others" simply don't exist, and there are no "spiritual advocates of every furtive taboo."[94] Right? In a few short paragraphs, though, we watch as Fry shows us the incipient religious imagination at work, the resilience of the unnatural in the face of attempts to naturalize it, an inexorable drift forcing the movement from skeptic to believer, from unambiguous cynicism to dread certainty. First comes cool rationalization: something happened in the cave, and Lily's father was changed when he emerged. Unable to explain it, her six-year-old mind structured an explanation commensurate with age and circumstance.

That must be it.

"The girl would have first noticed this while holidaying in the area," Glenn tells himself, reaching back to coursework in lifespan development, "her childish mind, with all its innate capacity for animism, attributing the chance to such a rich environment."[95] Warming to the comfort of his diagnosis, the intuitive correctness of his explanation, he continues: "Later, while researching the experience with credulous need, she'd learnt about the age-old myth associated with this small cave, the way the moon passed over its hole, and the *thing* that allegedly dwelt there." Satisfied for the moment, he turns to follow her toward the entrance to the cave. "It was all nonsense, of course."[96] The Loch Ness Monster, the

Jersey Devil, Igopogo, Bigfoot, and the god of Mooncap Cave—all of a psychological piece.

As he enters the cave, however, his training as a psychologist, his intellectual positioning as a rationalist, his utter lack of belief in the host of invisible forces that have haunted humankind's religious imagination for millennia—all these begin to erode before the singular power of the horror mode, the relentless force of the question, *But what if she's right?* "He considered his own youth" as he makes his way through the inky darkness, "and all the commonplace events he has similarly misinterpreted, imbuing them with magic and other primitive modes of thought."[97] Though Glenn insists repeatedly that he is not a Freudian, his story is redolent both with the Vienna Circle and with the superstitious notion of agency attribution. "Lately," he thinks, as though trying to convince no one so much as himself, he is "afraid of hardly anything . . . until today, of course, standing in this spooky cave with only a perverted fairy story to make sense of it."[98] However many thousands of generations separate the therapist from his protohuman ancestors do nothing to mitigate the sense of potential danger, his primordial alert system already set in motion by Lily's story. Indeed, he wonders, perhaps peering into the dark, suddenly afraid to take the next step, "would his reptilian self, the Freudian beast that allegedly existed inside all people, be roused from its depths?"[99] Shaking himself, knowing that "that was stupid, *stupid*," he looks into the dark.

"That was when he saw *it*."[100]

This is the moment when Glenn's mind points to a slight movement in the shadows and demands, "Then what the fuck is *that*?" He sees it, this strange, ancient god. He hears it speak, "the aged utterances of something beyond such petty concerns as life and death."[101] And he realizes in that singular moment that "everything she'd told him was true."[102] The monstrous god-thing that "was as large as himself, but considerably fleshier" was supposed to be a delusory explanation covering the unbearable pain of childhood trauma. But, no, because nothing in that explanation could prepare him for what he actually sees. Pallid flesh in "great folds hanging off a combination of bones that seemed too slipshod to sustain any movement" supported a "face, insofar as this could be described, [that] was a hybrid travesty of knotted skin and squashed features: eyes fought for supremacy amid a twisted nose and a razor-sharp mouth."[103] Feeling "his psyche flinch" and "sensing a shriek of terror building inside him," Glenn still cannot look away. "The whole of it appeared to thrum with incipient motion, even though it remained remarkably stationary; its elongated limbs, little more than sockets held together by stretches of sinew, hung laxly beside a corrugated torso, like wax dripping from a misshapen candle. It smelled like a zoo, foul and intense."[104]

Once again, the urge to rationalize is as strong in us as the religious imagination—both because the two are so intimately linked, the one a species of the other, and because the alternative is often too terrifying to entertain. What Glenn does not realize is that his interpretive drift has led him on a classic ritual journey. With Lily as his guide and ersatz initiator into the mysteries of Mooncap Cave, they have left the security and taken-for-granted nature of the everyday world. Moving down "the damp, snaking tunnel" into the heart of the cave and encountering the god-thing within constitute the liminal space between one way of understanding the world and the next.[105] According to anthropologist Victor Turner's standard model of the ritual journey, as a state of being, liminality is "necessarily ambiguous," an in-between condition that "[slips] through the network of classifications that normally locate states and positions in cultural space."[106] And, because those in this space have none of the conventional symbols, normative customs, or cultural markers that allow them interpretive purchase on the "before" side of their journey, they are forced to rely on whatever their guide has provided.[107] In this case, a psychologically damaged young woman's second-hand memory of "*a god of desire, a master of rage, a spiritual advocate of every furtive taboo.*"[108]

By the time Glenn has retreated in terror, stumbled back out of the cave and reentered consensus reality, he knows that he is irrevocably changed. Still unwilling to accept his shift in cosmic circumstances, however, he makes two additional attempts to regain reality as it was before his encounter in the cave. On the one hand, "he'd already decided that he'd suffered some kind of pot-induced hallucination in the cave; that was a rational interpretation, the only explanation that made sense now that his emotional engagement with the event had diminished."[109] Lily, however, desperate to hear what happened to him, won't settle for "such a humdrum account."[110] Of course it was not the drugs, because, if it was, any comfort she took in her childhood memories would evaporate. Of course there was a god-thing in the cave, slipping easily into the fallacy of personal incredulity, because, if there wasn't, what could possibly explain the change in her father all those years ago?

Glenn's next interpretive refuge is to make the experience about *him*. As with Luke Skywalker in the Dark Side Cave on Dagobah, as with Sam Gamgee navigating the caverns of Mount Doom, what Glenn confronts in the Mooncap Cave is the shadow-side of himself. That must be it. Mustn't it? A last desperate attempt to naturalize the unnatural invokes the shades of both Freud and Jung. That is, "Was there something *deeper* in his existence, something of which the *thing* he'd seen less than an hour earlier had been a subconscious symbol?"[111] Of course, it was all so clear now, the lexicon of psychoanalysis taking hold. "The entity lurking in that shadowy place, a vision conjured from inaccessible memories and sustained by perverse captivation, had tried telling him something."[112] "The creature was certainly delusional," he reasoned, a primeval revenant extruding for the moment from the depths of his subconscious, "but no less true in its meaning."[113]

Delusional, but no less true in its meaning.

What happens next is almost anticlimactic. In the throes of pent-up passion, Lily claws at Glenn, begging him to tell her what he saw, "her tongue darting in her mouth like some forked appendage."[114] As she frantically straddles him, reaching for his penis, he abandons any pretense to such "neutral logic and professional distance" as he might have left. "It knows about *us*, Lily," he tells her, and more than that, "it knows that functioning in everyday life involves suppression of desire, and that perversion is just blocked engagement."[115] Worst of all, it knows that "buried secrets can be released," as Lily finally tugs his member free and mounts him. In a frenzy of *lustmord*, they both reach for the "heavy mallet Glenn had used earlier to knock in those lethally sharp tent pegs."[116]

Lily gets there first.

On the one hand, in terms of a narrative postmortem, we could side with Glenn before his ritual encounter in Mooncap Cave and read the story psychologically. In fact, through his consistent attempts at rationalization, Fry hints throughout that this is how the story should be read, even as the story itself resists that reading. The easiest explanation is to see this as the murderous closure of Lily's childhood sexual assault, a horror-mode rape-revenge fantasy and PSA on the consequences of incest. But if so, again, so what? What does that tell us that we did not already know? That childhood sexual abuse is horrifying and horrific, leaving its victims scarred in ways that others cannot begin to imagine, let alone understand? Do we really need this story to tell us that? Because that is what a psychological reading—one that treats Lily and Glenn as riddles to be solved—asks us to accept. And, if that is the case, what does that say about *us*? Because if it is little more than a violently sexualized Scooby-Doo mystery, and the man under the bedsheet is Lily's long-dead father, whom she has longed to kill so much since she was six years old that she sought out a physical surrogate, how much more do we really know?

On the other hand, we could consider both the Inishwrack ashram and Mooncap Cave as examples of the numinous, and what David Hartwell calls the horror-mode problem of "third-stream stories."[117]

The Enigma of the Holy

For Hartwell, third-stream horror stories are enigmatic by nature, and rely for their narrative tension on ambiguity, ambivalence, uncertainty, and the problem of nonimpossibility. They "lack any explanation that makes sense in everyday reality—we don't know, and that doubt disturbs us, horrifies us."[118] Stories of aberrant human psychology, on the other hand, Hartwell's "second stream," place a recognizable monster at the center of the action, whether through long-repressed trauma that explodes in a frenzy of sexual violence or the hallucinogenic effects of this or that drug, be it mushrooms or marijuana. Even here, though, in stories that should be reserved for the unfathomable evil that lurks within the human heart and mind alone, and that should require no more motivation than that, Hartwell finds it difficult to avoid the problem of the supernatural, the enigma of the holy. Second-stream stories present the quintessential naturalized narrative, the horror story with a logical, if terrifying (but often wholly unsatisfying) rationalization.

In Caitlín Kiernan's "Houses Under the Sea," for example, rather than the ambiguous (im)possibility of the existence of the Old Ones and their inevitable pull on humankind, the group-brainwashing hypothesis provides this second-stream rationale for the mass self-drowning of the "controversial Open Door of Night cult."[119] That is, while it provides an *explanation* that supposedly helps the rest of us sleep better, it does not begin to *explain* the events of the story. Although Kiernan does not say it, "Houses Under the Sea" appears almost explicitly based on the mass suicides of Heaven's Gate in 1997, substituting the marine trench off California for "The Evolutionary Level Above Human," and the mysterious "Jacova Angevine" for Marshall Herff Applewhite.[120] That said, though, the question remains in each of these cases—storyworld and real world: What makes this "aberrant" when compared to the willingness of so many people to die (or kill) for a cause in which they believe absolutely and for whatever reason? Those who insist that the events in Kiernan's story, or many of the others we have considered to this point, could never happen need look no further than real life, and the confusion of consensus realities that it regularly and repeatedly presents.

In each of these third-stream stories, however, we encounter what theologian Rudolf Otto called "the numinous." Arguably the central concept animating his most influential work, this is "the idea of the holy" stripped of all moral considerations, ethical frameworks, or rational explanations. Derived from the Latin "*numen*," the "numinous" is "a spiritual force or influence often identified with a natural object, phenomenon, or place," and Otto maintained that "there is no religion in which it does not live as the real, innermost core."[121] While he recognized that over thousands of years "the holy" came to be identified with "the absolute moral attribute," "the consummate moral goodness," he insisted that not only was this not its original implication, it "never constituted the whole meaning of the word."[122] That we so often forget this fact is the essence of religion's good, moral, and decent fallacy. Rather, Otto traces the development of the numinous back to the primeval fears with which our ancestors lived, and which, for good or ill, they have bequeathed to us. This is "'fear' that is more than fear proper," he continues, and in the numinous we experience "terror fraught with an inward shuddering such as not even the most menacing and overpowering created thing can instil."[123] (He's talking about *you*, Bruce the shark.)[124] Rather, "it has something spectral to it," and "forms the starting point for the entire religious development in history. 'Daemons' and 'gods' alike spring from this root."[125] And, not to put too fine a point on it for our purposes, this ubiquitous form of primordial dread is demonstrated nowhere more than in "the potent attraction again and again exercised by the element of horror and 'shudder' in ghost stories, even among persons of high, all-round education."[126]

Although it does not deal with the sexual aspect of human being, award-winning horror writer Anna Tambour's short story "Simply, Petrified" tacks between Luhrmann's notion of "interpretive drift" and Otto's "idea of the holy," charting its ambiguous course between "religion and neuroses."[127] "Both hold minds in dark, fear-driven thrall," Tambour writes in her introduction to the story, "despite science's sparks of enlightenment and reason."[128] For example, reminding people that correlation is not causation does little to relieve their anxiety at the sudden flurry of bad things in their lives. We all want to know, What has changed? And it does no good to proclaim the metaphorical nature of demons when they are knocking at the church door, or blame cerebral chemical imbalances when we are confronted by "a god of desire, a master of rage." Science cannot explain away the "nameless dread" that lies at the heart of weird fiction, the sphincter-tightening horror at the thought of bodies wrenched violently out of place.[129] Indeed, Tambour concludes, contra Freud, Foucault, and all the rest, that "maybe knowledge isn't power, for science is weak against that certain something that Lovecraft, and the normal, irrational human mind all do so dreadfully well."[130] In this case, "Simply, Petrified" highlights the social construction of religious reality, as well as the relentless momentum of conversation when others come to believe the same things we do. Connecting this to the numinous, which Otto also called "*mysterium tremendum et fascinans*," the enigma by which we are both overwhelmed and enchanted, only deepens and intensifies this feeling—no matter how believers try to sugar-coat the problem.

More than that, Tambour's story is a search for meaning, especially meaning in the face of tragedy. With the exception of prosperity gospel preachers and their myriad followers, few of us look very hard for meaning in the context of unexpected success, lottery windfalls, and bequests from hitherto unknown aunts, and fewer still see these as personal vindication or explicit reward by the unseen forces of the universe. Conversely, most of us, whether implicitly or explicitly, do try to explain the bad things that come our way, and we fill in the blanks of our various tragedies with the thinnest of evidence, conjecture, and suggestion.

Most significantly, perhaps, we attempt to ensure that our suffering is not meaningless, that our plaintive cries of "Why me, Lord?" have an answer, even if it is one we don't want to hear. The reality is, though, that bad luck, misfortune, calamity are all things that can happen *for no good reason at all*. But, for some reason, we are incapable of leaving it there. "No reason" is not good enough, and we must fashion a reason if one is not readily on offer. We may not, as Lovecraft notes, be able to correlate the contents of our minds, to reconcile them with reality, but that doesn't mean we aren't going to try. We create the pretext, and thus the context, for *meaning*. We grasp at explanations, however tenuous and ephemeral they turn out to be. And, when that happens, Tambour suggests, it's a different story altogether.

In "Simply, Petrified," we watch the numinous play of conversation and interpretive drift, two principal forces operating on the religious imagination, both of which conspire to convince us that the most fantastic things are real, all while underpinning our belief in their reality. That is, once the insanity plea is thrown out, once the possibility of senile dementia or early-onset Alzheimer's is eliminated, in this instance we are left with the enigma of the religious imagination. In fact, it becomes far more than what geologist Hugh Krey thinks "religion should be, mushed myth to the pap of rubes," useless prayers offered to nonexistent gods in the hope of currying favor or forestalling judgment.[131] When his erstwhile partner, psychiatrist Walter Wilder, brings up the possibility of the gods—real, imagined, or some unimaginable combination of the two—Krey responds derisively, "You collect myths, too?" Sensing the other's plan, Krey wonders, finally, "So you're going to fake some story of the god who looks after the petrified forest?" Here, Tambour presses on the central nerve cluster of the religious imagination—the principle of evidence, the fallacy of authority, and the emotional power of nonfalsifiability—especially when these conspire to create that "nameless dread." "Better than that," Wilder replies. "Fake? What *is* reality? I'll implant the scholarly records. Remember, I have a reputation."[132]

Concerned with the damage done by souvenir hunters and treasure seekers to Arizona's Petrified Forest National Park, Wilder concocts the fiction of a myth warning of great danger to anyone foolish enough to take pieces of petrified wood with them when they leave the park. It is an important distinction, "the fiction of a myth." That is, Wilder had "put much thought into his faux myth," but "he hadn't reached the stage of myth invention."[133] Which is to say, he did not need to create the myth itself, because the story of the myth's existence was enough. Given the cultural currency of curses, hexes, and ritual taboos in the religious imagination, it takes no more than that to inspire the terrifyingly numinous that gradually takes over both the story and Wilder's life. From legends of dire punishment visited upon those who dared touch the Ark of the Covenant to curses promised to violators of the Valley of the Kings, from sacred places forbidden to all but the elect to simple charms bought from cunning folk at the edge of the village, we have always imagined some measure of control over the dark currents of the unseen order—and some consequence for transgression. As head of the Petrified Forest museum, Wilder constructed his faux myth with care, and soon a growing collection of artifacts, testimony, and incipient terror emerges.

"'Superstitious, I wasn't,' reads a penciled crumpled scrap of butcher paper. 'However, more bad luck has happened to me than any one person could rationally have experienced. Take this back.' It is signed, 'A cynic no more. Scranton, Pennsylvania.'"[134] A small, broken piece of petrified wood lies in the display case beside the hastily scrawled note, one of dozens of similar shards and scraps—"the great pile of letters and pieces of petrified stone"—none of them real, of course, none of them anything other than a forgery, a fraud. In fact, they are "all Krey and Wilder productions."[135] But, in the same way myths and urban legends grow, in the same way the religious imagination occasionally extrudes into consensus reality and becomes "the way things are," with each telling this tale takes on a life of its own. With each visitor who leaves the park, it travels further and further, gathering momentum with each repetition, gaining precisely the imprimatur of popular imagination its creators intended.

Soon, packages begin to arrive, each with a similar crumpled note, the same kind of plaintive awakening, and a bit of petrified wood returned to its rightful place. After a while, a second display case is added to accommodate the volume of submissions. A local newspaper, hungry perhaps for a human-interest story, all the more so if it boosts tourism, contributes to the fiction, without actually lying. Citing "Dr. Walter Wilder, head of the museum and a noted authority on myth"—none of this is false, even if, in the context of the situation, it is not exactly true—reinforces the legitimacy of the curse.[136] "Some myths," the enthusiastic young reporter continues, "like this one about the curse of taking petrified wood from the park, are so old that they predate historical knowledge"—again, not completely true, but not entirely false either.[137] Preying on basic ignorance, the mythic illiteracy of the audience, and the presumed authority of the expert (about which Wilder is hardly disingenuous), the myth neatly fills in the blanks on "why bad things happen to good people."

Many years later, though, long after they had lost touch, Wilder demands Krey visit him one last time. Perhaps it is senility, perhaps Alzheimer's, but Wilder tells his erstwhile partner, "'I asked you here because I want to warn you.' He rises up on his sticklike arms. 'Get rid of your pieces . . . get rid of them. There might be something left in your life.'"[138] To which, not surprisingly, Krey responds with a laugh, "You sound like a believer." "There *is* a curse," Wilder insists, recounting just a few of the recent tragedies in his life. "I just didn't believe it before."[139] Krey stares at the other man, incredulous, in the story's penultimate scene, suddenly desperate to remind him: "You made it—*We* made it up, Walter. Remember?"

"Men forget," wrote Peter Berger in his classic text, *The Sacred Canopy*, meaning, of course, both men and women. "They must, therefore, be reminded over and over again."[140] In fact, Berger argues that "one of the oldest and most important prerequisites for the establishment of culture is the institution of such 'reminders'"—even, and perhaps especially, when we are reminded of things that are not strictly true, but become so through the process of ongoing recollection.[141] Indeed, this is the foundation of the externalization-objectivation-internalization arc Berger and Luckmann describe in *The Social Construction of Reality*.[142] By this they mean the fact that, because we lose sight of the constructed—which is to say, fabricated—nature of our social and cultural worlds, they must be constantly tended, buttressed, and underpinned. Because, in many ways, this is our only defense against the precariousness of existence. Gradually, especially as more and more people come to agree with us, our worldviews take on an objective quality, as though we are presented with them, rather than having a hand in their initial construction and ongoing reinforcement. Which is why we seem constantly to be seeking the great god Pan.

Indeed, from Arthur Machen's "The Great God Pan" to H. P. Lovecraft's "From Beyond" and stories such as Stephen King's "N" and Simon Strantzas's "Thistle's Find," the concept of an order of reality that we can scarcely imagine but that beckons us nonetheless has dominated the horror mode. While we may be convinced (or we convince ourselves) that we should quite properly fear this unseen order, we are still inexorably drawn to it. Things we cannot explain, but whose effects on our lives we cannot deny, have an almost irresistible pull. Which is to say, we seek out the *call* of Cthulhu, the darkness without rather than within, and to which we turn next.

Darkness Without

Sex, Transcendence, and the Monstrous Body

There's low budget, and there's *low* budget. And then there's *Call Girl of Cthulhu.*

Four hundred backers raised nearly thirty thousand dollars on Kickstarter for Chris LaMartina's splatter-horror sex comedy, which fairly epitomizes Ado Kyrou's advice that we "learn to look at 'bad' films."[1] Riffing on such Lovecraft classics as "The Dunwich Horror," "The Haunter of the Dark," "The Horror at Red Hook," and the all-but-eponymous "Call of Cthulhu," this 2014 indie release claims its place in the ever-expanding, if loosely connected narrative multiverse developed by writers, poets, artists, filmmakers, game designers, pornographers, and a host of others who work in the Lovecraftian mode. From the main character's favorite Chinese restaurant, "Dagon-Wok," to "Cool Air" room freshener and a band t-shirt for the "Ulthar Cats," and from "Deep Ones" condoms to a television ad for "Celephais," the film's stand-in for Viagra or Cialis, *Call Girl of Cthulhu* is a nonstop homage to all things Lovecraft.[2] Indeed, as Detective LaGrassi says to the unfortunate Carter Wilcox in the film's opening scene, "Human sacrifices . . . alien gods . . . hookers giving birth to mutant babies. You see, Mr. Wilcox, we have forty-three dead bodies."[3]

What more could you want?

We've encountered the film's basic plot any number of times throughout our storyworld history as *Homo religiosus.* We see it in Greek mythology where, whether as a swan, an eagle, a bull, or a rain of gold, the pansexual Zeus continually proves himself the randiest of the Olympian gods. We see it in Genesis 6, where "the sons of God went in to the daughters of humankind, who bore children to them." And we see it a testament later when an angel tells a young peasant woman not to be afraid, because she has found favor with God and will shortly give birth to the savior of the world—whether she wants to or not. While millions of Christians insist on the uniqueness of this event as the theological guarantee of their salvation, in reality myths, legends, and folktales around the world are ripe with the unusual offspring of divine-human sexual relations. Whether we understand these births as virgin, miraculous, immaculate, or, as in *Call Girl of Cthulhu*, monstrous, whether they are in any way consensual or, instead, the horrific product of celestial rape, and whether ideas of the supernatural originate in the myth itself or develop as the story grows in the telling, the point here is that we find experiences such as these recorded on almost every continent and from the dawn of the historical horizon. We don't know how the "daughters of humankind" felt about the whole thing, and Christians tend to sanitize Mary's response as "much perplexed," but it's not difficult to imagine many of these women reacting the way *Call Girl of Cthulhu's* Riley Whatley does.[4]

"What the fuck did you do to me?" she gasps, as fangs sprout from the side of her face and boils erupt on her skin.[5]

Led by its high priest, Sebastian Suydum, the Church of Starry Wisdom has identified Riley, a young hooker with a heart just a few boxes below gold on the periodic table, as the one destined to bear their eldritch messiah.[6] "The cosmos has summoned you, Riley," Suydum says, as they kidnap her from the strip club where she earns a bit of extra money, "and you must answer the call."[7] Dragged to a crudely constructed ritual space, Riley struggles as Starry Wisdom acolytes in black rubber and gas masks mumble words familiar to every Lovecraft fan: "*Iä! Cthulhu fhtagn! Iä! Cthulhu fhtagn!*"[8] Their chanting intensifies as a crack opens between the worlds, and the Great Dreamer's terrifying tentacular form writhes in to greet his chosen mate.[9] Unlike the poor anonymous nun trapped in *The Convent of Hell*, however, this is no accident, but sexual assault by sacred design.

Awakening in her bed the next morning, Riley finds herself covered in cuts, bruises, and circular welts—the aftermath of her divine rape at the "hands" of Cthulhu. Rather than healing, though, her body begins to undergo horrifying changes. Mutating and transforming, Cthulhu seeks to manifest himself through her flesh. As the "'Sleeper of R'lyeh" gradually awakens and takes control, Riley embarks on a sex murder rampage based on each of her regular clients' particular kink.[10] Feeding her a

Dorito, an obese foodie whispers, "Oh, darlin', I could just eat you up." "Ditto," she responds—and does. A golden shower turns to acid on one trick's face, while a gynecological fetishist's oral fixation ends, well, as we might expect.

Later, as her transformation increases, becoming ever more monstrous, Suydum makes what amounts to the Annunciation. His minions hovering like rubber-clad angels, he exults, "You've been chosen, Riley! These changes that are happening to your body, it's a metamorphosis, an evolution. Consider your former self a caterpillar. Now, you are changing into a beautiful butterfly."[11] Mewling with horror as her humanity sloughs away and her new reality sinks in, she stares at him, wide-eyed. "This is merely a cocoon," the high priest of Starry Wisdom coos. "Cthulhu has chosen you to bear his child. It's a new chapter in your destiny!"[12]

That is, don't worry, be happy.

Whatever it lacks in production value, screenwriting, direction, editing, set design, and acting (with the exception of Melissa O'Brien as the ill-starred Riley Whatley), *Call Girl of Cthulhu* does draw together a number of the conceptual threads we have tugged at to this point in the book. In Cthulhu we see the predatory sexuality of the gods, and the paradox of humankind's powerlessness and instrumentality in the furtherance of the divine agenda. That is, it seems that the gods often cannot act on their own, and still require the devotion of human servants to manage the ceremonial aspects of celestial sexual assault. Since very few things come without cost in our species' religious storyworlds, cosmological rebirth comes here only in the context of venereal sacrifice. In this, Riley's story highlights once again the disturbing fact that the ritual emplacement of our bodies, like religion itself, is always perspectival.

Principia Lovecraftica: Varieties of Lovecraftian Religious Experience

Like horror itself, Lovecraftian fiction has grown into something that is neither a subgenre (a label aficionados despise) nor a genre unto itself (as some others see it). We are not talking about Lovecraft's own writings, though they continue to appear in ever more elaborate editions, but about those who have carried on his tradition of weird fiction, whether in short story form, as graphic novels or role-playing games, or as low-low-budget video. That is, in keeping with Hartwell's notion of horror as an emotional transaction between the author and the reader, Lovecraftian fiction is a mode of creative production, one that encompasses a wide range of styles, topics, themes, representations, mash-ups, and send-ups, all held together by the loosely structured themes of what we might call the *Principia Lovecraftica*.

The Lovecraft Principles.

Many chroniclers and critics of Lovecraftian fiction go to great lengths to explain that writing in this mode does not simply mean name dropping gods from the Cthulhu Mythos, finding this or that narrative waypoint in the Lovecraft gazetteer, or depending on shadowy religious movements like the Church of Starry Wisdom or the Open Door of Night to carry the story. Although it can certainly include these, and some of the best of it does—I'm thinking, for example, of David Hambling's "Question of Blood," Jason Eckhardt's "And the Sea Gave Up the Dead," or Kiernan's "Houses Under the Sea"—but the Lovecraftian mode does not have to be so . . . literally Lovecraft.[13] Rather, as S. T. Joshi insists, since "the Lovecraftian idiom is capable of almost infinite extension and adaptation," its emotional transaction is oriented around a set of binary principles that mark something out as "Lovecraftian."[14] Some of these we find in *Call Girl of Cthulhu*, others we have already seen elsewhere: the terror of alien invasion and bodily transformation; a fascination with forbidden knowledge and archeological secrets; the dread of an unseen order that challenges anything we think we recognize as consensus reality; and, most significantly, the horror of human insignificance in the face of cosmic indifference. Rather than attempt to survey the literally thousands of entries into the Lovecraftian shared storyworld, let us consider a few examples of what we might call "varieties of Lovecraftian religious experience," modal moments that illustrate ways in which the problems of sex, horror, and the religious imagination have been approached.[15]

Alien Invasion and Bodily Transformation

It's easy to get caught up in imagining Cthulhu, wondering what a being like that must look like, must *be* like—as if, with our limited faculties, we could ever really comprehend it. Trouble is, in doing so we tend to forget the equally important first part of Lovecraft's title, that is, "The *Call* of Cthulhu." Which is to say, the irresistible pull of the Great Old One, what Caitlín Kiernan calls in "Black Ships Seen South of Heaven" the "siren song" that went out into a doomed world after "R'lyeh rose, and the one sleeping there awoke."[16] Rudolf Otto might have labeled this "siren song" the dread attraction of the *mysterium tremendum et fascinans*, although his Christianity would have bade him imagine this as a good thing, perhaps because the alternative was simply too awful to contemplate. Not so for those who write in the Lovecraftian mode. Not so for those within Lovecraftian storyworlds who seek, whether for their own reasons or at the behest of powers beyond their comprehension, the destruction of this reality through the advent of another.

In "Black Ships Seen South of Heaven," the return of Earth's primal gods ushers in "the beginning of the End," as Kiernan's narrator, Susannah, tells us, although this is an event "which some will say is simply the Beginning."[17] Because, hidden behind ranks of artillery, rocket launchers, and anti-aircraft batteries, "even within the ragged fortress of Chicago" there are traitors to our species, "zealous priests and necromancers who pray day and night to the Old Things for the fall of all mankind. They have the books. They know the names. They spill blood on secret altars."[18] All in the name of gods that cannot but exist beyond comprehension.

Consider: even if we credence the basics of what the biblical texts relate, even if we stipulate to the least objectionable interpretations of the Jewish and Christian god, let alone the more triumphalist portrayals that have rung from chancels and choir lofts the world over, is it possible to imagine a being more *alien*, one *less like us*, than Yahweh? As theologian Paul Tillich famously, if cryptically, wrote in *Dynamics of Faith*, "God is [a] symbol for God," continuing elsewhere that "the notions implied in the idea of a highest being"—which Tillich considers another placeholder description for "God"—"make it adequate to stand for the ground and abyss of being."[19] Rather than Tillich's equally oft-quoted "ground of being," though, what if we imagine this "God," this "expression of our ultimate concern" as the "abyss of being"? As a cosmic force that has anything but our best interests in mind. Because how would we know? Perhaps this abyss would be the creatures out beyond the Chicago wall, the ones whom Susannah and the other survivors of the Cthulhian holocaust dread. And, bearing in mind the warning with which Lovecraft opens his own story—"The most merciful thing in the world, I think, is the inability of the human mind to correlate all its contents"—how do we even begin to understand the *call* of a being like Cthulhu, even as we acknowledge its effects?[20] Indeed, the nonbeliever Susannah's words are found on the lips of every person ever confronted by alien gods. "'They're not gods,' she said on the Worstday she met the boy when he wouldn't shut up about the monsters. 'They're just shit from other places. That's all they are.'"[21]

That may be, but whatever they are, the power of their call remains undeniable, in this case challenging any pretension we might have to free will, a principal enigma especially in the context of all-powerful, all-knowing creator deities. Because no matter what she thinks now, no matter how hard she fights it, Susannah "knows that in another week or two she'll be one of the alley lurkers, and by next month she'll be staggering out the gate, unable to resist the siren song, dragging what's left of her body towards the forest."[22]

This call, however, is not simply mind control by a being of unimaginable—which is, to us, the functional equivalent of "unlimited"—power. Nor is it the unsophisticated notion of brainwashing so beloved of armchair cult watchers and anticult activists. There is something far subtler at work here, something far more closely aligned with basic structures of our religious imagination. *It makes things make sense.* In this particular telling, the *call* of Cthulhu provides meaning and purpose, substance in a world that is suddenly insubstantial, security as everything we have taken for granted grows more precarious. To reimagine Yeats, it becomes the center that holds when all else falls apart.[23] And, despite her position guarding the eastern wall, the alien voices have already begun to invade Susannah's consciousness. Regardless of her avowed atheism, her certainty that whatever these beings are they are not *gods*, she can feel the changes they herald taking hold. Although the call comes in myriad forms, different for every person, Susannah understands it as one of the signs of "the Eyes and Mouths and Hands of the Black Pharaoh," a messenger of the new gods of this world, "the tall, dark man lingering in the doorway of a burned-out house."[24] At first, the message is subtle, teasing almost, but "more than enough to seduce."[25]

And, once the seduction begins, everything starts to make sense. Consensus reality shifts.

Suddenly, "She is among the hundreds in the city who have answered his call, and that seems a far, far greater purpose than numbering among the paper tigers who go through the motions of watching over the ignorant, the unseeing, the souls just counting off the days until deaths or fates much worse than death."[26] Susannah sees the difference between the saved and the damned from a new perspective, and, for her, those who now exist in hell and those who aspire to heaven have exchanged cosmic places. "Unlike them, her existence has *true* meaning, even if only a shred."[27] And is this not the quintessence of the religious imagination, to imbue our ephemeral being with "*true* meaning, even if only a shred," and even if in the context of the abyss?

When the day finally comes for Susannah, she is left with the only vocabulary she has, the meager lexicon of human imagination. "She finds her place among those who have come before her, a gaping wet vulvic nook in one of the stalks, and she allows that honeyed cleft to receive her. If this is Dante's Wood of the Suicides, William Blake's Forest of Self-Murderers, at least there are no harpies to tear at the bodies of the damned. And there is peace in unity."[28] Even in the end, as the world dies around her and "the stars are winking out, one by one," she finally looks and sees and understands.[29]

Forbidden Knowledge and Archeological Horror

Through much of horror literature runs the notion of the sideways glance, the oblique glimpse that precludes, but just as often warns against anything so direct as the gaze. A ghost caught out of the corner of our eye, a shadow we are not quite sure *didn't* move, a dark space we refuse to investigate, believing that ignorance keeps the illusion of safety intact. Because *looking* is the almost inevitable precursor to *knowing*, and, worse than that, having *what we think we know* ripped apart and cast out on "the black seas of infinity."[30] The sideways glance, on the other hand, glides over the shadows but refuses to probe their depths. It allows us to walk the shoreline without letting the turbid waters at our feet become a Rubicon, the boundary of a thing that, once known, can never be unknown. "I cannot see the world around me the way I once did," laments the unnamed narrator in "Pickman's Other Model (1929)," "for having beheld certain things there can be no return to the unprofaned state of innocence or grace that prevailed before these sights."[31] Only insanity, it seems, "merciful cases of shock and hysterical amnesia," are sufficient to permit the ones who now *know* to "forget the weird revelations visited upon those men and women who choose to ask forbidden questions."[32]

In Stephen King's *Revival*, his nod both to *Frankenstein* and to the Lovecraftian notions of forbidden knowledge and cosmic insignificance, the central characters are concerned with the one mystery that has occupied our religious imagination more than any other: What happens after we die?[33] In *Flatliners*, whether the Joel Schumacher original or Niels Arden Oplev's technologically updated remake, the answer to that question is always, "The only way to find out is to see for ourselves."[34] In the Lovecraftian mode, we've already met two of those who sought forbidden knowledge and paid the price for it: Dr. Thistle, he of the interdimensional brothel, and the ill-fated Vera Endecott. In "Houndwife," Caitlín Kiernan's homage-cum-sequel to Lovecraft's "The Hound," she introduces us to another unnamed narrator, one whose story begins, simply, "Memory fails."[35]

"Houndwife" is told episodically and nonchronologically—sometimes within the context of a single sentence, a device that keeps the reader consistently off-balance—and its key passage reads, "I've returned with absolutely no conscious knowledge of anything I may have experienced in death. Whatever secrets the Starry Wisdom sent me off to discover remain secrets."[36] Despite the fact that she lay in her "grave, fully cognizant but immobile," she was brought up with "no revelation to offer my fellow seekers. They'll ask questions, and I'll have no answers."[37]

While "The Hound" offers us grave robbery driven by a toxic mix of indolence and decadence, "Houndwife" essentially presents an occult telling of *Flatliners*. "Necromancy," and its more intimate cousin, necrophilia, have replaced neurology and pharmacology, while the Lovecraftian "Church of Starry Wisdom" stands in for some unnamed medical school.[38] "Dark figures in robes of half a dozen other shades of red and black and grey" are exchanged for the lab coats and surgical scrubs of an equally arrogant new clergy.[39] A rough stone altar fills in for the hospital gurney, while murmured "blessings and blasphemies," "mantras borrowed from the *Al Azif*," substitute for the unmistakable sounds and terse patois of an operating theater.[40] Surrounded by smells of "frankincense, galbanum, sage, clove, myrrh, and saffron," a "bitter ecru tincture" is offered in place of anaesthetic, defibrillator, adrenaline, and disinfectant.[41] In one telling, medical students scurry about, injecting their potions, attaching their machines, shouting at each other in their particular brand of arcane jargon as they seek to bring back The One Who Has Gone On. In the other, "Isobel Endecott is straddling me, and her right hand goes to my vagina. With her fingers, she scoops out the slimy plug of soil and minute branches of fungal hyphae that has filled my sex during the week and a half that I've spent below."[42]

Forgive, for a moment, that the different settings plumb the gulf between the religious imagination and the scientific method. Remember only that the questions are identical. And the answers they seek are the same. Despite its inevitability, despite the fact that we can do nothing to stop it, merely stave it off for a time, what happens to us after death *matters immensely*, yet constitutes the sine qua non of forbidden knowledge that religious traditions without number claim to understand. Instead of *Gray's Anatomy* and *Clinical Procedures in Emergency Medicine*, the Church of Starry Wisdom has the *Al Azif* (the original Arabic name for the *Necronomicon*) and one of the most popular tools for the excavation of the occult, the Tarot.[43] The Hermit, the Hierophant, the Ace of Pentacles, all the Major and many of the Minor Arcana are here, as is the Wheel of Fortune, the only name by which we eventually know the young woman who is the story's narrator.

Describing this card in his *Necronomicon Tarot*, Donald Tyson writes that through the Wheel of Fortune, "the face of the god shines above a beam of light that rises from the recumbent altar stone of Stonehenge, where a naked youth has been sacrificed with a stone blade."[44] In the night sky directly above the massive lintel, a glowing "vortex forms" as the ritual sacrifice "opens the way between the worlds."[45] In Kiernan's telling, however, the Wheel of Fortune is not a victim, but a volunteer. "'This is our daughter,' barks the High Priestess, the old one crouched near the base of the altar. Her voice is phlegm and stripped gears, discord and tumult. 'Of her own will does she come, and of her own will and the will of the Nameless Gods will she make the passage.'"[46] Indeed, as a ritual prelude to her "corporeal undoing," she is "led to the altar on the dais in the sanctuary of the Church of Starry Wisdom, to be bedded and worshipped and bled dry."[47] In her role as the Empress—the "dark goddess of endless fecundity" whose "dance is the dance of life and death"—"Isobel rises and kisses me," though "it's no more than the palest ghost of all the many kisses we've shared."[48] And, as the ritual proceeds, "burning, I lie down upon the cold, granite altar," as "my lover, the Empress, climbs on top of me—straddling my hips—while the High Priestess snarls her incantations."[49]

Days later, upon her return from the other realms, "on the altar, beneath those smoking braziers, the Empress has begun to clean the mud and filth and maggots from my body. The Priestess mutters caustic sorceries, invoking those nameless gods burdened with innumerable names. The congregation chants. I am delirious, lost in some fever that afflicts the risen, and I wonder if Lazarus knew it, or Osiris, or if it is suffered by Persephone every spring?"[50] Later, Isobel asks the Houndwife, the woman chosen only once every millennium, "How does it end? Do you even know?"[51]

In much of the Lovecraftian mode, forbidden knowledge follows the pattern of William James's four hallmarks of mystical experience: passivity, transiency, noesis, and ineffability.[52] Although she can prepare for the ritual, what happens to the unnamed Wheel of Fortune is out of her control; death overtakes her and she is its passive participant. Since she is expected to venture into the dark and return with knowledge denied all others this side of death, her experience is also transient. And, although it is clear that she comes back with "some depth of truth unplumbed by the discursive intellect," she has no answers for the Church of Starry Wisdom.[53] Ineffability, the last of James's four traits, prevents her. How can she possibly share her story with those who have not seen what she has seen, the ones who still cling to paltry notions of the world-as-it-is?

The Unseen Order and the Challenge to Consensus Reality

Consensus reality hinges not only on our agreement about reality but on our ability to explain challenges to what we agree is "real," thus keeping "consensus" in its proper place. Unlike "Houndwife" or "Black Ships Seen South of Heaven," Nicole Cushing's "Diary of a Sane Man" offers us a way to do this, a way out of the Lovecraftian mode if we want to take it and keep our consensus reality in place.

Stressed about his job and progress through the ranks as a middling academic, worrying over the security of his home and family, Jason goes for an evening walk in the snow to clear his head. *"Maybe this was just what I needed to inspire myself,"* he thinks, ambling through the neighborhood, the cold air "pleasant, like a love nibble."[54] Then, something happens, something so ordinary that, apart from the odd broken hip or sore back, it happens countless times every snowy winter day. "As I turned the corner to another side street," he tells us, "I slipped, wobbled, and—'Whuh!'—landed hard. My face felt sore and cut, but I found no blood in the snow."[55] And, in terms of what happens next, any number of perfectly mundane explanations present themselves, only the most obvious of which is concussion, which can result in minor symptoms such as irritability and confusion, though it can lead to profound personality changes and perceptual shifts. The moon, for example, could become "a single, filmy white eye" or, more than that, Jason could be sure that this "moon-eye" was "spying on me."[56] And when it spoke, it had "a voice like shrill violins. 'Beyond-yond! Beyond-yond!'"[57]

A finalist for the Shirley Jackson Award and a Bram Stoker Award winner, Cushing offers us traumatic brain injury as a way out. Just like 'Becka Paulson, who received her scandalous revelations from a 3-D picture of Jesus courtesy of a .22-calibre bullet. But, if that's the way we want it, we should stop reading the moment Jason tells us, "I let out a whimper and work to get back on my feet."[58] The point of exploring the religious imagination, especially through the horror mode, is that if you think something as simple as head trauma explains what happens next, you should probably get off at this stop. There is nothing for you further down the line, if for no other reason than that it begs the question of how to explain the countless millions of people who have similar experiences, but did not slip and fall and hit their heads. Yet, they are as convinced as Jason that *something* has changed. Something is not as it was. He begins to realize the presence of the *unseen order*, something *more* than what we perceive around us every day, something *other* than ice and snow and slippery steps. Something that feels oddly familiar, yet profoundly strange, what Freud would have called *"das Unheimlich."* Uncanny.[59]

Everything around him begins to feel "ephemeral," tenuous, fugitive, as though the life he had known to that moment—his wife and family, his professorial career, the position as department chair that he so desperately wants—was itself the dream from which he is just now struggling to awaken. It is not too much to say that he is losing his grip on what the rest of us consider consensus reality—but feels much the better for it. Even his "house felt too unstable to dwell in. I felt the need to live in a more durable reality."[60]

As far as Jason is concerned, and whatever the proximate cause, "insanity is the launching pad to one's further evolution to something *better* than human."[61] Descending further into madness or rising through higher levels of reality—it depends on your perspective—he comes to resent more and more the imposition of the mundane and the demands of the flesh, particularly those the flesh of others make on him. For Jason, almost by definition his body is now continually out of place. "To be sane," his newfound guide, "the moon-eye," tells him, "means to have one's mind firmly chained to the mental constructs of the human species."[62] Among other things, this "means suffering the distraction-of-attraction to other members of the species and succumbing to mating impulses, so that the whole thing perpetuates itself, *ad infinitum!*"[63]

As it is on Inishwrack, the commitment to chastity as a way of clearing the path to spiritual advancement is found in many religious traditions. Here, Lovecraft's well-documented aversion to all matters of the body recreates the Aristotelian dualism that for untold millions of Christians forever divorced the elevation of the spirit from the tedium of the flesh— all played out on the icy back streets of Providence. Once again, it would be relatively easy to take Cushing's off-ramp, or shelve poor Jason's experience as her short-story version of a Lovecraftian roman à clef, her way of solving the puzzle of Lovecraft himself. Here, though, not unlike in *The Wicker Man*, we see once again the importance of perspective. Presented in the horror mode, the story contains nothing particularly horrific. We are meant, however, to see Jason's experience as somehow negative. Yet, from the perspective of religiously mandated abstinence, while he might take the "distraction-of-attraction" too far, he is not wrong, or at least as far as he is concerned, he is not on the wrong path.

As Jason continues to live "the diary of a sane man," as he follows the "moon-eye" further and further along that path, he becomes ever more distanced—or disconnected, if you prefer—from consensus reality, from the life he shares with other beings of flesh and blood and need. He comes to loathe the forced vacillation between his new state of being and his old way of life. "The female mate I mistakenly acquired years ago," he tells us, "used her communication device to try and reach me. I wouldn't answer."[64] That is, when his "female mate," Becca, not unreasonably demands an explanation for his increasingly odd behavior, he tells her simply, "I'm through with being human. Through with eating and shitting and sleeping and shoving my ridiculous monkey append-age inside of your ridiculous monkey hole!"[65] Later, as he evolves even further, he "couldn't stop giggling" whenever his wife tries to talk to him. After all, "What are you supposed to do when a human female makes monkey noises at you on the phone?"[66] To whatever Jason feels he has become, it all just seems so insignificant.

Cosmic Indifference and Human Insignificance

For those familiar with new religious movements of the late twentieth century, the Children of God (also known as The Family, and now The Family International) will be remembered, among other things, for their controversial views on sexuality. Reclaiming what founder David Berg considered the rightful place of "proper" religion in society, the Children of God celebrated sexuality rather than repressed it, recognizing the centrality of sex in the social and family structures ordained by God rather than exiling it to the moral margins or excluding it altogether. Among their more provocative innovations were open sexual relationships within local Children of God communal homes, behavior that led to multiple accusations of sexual abuse and assault, especially child sexual abuse.[67] This also meant the practice of "flirty fishing." Attractive young Children of God women (and, occasionally, men) used attention, affection, and the teasing possibility of sex as a way of recruiting potential converts to the group. Indeed, the more-than-a-little misogynistic cover of one of Berg's *True Komix*, part of the vast epistolary record by which he communicated with Children of God groups spread all over the globe, depicts a bare-breasted young mermaid perched on a large fish-hook, arms back, bosom prominent, "come-hither" smile on her face.[68] Drawn by "Philippe la Plume" and clearly based on the work of such fantasy artists as Frank Frazetta, Boris Vallejo, and especially Rowena Morrill—whose work Family leadership have admitted their artists plagiarized—the image could easily be adapted for Sam Gafford's Lovecraftian short story, "Weltschmerz."

Coined by nineteenth-century German romanticist Jean Paul, "*weltschmerz*" translates literally as "world-pain," a kind of lethargic apathy that infects and overwhelms us with a sense of meaninglessness and pessimism. "A mood of weariness or sadness about life," writes philosopher Frederick Beiser, "pessimism is the thesis that life is not worth living, that nothingness is better than being, or that it is worse to be than not to be."[69] Although he concludes that German pessimism "essentially grew out of a rediscovery of the problem of evil," what does it mean for Doug Marsden, Gafford's main character, who begins his tale, "I woke up again today" and "silently cursed the fact that I hadn't died in my sleep"?[70]

A middle-aged office drone who has no real identity beyond this arbitrary set of social labels, Doug leads a life capable of being summed up in a few key phrases. His wife, Ann, whom he has long since stopped loving, he describes as "an amorphous blob."[71] And that morning "was the same as every morning had been for the last twenty years."[72] His work processing dividends for people who will always have more money than he "was tedious and laborious and mind-numbing," though his "cubicle in hell is a clean one."[73] So at least there's that. Even his lunch is the same: "plain turkey on white bread. No lettuce, tomato, or mayo."[74] For Doug, *weltschmerz* is not a function of the problem of evil. A little evil might actually spice up his life, or at least add a fleeting dollop of interest. No, his problem is futility, meaninglessness, the clear and unavoidable sense that *nothing really matters*.

Nothing, that is, until he meets Maya.

All it takes is a wink and a nod from the new girl in the office, whom the air conditioning told Doug "wasn't wearing a bra as two points started to rise up under her shirt."[75] All it takes is the appearance of her interest in him, and the barest hint that her attentions might continue: "Same time tomorrow, Doug?"[76] Suddenly, as if a light switch had flipped, the world doesn't seem so grey, so pointless, and, rather than simply enduring the afternoon's tedium, Doug Marsden finds himself "looking up every time someone came into the room."[77] Suddenly, there

Figure 7.1. Cover art for *True Komix* (No. 93), "The Little Flirty Fishy." Source: XFamily.org.

is something to look forward to, a reason to get up in the morning. Perhaps he even smiles at Ann the next morning as he "gulped down a few bites of something."[78]

Among other things, this brief interchange indicates the transactional and situational relationship we have with concepts like meaning and purpose and value. We may not think of an interoffice romance in this way, but consider what those four words mean: "Same time tomorrow, Doug?" Objectively, Doug's life has not changed, and his "regular routine was no different."[79] Because of Maya, though, whose very name means "illusion," particularly the illusion of the world as a phenomenological reality, "for the first time in years, [he] did not greet the morning with anger."[80] Indeed, the next day, when he tells Maya that he has watched her admittedly amateurish YouTube videos—little more than short clips of her dancing while "screaming and yelling and chanting" strange "words like Ktooloo and Daygon"—the young woman is delighted, and her reaction fills him with elation. Here, Gafford carefully juxtaposes Maya's exuberant Lovecraftian mythos language with Ann's staid commitment to her traditional Christian church. For Doug, though, any notion of *weltschmerz* vanishes, at least momentarily, when Maya "leaned forward and hugged me. Her breasts pushed into my arm and I felt a pleasant warmth growing within me."[81] Which is to say that he *can* feel, he *has* feelings where for twenty years there had been only emptiness.

When she invites him over to her place that weekend—promising him "more fun than mowing the fucking lawn"—propriety initially insists that he hesitate, but he knows that he will go to her in the end.[82] As she leaves the office, his eyes follow her with a hunger he has not known in decades—if ever. "I was watching her ass," he tells us, "and wanted desperately to touch it."[83] Whether, for Doug, this is the issue of sex as human connection, or a human connection that might blossom into sex, is not immediately clear. For Maya, like Summerisle's Willow, it could be not only that those boundaries are unimportant but that they don't exist as boundaries. There is no transgression because there are no limitations to transgress.

In college, before he acquiesced to the life he felt had been laid out for him and that he believed himself ill equipped to refuse, a "professor had asked everyone to think about what their personal philosophy was and how it impacted your life."[84] "After much thought," Doug recounts, "I decided that I had no personal philosophy. I'd never been religious," an admission that also places him in tension with the story's constant references to Ann's church activities.[85] "I was an existentialist," he concluded eventually. "I didn't care about anything. Nothing was important, least of all, me."[86]

Now, for the first time perhaps in his entire life, a girl he dreams about meeting naked in a forest clearing has intimated that there is something real in the world, something worth caring about. A girl on whose "naked back" was "a large tattoo . . . greenish . . . a humanoid figure with tentacles on its face and wings on its back."[87] Waking from his dream, he realizes that Maya exists in complete contrast to his wife, whose "church group got together with other church groups in the state and had meetings and elections and such."[88] That is, through these two women, Gafford sets the meaningless organizational detritus of *religion*, which constitutes nothing more than the ongoing attempt to convince believers that they are doing something important and that, therefore, they matter, against the almost limitless freedom of the *religious imagination*, exemplified for Doug Marsden in a young woman who "was wearing a kind of tank top that pressed her breasts up and together," a girl who "had tattoos on her arms."[89]

Most significant, though, for Doug, is the sex. Finally alone in her apartment, which just happens to be in Lovecraft's old rooming house on "Barnes Street on the east side of Providence," they watch Stuart Gordon's *Dagon* together.[90] Since he is unfamiliar with the Lovecraft canon and the stories on which the 2001 film is loosely based, she explains the mythos to him.[91] Soon, they are having sex in a way that, clearly, he never imagined, and which Gafford describes in sufficient detail to mirror Doug's initial description of *weltschmerz*. Not least, "the piercing in her tongue flicked over the head of my penis," he writes, and "on her back there was the same tattoo from my dream, the green monster with an octopus face and wings. As she moved back and forth, I could swear the wings were flying."[92]

Like Nicole Cushing, however, Sam Gafford also offers us a way out if we want to take it, or at least he presents the potential in a very un-Lovecraftian way. Unwilling simply to let the Cthulhian monstrosity of their relationship—Maya's "flirty fishing" Doug to the cause of the Great

Old One—be what it is, he lets us off the hook, as it were. "Maya held out her hand," Doug tells us, "and, lying in her palm, were two black pills. I'd never seen anything so black. Each one had a large 'N' on it in white."[93] This is the fork in the narrative trail, a riddle on the right, a more sinister enigma on the left. Take one path and, all of a sudden, this is not about the Old Ones and only peripherally about Lovecraft. At most, for Maya, it is about a young woman's sexualized attempts to connect with another human being, while, for Doug, it is probably the best sex he has ever had, and not any more complicated than that.

In this context, though, "N" almost certainly stands for Nyarlathotep, "the Soul and Messenger of the Outer Gods."[94] Although this entity or force goes by various names in the Cthulhu Mythos, whoever and whatever Nyarlathotep is operates principally as "an intermediary between the Great Old Ones and the worshipers."[95] Ritual experience, mystical revelation, and drugs ranging from ayahuasca to peyote, and from mescaline to DMT have been connected to revelation and the religious imagination for as long as we have records.[96] Performing precisely this mediating function, by disconnecting the discursive mind, they force open, as Aldous Huxley said, "the doors of perception."[97] In the Lovecraftian mode, however, we not infrequently wish we could slam those doors shut again, and forget whatever we saw behind them. Because in Maya's small apartment, it's not difficult to grasp what happens next.

After a round of drug-fueled sex during which he imagines a bifurcated consciousness between himself and the Old Ones, when Doug "awoke, Maya was in pieces on the floor. A blood-stained butcher's knife was in my hand. I looked at her and felt only envy."[98] We are back to the anger and bitterness—the meaninglessness—he feels each morning. With the black pill, however, goes any necessary narrative connection to the supernatural or the metaphysical, any real connection to the Mythos beyond Maya's clearly misguided devotion to it. Bleeding out, she leaves behind only her hallucinogenic obsession with a long-dead writer of weird tales, and a lonely man's resurgent conviction that *weltschmerz* is the only reality. Even the primeval beings she believed lay at the heart of Lovecraft's work Gafford leaves nonexistent. "The 'gods' and 'monsters,'" Doug tells us, were little more than "something for the earth-centric minded ones to latch on to."[99] For him, the logical extension to the proposition that *nothing matters* is that *nobody matters*, and from this it follows that "laws, rules, and morality were mere trappings man clothed himself in while he tried desperately to convince himself that he mattered at all."[100] Which is to say, the answer to the most persistent of those properly human questions—*Do we matter?*—is not "No," but nothing. An eternal, haunting silence, not because no one is speaking but because there is nothing there to speak.

Why Lovecraft, or Why Lovecraft *Still*?

"Why Lovecraft?" is a simple but hardly unimportant question in the context of sex, horror, and the religious imagination. After all, Lovecraft died young, in 1937 at the age of forty-six from stomach cancer. While something of a celebrity within the pulp horror and weird fiction community, with whose members he carried on a voluminous correspondence, during his lifetime he was only marginally popular beyond that, and departed this plane nearly penniless.[101] He may have named the Great Old Ones who populate his stories, the primal gods who wait with terrible patience in the outer darkness, but he did not gather them together into anything like a coherent pantheon. That was left to others, such as August Derleth, a fellow writer of weird fiction and the anthologist who first promoted stand-alone editions of Lovecraft's works.[102] Lovecraft himself was an unrepentant materialist who, as a child, had self-published nearly seventy issues of an astronomy newsletter, yet whose fiction wove visions of a horrifying supernatural order, a cosmic reality in which humankind is entirely inconsequential. He was also notoriously asexual, if not antisexual, a man who seemed profoundly uncomfortable in his own skin, and much of his work—as well as of those who work in the Lovecraftian mode—turns on the problem of bodies out of place.

In correspondence with Reinhart Kleiner, a member of the Kalem Club, Lovecraft's literary circle during his brief sojourn in New York City, Lovecraft wrote that "eroticism belongs to a lower order of instincts, and is an animal rather than a nobly human quality."[103] While he eventually came to recognize—if not necessarily appreciate—the libido's power in human affairs, such that "its overthrow by higher interests [is] impossible," he maintained his basic positions, including "the acknowledged repulsiveness of direct erotic manifestations"; "the obvious kinship of erotic instincts to the crudest and earliest neural phenomena of organic nature"; "the apparent connexion betwixt erotic interest and national decadence"; and, for good measure, the fact that, as far as he "could judge erotic interests are overrated, being in truth mere trifles which engross crude minds."[104] He even called the queen of pulp cover art onto the carpet. Although he insisted that he was not put off "by mere nudity in artwork," as long as it served some higher artistic purpose, "I don't see what the hell Mrs. Brundage's undressed ladies have to do with weird fiction."[105] More than that, he complained in a letter to August Derleth, "You'll recall that [Weird Tales illustrator Hugh] Rankin made ample-bosomed wenches of my *male* orgiasts in the Louisiana swamp scene of 'Cthulhu'!"[106]

On the one hand, nearly three generations after his death, it is difficult to overstate the influence of Lovecraft and his work, either on those who have become staples of the modern horror genre (e.g., Stephen King) or on those who toil in relative obscurity, yet still produce endless reams of Lovecraftiana. Numerous films and television adaptations tell versions of his stories, contribute to the evolution of the Cthulhu Mythos, or use aspects of philosophy embedded in his fiction to color the spaces of their own transmedial storyworlds.[107] Since fellow writer Clark Ashton Smith first wrote a short story using elements of Lovecraft's nascent cosmology—1931's "Return of the Sorcerer" in the inaugural issue of *Strange Tales*—a continuous stream of short fiction, novels, and anthologies have contributed to the flow of Lovecraft's influence.[108] Some have concentrated on the problem of insanity and the tipping point between what we imagine is real and what we learn is reality, while others have focused more directly on Lovecraft's monstrous pantheon.[109] Still others spend their time exploring the geographic locales special both to Lovecraft and to his work: from Innswich to Dunwich, from gloomy Arkham and fabled Miskatonic University to his beloved Providence, Rhode Island.[110] At least one best-selling author wonders how Sherlock Holmes would solve the mysteries of a Lovecraftian world.[111]

Scholars and critics have examined Lovecraft's work from perspectives ranging from object-oriented ontology and speculative realism to continental philosophy and critical theory, from his trenchant atheism to his influence on everything from modern occultism to pop-culture extraterrestrials.[112] In *Sex and the Cthulhu Mythos*, weird fiction scholar

Bobby Derie offers the most comprehensive exploration of the titular topic available, not only discussing Lovecraft's own problematic relationship with the sexual but cataloguing entries into the Lovecraftian canon ranging from *Cthulhu Sex Magazine* to such collections of Cthulhian erotica as *Eldritch Blue, Cthulhurotica,* and *Whispers in Darkness.*[113] And, finally, despite Lovecraft's clear and unambiguous dismissal of the mystical, the magical, and the supernatural, others remain convinced that he was, well, onto something.

Forty years after Lovecraft died, the first (though hardly the only) volume claiming to be the authentic *Necronomicon* appeared, an actual version of the dread grimoire that lies at the heart of humankind's efforts to engage the Old Ones. Followed nearly a generation later by corresponding ritual texts, books such as these give otherworldly life to the belief that Lovecraft was, indeed, in touch with ancient truths and primeval forces.[114] I say the "first volume" because, beginning in 2004, Canadian writer and occultist Donald Tyson—who also pens rather good Lovecraftian fiction—made good on his claim that "the public wants the Necronomicon to exist, indeed, it demands that it exist."[115] Although he acknowledges in his foreword to *The Necronomicon Files* that "it seems almost a crime to debunk the living and growing myth of the *Necronomicon*," he recognizes that "it is arguably a greater crime to sell books claiming that they are the genuine *Necronomicon* when no such text ever existed."[116]

Remember that last phrase and fast-forward five years.

Working with popular New Age and modern Pagan publisher Llewellyn, Tyson released his own version of the *Necronomicon*, which begins, "You who would learn the wisdom of hidden things and traverse the avenues of shadows beneath the stars, heed this song of pain."[117] He followed this a year later with a massive fictional biography of the "mad Arab" Alhazred, the putative eighth-century Yemeni mystic who first wrote down the terrible "Book of Names of the Dead."[118] Within a few years, Tyson added the *Grimoire of the Necronomicon*, a handbook of ritual magic and the initial organizational structure for a magical order devoted to the Cthulhian pantheon.[119] Leveraging the enormous popularity of all things Tarot, he released a nicely illustrated *Necronomicon Tarot*, as well as its almost de rigueur companion volume, *Secrets of the Necronomicon*.[120] As I have written elsewhere, and per Jean Baudrillard, material culture such as this is "the excerpted reflection of a larger, more totalizing conceptual order. In this sense, every object functions as a metonym for the system of object-ideas within which it is located and to which it contributes"—in this case, the Lovecraftian narrative universe.[121]

Finally, in 2013, Tyson published his own biography of Lovecraft, which explicitly reimagined much of the writer's well-documented skepticism of mysticism, religion, and the occult. Indeed, writing to August Derleth in 1932, Lovecraft declared that "the fact that nearly all claimants to supernatural powers and prophetic endowments are seedy, illiterate, and rather disreputable offshoots of a semi-underworld, is in sober fact a perfectly effective answer to all their claims."[122] Nonetheless, Tyson argues that Lovecraft's active and often disturbing dream life contributed far more to the Cthulhu Mythos than other biographers allow and reveals more about the reality of the shadow world his stories describe.[123] Rather, Tyson casts Lovecraft as a prophet in the manner of Edgar Cayce. "I have come to believe," he confesses in the *Grimoire of the Necronomicon*, that Lovecraft "was a sleeping seer who drew forth from his dreams archetypal realities that lie on the verge of human consciousness, and which have found expression in various veiled forms in our religious myths."[124]

Tyson's Lovecraftian spirituality is an excellent example of what sociologist Adam Possamai calls "hyper-real religion," "a simulacrum of religion, created out of, or in symbiosis with, popular culture, which provides inspiration for believers/consumers."[125] And Tyson's efforts, nothing in which gives anything other than the impression that he expects to be taken seriously, haunt the liminal spaces between fiction and belief, the narrative embodiment of Stephen King's claim that "the only two useful artforms are religion and stories."[126]

On the other hand, working in the Lovecraftian mode is not without its complications. For decades, the World Fantasy Convention awards were memorialized by a small bust of Lovecraft designed by cartoonist of the macabre Gahan Wilson. "I am conflicted," however, writes Nnedi Okorafor of her 2011 World Fantasy Award for Best Novel (for *Who Fears Death*). The award itself, "a statuette of this racist man's head is in my home," she continues, and "a statuette of this racist man's head is one of my greatest honors as a writer."[127] Another WFA honoree, China

Miéville, whose *The City & the City* won for best novel the year before, told her that he dealt with the issue this way: "The statuette of the man himself? I put it out of sight, in my study, where only I can see it, and I have turned it to face the wall. So I'm punishing the little fucker like the malevolent clown he was."[128]

While others pushed back on Okorafor and her colleagues, some shared similar stories, and a few just tried to calm the waters. "All I can say, I guess," commented fellow writer Nick Mamatas, trying to find the silver lining, "is that the greatest Lovecraftian writers today are a transgender woman and a cross-dressing gay punk rocker (Caitlín Kiernan and Wilum Hopfrog Pugmire), his biographer and main editor is a literary critic born in India (S. T. Joshi) and the director most likely to finally make a major Hollywood film of Lovecraft's work is Mexican ([Guillermo] del Toro). So . . . ," Mamatas concludes, "we won."[129] And, indeed, by 2017 the Lovecraft statuette was retired in favor of a new award, a leafless tree in front of an enormous full moon, created by sculptor Vincent Villafranca.

Not everyone was happy with the change, though. Editor and critic S. T. Joshi, who has done more to promote the cause of weird fiction than anyone else, and has himself been twice honored with the World Fantasy Award for his contributions to the field, was dismayed by the decision, to say the least. Calling the change "a craven yielding to the worst sort of political correctness" that was meant to do nothing more than "placate the shrill whining of a handful of social justice warriors," he returned his own two awards in protest.[130] Telling World Fantasy Convention cochair David Hartwell that not only would he boycott the convention himself but he would try to convince as many others as possible to do the same, Joshi concludes that "if anyone feels that Lovecraft's perennially ascending celebrity, reputation, and influence will suffer the slightest diminution as a result of this silly kerfuffle, they are very much mistaken."[131] And he's not wrong.

None of which solves the problem, really, nor addresses why Lovecraft remains so inescapably popular, especially in an age when an inadvertent tweet, an unguarded moment, an off-color comment caught on a hot mike can (and does) cost (some) people their jobs. How do those who write in the "mode" or the Lovecraftian context deal with the more unsavory aspects of his character, including what Miéville calls "the depth and viciousness of Lovecraft's racism," his deeply seated "race hatred"?[132] Rick Dakan's "Correlated Discontents" is one of the few Lovecraftian stories that confronts "the dead author's century-old nastiness" directly.[133] It also resonates with another icon of twentieth-century speculative fiction, Philip K. Dick, and an animatronic head that was reputed to be able to answer questions as though it was Dick himself.[134] Indeed, Dakan's story meets the most trenchant criticism of Lovecraft head on, as it were.

The speculative question is simple: If you upload everything an author wrote, including notes, letters, and ephemera, backstop it with biographies, commentaries, and editorial marginalia, can you create a reasonable simulacrum of the person? It's a bit like H. P. Lovecraft meets the Turing Test meets Philip K. Dick, all by way of uploaded transhumanism. Through the "Revenant Project"—"revenant" being the word for a haunting spirit, and rarely used in anything other than a horrific sense—the program operator, who is little more than a technologically facilitated medium, has an "ability to synthesize everything Mr. Lovecraft ever wrote [that] far exceeds the ability of even the most diligent literary scholar. The program, with its perfect recall, has all the facts at hand in a way no one has since the living subject died in 1937."[135] Once again, what could possibly go wrong?

As the boundaries between operator and author inevitably blur, the computerized Lovecraft-revenant gradually takes over, while the medium begins not only to quote from Lovecraft but to extrapolate what he might have said in any given situation. How he might have answered questions. "Are you alive?" asks one audience member at a Revenant Project performance. "My body died in 1937," the medium/revenant responds, "but wandering energy always has a detectable form."[136] Another audience member, a "plump woman [who] was dressed in a three-piece suit that put me in mind of a Victorian Egyptologist," names the elephant in the room: "Many people have called you a racist . . . would you agree?"[137] From the choices offered by the Revenant Program, the operator "picked the slightly more circumspect answer," and "Lovecraft" responds.[138] "Race prejudice is a gift of nature, intended to preserve in purity the various divisions of mankind which the ages have evolved," he replies. "The problem of race and culture is by no means as

simple as is assumed either by the Nazis or by the rabble-catering equali-
tarian columnists of the Jew-York papers."[139]

Not surprisingly, "The room went silent."

Put differently, perhaps Lovecraft were to somehow show up at a
World Fantasy Convention. What would he say, and what would be
said? "Someone else followed up with a query about miscegenation,"
continues Jannowitz, the young man who proposed Lovecraft for the
Revenant Project in the first place and who acts as his operator/me-
dium, "followed closely by another about the people living in New York.
Every answer [Lovecraft gave] appalled me, but they came fast and natural. . . . The more they failed to trip me up, the more racist things they
got Lovecraft to say, the more enthusiastic they became."[140] Which is to
say, Dakan proposes, how far off the mark was Lovecraft in his disdain
for people precisely because of their demonstrated penchant for philis-
tine behavior?

Reviews of the Revenant Project performance were mixed, to say the
least. "Of course plenty of people with no affection for Lovecraft railed
against his racism and against us for parroting it back to modern ears.
Among the fans it was more divided, with some holding forth that it was
bad for other Mythos and Lovecraft writers to have such associations,
while others pointed to much worse things said by much more famous
authors."[141] Indeed, it is not difficult to read this as a fictionalized version of Nnedi Okorafor's blog post on Lovecraft's racism, seeing here
the factions represented by, among others, Miéville, Joshi, and Okorafor
herself. Jannowitz tries to defend the project, but winds up inadvertently
defending Lovecraft himself when he writes on a message board, "You
were fine with Lovecraft's racism before you heard him say it live."[142]
While this does not go a long way toward calming the mood, Jannowitz explains that he "just meant that the racist thing shouldn't surprise
anyone."[143] Instead, though, "They thought I was saying they were all
racists."[144]

Later, in an online chatroom, the Revenant Program takes more and
more control of the conversation, placing before the reader a number
of Lovecraft's less popular views, implicitly indicting them along with
the chatroom participants. "It is the frank and cynical recognition of
the inevitable limitations of people in general," continues the Lovecraft

simulacrum, "which makes me absolutely indifferent instead of actively hostile toward mankind. Of course, so far as personal taste goes, I'm no lover of humanity."[145]

If one of the central themes of the Lovecraftian mode is alien invasion, then "Correlated Discontents" turns this on its head—or at least inside out—since the Lovecraft revenant is the invader, eventually taking complete control of Jannowitz, for whom it appears to have no more concern than the Old Ones have for any of us. "Nothing really matters," the simulacrum says near the end of the story, becoming in effect the personification of cosmic indifference, "and the only thing for a person to do is take the artificial and traditional values he finds around him and pretend they are real."[146] Reading like the externalization, objectivation, and internalization arc described by Peter Berger and Thomas Luckmann, the means by which we create cultures that appear to us as self-existent, it actually comes from one of Lovecraft's letters.[147] We do all of this for one reason: "to retain that illusion of significance in life which gives to human events their apparent motivation and semblance of interest."[148] Few comments cut closer to the bone of the religious imagination. Which is to say, how do we make meaning in the face of cosmic indifference?

Despite what devoted fans of pulp horror, tabletop roleplayers enchanted by the growing array of games based explicitly in the Lovecraftian world, or casual observers of the horror scene might think, what stories such as these suggest, and Joshi insists, is that "Lovecraft was an intensely serious writer who, as his letters and essays suggest, continually grappled with the central questions of philosophy and sought to suggest answers to them by means of horror fiction."[149] While we can hardly be expected to agree with everything he says, like M. R. James's classic essays on the ghost story, Lovecraft's *Supernatural Horror in Literature* remains required reading for any serious horror fan.[150] Revere him as the master of weird fiction or dismiss the "little fucker like the malevolent clown he was," grapple directly with his racism and incipient misanthropy or reject both as easily as sticking his bust in the bathroom, he is not going away anytime soon, and neither are those who pursue him down the dark rabbit holes of the imagination. Throughout his work, Lovecraft continually sought to explore the properly human questions that have animated our species both as *Homo narrans* and as *Homo religiosus*. And, although many of his protagonists survive the horrors of their experience to tell their stories, Lovecraft's answers often make us distinctly uncomfortable. Is there a god? Perhaps, but not like any you know, or would ever want to meet. Why do we suffer? Sometimes to no purpose at all; other times as the bride-price of another's enlightenment. Do we matter? Put bluntly, not in the least.

As New Testament scholar and Lovecraft expert Robert Price notes, "One big reason Lovecraft's fiction is so hypnotically effective for many of us is that we see ourselves reflected in the mirror it holds before us."[151] And isn't that what all good stories do? Price explicitly criticizes those who "assume, as Paul Tillich did, that a religion must centre about, and must symbolize, one's ultimate concerns, and that these concerns must be appropriately ultimate in scope, dealing with issues of timely relevance and eternal significance. This is a sad and Puritanical definition of religiosity. It gets the focus wrong and neglects the role of the imagination in religion, i.e., myth."[152] Which is to say, story. As numerous commentators and critics have noted, however uncomfortable Lovecraft may have been in personal relationships, he assiduously supported the literary pursuits of any number of writers, both established and aspiring. That is his continuing legacy, and those who write in the Lovecraftian mode, whether "in the spirit of homage, debate, critique, memorial, or philosophical inquiry," continue the quest.[153]

Rarely, either in the Lovecraftian mode or in Lovecraft's work itself, do things turn out alright in the end. In fact, the nature of his questioning is underpinned by "a sensibility that keenly etches humankind's transience and fragility in a boundless universe that lacks a guiding principle or direction."[154] Indeed, at the dark heart of the mode is Lovecraft's own "fundamental premise," detailed in a 1927 letter to *Weird Tales* editor Farnsworth Wright, "that common human laws and interests and emotions have no validity or significance in the vast cosmos-at-large."[155] Our most abiding fear is that we do not matter, and those who write in the Lovecraftian mode seek to work out the implications of what that means. Contrary to the pleasant fiction of Psalm 8, and *pace* Einstein's famous wonderings about the friendliness of the universe, for Lovecraft's artistic descendants not only is the universe not a friendly place; it is often so radically different from our comprehension that concepts such as "friendly" and "unfriendly" lose any meaning they might have had. In those stories where they appear to do so, there is always the fear that still lurks, the warning never to visit this place or that again, the seemingly endless night that stretches before the survivors every time the sun goes down. Even in a story such as "The Dunwich Horror," in which, unlike "Black Ships Seen South of Heaven," the immediate threat of apocalypse appears to have been averted, the Old Ones still wait with dread patience; the *Necronomicon* by which they are called still exists. We are secure for the moment, but we are never, ever safe.

8

Going Monstering

The End of the Beginning

Ask "Who, or what, is God?" and we answer inevitably with a story.

God is a god of love, we say confidently, who brought about an extinction-level event because he wasn't happy with the behavior of a relative few of his creations. We tend to remember the ending of this one, the olive branch and the dove, gestures of alleged mercy offered from above, but we do so thankful that the terrified screams of the dying are silenced beneath the waves. God is a god of love, we tell each other, who stopped a man from gutting his only son just to prove how much he loved this god. Well, that's one way of telling it, anyway. What would have happened, though, if Abraham had been so intent on the sacrifice that he didn't notice the conveniently placed ram in the thicket? God is a god of love, we remind the next generation, who commanded the wholesale slaughter of men, women, and children because, as one particularly unctuous explanation insists, "it was the best of the bad options available in the time and with the people he had. The total war against the Canaanites minimized their pain by ending it quickly."[1]

Perhaps God is a monster, and the religious imagination a millennia-long exercise in going monstering.

"So, how are we supposed to worship God?" is another question, one that comes packed with a laundry list of assumptions, at least as Don Webb proposes it in his short story, "The Megalith Plague." Central to these is the question behind nearly every shift in the divine/human relationship, and the metric by which proper allegiance is determined: *Did we get it right this time?* In Flapjack, Texas, it turns out, a local farmer named Fenster was sinking "a well where an old church was and he found a little metal box. Inside was a small book called *How to Worship God Correctly*. Seems like we've been doing it all wrong for years."[2] Richard Scott, the storyteller, is a short man with "gray beetle brows," "bloodshot slate blue eyes," "who smelled of welding."[3] Despite being a walking pharmacopeia of "anti-psychotics, anti-convulsants, mood stabilizers, anti-depressants, typical and atypical neurolyptics," Scott also freely admits that he is "crazy, bugfuck crazy," but the meds keep him from hearing divine voices at all hours of the day and night.[4] According to Scott, though, it appears that our Neolithic ancestors had it right all along and the answer to the question, "So, how are we supposed to worship God?" was with "megalithic stone circles. Mankind apparently hit the mark with Stonehenge," he tells his new doctor. "That's what God wants."[5]

"I'll bet that went over big with the Baptists," says Dr. Huff, rapidly calculating which combination of meds led Scott down that particular yellow brick road. Well, "you'd think not," the little man replied, "but everyone seemed pretty positive about it."[6] In fact, shortly after "the *Flapjack Recipe* ran the complete text of *How to Worship God Correctly,*" stone circles began to appear in small towns all up and down I-35 between Austin and Dallas. "In my opinion, it caught on."[7] "For the love of God," Huff explodes, "are they all crazy?"[8] Well, Scott replies laconically, "weeks before this they were all worshipping a dead carpenter. I think the movement toward sculpture is healthy."[9]

What Scott does not tell his doctor, at least not until it is far too late, is that he "made the little box for Fenster to find" and, more than that, he cooked up *How to Worship God Correctly* himself, combining elements from "an old Baptist hymnal with the *Typhonian Tablets* with simple diagrams showing all the angles" for what turned into the megalith plague in southern Texas.[10] In fact, stone circles multiplied at an alarming rate around Flapjack, consuming so much of the town's psychic and emotional energy—not to say mental stability—that Huff seeks only to escape.

Alas.

"They dragged me to the center of town," he tells us, bare minutes before becoming this story's Neil Howie, and brought him "to the middle of the largest circle, where Scott was their king. He wore a crown made of stainless steel knives and forks that he had welded together in a strange fashion"—apparently some stories, stories about "a dead carpenter," are not so easily replaced after all.[11] "Do you know what your problem is,

Dr. Huff?" Scott asks, as though addressing "the dull pupil who couldn't quite do the lesson," "You don't ask the right questions."[12] *Who, or what is "God"? How are we supposed to worship "God"?* "I had a Question," he continues. "All great Quests start with a Question"—which is far more important than an answer, something even someone as "bugfuck crazy" as Richard Scott knows.[13]

The short-lived journal *Zetetic Scholar*, which was a labor of love for sociologist Marcello Truzzi (d. 2003), was interested in mediating the "sociology and psychology of disputes" between "proponents and critics of claims of the paranormal."[14] That is, Truzzi set out from the very first paragraph to do something that more overtly critical magazines and journals tend to avoid: understand the persuasive power of paranormal and/or supernatural beliefs, and even the need to understand why people believe at all. Which is to say, to begin with questions, rather than answers. "We will seek," Truzzi continued, "to balance proper skepticism towards extraordinary claims with the need for objectivity and fairness," identifying the two qualities so often lacking in the skeptical community in its gleeful rush to point out gullibility and the intellectual failings of others.[15] And this, despite the fact that such criticism is often based on believers' own presumed lack of objectivity and fairness. Truzzi, however, sought a better way of talking about what he called the "integrated anomalies."[16] What I call the ambivalent, ambiguous storyworld spaces where we engage the questions that matter to us most. Grounding his approach, Truzzi quotes the founder of pragmatism, philosopher Charles Pierce, and his "first rule of reason": "In order to learn you must desire to learn, and in so desiring not be satisfied with what you already incline to think." Or, more succinctly, "Do not block the way of inquiry."[17]

In terms of the monstrous cartography of sex, horror, and the religious imagination, this particular quest is drawing to a close, but the inquiry continues. Rather than a conclusion, though, I propose that this is the end of the beginning, and, from among the myriad paths we could take, I would like to focus for a moment on three of the many potential avenues deserving of further exploration: splatter-horror and the grotesque; the queering of horror; and, finally, the vast, bleak expanse of the Sadeian imagination.

Splatter-Horror: The Gospel According to Edward Lee

It is doubtful that anyone will be tempted to do for Edward Lee (b. 1957) what writers such as John McDowell, Connie Neal, and Ralph Wood have done for George Lucas, J. K. Rowling, and J. R. R. Tolkien, respectively.[18] That is, the likelihood approaches zero that a book entitled "The Gospel According to Edward Lee" will ever see print, or even that his brand of splatter-horror could be made theologically palatable to the Christian faithful, however explicitly many of his storyworlds are located at the margins of Christian belief and engage the questions that have animated that belief for two millennia.

Author of nearly fifty novels, some in mass-market edition, others through small independent horror houses such as Deadite Press and Necro Publications, Lee specializes in occult-inspired gore, religiously inflected pornography, and a prose style that one critic describes as "fast and mean as a chain saw revved up to full-tilt boogie." In *Witch Water*, scopophile Stewart Fanshawe has come to a New Hampshire village to escape his voyeuristic temptations and recover a socially appropriate sexual equilibrium. What he finds there, however, is the horror-mode quintessence of the witches' orgy. Watching through a telescope one night, for instance, he spies "a moon-lit crush of naked bodies, churning, squirming, and writhing," members of the local coven "exploring every sexual position conceivable—and some not conceivable—as a taller almost block-like figure looked on from between two trees."[19] In *Succubi*, Lee takes on the famous "witch-cult" hypothesis proposed by anthropologist Margaret Murray: that the medieval witch hunts were specifically intended to expose and exterminate a pagan tradition that survived the forced Christianization of the British Isles.[20] In Lee's case, though, before the witches, before the Druids, there were the Ur-locs, a cannibalistic matriarchy that traces its origins back to the Ardat-lil, the ur-succubus, Lilith. And, in *Trolley No. 1852*, part of Lee's triptych homage to H. P. Lovecraft, descendants of a mythological Egyptian witch-priestess operate a clandestine brothel for the sole purpose of harvesting semen for the pleasure of their mistress. She, in turn, is beholden to a race of ageless beings, "more than *creatures*" and "so much more than *gods*," who subsist on "the blatant molestations and torture of the human race." For these "Pyramidiles," our sexual and "psychic horror" is literally the food of the gods.[21]

While each of his niche horror writings, whether Lovecraftian, southern gothic horror, or grotesque erotica, has its fan base, Lee is best known beyond these for his four-volume *City Infernal* series. "It stretches, literally, without end," he writes in *Infernal Angel*, "a labyrinth of smoke and waking nightmare. Just as endlessly, sewer grates belch flame from the sulphur fires that have raged beneath the streets for millennia. Clock towers spire in every district, by public law, but their faces have no hands; time is not measured here in seconds or hours but in atrocity and despair."[22] That said, though, Mephistopolis is a lot like any other big city. Although "screams rip down streets and through alleys," still "the people of this place trudge the sidewalks back and forth, to home, to work, to stores, etc., just as they do in any city. There's only one dissimilarity. In this city, the people are all dead."[23]

Lee takes extraordinary delight in imagining the gory excesses and religious inversions of the vast city that Hell became. In a city literally powered by terror, "suffering serves as convertible energy," while "barges manned by Golems float atop the brown, lump-ridden surface of a river called Styx, pumping raw sewage into the city's domestic reservoirs."[24] It has all the landmarks associated with any great metropolis, though these Lee obviously delights in presenting as a kind of "who's who" of historical allusion and cultural critique. "De Rais University extended over countless acres and appeared almost campus-like in its layout. Here, the finest Warlocks in the land taught their pupils in the blackest arts."[25] "The Rockefeller Mint provided the city with all its currency," while "Osiris Heights stood proud and posh," its luxury apartments equipped with "the latest conveniences: harlot cages, skull-presses, iron-maidens, and neat personal-sized crematoriums."[26] "Boniface Square," named for the notorious tenth-century antipope, "encompassed whole city blocks in its leisure services," and "all manner of abyssal entertainment." As far as law enforcement goes, "the J. Edgar Hoover Building existed in the Living World as it did in Lucifer's."[27] The sick are treated at "Tojo Memorial Hospital," while scholars can browse the stacks at "the John Dee Library and Infernal Archives," and the more spiritually minded find inspiration at "St. Iscariot Abbey."[28]

For all this, however, "the city of Hell" presents a fairly conventional religious worldview, the fiendish delights and unending torments reflecting little more than the nightmares of conservative Christians everywhere—not least of which is the fact that the vast majority of punishments are either meted out for common sexual offenses or executed by gruesome sexual means.

In *Teratologist*, on the other hand, written with fellow splatter-horror author Wrath James White, an eccentric billionaire is consumed with the search for God. But, rather than prayer or meditation, Farrington wants to force God's hand through the most appalling sex acts imaginable—all perpetrated against those who have explicitly committed their lives to God. "Show yourself!" he screams as he sexually abuses a captive Roman Catholic nun in the most brutal fashion imaginable. "Show yourself to me! How many of your slaves do I have to humiliate before you will face me?"[29] A man obsessed with understanding the divine, Farrington's theological calculus is simple: if acts as vile and heinous as these do not provoke the Creator to anger, do not demand some form of divine intervention, then whether he exists or not becomes, essentially, immaterial.

There is, however, another option.

"The entity materializing before him could not have been God," Farrington's mind tells him feverishly, surely not something "so profane and hideous. The monstrous thing was a chaos of limbs and mouths, genitals of every sex and species, and suppurating orifices with purposes that seemed beyond appetite and reproduction."[30] "Delirious with fear," Farrington gibbers, "but I didn't call you. I called for GOD!" "GOD?" the entity responds. "BUT I AM GOD. I AM THE GOD OF MAN . . . ALL THAT MAN HAS WROUGHT HAS BEEN WITH MY INSPIRATION."[31]

Teratologist epitomizes the concept of bodies out of place, one Amazon review proclaiming it "a total debauchery towards any and everything religious and holy. You will feel uncomfortable in your own dirty skin," while, on the other hand, another suggests that it does "contain a significant message about the redeeming qualities of God." Although not disputing the novel's grotesque character, this reviewer concludes that it "isn't a horror story per se, but rather an extreme form of social critique regarding the despicable conditions of our world and how most of us have fallen away from the one thing that could save us." That is,

Lee and White have produced a theological meditation on theism and antitheism set in the midst of a narrative Grand Guignol.

The Next Exorcism: Queer Horror and the Religious Imagination

Consider next a very different kind of exorcism than the one with which we began this book. Consider "Tamara's Last Exorcism."

In this Wrath James White short story, a young woman raised in a conservative religious home attributes her homosexuality to demonic possession, and undergoes sex reassignment surgery as her "last exorcism," a final attempt to keep her body in place—neither of which are unreasonable propositions, given the virulent antipathy many religious communities feel toward homosexuality in any form.

From her earliest sexual awakenings, before she even knew what those strange, discomfiting urges were, Tamara "could feel the demon inside of her like a parasite wriggling around in her skull."[32] Now, that demon "wanted the woman in the tight red pants," and "Tamara could feel the demon's lust radiating up from within her."[33] Time and again, "*it* had taken physical control over her," and "*its* twisted imagination" sought to satisfy "*its* perverse desires."[34] "Flesh was what the evil wanted," she knew. "The flesh of the beautiful, the flesh of woman, and it would use her to get it."[35] Now, as she had so many times over the years, Tamara struggles to keep the demon at bay, to renounce its hold on her body, to keep her proper place in the order of things. She does all the things she has been taught. She "tried reciting bible verses in her head. She whispered the Lord's Prayer but the demon's voice drowned it out with laughter and perverse obscenities."[36]

It doesn't matter. The result is always the same. Hours later, "ashamed at what she had done," Tamara flees the scene of her apostasy, the "taste of the woman's flesh" and "her musky sweet scent" still strong in her mouth and on her skin. Even worse, though, she knows, is that "the demon had claimed another victim, another soul for the inferno, and it had been Tamara's fault."[37] She begs the Lord for deliverance, but heaven is silent. *Deus absconditus.* God is not there. It's all up to her. She must "release the abomination from her flesh."[38]

Not that she hadn't tried before. "Her teenage years had been a seemingly endless parade of wrinkled old Jesuits tying her to her bed and dousing her with holy water, hurling bible verses at her and painting crucifixes on her forehead. There had been floggings and beatings as well, all with her parent's [sic] consent and encouragement. 'Evil!' 'Abomination!' 'Sinful!'"[39]

And then, there was the last exorcism but one, that vile, penultimate ritual "when her parents had held her down as the old priest had climbed on top of her and entered her, raping her while her parents held her wrists and told her not to fight. . . . 'We've tried everything else,' he had told her parents. 'This is the only way. We have no other choice.'"[40]

Tamara isn't real, of course, but she is real-ish. That is, she is *true*, given that, through the grammar of horror, we see in her any number of people who struggle with the same demons, who find themselves bound by the same chains, who suffer the same daily torment. Or, at least, what they have been warned are demons and taught are chains and told is their daily torment. Because so much of our religious behavior has been predicated on fear of the gods, our desperate attempts to keep bodies in place become the constant site of cruelty and horror. Our cross to bear. The karma we have earned. The just punishment of a loving god. The same things that Tamara "could never unsee or unfeel" are seen and felt daily by any number of men and women who *are* real.[41] The same things that she was taught "had wounded her soul and made her fear the church even more than the hell-spawned thing that had married its soul to hers" are wounds and fears experienced around the world.[42] Indeed, what makes this tale truly horrifying is that, while Tamara is a fictional character, for hundreds of millions of people her story is not. A story such as this could easily be the confession of a young woman trying in vain to deny her feelings for a female classmate or a young man struggling with transgender issues in the face of gross parental disapproval, each wrestling with the better angels of their nature as they try to escape what others have told them is the demon of their embodied apostasy.

Despite the fact that queer theory has been a part of horror studies for more than twenty years, it is a reality that much of horror remains, in one way or another, heteronormative. Nunsploitation cinema and European vampire erotica often rely on lesbianism for their titillating tension, but both signify homosexuality either as the sexual temptation to be avoided or the sexualized manifestation of evil. Male homosexuality, or at least homosociality, excavated from cinematic texts such as *The Exorcist*, often points us in other directions.[43] But, from works ranging from Harry Benshoff's *Monsters in the Closet*, his penetrating study of *Homosexuality and the Horror Film*, to Darren Elliott-Smith's *Queer Horror Film and Television* and his edited collection, *New Queer Horror Film and Television*, queer theory continues to emerge as one of the most important waypoints in the cartography of sex, horror, and the religious imagination.

The Sadeian Imaginary: From the Abbey to the Château

In Matthew Lewis's gothic classic, *The Monk*, a young woman, Matilda, has fallen hopelessly in love with the handsome, eponymous monk, Ambrosio. In a Shakespearean *Twelfth Night* gender-swap, she enters the abbey as "Rosario" but cannot bear the erotic pain of deception, and longs to confess her love. Finally, quite literally revealing the truth, "she tore open her habit and her bosom was half exposed."[44] Unable to countenance a woman's presence in the abbey, Ambrosio is fully prepared to send Matilda away. That is, until the point of the slim dagger with which she threatens suicide "rested upon her left breast: And Oh! that was such a breast! The Moon-beams darting full upon it, enabled the Monk to observe its dazzling whiteness. His eye dwelt with insatiably avidity upon the beauteous Orb."[45]

Recall that, whether we are in the habit or not, as it were, we are hardwired to notice sexually relevant information. "The religious breast prohibits abstraction," writes theologian Margaret Miles. Indeed, "the revelation of a naked breast startles viewers into attentiveness to the concrete."[46] Although Miles connects this particular revelation to the "reality of the feeding breast," her observation aptly describes its erotic effect on Ambrosio. Confronted with even the hint of Matilda's breast, that is, and he is dragged headlong from the spiritually abstract—the prayer grotto to which he has retreated—to the carnally unavoidable.

"A sensation till then unknown filled his heart"—and, we can imagine, regions further south—"with a mixture of anxiety and delight: A raging fire shot through every limb; The blood boiled in his veins, and a thousand wild wishes bewildered his imagination."[47] Later, in his cell, sleeping only fitfully, "his inflamed imagination had presented him with none but the most voluptuous objects."[48] Not surprisingly, Matilda walks in his dreams, "and his eyes again dwelt upon her naked breast."[49] This time their dream-embrace is passionate, lustful in its intensity, though soon to be replaced by the image of the Virgin from his favorite painting. "He pressed his lips to hers, and found them warm: The animate form started from the Canvas, embraced him affectionately, and his senses were unable to support delight so exquisite."[50] The one place in all the abbey that ought to be his sanctuary is now the dreamscape of his sexual torment. Lewis gives us only these two brief glimpses, but "such were the scenes, on which his thoughts were employed while sleeping: His unsatisfied Desires placed before him the most lustful and provoking Images, and he rioted in joys till then unknown to him."[51]

While Lewis makes abundantly clear that Ambrosio suffers the sin of pride, as we find out nearly four hundred pages later, from the moment he catches sight of Matilda's breast, his long, hard fall from grace is actually the result of demonic temptation. "I watched the movements of your heart," Satan tells the stricken monk, who has just signed away his soul in return for escape from the Inquisitor's torture chamber.[52] "I saw that you were virtuous from vanity, not principle, and I seized the fit moment of seduction. I observed your blind idolatry of the Madonna's picture. I bade a subordinate but crafty spirit assume a similar form, and you eagerly yielded to the blandishments of Matilda."[53]

In the abbey, the evil is supernatural. It enters from outside. It invades and corrupts. Not so with Lewis's contemporary, the Marquis de Sade. Particularly in *Justine* and *The 120 Days of Sodom*, which should be seen as the foundation of Sade's work rather than its culmination, there is no diabolical temptation, no satanic justification for the horrifying behavior of the libertines. Whether we find them in the monastery, where the virtuous Justine is reduced to a sex slave for the monks and priests, or the Château de Silling, site of the worst Sadeian monstrosities, they are who they are by no virtue other than being human, than succumbing to the desires of the flesh bred within us all. Reading Sade, however, especially in the horror mode, presents us with two additional complications: the Sadeian imaginary and the Sadeian principles.

Not surprisingly, most people know little of Sade's life, and relatively few have read his work. More than that, though, even when they learn the facts—only the least of which is that he spent most of his adult life

in prison, much of that time under *lettres de cachet* from his odious
mother-in-law—many people find some way to hold on to their beliefs
and prejudices about him. Seeing the man in his works, they inhabit
their own version of the Sadeian imaginary, perhaps because it suits
ideological purpose, perhaps because too many other aspects of their
worldview are placed at risk by imagining Sade differently. For whatever
reason, Sade becomes "Sade."

In her preface to *Screening the Marquis de Sade*, Lindsay Anne Hallam
provides a valuable theoretical positioning for a Sadeian view of horror. Eschewing any obligation to "psychoanalysis, feminism, semiotics,
and post-structuralism," disciplines in which it is de rigueur to regard
religious imagery as anything but religious, and recognizing that "many
analyses use theory to excuse and thus dilute the power of sexual and
violent images, the application of Sadean philosophy to film is deliberately transgressive and confrontational."[54] Which is to say, the process
of interpretation is decidedly not about solving the problem or picking
the lock. It is not about mitigating, and thus dismissing the transgressive power of this film, that novel, or one or another short story. It is
about examining our reactions in the face of the unnatural that cannot
be naturalized, the abnormal that cannot be normalized, the anomalous
that cannot be reconciled with consensus reality.

Subtitling *The Witch* "A New England Folk-Tale" no more dilutes the
power of its disturbing imagery and somber storyline than saying "Remember, it's only a movie" will keep audiences from turning away as
poor Sam is ground to jelly in the witch's mortar-and-pestle. And if it
did, what would that say about the human capacity to endure the suffering of others—and to do so explicitly for our enjoyment? The urge to
naturalize, to approach the horror mode as a relentless social allegory,
to make everything alright in the end and for everyone to "live happily
ever after," is our desire to retreat in the face of the overwhelming, or
the imagined fear that we will be overwhelmed, and that therefore the
boundaries of body and society cannot be maintained.

Rather than let us off the interpretive hook, a Sadeian analysis forces
the overwhelming upon us, and invites us to look at artistic "representations of human relations as unflinchingly as Sade did in his novels."[55]
In this, Sade's "philosophy provides a *method of thinking* that uncovers
the ways in which cinema challenges bodily norms in order to suggest

broader cultural and political transgressions."[56] By "Sade's philosophy," Hallam means four organizing principles of the Sadeian imaginary.

First, for Sade, everything both begins with and reduces to the body, "the thing through which his ideas are expressed. In Sade's thought, there can be no ideas without the body."[57] Not unlike the cosmic indifference that lies at the heart of Lovecraft's horror, "Sade's basic principle is that we are all isolated beings, that our bodies are all that we have."[58] Second, foreshadowing Freud by a full century, "in Sade, sex is the driving force of all actions."[59] Contrary to a good friend of mine, who asked, "How many people did Sade kill, anyway?" Hallam reminds us that "the sexual sadism described by Sade is a textual action, that is, only occurring within the realm of fiction"—that is, within the horror mode.[60]

The third principle, the one toward which the others inevitably bend, is the value of transgression, an individualist anarchy that responds to the demands of society only as and when its own purpose is served. Sade, as Hallam puts it, "presents a philosophy that presents all aspects of the transgressive body," places all angles of the body out of place on display.[61] "In Sade's view," she continues, "society's norms are cultural constructions imposed upon the body and not naturally exhibited by it. In order to stem the natural urges—carnal desires and violent impulses—both church and state have condemned them as evil."[62] This makes the Sadeian imaginary a rich theoretical approach to the problem of sex, horror, and the religious imagination—which is as much about probing our efforts to escape these theological and cultural constraints as it is about describing the manner in which these constructions are established and maintained in the first place.

This leads to the fourth principle, the principle of the imagination, the willingness not simply to indulge on a whim. Hallam points out that "although nature has given the Sadean libertine the desire to commit violent, carnal or criminal acts, for Sade it is the *idea* of these actions and the transgressiveness of the activity that create pleasure."[63] This is the power of expectation over experience, the reality that the brain's reward system is triggered far more by anticipation than by participation. As neurologist Robert Sapolsky puts it, "Dopamine is not about pleasure, it's about the anticipation of pleasure. It's about the pursuit of happiness rather than happiness itself."[64] Or, to speak with Noël Carroll once again, the paradoxical pleasures of scary movies and spooky stories.

To these principles, however, must be added a fifth, drawn explicitly from the rules laid down for the poor unfortunates gathered as libertine playthings in the Château de Silling: Any appeal to religion is expressly forbidden. "The slightest religious act on the part of any subject," read the Silling statutes, "whomsoever he be, shall be punished by death."[65] Not only should their language be "the most lascivious," "indicative of the greatest debauchery," the "filthiest, the most harsh," it must also be "the most blasphemous."[66] To that end, "The name of God shall never be uttered save when accompanied by invectives or imprecations, and thus qualified it shall be repeated as often as possible."[67]

Sadeian philosophy indicts the God-who-is-not-there rather than justifies the one who is. And, presaging *Teratologist* by more than two hundred years, the Duc de Blangis puts the singular question of theodicy and the (im)possibility of divine benevolence to the doomed participants: "Were there a God and were this God to have any power, would he permit the virtue which honors him, and which you profess, to be sacrificed to vice and libertinage as it is going to be? Would this all-powerful God permit a feeble creature like myself . . . to insult him, to flout him, to defy him, to challenge him, to offend him as I do?"[68]

In his own introduction to *The 120 Days*, Sade tells his readers that they will disapprove of much that takes place in the Silling banquet hall. Here, he allows the briefest moment of normality. Deviance and debauchery there will be, he continues, the likes of which we have never seen. And, of course, we would disapprove; that is only to be expected. In this, he appears the ringmaster of the normal. But, while Sade tells us that "many of the perversions you will soon see depicted will displease you," others will "excite you to the point of costing you some sperm, and that is all we need."[69]

That is all we need to challenge the plausibility of the worldviews to which we so desperately cling—whatever they are. That is all we need to shake the foundations of inevitability—however we have laid them. That is all we need . . . because when this happens, when the sperm is spent or vulvic juices expelled, indeed when even a tickle of arousal moves in our loins, however much distance we have convinced ourselves exists between the reader and the château is annihilated. The shattering emotional transaction that lies at the heart of sex, horror, and the religious imagination rouses itself once again.

NOTES

INTRODUCTION

1 Craven, *Scream*.
2 See Kendrick, *The Thrill of Fear*.
3 Cartwright, *Vexed*.
4 See Koike, *The Graveyard Apartment*; Jackson, *The Haunting of Hill House*; Straub, "Blue Rose," *Ghost Story*.
5 See King, *Pet Sematary*; Cowan, *America's Dark Theologian*, 74–77, 125–38.
6 See Cowan, *Sacred Terror*, 184–89.
7 Clasen, *Why Horror Seduces*, 4.
8 Clasen, *Why Horror Seduces*, 29.
9 For a variety of perspectives on the subject of human fearing, see, for example, Altheide, *Creating Fear*; Cohen, *Monster Theory*; Cowan, *Sacred Terror*; Freud, *The Uncanny*; Furedi, *Culture of Fear Revisited*; Gilmore, *Monsters*; Glassner, *The Culture of Fear*; Hankiss, *Fears and Symbols*; Kearney, *Strangers, Gods, and Monsters*; Ligotti, *The Conspiracy against the Human Race*; Scruton, *Sociophobics*; Thacker, *In the Dust of This Planet, Starry Speculative Corpse*, and *Tentacles Longer Than Night*.
10 *Pontianak* and *kuntilanak* are the quintessential South Asian haunting spirits, often styled as beautiful young women who have died in tragic circumstances, and who either do not yet realize they are dead or seek revenge for their deaths (see, for example, Duile, "Kuntilanak"; Kusumaryati, "The Feminine Grotesque in Indonesian Horror Films"; Tan, "*Pontianaks*, Ghosts, and the Possessed"). *Yurei* and *yokai* are Japanese ghosts and monsters, respectively (see, for example, Davisson, *Yūrei*; Foster, *The Book of Yōkai* and *Pandemonium and Parade*).
11 See Cowan, *America's Dark Theologian*, esp. 6, 27–28, "The Crack in the World," *Magic, Monsters, and Make-Believe Heroes*, esp. 191–94, and *Sacred Terror*, esp. 259–64.
12 For further thoughts on this, see Cowan, "Re-Iterations."
13 Stone, "The Sanctification of Fear," 1; see Cowan, *Sacred Terror*, 42–47.
14 Etchison, in Winter, *Faces of Fear*, 62.
15 Stone, "The Sanctification of Fear," 12.
16 Stone, "The Sanctification of Fear," 12.
17 Craven, *Scream*.

18 One of North American cinema's most recognizable scream queens, Curtis also appeared in *The Fog, Prom Night, Terror Train*—all released in 1980—*Halloween II*, and *Road Games* (both 1981). Decades on, she reprised her *Halloween* role as Laurie Strode in three sequels/reboots: *Halloween H2o: 20 Years Later* (1998), *Halloween: Resurrection* (2002), and *Halloween* (2018).

19 Craven, *Scream*.

20 Craven, *Scream*. The question of whether sex really does equal death, particularly in slasher movies and especially for women, has evolved from cinema horror trope to pop culture cliché. It has, however, come under significant scrutiny in recent years. For a variety of perspectives on the debate, see Linz and Donnerstein, "Sex and Violence in Slasher Films"; Molitor and Sapolsky, "Sex, Violence, and Victimization in Slasher Films"; Sapolsky, Molitor, and Luque, "Sex and Violence in Slasher Films"; Welsh, "On the Perils of Living Dangerously in the Slasher Horror Film" and "Sex and Violence in the Slasher Horror Film."

21 Scott, *Alien*.

22 Freud, *Three Essays on the Theory of Sexuality*, 108. In Western psychology, a "paraphilia" is generally regarded neutrally, unless the person experiences a level of discomfort or impairment associated with it, at which point it becomes a "disorder." The various debates on this, though, continue, often informed less by empirical evidence than by ideological commitment. This is most obviously on display in the current fashion of so-called sex addiction. For a variety of perspectives on this, see Bering, *Perv*; Best and Bogle, *Kids Gone Wild*; Klein, *America's War on Sex*; Levy, *Female Chauvinist Pigs*; Ley, *The Myth of Sex Addiction*; Maltz and Maltz, *The Porn Trap*; Peele, *Diseasing of America*; Struthers, *Wired for Intimacy*.

23 Tisdale, "Talk Dirty to Me," 45.

24 For Tisdale, this is the principal message of pornography, for example, that "by its very existence," pornography in any and all its forms forces us to confront the fact "that our sexual selves are real" ("Talk Dirty to Me," 44).

25 Freud, *Three Essays on the Theory of Sexuality*, 108. See also, for example, Bullough, *Sexual Variance in Society and History*; Bullough and Bullough, *Sexual Attitudes*; Ogas and Gaddam, *A Billion Wicked Thoughts*; Ryan and Jethá, *Sex at Dawn*; Symons, *The Evolution of Human Sexuality*.

26 Slung, *I Shudder at Your Touch*, xiii.

27 Winner, *Real Sex*, 123.

28 Augustine, *City of God*, 14: 16; Tertullian, *On the Apparel of Women*, 1; Daly, *Pure Lust*.

29 Winner, *Real Sex*, 123–24.

30 See, for example, Bromley, *Falling from the Faith: Causes and Consequences of Religious Apostasy* and *The Politics of Religious Apostasy: The Role of Apostates in the Transformation of Religious Movements*.

31 See Cowan, *Bearing False Witness?*

32 See Laquer, *Making Sex* and *Solitary Sex*.

33 On Clinton and Lewinsky, see Berlant and Duggan, *Our Monica, Ourselves*.
34 See Orwell, *1984*.
35 Winner, *Real Sex*, 35.
36 King, "The Revelations of 'Becka Paulson," 1.
37 King, "The Revelations of 'Becka Paulson," 8.
38 King, "The Revelations of 'Becka Paulson," 18.
39 King, "The Revelations of 'Becka Paulson," 18–19.
40 King, "The Revelations of 'Becka Paulson," 19.
41 See King, *Carrie*; Cowan, *America's Dark Theologian*, 139–48.
42 See King, *The Dead Zone*; Cowan, *America's Dark Theologian*, 148–56.
43 King, "The Revelations of 'Becka Paulson," 9.
44 King, "The Revelations of 'Becka Paulson," 9.
45 King, "The Revelations of 'Becka Paulson," 9.
46 King, "The Revelations of 'Becka Paulson," 10.
47 King, "The Revelations of 'Becka Paulson," 11.
48 King, "The Revelations of 'Becka Paulson," 9.
49 Katz, "Language, Epistemology, and Mysticism," 26; emphases in the original.
50 Katz, "Language, Epistemology, and Mysticism," 26.
51 Cowan, *Sacred Space*, 217; see 215–19.
52 King, "The Revelations of 'Becka Paulson," 3.
53 King, "The Revelations of 'Becka Paulson," 8.
54 King, "The Revelations of 'Becka Paulson," 9
55 King, "The Revelations of 'Becka Paulson," 9.
56 King, "The Revelations of 'Becka Paulson," 9.
57 King, "The Revelations of 'Becka Paulson," 10.
58 See King, *Needful Things*; Cowan, *America's Dark Theologian*, 109–14.
59 King, "The Revelations of 'Becka Paulson," 10.
60 Slung, *I Shudder at Your Touch*, xiii.
61 King, "The Revelations of 'Becka Paulson," 12.
62 King, "The Revelations of 'Becka Paulson," 12.
63 King, *Danse Macabre*, 41.
64 See King, *Desperation, Duma Key, Revival*, and *Under the Dome*. For discussions of each of these, see Cowan, *America's Dark Theologian*, 165–71, 195–201, 159–64, and 182–85, respectively.
65 King, *Danse Macabre*, 185.
66 *Penny Dreadful*, "Night Work."
67 Van Hollander, "Susie," 499. Many of those who write in the Lovecraftian mode regularly weave aspects of Lovecraft's life as well as his fiction into their own work. In 1893, Lovecraft's father suffered a seizure while on a business trip and was placed in Butler Hospital in Providence, Rhode Island. He would remain there until his death five years later.
68 Van Hollander, "Susie," 499.
69 Van Hollander, "Susie," 503.

70 Van Hollander, "Susie," 504.

71 Van Hollander, "Susie," 501.

72 Van Hollander, "Susie," 501–2.

73 Van Hollander, "Susie," 502.

74 Van Hollander, "Susie," 502.

75 Van Hollander, "Susie," 502–3.

76 Van Hollander, "Susie," 503. For fans of the Lovecraft mythos, "its truest name" is, of course, Cthulhu, High Priest of the Old Ones, also known as the Great Dreamer, and the Sleeper of R'lyeh (see Lovecraft, "The Call of Cthulhu").

77 Paton, *The Greek Anthology*, vol. 1, book 5, 353.

78 Gilliam and Jones, *Monty Python and the Holy Grail*.

79 See Bate, *Photography and Surrealism*, 21–23.

80 Clasen, *Why Horror Seduces*, 4. This process is very similar to the argument made more than two hundred years ago by Immanuel Kant in *Critique of Judgment*; on modern iterations of the "reality simulation model" of storytelling, see, for example, Boyd, *On the Origin of Stories*; Gottschall, *The Storytelling Animal*; Pinker, *How the Mind Works*.

81 Clasen, *Why Horror Seduces*, 46. Something of a conventional piety in the emerging cognitive science of religion, on agency-attribution and the supernatural, see Atran, *In Gods We Trust*; Barrett, *Why Would Anyone Believe in God?*; Boyer, *The Naturalness of Religious Ideas* and *Religion Explained*; Pyysïainen, *Supernatural Agents*; Tremelin, *Minds and Gods*.

82 Clasen, *Why Horror Seduces*, 46.

83 Gladwin, "Witches, Spells, and Politics," 219; see also Kusumaryati, "The Feminine Grotesque in Indonesian Horror Films."

84 See, for example, Onoh, *The Sleepless* and *Unhallowed Graves*; Tutuola, *My Life in the Bush of Ghosts*.

85 On *mizuko kuyo*, see Hardacre, *Marketing the Menacing Fetus in Japan*; Wilson, *Mourning the Unborn Dead*.

86 For a variety of these approaches, see, for example, Grant, *Planks of Reason*; Hendershot, *I Was a Cold War Monster*; Jancovich, *Rational Fears*; Skal, *Screams of Reason*; Tsutsui, *Godzilla on My Mind*; Tudor, *Monsters and Mad Scientists*.

87 See, for example, Douglas, *Purity and Danger*; James, *Varieties of Religious Experience*.

88 For a variety of perspectives on this, see, for example, Biale, *Eros and the Jews*; Boswell, *Christianity, Social Tolerance, and Homosexuality*; Boyarin, *Carnal Israel*; Daichman, *Wayward Nuns in Medieval Literature*; Daly, *The Church and the Second Sex*; Elliott, *Fallen Bodies*; Faure, *The Red Thread*; Hanegraff and Kripal, *Hidden Intercourse*; Jordan, *The Invention of Sodomy*; Meigs, *Food, Sex, and Pollution*; Miles, *Carnal Knowing*; Ranke-Heinemann, *Eunuchs for the Kingdom of Heaven*; Urban, *Magia Sexualis*.

89 James, *The Varieties of Religious Experience*, 61.

90 Boyd, *On the Origin of Stories*, 129.

CHAPTER 1. BODIES OUT OF PLACE

1 Friedkin, *The Exorcist*.
2 McCabe, *The Exorcist*, 100.
3 Blatty, *The Exorcist*, 189, 190.
4 McCabe, *The Exorcist*, 101. See Phillippe, *Leap of Faith*.
5 "The Exorcist (1973) Crucifix *13+*."
6 McCabe, *The Exorcist*, 100.
7 Clover, *Men, Women, and Chain Saws*, 87.
8 Clover, *Men, Women, and Chain Saws*, 88.
9 Beit-Hallahmi, "'The Turn of the Screw' and 'The Exorcist,'" 296.
10 Beit-Hallahmi, "'The Turn of the Screw' and 'The Exorcist,'" 296.
11 Williams, "The Power of Christ Compels You," 223.
12 Williams, "The Power of Christ Compels You," 228.
13 Hogan, *Dark Romance*, 20.
14 See Douglas, *Purity and Danger*; Flood, *The Tantric Body*; McDaniel, *Offering Flowers, Feeding Skulls*; Simmer-Brown, *Dakini's Warm Breath*; Urban, *Tantra*.
15 McDaniel, *Offering Flowers, Feeding Skulls*, 124; see 123–32.
16 For differing views on this, see Bhattacarya, *History of the Tantric Religion*, and McDaniel, "Death Visions of the Goddess Kali."
17 Reitman, *Ghostbusters*.
18 See, for example, Chesters, *Ghost Stories in Late Renaissance France*; Downey, *American Women's Ghost Stories in the Gilded Age*; Felton, *Haunted Greece and Rome*; Goldstein, Grider, and Thomas, *Haunting Experiences*; Handley, *Visions of an Unseen World*; Ross, *Japanese Ghost Stories*.
19 See *The Epic of Gilgamesh*, XI–XIII.
20 See "Biting a Ghost" and "The Southern Wutong-Spirit," in Songling, *Strange Tales from a Chinese Studio*, 31–33, 421–26.
21 Hearn, *Kwaidan*; see also Brown, *Japanese Horror*; Choi and Wada-Marciano, *Horror to the Extreme*; Davisson, *Yūrei*; Kalat, *J-Horror*; Maseo, *Kaiki: Uncanny Tales from Japan*; McRoy, *Nightmare Japan*.
22 On this, see, for example, Barzun, "The Art and Appeal of the Ghostly and Ghastly"; Cowan, *America's Dark Theologian*, 63–87, and *Sacred Terror*, 126–33; Hall, "The Ghost."
23 Barker, *The Scarlet Gospels*, 173; see Cowan, "The Crack in the World."
24 See Shelley, *Frankenstein*; King, *Pet Sematary*.
25 Kirkman, in Davies, "The Walking Dead"; see Kirkman, *The Walking Dead*.
26 See, for example, Heinlein, "They"; Jones, "The Last Ones"; Kiernan, "Houses under the Sea"; Lee, *The Innswich Horror*.
27 Howard, "Black Hound of Death," 418.
28 Howard, "Black Hound of Death," 420–21.
29 Howard, "Black Hound of Death," 410.
30 Howard, "Black Hound of Death," 426.

31 Howard, "Black Hound of Death," 425.

32 The term "culturfact" is defined later in this chapter.

33 "Americans Escape from Tibet"; "Roof of the World."

34 "Black Bon Po Rites Rampant in Tibet"; "Demonology and Witchcraft Now Rule Tibetan Buddhism [*sic*]."

35 "Roerich Expedition Reaches Civilization."

36 "Black Art in Tibet."

37 "Black Art in Tibet."

38 On the Sadeian body in horror, see Hallam, *Screening the Marquis de Sade*; Siddique and Raphael, *Transnational Horror Cinema*.

39 Farmer, *The Image of the Beast*. See also, Farmer, *Blown* and *Flesh*.

40 Strantzas, "Thistle's Find," 340, 341; Lovecraft, "From Beyond."

41 Strantzas, "Thistle's Find," 345.

42 Strantzas, "Thistle's Find," 55. On "thin spots" in horror fiction, see Cowan, *America's Dark Theologian*, 36–62.

43 Strantzas, "Thistle's Find," 345.

44 On ghouls in Lovecraft, see especially "The Dream-Quest of Unknown Kadath" and "Pickman's Model."

45 Strantzas, "Thistle's Find," 347.

46 Strantzas, "Thistle's Find," 347.

47 Strantzas, "Thistle's Find," 347.

48 See Blanchard et al., *Human Zoos*; Qureshi, *People on Parade*.

49 Strantzas, "Thistle's Find," 348.

50 Daly, *Pure Lust*, 2.

51 Ryan and Jethá, *Sex at Dawn*, 85.

52 Ryan and Jethá, *Sex at Dawn*, 85.

53 Wyndham, *The Chrysalids*, 13; see also Miller, *A Canticle for Liebowitz* and *Saint Liebowitz and the Wild Horse Woman*.

54 For a list of sexual sins covered by the so-called Holiness Code, as well as the relevant punishments, see Leviticus 18–21; see also Biale, *Eros and the Jews*, 17–20.

55 Salmonson and Pugmire, "Underneath an Arkham Moon," 77, 78, 81.

56 Salmonson and Pugmire, "Underneath an Arkham Moon," 78.

57 Salmonson and Pugmire, "Underneath an Arkham Moon," 77.

58 Salmonson and Pugmire, "Underneath an Arkham Moon," 83.

59 Salmonson and Pugmire, "Underneath an Arkham Moon," 82, 83.

60 Hickox, *Hellraiser III: Hell on Earth*. On the Cenobites and the *Hellraiser* mythos, see Barker, *The Hellbound Heart* and *The Scarlet Gospels*; Cowan, *Sacred Terror*; Kane, *The "Hellraiser" Films and Their Legacy*.

61 Hickox, *Hellraiser III*.

62 Hickox, *Hellraiser III*.

63 Barker, *Hellraiser*.

64 Blatty, "'The Exorcist's' Secret Message." On the problem of genre and preconception, this time in terms of Stephen King, see Cowan, *America's Dark Theologian*, ix–xiii.

65 Cowan, *Sacred Terror*, 17.

66 Hartwell, *Shadows of Fear*, 2.

67 Hartwell, *Shadows of Fear*, 2.

68 Hartwell, *The Dark Descent*, 5.

69 Hartwell, *The Dark Descent*, 5.

70 On this, see Whitehouse, "Terror," esp. 270–71.

71 Barzun, "The Art and Appeal of the Ghostly and Ghastly," xxi.

72 Smithee, *Hellraiser: Bloodline*.

73 Burton, *Sleepy Hollow*.

74 Ulmer, *Daughter of Dr. Jekyll*.

75 See Cowan, "Pulp Evangelism and Narrative Structure in Evangelical Fiction."

76 Potassium permanganate powder stains skin a deep, long-lasting brown color; see also, Hill, *Paranormal Media*.

77 Murphy, *The Awakening*. See also Hill, *Paranormal Media*.

78 Kiernan, "Pickman's Other Model (1929)," 17. Kiernan, who has been called Lovecraft's literary granddaughter, wrote this story as something of an homage to the Lovecraft classic, "Pickman's Model," originally published in 1927.

79 Kiernan, "Pickman's Other Model (1929)," 17.

80 Kiernan, "Pickman's Other Model (1929)," 14.

81 Kiernan, "Pickman's Other Model (1929)," 29.

82 Kiernan, "Pickman's Other Model (1929)," 26, 37; see also Dijkstra, *Evil Sisters*; Golden, *Vamp*. Although Kiernan's narrator associates these images with "J. Edward Gordon's *Salomé*," a change that better suits the sexualized nature of Kiernan's story, the Bara stills were actually shot for the 1915 film version of Porter Emerson Brown's controversial stage play, *A Fool There Was*.

83 Dijkstra, *Evil Sisters*, 267.

84 Kiernan, "Pickman's Other Model (1929)," 37–38.

85 Kiernan, "Pickman's Other Model (1929)," 29.

86 Carpenter, *The Thing*; see Neale, "You Got to Be Fucking Kidding!"

87 *Penny Dreadful*, "Night Work."

88 Hickox, *Hellraiser III*.

89 Grigg, *Science Fiction and the Imitation of the Sacred*, 11. For a rejoinder to Grigg, see Cowan, "Review of *Science Fiction and the Imitation of the Sacred*."

90 On this, see, for example, Boyd, *On the Origin of Stories*; Cowan, *Magic, Monsters, and Make-Believe Heroes*; Davidsen, "Fiction and Religion" and "The Religious Affordance of Fiction"; Petersen, "The Difference between Religious Narrative and Fictional Literature."

91 James, *Varieties of Religious Experience*, 36.

92 James, *Varieties of Religious Experience*, 61.

93 Prominent UFO researcher Jacques Vallée is among those who have proposed that the beings commonly represented as "extraterrestrial" are, in fact, interdimensional travelers; see *Dimensions*, *The Invisible College*, and *Messengers of Deception*.

94 Cowan and Bromley, *Cults and New Religions*, 8.

95 In the *Warhammer 40K* storyverse, see, for example, the narrative arcs of "Inquisitor Gregor Eisenhorn" (Abnett, *Xenos, Malleus, Hereticus,* and *The Magos*) and the "Adepta Sororitas," the Sisters of Battle (Swallow, *Sisters of Battle*).

96 In addition to the video games, see, for example, Bear, *Halo: Cryptum, Halo: Primordium,* and *Halo: Silentium.*

97 Durkheim, *Elementary Forms of Religious Life,* 42; cf. Cowan, *Magic, Monsters, and Make-Believe Heroes,* 64–66.

98 See DuQuette, *My Life with the Spirits.*

99 Farrar and Farrar, *The Witches' Way,* 105.

100 Weinberg, *Facing Up,* 242.

101 King, "Children of the Corn," in *Night Shift,* 265; Lovecraft, "The Shadow over Innsmouth," 277.

102 Barker, *Hellraiser.*

103 Kiernan, "Pickman's Other Model (1929)," 45.

104 Kiernan, "Pickman's Other Model (1929)," 45.

105 Herbert, in Winter, *Faces of Fear,* 106; see Cabell, *James Herbert*; Jones, *James Herbert.*

106 McDowell, in Winter, *Faces of Fear,* 185. "Lovecraftian," in this context, means in the manner of Lovecraft's weird fiction, not the personal beliefs of Lovecraft himself, who was a thoroughgoing materialist.

107 Burleson, "Desert Dreams," 49.

108 Barker, in Jones, *Clive Barker's Shadows in Eden,* 1.

CHAPTER 2. CRAB MONSTERS AND GIANT LEECHES

1 Corman, *Attack of the Crab Monsters.*

2 Among his nearly forty credits as a screenwriter, Griffith is best known for *Little Shop of Horrors,* which revisits some of the tropes in *Attack of the Crab Monsters,* as well as an uncredited collaboration on Roger Vadim's science fiction sex comedy, *Barbarella.*

3 See Gray, *Roger Corman*; Silver and Ursini, *Roger Corman.*

4 Corman, *Attack of the Crab Monsters.*

5 Gottschall, *The Storytelling Animal,* 34.

6 Gray, *Roger Corman,* 48.

7 Gray, *Roger Corman,* 48.

8 While they are rarely considered "exploitation," it is clear that the vast majority of action-adventure movies, superhero films, and a good deal of Japanese anime exploit Joseph Campbell's well-known "hero's journey" both for their narrative structure and their cultural appeal; see, for example, Campbell, *The Hero with a Thousand Faces*; Cowan, *Magic, Monsters, and Make-Believe Heroes*; Vogler, *The Writer's Journey.*

9 Searing, "B Movies," 18.

10 Tsutsui, *Godzilla on My Mind,* 82.

11 Searing, "B Movies," 18.

12 Searing, "B Movies," 18.

13 Huizinga, *Homo Ludens*, 3; see also Sicart, *Play Matters*.

14 In terms of global reach of the "king of monsters" and Japanese popular culture, see Tsutsui, *Japanese Popular Culture and Globalization*; Tsutui and Michiko, eds., *In Godzilla's Footsteps*.

15 Kyrou, *Le surréalisme au cinéma*, 276.

16 Kyrou, *Le surréalisme au cinéma*, 276.

17 Kyrou, *Le surréalisme au cinéma*, 90.

18 Kyrou, *Le surréalisme au cinéma*, 279.

19 Searing, "B Movies," 20; see Hendershot, *I Was a Cold War Monster*; Jancovich, *Rational Fears*; King, *Danse Macabre*; Skal, *Screams of Reason*. For "free-floating social anxieties" that are particularly concerned with religion, and the fears it both engenders and reflects, see my *Sacred Terror: Religion and Horror on the Silver Screen*.

20 Scorcese, in Sanders and Sanders, *The American Drive-In Movie Theater*, 118. Generous with his knowledge and experience, Corman is also credited with helping to launch the careers of such directors as James Cameron, Francis Ford Coppola, and Steven Spielberg.

21 Sanders and Sanders, *The American Drive-In Movie*, 118–19. In Japanese manga and anime, this principle is known as "fan service": highly sexualized aspects of the story that may or may not relate to the plot, but that are explicitly intended to appeal to the audience's more prurient interests (see Brenner, *Understanding Manga and Anime*, 88–89; Lamarre, "Platonic Sex"; Thompson, *Manga*).

22 See Newell, *The Art of the B-Movie Poster*.

23 Sorrow, "Magazine Trends Study Finds Increase in Advertisements Using Sex."

24 Reichert and Lambiase, *Sex in Consumer Culture*, xiii. See also Reichert, *The Erotic History of Advertising*; Reichert, Heckler, and Jackson, "The Effects of Sexual Social Marketing Appeals on Cognitive Processing and Persuasion."

25 To see this on full display, one need only review recent panic literature on the so-called scandal of hypersexualization in society, especially as it is represented in adult entertainment: Barton, *The Pornification of America*; Dines, *Pornland*; Jensen, *Getting Off*; Levy, *Female Chauvinist Pigs*; Paul, *Pornified*; Sarracino and Scott, *The Porning of America*.

26 Berger and Luckmann, *The Social Construction of Reality*, 83.

27 Berger and Luckmann, *The Social Construction of Reality*, 83.

28 Sex therapist Marty Klein argues that perceiving sex toys "as some kind of threat is really page 1 in the sexual misunderstanding textbook" (*America's War on Sex*, 89).

29 On the Gathings Committee, which was technically known as the House Select Committee on Current Pornographic Materials, see Rabinowitz, *American Pulp*; on Wertham's anti-comic crusade, see Barker, *A Haunt of Fears*; Hadju, *The Ten-Cent Plague*.

30 The seminal works on the efforts to censor motion pictures during this period remain Gregory Black's *Catholic Crusade against the Movies* and *Hollywood Censored*.

31 Black, *The Catholic Crusade against the Movies*, 26.

32 "The Production Code," 138.

33 "The Production Code," 145; emphases in the original.

34 "The Production Code," 141.

35 "The Production Code," 141.

36 "The Production Code," 147, 139.

37 "The Production Code," 139.

38 Later, the code refers to homosexuality as "*impure love*, the love which society has always regarded as wrong and which has been banned by divine law" ("The Production Code," 148).

39 "The Production Code," 140; emphasis in the original.

40 "The Production Code," 140, 148; emphasis in the original.

41 "The Production Code," 140.

42 "The Production Code," 148.

43 "The Production Code," 148.

44 King, *Danse Macabre*, 143.

45 See Brunvand, *The Vanishing Hitchhiker*.

46 Corman, *The Undead*.

47 On the off-screen reality of this prejudice, see, for example, Chateauvert, *Sex Workers Unite*; Pheterson, *A Vindication of the Rights of Whores*; Weitzer, *Sex for Sale*.

48 Corman, *The Undead*.

49 Huddleston et al., "The 50 Best Monster Movies."

50 Cohen, *Q: The Winged Serpent*.

51 Cohen, *Q: The Winged Serpent*.

52 Corman, *Attack of the Crab Monsters*.

53 Maltin, *Leonard Maltin's Classic Movie Guide*, 32.

54 Kowalski, *Attack of the Giant Leeches*.

55 Mallon, "Attack of the Giant Leeches." In *Attack of the 50-Foot Woman*, Vickers played a not-dissimilar role, this time as the sexual temptress who breaks up a marriage. The end, though, is the same as in *Giant Leeches*: both Vickers and the cheating husband are dead, as well as the man's wife.

56 Kowalski, *Attack of the Giant Leeches*.

57 Kowalski, *Attack of the Giant Leeches*.

58 Kowalski, *Attack of the Giant Leeches*.

59 Thankfully, producer Gene Corman moved on to other television projects, although a Canadian independent film company did remake *Attack of the Giant Leeches* in 2008. Sticking fairly closely to the original script, but featuring lower production values and even worse performances than the Kowalski original (if that's possible), the last few seconds are, nonetheless, worth a watch.

60 Kowalski, *Attack of the Giant Leeches.*

61 Arakawa, *Never-Ending Man.*

62 "The Production Code," 139; Kowalski, *Attack of the Giant Leeches.*

63 Cowan, *Magic, Monsters, and Make-Believe Heroes,* 71.

64 Hogan, *Dark Romance,* xi, xiii.

65 Stoker, *Dracula,* 10.

66 See Cowan, *Sacred Terror,* 123–66.

67 Browning, *Dracula.*

68 In addition to the 1931 *Dracula,* these classic Universal films include *Creature from the Black Lagoon* (1954), *Frankenstein* (1931), *The Invisible Man* (1933), *The Mummy* (1932), and *The Wolf Man* (1941).

69 Campbell, "The Rules of the Beast."

70 The Norton critical edition of *Dracula* notes that Stoker's description of the Count's hairy palms could refer to Victorian abhorrence of masturbation, which was commonly believed to drain the life essence from those addicted to "self-abuse" (Stoker, *Dracula,* 24 n. 8); see also Gordon and Hollinger, *Blood Read.*

71 From the hundreds on offer and in a variety of genres, see, for example, Adler, *Bordello of Blood*; Baker, *The Vampire Lovers*; Fisher, *The Brides of Dracula*; Landis, *Innocent Blood*; Lussier, *Dracula 2000*; Rodriguez, *From Dusk till Dawn*; Rollin, *The Nude Vampire* and *Requiem for a Vampire*; Sangster, *Lust for a Vampire*; Sasdy, *Countess Dracula*; Scott, *The Hunger*; Wynorski, *Vampirella.*

72 See, respectively, Browning, *Dracula*; Badham, *Dracula*; Marshak, *Dracula Sucks*; Hillyer, *Dracula's Daughter.* Two of the standard references for all things vampiric are Melton, *The Vampire Book* and *Videohound's Vampires on Video.*

73 Stoker, *Dracula,* 42.

74 Stoker, *Dracula,* 42.

75 Stoker, *Dracula,* 43.

76 Shimizu, *Ju-on* and *The Grudge*; Nakata, *Ringu*; Verbinski, *The Ring*; see Cowan, *Sacred Terror,* 128–33.

77 Skal, *Hollywood Gothic,* 162.

78 In the English version, Lucy Weston was played by Frances Dade, and Mina Seward by Helen Chandler; in the Spanish version, Carmen Guerrero portrayed Lucía Weston, while Lupita Tovar played Eva Seward.

79 Tovar, "Introduction to the Spanish Version."

80 Tovar, "Introduction to the Spanish Version."

81 Smith, *Imagining Religion,* 21.

82 Smith, *Imagining Religion,* 21.

83 Cowan, *Magic, Monsters, and Make-Believe Heroes,* 37.

84 Smith, *Imagining Religion,* 35.

85 Smith, *Imagining Religion,* 35; emphasis added.

86 Browning, *Dracula.*

87 On the difference in sexual arousal cuing, see Barton and Hardesty, "Spirituality and Stripping"; Critelli and Bivona, "Women's Erotic Rape Fantasies"; Ellis and

Symons, "Sex Differences in Sexual Fantasy"; Gallup and Frederick, "The Science of Sex Appeal"; Ogas and Gaddam, *A Billion Wicked Thoughts*, 108–13.

88 Campbell, "The Rules of the Beast."
89 Campbell, "The Rules of the Beast."

CHAPTER 3. ALTARED BODIES

1 Amendola, "The Secret War."
2 Amendola, "The Secret War."
3 Zorkóczy, "The Secret War."
4 Zorkóczy, "The Secret War."
5 Zorkóczy, "The Secret War." "Kolyak" may be Amendola's misreading of "Koryak," an indigenous people living in the far northeast of Siberia.
6 Amazon, "The Secret War."
7 Amendola, "The Secret War."
8 Recall Kiernan, "Pickman's Other Model (1929)."
9 Sales, "Human Sacrifice in Biblical Thought," 112.
10 Carrasco, "Sacrifice/Human Sacrifice in Religious Traditions."
11 See, for example, Beal, *Religion and Its Monsters*, 90.
12 King, *Danse Macabre*, 264; on this, see also Boyd, *On the Origin of Stories*, esp. 129–31.
13 Thomas, "The King of Cat Swamp," 90; though it seems there are words missing here, Thomas's prose is meant to evoke an invoice or shipping manifest, a checklist of catalogue-purchased style.
14 Thomas, "The King of Cat Swamp," 94.
15 Thomas, "The King of Cat Swamp," 90, 91.
16 Thomas, "The King of Cat Swamp," 95.
17 Booth, "Human Sacrifice in Literature," 7.
18 Ingham, "Human Sacrifice at Tenochtitlan," 379; see also Rives, "Human Sacrifice among Pagans and Christians."
19 Ingham, "Human Sacrifice at Tenochtitlan," 379.
20 Ingham, "Human Sacrifice at Tenochtitlan," 379.
21 Leeson, "Human Sacrifice," 138.
22 Scodel, "Δόμων ἄγαλμα: Virgin Sacrifice and Aesthetic Object," 111; see also Burkert, *Homo Necans*, esp. 58–72.
23 Scodel, "Δόμων ἄγαλμα: Virgin Sacrifice and Aesthetic Object," 111.
24 Scodel, "Δόμων ἄγαλμα: Virgin Sacrifice and Aesthetic Object," 111–12.
25 Harner, "The Ecological Basis for Human Sacrifice"; cf. Price, "Demystification, Enriddlement, and Aztec Cannibalism." On Harner's neo-shamanism, see *The Way of the Shaman*.
26 Winkelman, "Aztec Human Sacrifice," 286–87.
27 Smith, *Imagining Religion*, 110.
28 Smith, *Imagining Religion*, 110.

29 A similar case could be made for taking one's own life: Not all ritual suicide serves a sacrificial function.

30 Newton, "Written in Blood," 104; emphasis added.

31 Newton, "Written in Blood," 104.

32 Shea, *Demiurge*, 41–64; Kiernan, "Houndwife." For further perspectives on the problem of human sacrifice, see Burkert, *Homo Necans*; Girard, *The Scapegoat*; Obeyesekere, *Cannibal Talk*.

33 Newton, "Written in Blood," 104.

34 On the precarious nature of religion, and the legitimation strategies undertaken to address this, see Berger, *The Sacred Canopy*, 29–51; Berger and Luckmann, *The Social Construction of Reality*, 65–146.

35 One of the most trenchant statements of this position is H. L. Mencken's 1922 column "Memorial Service," first printed in the literary magazine, *The Smart Set*.

36 This is also known as the "failure of prophecy" problem, which led to the development of the concept of "cognitive dissonance"; the seminal text on this remains Festinger, Riecken, and Schachter, *When Prophecy Fails*.

37 I owe this particular formulation to Matt Dillahunty, of *The Atheist Experience* (www.axp.show).

38 Schallert, "'King Kong' Stirring Film"; Merrick, "Fifty-foot ape central figure in 'King Kong.'"

39 Tinee, "Monster ape in N.Y. setting packs thrills in new talkie"; emphasis in the original.

40 Looking back, it is also difficult not to see the wild-eyed, homicidal Kong reflected in Robert E. Howard's profoundly racist description of murderer Tope Braxton in "Black Hound of Death."

41 Scott, "Fantastic film sets new pace," A1.

42 Harryhausen, of course, is remembered for the stop-motion special effects in such favorites as *20 Million Miles to Earth*, *Jason and the Argonauts*, and *Clash of the Titans*, while Burton and Selick have elevated the form, collaborating on such films as *The Nightmare before Christmas*, *Corpse Bride*, and *Coraline*; Travis Knight helmed the magnificent *Kubo and the Two Strings*.

43 Jordan Vogt-Roberts's 2017 *Kong: Skull Island*, which is better understood as a story told from within the Kong universe rather than a different version of the original, explicitly presents Kong as the hero. The epitome of the perspectival sentiment on the monstrous, though, is Ellen Ripley's grating riposte to the company man, Carter Burke, in James Cameron's *Aliens*: "You know, Burke, I don't know which species is worse. You don't see them fucking each other over for a goddamn percentage."

44 Smith, *Imagining Religion*, xi.

45 Smith, *Imagining Religion*, xi; emphasis in the original.

46 Smith, *Imagining Religion*, xi.

47 Smith, *Imagining Religion* xi.

48 Smith, *Imagining Religion*, xi.

49 In addition to LaHaye and Jenkins, *Left Behind*, see, for example, Forbes and Kilde, *Rapture, Revelation, and the End Times*; Frykholm, *Rapture Culture*; Gribben, *Writing the Rapture*; Shuck, *Marks of the Beast*.

50 In addition to Brown, *The Da Vinci Code*, see, for example, Bock, *Breaking the Da Vinci Code*; Lutzer, *The Da Vinci Deception*; Rhodes, "Crash Goes the Da Vinci Code"; Witherington, *The Gospel Code*.

51 See Baigent, Leigh, and Lincoln, *Holy Blood, Holy Grail*. In 2005, Henry Baigent and Richard Leigh unsuccessfully sued both Brown and his publisher, Random House, for plagiarism and copyright infringement.

52 Other social psychological processes that work with source dissociation and the availability heuristic, and contribute to the meaning-making process, include the validity effect; confirmation, expectation, and hindsight biases; the in-print fallacy; the problem of authority; and the false-consensus effect. Curiously, a review of the American Theological Libraries Association database reveals that *none* of these are used with any regularity to help explain the religious imagination and its power over us.

53 Feil, "From the Classical *Religio* to the Modern *Religion*," 32.

54 Feil, "From the Classical *Religio* to the Modern *Religion*," 32.

55 Feil, "From the Classical *Religio* to the Modern *Religion*," 32.

56 Feil, "From the Classical *Religio* to the Modern *Religion*," 32. One of the best short-story expositions of this principle is Stephen King's "Rainy Season" (see King, *Nightmares and Dreamscapes*, 453–79; Cowan, *America's Dark Theologian*, 115–18).

57 Cooper, *King Kong*.

58 This aspect of the Kong story is made explicit in *Kong: Skull Island*, where the great ape protects his domain from terrifying lizard-creatures known as the "Skullcrawlers."

59 The classic anthropological statement of the problem of "rationality" and the outsider perspective remains E. E. Evans-Pritchard's *Witchcraft, Oracles, and Magic among the Azande*.

60 Cooper and Schoedsack, *King Kong*.

61 Symons, *The Evolution of Human Sexuality*, 150–51; see Lévi-Strauss, *The Elementary Structures of Kinship*, 38.

62 Lovecraft, "The Call of Cthulhu," 139.

63 Nietzsche, *Twilight of the Idols/The Anti-Christ*, 185.

64 See Castiglia, *Bound and Determined*; Ebersole, *Captured by Texts*.

65 See Prothero, *Religious Literacy*.

66 Kozlovic, "Structural Characteristics of the Christ-Figure," pars. 41, 65. For a trenchant rebuttal to Kozlovic's position, see Deacy, "Reflections on the Uncritical Appropriation of Cinematic Christ-Figures."

67 Kozlovic, "Structural Characteristics of the Christ-Figure," par. 51.

68 Cowan, *Sacred Space*, 268; see also my "Seeing the Saviour in the Stars."

69 Another example of the explicit nature of the cruciform pose is the death of Ripley scene in David Fincher's *Alien³*.

70 Jackson's *King Kong* makes much more of the cultural and class differences between rich and poor. Indeed, some of these sequences call to mind nothing so much as Arthur Fellig's famous 1943 photograph *The Critic*, which was used as the cover image for the Anchor Books paperback edition of Erving Goffman's *Presentation of Self in Everyday Life*.

71 "I'm Dwan," she tells her rescuers. "D-W-A-N, Dwan. That's my name. You know, like Dawn, except that I switched two letters to make it more memorable" (Guillermin, *King Kong*).

72 Guillermin, *King Kong*.

73 See Gerard, *Deep Throat*.

74 On the rise of feminist antiporn activism in the 1970s, see, for example, Bronstein, *Battling Pornography*; Brownmiller, *Against Our Will*; Strub, *Perversion for Profit*.

75 Guillermin, *King Kong*.

76 Guillermin, *King Kong*.

77 Guillermin, *King Kong*.

78 Guillermin, *King Kong*.

79 Weinberg, "Illustration," 215; see also Weinberg, *A Biographical Dictionary of Science Fiction and Fantasy Artists*.

80 See Pendarves, "The Altar of Melek Taos"; Quinn, "The Hand of Glory." "G. G. Pendarves" was the *Weird Tales* pen name of British novelist and screenwriter Gladys Gordon.

81 See Korshack and Spurlock, *The Alluring Art of Margaret Brundage*, 11–12; Weinberg, *The "Weird Tales" Story*.

82 Weinberg, *The "Weird Tales" Story*, 65.

83 Weinberg, "Brundage, Margaret (1900–1976)," 61.

84 Weinberg, *The "Weird Tales" Story*, 66.

85 Weinberg, *The "Weird Tales" Story*, 66.

86 Weinberg, "Brundage, Margaret (1900–1976)," 61.

87 Weinberg, *The "Weird Tales" Story*, 67; see also Jones, *The Shudder Pulps*.

88 Weinberg, "Brundage, Margaret (1900–1976)," 61.

89 Vanderburgh and Weinberg, "Introduction," x.

90 Howard, "Red Nails," 349; emphasis added. Where the third installment ends, the rest of the page in that issue is taken up by R. H. Barlow's poem, "R. E. H.," a tribute to Howard, who took his own life the month before the first part of "Red Nails" appeared.

91 "The Production Code," 140.

92 "The Production Code," 141.

93 Ryan and Jethá, *Sex at Dawn*, 97.

94 See Magilow, Vander Lugt, and Bridges, *Nazisploitation*; Pentangeli, *Soft Brides for the Beast of Blood, Soft Flesh and Orgies of Death*, and *Soft Nudes for the Devil's Butcher*.

95 On *giallo* horror art for such films as, respectively, *Satan's Doll*, *The Devil's Rain*, *Death Falls Softly*, and *Blood of the Virgins*, see Alfrey, *Sex and Horror: The Art of Alessandro Biffignandi* and *Sex and Horror: The Art of Emanuele Taglietti*; Janus, *Voluptuous Terrors* and *Voluptuous Terrors 2*. On horror paperback art, see Delving, *The Devil Finds Work*; Hendrix, *Paperbacks from Hell*; Streiber, *The Night Church*; Sutton, *The Sacrifice*.

CHAPTER 4. SACRED FLESH

1 Noé and Barreiro, *The Convent of Hell*.
2 Noé and Barreiro, *The Convent of Hell*, 1.
3 Noé and Barreiro, *The Convent of Hell*, 2.
4 Noé and Barreiro, *The Convent of Hell*, 4.
5 Boccaccio, *Decameron*, 159; see Chaucer, *The Canterbury Tales*.
6 See Brakke, *Demons and the Making of the Monk*; Daichman, *Wayward Nuns*; Fentone, *AntiCristo*; Steele, "Fashion, Fetish, Fantasy."
7 Jenkins, *Convergence Culture*, 93–134; Cowan, *Magic, Monsters, and Make-Believe Heroes*, 139.
8 Russell, "A Scary Nonlinear Curse"; Westbrook, "Retro Chill Factor."
9 See Cowan, *Sacred Terror*, 128–33.
10 Walking in my neighborhood one day while writing this book, I passed a young man who was wearing a sweatshirt that read "Virgins live longer." While this is a horror trope lodged specifically in slasher movies of the 1980s and 1990s, in this case it has been coopted in support of the teen sexual-abstinence program promoted by the young man's conservative Protestant megachurch.
11 See Considine, "Bored at Work?"; Roy, "Behind Creepypasta."
12 Cowan, *Magic, Monsters, and Make-Believe Heroes*, 139. Nearly half a century after *The Exorcist* was first released, for example, its intertextuality still resonates. When the main characters in the 2020 British comedy-horror series *Truth Seekers* ask a medium for help with some troublesome spirits, she warns that if the young woman's head spins around, or "you stick a crucifix up your what's-it," she'll end the session immediately—presumably with no refund (Smith, "The Girl with All the Ghosts").
13 Goldberg and Schneider, "Sex and Death, Cuban Style," 90.
14 Noé and Barreiro, *The Convent of Hell*, 1. Other intertextual references include Nahum Tate's famous Christmas hymn, "While Shepherds Watched Their Flocks by Night" (Noé and Barreiro, *The Convent of Hell*, 42), and *The Rocky Horror Picture Show* (Noé and Barreiro, *The Convent of Hell*, 49–57).
15 Noé and Barreiro, *The Convent of Hell*, 12.
16 Noé and Barreiro, *The Convent of Hell*, 20.
17 Noé and Barreiro, *The Convent of Hell*, 13.
18 Noé and Barreiro, *The Convent of Hell*, 16.
19 Noé and Barreiro, *The Convent of Hell*, 16.

20 See Deiss, *Herculaneum*; Johns, *Sex or Symbol?*, 19–21; *Pornography: The Secret History of Civilization*; Vout, *Sex on Show*, 209–11.

21 Noé and Barreiro, *The Convent of Hell*, 21–26.

22 Noé and Barreiro, *The Convent of Hell*, 38.

23 Also known as *Les Diaboliques*, see Julliann, *Dreamers of Decadence*, 106; Black, *Lust for the Devil*.

24 Julliann, *Dreamers of Decadence*, 92–93. See also Black, *Lust for the Devil*, 16–23; Wood, *Art Nouveau and the Erotic*, 72–74, 82.

25 Noé and Barreiro, *The Convent of Hell*, 44.

26 Davis and Javor, "Religion, Death, and Horror Movies," 13.

27 Davis and Javor, "Religion, Death, and Horror Movies," 17.

28 Scruton, "The Anthropology of an Emotion," 9.

29 See Cowan, *Sacred Terror*, 123–65.

30 Scruton, "The Anthropology of an Emotion," 9.

31 Nietzsche, *Twilight of the Idols/The Anti-Christ*, 185.

32 Nietzsche, *Twilight of the Idols/The Anti-Christ*, 185; see 178–85.

33 See Royal Collection Trust, *High Spirits*.

34 On this, see especially Bataille, *Erotism* and *The Tears of Eros*.

35 Further examples of Trouille's connections among sex, death, and the religious imagination include, but are hardly limited to, *Remembrance* (1930), *Bikini* (ca. 1930), *My Funeral* (1940), *My Grave* (1947), *The Stigmata of the Devil* (1960), and *The Good Confessor* (n.d.).

36 Gammon, *Desire, Drink, and Death in English Folk and Vernacular Song*, 18.

37 Gammon, *Desire, Drink, and Death in English Folk and Vernacular Song*, 18.

38 Gammon, *Desire, Drink, and Death in English Folk and Vernacular Song*, 18.

39 Gammon, *Desire, Drink, and Death in English Folk and Vernacular Song*, 18.

40 Tertullian, *On the Apparel of Women*, book 1, chapter 1.

41 Ranke-Heinemann, *Eunuchs for the Kingdom of Heaven*, 76.

42 Ranke-Heinemann, *Eunuchs for the Kingdom of Heaven*, 127.

43 Jowett and O'Donnell, *Propaganda and Persuasion*, 54, 55, 56.

44 Ellul, *Propaganda*, 33. For a more in-depth discussion of propaganda theory, see Cowan, "Bearing False Witness," 127–270.

45 Monk, *Awful Disclosures of Maria Monk*, v.

46 Monk, *Awful Disclosures of Maria Monk*, v.

47 Monk, *Awful Disclosures of Maria Monk*, v.

48 O'Gorman, *Convent Life Unveiled*, iii.

49 O'Gorman, *Convent Life Unveiled*, iii.

50 O'Gorman, *Convent Life Unveiled*, iv.

51 Chiniquy, *Fifty Years in the Church of Rome*, 5.

52 Chiniquy, *Fifty Years in the Church of Rome*, 5.

53 Fresenborg, "Thirty Years in Hell," 33.

54 Fresenborg, "Thirty Years in Hell," 3; all emphases in the original.

55 Fresenborg, *"Thirty Years in Hell,"* 31.

56 Dijkstra, *Idols of Perversity*, 13–24.

57 Fresenborg, *"Thirty Years in Hell,"* 83.

58 Fresenborg, *"Thirty Years in Hell,"* 84.

59 Fresenborg, *"Thirty Years in Hell,"* 85.

60 Fresenborg, *"Thirty Years in Hell,"* 85–86.

61 Fresenborg, *"Thirty Years in Hell,"* 86.

62 On Protestant anti-Catholicism, see Cowan, *Bearing False Witness?*, 171–90.

63 Chiniquy, *The Priest, The Woman, and the Confessional*, 21.

64 Chiniquy, *The Priest, The Woman, and the Confessional*, 21.

65 See McGowan, "Convents and Conspiracies." This practice has not changed, and has developed into a niche group of conservative Protestants, the Christian counter-cult, whose faith identity is formed and maintained by virtue of their opposition to any religious group different from their own; see Cowan, *Bearing False Witness?*

66 O'Gorman, *Convent Life Unveiled*, 36.

67 O'Gorman, *Convent Life Unveiled*, 38.

68 O'Gorman, *Convent Life Unveiled*, 37.

69 O'Gorman, *Convent Life Unveiled*, 37.

70 O'Gorman, *Convent Life Unveiled*, 37.

71 O'Gorman, *Convent Life Unveiled*, 37.

72 O'Gorman, *Convent Life Unveiled*, 37.

73 O'Gorman, *Convent Life Unveiled*, 37.

74 Monk, *Awful Disclosures of Maria Monk*, 52.

75 Monk, *Awful Disclosures of Maria Monk*, 53.

76 Monk, *Awful Disclosures of Maria Monk*, 58.

77 Monk, *Awful Disclosures of Maria Monk*, 58–59; "accouchement" is an archaic term for the process of giving birth. The numbering of the paragraphs suggests that some editions of the book might have contained a crude map of the convent.

78 McGowan, "Convents and Conspiracies," 46; McGowan's unpublished PhD dissertation remains one of the best studies of the conventual memoir genre.

79 Monk, *Awful Disclosures of Maria Monk*, 53–59.

80 Monk, *Awful Disclosures of Maria Monk*, 59.

81 Monk, *Awful Disclosures of Maria Monk*, 136. According to her narrative, Maria participated, however unwillingly, in one such murder (Monk, *Awful Disclosures of Maria Monk*, 83–91).

82 Monk, *Awful Disclosures of Maria Monk*, 136.

83 Monk, *Awful Disclosures of Maria Monk*, 136.

84 Monk, *Awful Disclosures of Maria Monk*, 65.

85 Monk, *Awful Disclosures of Maria Monk*, 65–66.

86 Monk, *Awful Disclosures of Maria Monk*, 66.

87 Monk, *Awful Disclosures of Maria Monk*, 66.

88 If this sounds hyperbolic, consider that in 1834, less than two years before *Awful Disclosures'* publication, anti-Catholic hysteria boiled over in Charlestown,

Massachusetts, when Protestant gangs attacked and burned an Ursuline convent
and school overlooking Boston Harbor; see Donahoe, *The Charlestown Convent*;
Schultz, *Fire and Roses*; Whitney, *The Burning of the Convent*.

89 Monk, *Awful Disclosures of Maria Monk*, 58.
90 Slocum's book was also released as *Confirmations of Maria Monk's Disclosures*, to
which was appended *Further Disclosures of Maria Monk*.
91 Monk, *Further Disclosures of Maria Monk*, 155.
92 Monk, *Further Disclosures of Maria Monk*, 155.
93 Monk, *Further Disclosures of Maria Monk*, 155.
94 Pagels, *Adam, Eve, and the Serpent*, 140.
95 Much of books 13 and 14 in Augustine's *City of God* are taken up with these matters.
96 Fresenborg, "Thirty Years in Hell," 3.
97 "Apostate Priest Retracts Errors."
98 Poutanen, *Beyond Brutal Passions*, 154.
99 Sylvain, "Monk, Maria."
100 Poutanen, *Beyond Brutal Passions*, 155–57.
101 "Religious Lies," 22; From One Who Knows, "Maria Monk and Her Awful Disclosures," 59.
102 See Stone, *Maria Monk's Show-Up!!! or, The "Awful Disclosures," a Humbug*, the
frontispiece for which featured a caricature of the Reverend George Bourne, one
of the men who, with J. J. Slocum, actually wrote *Awful Disclosures*, taking dicta-
tion from Satan.
103 Editors, "Awful Disclosures of Maria Monk," 50; see also Stone, *A Complete
Refutation of Maria Monk's Atrocious Plot* and *Maria Monk and the Nunnery of the
Hotel Dieu*.
104 Editors, "Maria Monk's Awful Disclosures," 125.
105 Editors, "Awful Disclosures," 28.
106 "Maria Monk Dead"; Roy, "Maria Monk," 1.
107 Roy, "Maria Monk," 1.
108 Roy, "Maria Monk," 1.

CHAPTER 5. SKYCLAD

1 Eggers, *The Witch*.
2 For a much fuller treatment of *The Witch*, see Grafius, *The Witch*.
3 Reis, *Damned Women*, 93.
4 Contrary to popular belief, Puritans were not generally opposed to sex within its
proper social confines—the marriage bed—and considered unnatural abstinence
a vestige of the hated "popery." As long as sexual bodies were in their appropriate
place, everything was fine. Any sexual activity beyond that, though, was forbidden, and harshly punished; see Ben-Atar and Brown, *Taming Lust*; Bloch, "Changing Conceptions of Sexuality and Romance in Eighteenth-Century America"; Fessenden, Radel, and Zaborowska, *The Puritan Origins of American Sex*: Morgan,

"The Puritans and Sex"; Stone, *Sex and the Constitution*, 74–82; Verduin, "'Our Cursed Natures.'"

5 Reis, *Damned Women*, 93.

6 Joho, "*The Witch* isn't an empowerment narrative and that's why it's great."

7 See Ostling, "Babyfat and Belladonna."

8 See Callow, *Embracing the Darkness*, 59–77, 90–99; Sullivan, "The Witches of Dürer and Hans Baldung Grien"; Zika, "The Witch and Magician in European Art."

9 See Tal, "Demonic Possession in the Enlightenment." *The Witches' Flight* is part of a six-painting series related to witchcraft, including *The Spell*, *Witches' Kitchen*, *Witches' Sabbath*, *The Bewitched Man* (also known as *The Devil's Lamp*), and possibly *The Stone Guest*.

10 See Cowan, *Magic, Monsters, and Make-Believe Heroes*, 58–62.

11 See Cowan, *Sacred Terror*, 84–90.

12 Richter, *The Adventures of Buckaroo Banzai Across the 8th Dimension*.

13 Smith, *To Take Place*, 103.

14 Contrary to popular belief, Puritans rejected neither leisure in general nor dancing in particular—so long as they were conducted with appropriate decorum and did not disrupt the social order. "Dancing naked with the devil" would, presumably, transgress both these conditions. On the Puritan attitude toward dance, see Packard, "Dancing along the Tightrope of Pleasure," esp. 50–64.

15 Even this image points to the reduplicative nature of horror culture, recreating almost exactly the central figure in the poster for the Italian release of Dan O'Bannon's 1985 comedy-horror classic, *Return of the Living Dead* (It. *Il Ritorno dei Morti Viventi*; see Janus, *Voluptuous Terrors*, 121).

16 See Demos, *Entertaining Satan*; Karlsen, *The Devil in the Shape of a Woman*; Reis, *Damned Women*.

17 See Gray, *Show Sold Separately*.

18 Hutton, *The Witch*, 23.

19 Hutton, *The Witch*, 23.

20 Hutton, *The Witch*, 51.

21 Hutton, *The Witch*, 23.

22 See Lyons, "Paranormal Beliefs Come (Super)Naturally to Some"; Moore, "Three in Four Americans Believe in Paranormal"; Newport and Strausberg, "Americans' Belief in Psychic and Paranormal Phenomena Is Up over Last Decade"; Taylor, "The Religious and Other Beliefs of Americans."

23 Sullivan, "The Witches of Dürer and Hans Baldung Grien," 334.

24 Sullivan, "The Witches of Dürer and Hans Baldung Grien," 334.

25 On the changes related to the religious and secular manners in which artistic representation of the nude form was understood, see Clark, *The Nude*; Miles, *Carnal Knowing* and *A Complex Delight*.

26 For seminal work on the fairy tale as a social and cultural genre, see Zipes, *Breaking the Magic Spell*, *Fairy Tales and the Art of Subversion*, *The Irresistible Fairy Tale*, and *Why Fairy Tales Stick*.

27 Mannheim, *Ideology and Utopia*, 6.

28   Kramer and Sprenger, *The Malleus Maleficarum of Heinrich Kramer and James Sprenger*, 8.

29 Mannheim, *Ideology and Utopia*, 6.

30 Berger and Luckmann, *The Social Construction of Reality*, 172.

31 Berger and Luckmann, *The Social Construction of Reality*, 172.

32 Berger and Luckmann, *The Social Construction of Reality*, 172.

33 Berger and Luckmann, *The Social Construction of Reality*, 172.

34 Pears advertisement from *Punch*, 1895.

35 See Reichert, *The Erotic History of Advertising*, 45–66.

36 See Blacker, *Hex Wives*; Brown, *The Coven*; Bunn, *Harrow County*; Lovecraft, "The Dreams in the Witch House"; Myrick and Sánchez, *The Blair Witch Project*; Snyder and Jock, *Wytches*.

37 Brown, *The Coven*, front cover.

38 Cowan, *Magic, Monsters, and Make-Believe Heroes*, 63.

39 Cowan, *Magic, Monsters, and Make-Believe Heroes*, 63.

40 On the pop-culture domestication of witches and witchcraft, see Cowan, *Magic, Monsters, and Make-Believe Heroes*, 62–71.

41 Larson, *Larson's New Book of Cults*, 464.

42 Gage, *Women, Church, and State*, 247; Read, *The Burning Times*. For debunking of these claims, see Gibbons, "Recent Developments in the Study of the Great European Witch Hunt."

43 Larson, *Larson's Book of Spiritual Warfare*, 168.

44 Larson, *Larson's Book of Spiritual Warfare*, 169.

45 Larson, *Larson's Book of Spiritual Warfare*, 170. Kidman, of course, went on to play the film version of arguably the most famous television witch, Samantha Stephens, in *Bewitched*.

46 Larson, *Larson's Book of Spiritual Warfare*, 169.

47 As I write this in late 2020, pop-culture witchcraft is seeing another resurgence in the wake of the fading popularity of vampires and zombies.

48 Larson, *Larson's Book of Spiritual Warfare*, 170.

49 See Hahn, "Jessica: A New Life"; Stange, "Jessica Hahn's Strange Odyssey from PTL to *Playboy*."

50 Herszenhorn, "Witches Express Relief as Vexing Case Is Closed," B5.

51 Herszenhorn, "Witches Express Relief as Vexing Case Is Closed," B5.

52 Herszenhorn, "Witches Express Relief as Vexing Case Is Closed," B5.

53 Larson, *Larson's Book of Spiritual Warfare*, 170.

54 Alexander, *Witchcraft Goes Mainstream*, 226.

55 Howe, "Modern Witchcraft."

56 Baker, *Dewitched*, 184–89.

57 Baker, *Dewitched*, 160.

58 Baker, *Dewitched*, 160.

59 Demos, *Entertaining Satan*, xi.

60 Ball and O'Leary, "Witch Performs Pagan Rituals while Naked with Her Children."

61 Demos, *Entertaining Satan*, 275–312.

62 ACLU, "Hunter v. Salem Public Library Board of Trustees."

63 Patrick, "Missouri Librarian Agrees Not to Block Witch Websites."

64 ACLU, "Hunter v. Salem Public Library Board of Trustees."

65 Barner-Barry, *Contemporary Paganism*.

66 Barner-Barry, *Contemporary Paganism*, 129.

67 Barner-Barry, *Contemporary Paganism*, 131.

68 Barner-Barry, *Contemporary Paganism*, 131.

69 See Starr, "Mother Ocean." *newWitch* has since rebranded itself as *Witches & Pagans*.

70 Mama Roz, Letter to the editor, 5.

71 Niven, "Ban Nudity in *newWitch*?" 14; see Cowan, *Cyberhenge*, 42–43.

72 Niven, "Ban Nudity in *newWitch*?" 15.

73 Deeply Disturbed Old Witch, "*newWitch* Too Goth?" 5.

74 Raven, Letter to the editor, 8–9.

75 See, respectively, Penczak, "Sex, Magic, and Healing"; Ardrian, "Toying Around"; Filan, "The Magical, Mystical Phallus."

76 "The Mask of the Demon."

77 The less said about Neil LaBute's 2006 remake of Hardy's classic, the better. Really.

78 Hardy, *The Wicker Man*.

79 Hardy, *The Wicker Man*.

80 Hardy, *The Wicker Man*.

81 Hardy, *The Wicker Man*.

82 Hardy, *The Wicker Man*.

83 Cherry, "The Wicca Woman," 112; see Zillman and Weaver, "Gender-Socialization Theory of Reactions to Horror."

84 Cherry, "The Wicca Woman," 115.

85 Cherry, "The Wicca Woman," 114.

86 Cherry, "The Wicca Woman," 120.

87 Cherry, "The Wicca Woman," 114.

88 Indeed, Wikipedia lists *The Wicker Man* rather strangely as a "folk horror musical."

89 Hardy, *The Wicker Man*.

90 Cherry, "The Wicca Woman," 115. The first verse of "The Landlord's Daughter," also written by Paul Giovanni for the film, goes, "Much has been said of the strumpets of yore / Of wenches and bawdy house queens by the score / But I sing of the baggage that we all adore / The Landlord's Daughter."

91 Ovid, *Metamorphoses*, 389.

92 Cherry, "The Wicca Woman," 117, 120.

93 Cherry, "The Wicca Woman," 114.

94 Cherry, "The Wicca Woman," 117.

95 Durkheim, *The Elementary Forms of Religious Life*, 42; see Cowan, *Magic, Monsters, and Make-Believe Heroes*, 64–66.
96 Blanchard, "Magic and Religion," 51.
97 Blanchard, "Magic and Religion," 51.
98 Cowan, *Magic, Monsters, and Make-Believe Heroes*, 65.
99 Thomas, *Religion and the Decline of Magic*, 303.
100 Thomas, *Religion and the Decline of Magic*, 304.
101 Thomas, *Religion and the Decline of Magic*, 304.
102 Lévi-Strauss, *The Savage Mind*, 221.
103 Hutton, *The Triumph of the Moon*, 394.

CHAPTER 6. DARKNESS WITHIN
1 Barker, "Jacqueline Ess," 60.
2 Barker, "Jacqueline Ess," 58, 59.
3 Barker, "Jacqueline Ess," 59.
4 Barker, "Jacqueline Ess," 59.
5 Barker, "Jacqueline Ess," 60.
6 Barker, "Jacqueline Ess," 59.
7 Barker, "Jacqueline Ess," 60.
8 Barker, "Jacqueline Ess," 60.
9 Barker, "Jacqueline Ess," 60.
10 Barker, "Jacqueline Ess," 67.
11 Barker, "Jacqueline Ess," 61.
12 Barker, "Jacqueline Ess," 62.
13 Barker, "Jacqueline Ess," 62.
14 Barker, "Jacqueline Ess," 62.
15 Barker, "Jacqueline Ess," 62.
16 Barker, "Jacqueline Ess," 62.
17 Barker, "Jacqueline Ess," 63.
18 Barker, "Jacqueline Ess," 63.
19 Barker, "Jacqueline Ess," 63.
20 Barker, "Jacqueline Ess," 63.
21 In *Hellraiser III*, when Pinhead follows Joey Summerskill into a Catholic church, the resident priest shouts that the demon will burn in hell for his desecration of God's house. "Burn?" the Cenobite asks suavely, before killing the cleric. "Oh, such a limited imagination."
22 See Machen, "The Great God Pan," in *The Three Imposters*; Lee, *Succubi*; Haggard, *She*; Smithee, *Hellraiser: Bloodline*.
23 Barker, *Hellraiser*.
24 King, *Danse Macabre*, 180.
25 King, *Nightmares and Dreamscapes*, 882. Here, King refers to the original version of his 1977 short story "Children of the Corn"; see Cowan, *America's Dark Theologian*, 36–43.

26 See King, *Carrie*. While her mother's fanatical Christian fundamentalism and the cruelty of her classmates may explain why Carrie's telekinesis manifests, neither accounts for its origin; see Cowan, *America's Dark Theologian*, 139–48.

27 Circe's story has been told in a number of ways, from classical sources such as Homer's *Odyssey*, Hesiod's *Theogony*, and Ovid's *Metamorphoses* to Nathaniel Hawthorne's *Tanglewood Tales*, Thomas Disch's *The Sub*, and Madeline Miller's eponymous reimagining.

28 Barker, "Jacqueline Ess," 66.

29 Barker, "Jacqueline Ess," 67; Lovecraft, "Call of Cthulhu," 139.

30 Beit-Hallahmi, "'The Turn of the Screw' and 'The Exorcist,'" 296; Creed, "Horror and the Monstrous-Feminine," 53.

31 Scanlon, *Apparitions*, 123.

32 Scanlon, *Apparitions*, 6. In addition to the narrator being identified only as "S," Inishwrack is "one of scores of islands in Clew Bay," on another of which, Achill Island, Scanlon himself lives.

33 Scanlon, *Apparitions*, 13–14.

34 Desai, *Khajuraho*, 12. On the Kama Sutra, see Wendy Doniger, *Redeeming the Kama Sutra*.

35 Desai, *Khajuraho*, 12.

36 Carroll, "Kama Sutra."

37 Desai, *Khajuraho*, 12.

38 Lal, *The Cult of Desire*.

39 Lal, *The Cult of Desire*, 6–7. On "secret museums," the sexual and sexualized artwork and artifacts kept under lock and key by Victorian society, see Kendrick, *The Secret Museum*; Marcus, *The Other Victorians*.

40 Fleming, *The Wizard of Oz*.

41 Said, *Orientalism*, 6, 202–3; for a counterargument to Said's claims, see, for example, Irwin, *Dangerous Knowledge*.

42 Said, *Orientalism*, 42.

43 This orientalization of sex is on similar display in Scanlon's subsequent novel, *Black Ashes*. Though it is somewhat dated, on the issue of orientalism in Western cinema, see Bernstein and Studlar, *Visions of the East*; and, for a religious studies perspective on the issue, one of the seminal texts remains Cox, *Turning East*.

44 Scanlon, *Apparitions*, 10.

45 Scanlon, *Apparitions*, 15, 16.

46 Scanlon, *Apparitions*, 16.

47 Scanlon, *Apparitions*, 16.

48 Scanlon, *Apparitions*, 17.

49 Scanlon, *Apparitions*, 75.

50 Scanlon, *Apparitions*, 20.

51 Scanlon, *Apparitions*, 19, 20.

52 Scanlon, *Apparitions*, 19.

53 Scanlon, *Apparitions*, 19.

54 Scanlon, *Apparitions*, 90.
55 Scanlon, *Apparitions*, 90.
56 Scanlon, *Apparitions*, 91.
57 Scanlon, *Apparitions*, 91.
58 Scanlon, *Apparitions*, 91.
59 Scanlon, *Apparitions*, 92.
60 Scanlon, *Apparitions*, 134.
61 Scanlon, *Apparitions*, 134.
62 Scanlon, *Apparitions*, 150–51.
63 James, "Some Remarks on Ghost Stories," in *The Haunted Doll's House*, 260.
64 For a variety of perspectives on this, see, for example, Cowan and Bromley, *Cults and New Religions*, 99–119; Foster, *Religion and Sexuality*; Lewis and Melton, *Sex, Slander, and Salvation*; Neitz and Goldman, *Sex, Lies, and Sanctity*; Palmer, *Aliens Adored* and *Moon Sisters, Krishna Mothers, Rajneesh Lovers*; Williams, *Heaven's Harlots*.
65 Scanlon, *Apparitions*, 145.
66 Scanlon, *Apparitions*, 145.
67 Scanlon, *Apparitions*, 145.
68 Scanlon, *Apparitions*, 145–46.
69 Scanlon, *Apparitions*, 16.
70 Scanlon, *Apparitions*, 16.
71 Scanlon, *Apparitions*, 199.
72 Scanlon, *Apparitions*, 199.
73 Scanlon, *Apparitions*, 207.
74 Clasen, *Why Horror Seduces*, 18.
75 Fry, "Sealed by the Moon," 122.
76 Fry, "Sealed by the Moon," 122.
77 Luhrmann, *Persuasions of the Witch's Craft*, 335–52.
78 Luhrmann, *Persuasions of the Witch's Craft*, 340.
79 Luhrmann, *Persuasions of the Witch's Craft*, 340.
80 Luhrmann, *Persuasions of the Witch's Craft*, 341.
81 See Turner, *Forest of Symbols*, 97–11, *The Ritual Process*, 94–165.
82 Fry, "Sealed by the Moon," 128.
83 Fry, "Sealed by the Moon," 128.
84 Fry, "Sealed by the Moon," 128.
85 Fry, "Sealed by the Moon," 122.
86 Fry, "Sealed by the Moon," 129.
87 Fry, "Sealed by the Moon," 128–29.
88 Fry, "Sealed by the Moon," 128.
89 Fry, "Sealed by the Moon," 131.
90 Fry, "Sealed by the Moon," 131.
91 Fry, "Sealed by the Moon," 131.
92 Fry, "Sealed by the Moon," 132–33.

93 On the importance of story in *Peter Pan*, see Cowan, *Magic, Monsters, and Make-Believe Heroes*, 82–83.

94 Barker, *Hellraiser*; Fry, "Sealed by the Moon," 129.

95 Fry, "Sealed by the Moon," 134.

96 Fry, "Sealed by the Moon," 134.

97 Fry, "Sealed by the Moon," 134–35.

98 Fry, "Sealed by the Moon," 135.

99 Fry, "Sealed by the Moon," 136.

100 Fry, "Sealed by the Moon," 136.

101 Fry, "Sealed by the Moon," 136.

102 Fry, "Sealed by the Moon," 137.

103 Fry, "Sealed by the Moon," 136.

104 Fry, "Sealed by the Moon," 136.

105 Fry, "Sealed by the Moon," 137.

106 Turner, *The Ritual Process*, 95.

107 For an example of this in terms of Stephen King's work, see Cowan, *America's Dark Theologian*, 115–38.

108 Fry, "Sealed by the Moon," 137.

109 Fry, "Sealed by the Moon," 137–38.

110 Fry, "Sealed by the Moon," 138.

111 Fry, "Sealed by the Moon," 138.

112 Fry, "Sealed by the Moon," 138.

113 Fry, "Sealed by the Moon," 138.

114 Fry, "Sealed by the Moon," 139.

115 Fry, "Sealed by the Moon," 140.

116 Fry, "Sealed by the Moon," 140; for a compelling look at the phenomenon of sexual murder, see Tatar, *Lustmord*.

117 Hartwell, *Dark Descent*, 10; Hartwell's first- and second-stream horror stories are, respectively, the *moral allegorical* and stories of *aberrant human psychology*.

118 Hartwell, *Dark Descent*, 10.

119 Kiernan, "Houses under the Sea," 189.

120 Kiernan, "Houses under the Sea," 161; on Heaven's Gate, see Cowan and Bromley, *Cults and New Religions*, 141–60; Zeller, *Heaven's Gate*.

121 *Merriam-Webster's Collegiate Dictionary*, 10th ed., "numen"; Otto, *The Idea of the Holy*, 6.

122 Otto, *Idea of the Holy*, 5.

123 Otto, *Idea of the Holy*, 14.

124 "Bruce," as all creature-feature fans know, was the name affectionately given to the animatronic great white shark in Spielberg's classic, *Jaws*.

125 Otto, *Idea of the Holy*, 14.

126 Otto, *Idea of the Holy*, 16.

127 Tambour, "Simply, Petrified," 72.

128 Tambour, "Simply, Petrified," 72.

129 Tambour, "Simply, Petrified," 58.

130 Tambour, "Simply, Petrified," 72.

131 Tambour, "Simply, Petrified," 54.

132 Tambour, "Simply, Petrified," 57.

133 Tambour, "Simply, Petrified," 58.

134 Tambour, "Simply, Petrified," 59.

135 Tambour, "Simply, Petrified," 60.

136 Tambour, "Simply, Petrified," 61.

137 Tambour, "Simply, Petrified," 61.

138 Tambour, "Simply, Petrified," 69.

139 Tambour, "Simply, Petrified," 69.

140 Berger, *Sacred Canopy*, 40.

141 Berger, *Sacred Canopy*, 40.

142 See Berger and Luckmann, *Social Construction of Reality*, 63–204.

CHAPTER 7. DARKNESS WITHOUT

1 Kyrou, *Le surréalisme au cinema*, 276.

2 LaMartina, *Call Girl of Cthulhu*. While "Ulthar Cats" is rooted in Lovecraft's 1920 short story, "The Cats of Ulthar," as groupie clothing, it is also a reference to the house band in Alan Moore and Jacen Burrows's graphic novel, *Neonomicon*. Also, see Lovecraft, "Cool Air," "The Cats of Ulthar," "Celephaïs," and "Dagon."

3 LaMartina, *Call Girl of Cthulhu*.

4 Even the main character's name pays intertextual homage to Lovecraft. "Riley" is R'lyeh, the lost city described in "The Call of Cthulhu," where "dead Cthulhu waits dreaming," "hidden in slimy green vaults" until awakened by his human acolytes (Lovecraft, "Call of Cthulhu," 150, 165). "Whatley" is LaMartina's creative misspelling of 'Whateley,' the eldritch family at the center of "The Dunwich Horror."

5 LaMartina, *Call Girl of Cthulhu*.

6 On the Church of Starry Wisdom, also known as the Starry Wisdom Cult in both Lovecraft's work and those who write in the Lovecraftian mode, see Harms, *The Cthulhu Mythos Encyclopedia*, 269–70.

7 LaMartina, *Call Girl of Cthulhu*.

8 Lovecraft, "Shadow over Innsmouth," 304.

9 A very similar scene occurs when the "Cloistered Barefoot Marionite Sisters" first open the hidden door in the basement of the Convent of Hell. See Noé and Barreiro, *The Convent of Hell*, 19–24.

10 Another fairly common trope in religious-oriented horror cinema, this is similar, for example, to David Fincher's 1995 horror-thriller, *Se7en*.

11 LaMartina, *Call Girl of Cthulhu*.

12 LaMartina, *Call Girl of Cthulhu*.

13 See, respectively, Kiernan, "Houses under the Sea"; Eckhardt, "And the Sea Gave Up the Dead."

14 Joshi, "Introduction," in Joshi, ed., *Black Wings of Cthulhu 3*, 9.

15 For various considerations of those writing in the Lovecraftian mode, see Haefele, *A Look behind the Derleth Mythos*; Joshi, *The Rise, Fall, and Rise of the Cthulhu Mythos*; Poole, *In the Mountains of Madness*.

16 Kiernan, "Black Ships Seen South of Heaven," 85, 86.

17 Kiernan, "Black Ships Seen South of Heaven," 81.

18 Kiernan, "Black Ships Seen South of Heaven," 81.

19 Tillich, *Dynamics of Faith*, 46; "Symbol and Knowledge: A Response," in Grigg, "God Is a Symbol for God," 48.

20 Lovecraft, "The Call of Cthulhu," 139.

21 Kiernan, "Black Ships Seen South of Heaven," 84.

22 Kiernan, "Black Ships Seen South of Heaven," 85.

23 On this, see W. B. Yeats's famous 1919 poem, "The Second Coming."

24 Kiernan, "Black Ships Seen South of Heaven," 90.

25 Kiernan, "Black Ships Seen South of Heaven," 90.

26 Kiernan, "Black Ships Seen South of Heaven," 90.

27 Kiernan, "Black Ships Seen South of Heaven," 90.

28 Kiernan, "Black Ships Seen South of Heaven," 99.

29 Kiernan, "Black Ships Seen South of Heaven," 101.

30 Lovecraft, "The Call of Cthulhu," 139.

31 Kiernan, "Pickman's Other Model (1929)," 18.

32 Kiernan, "Pickman's Other Model (1929)," 18.

33 See King, *Revival*; Cowan, *America's Dark Theologian*, 159–64.

34 Schumacher, *Flatliners*; Oplev, *Flatliners*.

35 Kiernan, "Houndwife," 63; see Lovecraft, "The Hound."

36 Kiernan, "Houndwife," 79–80.

37 Kiernan, "Houndwife," 79, 80.

38 Kiernan, "Houndwife," 64, 81.

39 Kiernan, "Houndwife," 65.

40 Kiernan, "Houndwife," 67, 76.

41 Kiernan, "Houndwife," 65, 67.

42 Kiernan, "Houndwife," 82.

43 See Cowan, "Dealing a New Religion"; Decker, DePaulis, and Dummett, *A Wicked Pack of Cards*; Decker and Dummett, *A History of the Occult Tarot, 1870–1970*.

44 Tyson, *Secrets of the Necronomicon*, 51.

45 Tyson, *Secrets of the Necronomicon*, 51.

46 Kiernan, "Houndwife," 66.

47 Kiernan, "Houndwife," 64.

48 Tyson, *Secrets of the Necronomicon*, 35; Kiernan, "Houndwife," 66.

49 Kiernan, "Houndwife," 76.

50 Kiernan, "Houndwife," 77.

51 Kiernan, "Houndwife," 82.

52 See James, *Varieties of Religious Experience*, 413–68.

53 James, *Varieties of Religious Experience*, 414.

54 Cushing, "Diary of a Sane Man," 41, 42.

55 Cushing, "Diary of a Sane Man," 42.

56 Cushing, "Diary of a Sane Man," 43.

57 Cushing, "Diary of a Sane Man," 43.

58 Cushing, "Diary of a Sane Man," 42.

59 See Freud, *The Uncanny*, 123–34.

60 Cushing, "Diary of a Sane Man," 45.

61 Cushing, "Diary of a Sane Man," 47.

62 Cushing, "Diary of a Sane Man," 47.

63 Cushing, "Diary of a Sane Man," 47–48.

64 Cushing, "Diary of a Sane Man," 49.

65 Cushing, "Diary of a Sane Man," 49.

66 Cushing, "Diary of a Sane Man," 53.

67 See Williams, *Heaven's Harlots*.

68 See Cowan and Bromley, *Cults and New Religions*, 99–119, esp. 114–16.

69 Beiser, *Weltschmerz*, 1, 4.

70 Beiser, *Weltschmerz*, 5; Gafford, "Weltschmerz," 315.

71 Gafford, "Weltschmerz," 315.

72 Gafford, "Weltschmerz," 315.

73 Gafford, "Weltschmerz," 316, 318.

74 Gafford, "Weltschmerz," 320.

75 Gafford, "Weltschmerz," 321.

76 Gafford, "Weltschmerz," 322.

77 Gafford, "Weltschmerz," 322.

78 Gafford, "Weltschmerz," 315.

79 Gafford, "Weltschmerz," 324.

80 Gafford, "Weltschmerz," 324.

81 Gafford, "Weltschmerz," 325.

82 Gafford, "Weltschmerz," 327.

83 Gafford, "Weltschmerz," 328.

84 Gafford, "Weltschmerz," 328. This is not unlike the initial position paper I regularly ask students to write in a fourth-year course I teach called "Critical Encounters with Human Nature."

85 Gafford, "Weltschmerz," 328–29.

86 Gafford, "Weltschmerz," 329.

87 Gafford, "Weltschmerz," 329.

88 Gafford, "Weltschmerz," 329.

89 Gafford, "Weltschmerz," 330.

90 Gafford, "Weltschmerz," 330. See Gordon, *Dagon*; Cowan, *Sacred Terror*, 81–84.

91 Gordon's *Dagon* is based on Lovecraft's "Dagon" and "The Shadow over Innsmouth."

92 Gafford, "Weltschmerz," 333.

93 Gafford, "Weltschmerz," 334.

94 Harms, *The Cthulhu Mythos Encyclopedia*, 204.

95 Harms, *The Cthulhu Mythos Encyclopedia*, 204.

96 For a variety of perspectives on drugs and the religious experience, see, for example, Allegro, *The Sacred Mushroom and the Cross*; Davis, *The Serpent and the Rainbow*; McKenna, *Food of the Gods*; Partridge, *High Culture*; Strassman, *DMT*.

97 See Huxley, *The Doors of Perception*.

98 Gafford, "Weltschmerz," 335.

99 Gafford, "Weltschmerz," 336.

100 Gafford, "Weltschmerz," 336.

101 On Lovecraft's life, see among others Burleson, *Lovecraft*; De Camp, *H. P. Lovecraft*; Houellebecq, *H. P. Lovecraft*; Joshi, *H. P. Lovecraft*.

102 For a variety of perspectives on this, see Haefele, *A Look behind the Derleth Mythos*; Joshi, *The Rise, Fall, and Rise of the Cthulhu Mythos*; Poole, *In the Mountains of Madness*.

103 Lovecraft to Kleiner, in Derie, *Sex and the Cthulhu Mythos*, 28; on the Kalem Club, see Hart and Joshi, *Lovecraft's New York Circle*.

104 Lovecraft to Kleiner, in Derie, *Sex and the Cthulhu Mythos*, 28.

105 Lovecraft to Kleiner, in Derie, *Sex and the Cthulhu Mythos*, 30.

106 Lovecraft to Derleth, in Derie, *Sex and the Cthulhu Mythos*, 30; see Weinberg, *Biographical Dictionary of Science Fiction and Fantasy Artists*, 225.

107 See Migliore and Strysik, *Lurker in the Lobby*.

108 See Smith, "The Return of the Sorcerer."

109 On insanity in the Lovecraftian mode, see, for example, Joshi, *The Madness of Cthulhu*; on the monstrous pantheon, see Datlow, *Lovecraft's Monsters*; French, *The Gods of H. P. Lovecraft*; Guran, *The Mammoth Book of Cthulhu*; Lockhard, *Cthulhu Fhtagn!*

110 See, for example, Jones, *Shadows over Innsmouth*; Lee, *The Innswich Horror*; Lupoff, *The Doom That Came to Dunwich*; Moore and Burrows, *Providence*; Schweitzer and Ashmead, *Tales from the Miskatonic University Library*.

111 See Gresh, *Sherlock Holmes vs. Cthulhu: The Adventure of the Deadly Dimensions*, *Sherlock Holmes vs. Cthulhu: The Adventure of the Innsmouth Mutation*, and *Sherlock Holmes vs. Cthulhu: The Adventure of the Neural Psychoses*.

112 See, respectively, Harman, *Weird Realism*; Sederholm and Weinstock, *The Age of Lovecraft*; Joshi, *Against Religion*; Steadman, *H. P. Lovecraft and The Black Magickal Tradition*; Colavito, *The Cult of Alien Gods*.

113 Derie, *Sex and the Cthulhu Mythos*; see Blackmore, *Whispers in Darkness*; Cowin and Kirk; *Lovecraft after Dark*; Cuinn, *Cthulhurotica*; O'Brien, *Eldritch Blue*.

114 See Simon, *The Gates of the Necronomicon*, *Necronomicon*, and *Necronomicon Spellbook*. For a debunking of this, however, see Harms and Gonce, *The Necronomicon Files*.

115 Tyson, "*The Necronomicon*: Shadow in the Mind," xi; for an excellent example of Tyson's Lovecraftian fiction, especially in the context of the emergence of a new religious movement, see Tyson, "The Skinless Face."

116 Tyson, "*The Necronomicon*: Shadow in the Mind," xiii.

117 Tyson, *Necronomicon*, 3.

118 Tyson, *Alhazred* and *Necronomicon: Wanderings of Alhazred*. See Davies, *Grimoires*, 264–67.

119 Tyson, *Grimoire of the Necronomicon*.

120 Tyson and Stokes, *Necronomicon Tarot*; Tyson, *Secrets of the Necronomicon*.

121 Cowan, "Dealing a New Religion," 259; see Baudrillard, *The System of Objects*.

122 Lovecraft to Derleth, in Joshi, *Against Religion*, 176.

123 See Tyson, *The Dream World of H. P. Lovecraft*.

124 Tyson, *Grimoire of the Necronomicon*, xxii.

125 Possamai, "Yoda Goes to Glastonbury," 1; see Cowan, "Dealing a New Religion," 256–62.

126 King, "The Body," in *Different Seasons*, 399.

127 Okorafor, "Lovecraft's Racism."

128 Miéville, in Okorafor, "Lovecraft's Racism"; for a more detailed look at Miéville's views on Lovecraft's racism, see Sederholm and Weinstock interview with Miéville in *The Age of Lovecraft*, esp. 240–42.

129 Matamas, in Okorafor, "Lovecraft's Racism."

130 Flood, "HP Lovecraft biographer rages."

131 Flood, "HP Lovecraft biographer rages."

132 Miéville, in Okorafor, "Lovecraft's Racism."

133 Dakan, "Correlated Discontents," 298.

134 See Dufty, *Losing the Head of Philip K. Dick*.

135 Dakan, "Correlated Discontents," 300; see Bebergal, *Strange Frequencies*.

136 Dakan, "Correlated Discontents," 300.

137 Dakan, "Correlated Discontents," 300, 303.

138 Dakan, "Correlated Discontents," 303.

139 Dakan, "Correlated Discontents," 303.

140 Dakan, "Correlated Discontents," 304.

141 Dakan, "Correlated Discontents," 306.

142 Dakan, "Correlated Discontents," 307.

143 Dakan, "Correlated Discontents," 307.

144 Dakan, "Correlated Discontents," 307.

145 Dakan, "Correlated Discontents," 311.

146 Dakan, "Correlated Discontents," 312.

147 See Berger and Luckmann, *The Social Construction of Reality*.

148 Dakan, "Correlated Discontents," 312.

149 Joshi, "Introduction," in Joshi, ed., *Black Wings of Cthulhu 2*, 8.

150 In addition to Lovecraft, *The Annotated Supernatural Horror in Literature*, see James, "Ghosts—Treat Them Gently" and "Some Remarks on Ghost Stories."

151 Price, "Introduction," in Price, ed., *Acolytes of Cthulhu*, 10.

152 Price, "Introduction," in Price, ed., *Acolytes of Cthulhu*, 11; for a selection of Price's own Lovecraftian fiction, see Price, *The Selma Horror and Others*.

153 Newman, "Foreword," in Joshi, ed., *The Madness of Cthulhu*, volume 2, 9.

154 Joshi, "Introduction," in Joshi, ed., *Black Wings of Cthulhu 2*, 8.

155 H. P. Lovecraft, quoted in Joshi, *Black Wings of Cthulhu*, 9.

CHAPTER 8. GOING MONSTERING

1 Johnson and Reynolds, *Against All Gods*, 80.

2 Webb, "The Megalith Plague," 212.

3 Webb, "The Megalith Plague," 208.

4 Webb, "The Megalith Plague," 208–9.

5 Webb, "The Megalith Plague," 213.

6 Webb, "The Megalith Plague," 213.

7 Webb, "The Megalith Plague," 214.

8 Webb, "The Megalith Plague," 214.

9 Webb, "The Megalith Plague," 214.

10 Webb, "The Megalith Plague," 221.

11 Webb, "The Megalith Plague," 218.

12 Webb, "The Megalith Plague," 219.

13 Webb, "The Megalith Plague," 219.

14 Truzzi, "Editorial," 2.

15 Truzzi, "Editorial," 2.

16 Truzzi, "Editorial," 34.

17 "Pierce on the Paranormal," 31.

18 See McDowell, *The Gospel according to "Star Wars"*; Neal, *The Gospel according to Harry Potter*; Wood, *The Gospel according to Tolkien*. On mapping one's own theology onto pop culture products, see Cowan, *Magic, Monsters, and Make-Believer Heroes*, 68–71, *Sacred Space*, 264–69.

19 Lee, *Witch Water*, 135.

20 See Murray, *The God of the Witches* and *The Witch-Cult in Western Europe*.

21 Lee, *Trolley No. 1852*, 78, 79; other volumes in Lee's Lovecraftian series include *The Haunter of the Threshold* and *The Innswich Horror*.

22 Lee, *Infernal Angel*, 10.

23 Lee, *Infernal Angel*, 1.

24 Lee, *City Infernal*, 8.

25 Lee, *City Infernal*, 106.

26 Lee, *City Infernal*, 107.

27 Lee, *City Infernal*, 107.

28 Lee, *City Infernal*, 107.

29 Lee and White, *Teratologist*, 42.

30 Lee and White, *Teratologist*, 105–6.

31 Lee and White, *Teratologist*, 106.

32 White, "Tamara's Last Exorcism," in *Horrible Gods*, 33.

33 White, "Tamara's Last Exorcism," in *Horrible Gods*, 33.

34 White, "Tamara's Last Exorcism," in *Horrible Gods*, 33; emphases added.

35 White, "Tamara's Last Exorcism," in *Horrible Gods*, 34.
36 White, "Tamara's Last Exorcism," in *Horrible Gods*, 34.
37 White, "Tamara's Last Exorcism," in *Horrible Gods*, 35.
38 White, "Tamara's Last Exorcism," in *Horrible Gods*, 35.
39 White, "Tamara's Last Exorcism," in *Horrible Gods*, 36.
40 White, "Tamara's Last Exorcism," in *Horrible Gods*, 37.
41 White, "Tamara's Last Exorcism," in *Horrible Gods*, 35.
42 White, "Tamara's Last Exorcism," in *Horrible Gods*, 36.
43 See Humphrey, "Gender and Sexuality Haunt the Horror Film."
44 Lewis, *The Monk*, 65.
45 Lewis, *The Monk*, 65; on various Christian interpretations of the breast, see Miles, *Carnal Knowing* and *A Complex Delight*.
46 Miles, *A Complex Delight*, x.
47 Lewis, *The Monk*, 65.
48 Lewis, *The Monk*, 67.
49 Lewis, *The Monk*, 67.
50 Lewis, *The Monk*, 67.
51 Lewis, *The Monk*, 67.
52 Lewis, *The Monk*, 440.
53 Lewis, *The Monk*, 440.
54 Hallam, *Screening the Marquis de Sade*, 3. Writers are divided on whether the appropriate spelling is 'Sadean' or 'Sadeian.'
55 Hallam, *Screening the Marquis de Sade*, 3.
56 Hallam, *Screening the Marquis de Sade*, 3; emphasis added.
57 Hallam, *Screening the Marquis de Sade*, 5.
58 Hallam, *Screening the Marquis de Sade*, 5.
59 Hallam, *Screening the Marquis de Sade*, 5.
60 Hallam, *Screening the Marquis de Sade*, 5. The answer to my friend's question is, "None, that we know of."
61 Hallam, *Screening the Marquis de Sade*, 6.
62 Hallam, *Screening the Marquis de Sade*, 8.
63 Hallam, *Screening the Marquis de Sade*, 10.
64 Sapolsky, "Dopamine Jackpot!"; see also Sapolsky , *Why Zebras Don't Get Ulcers*, 37–43.
65 Sade, *The 120 Days of Sodom*, 248.
66 Sade, *The 120 Days of Sodom*, 248.
67 Sade, *The 120 Days of Sodom*, 248.
68 Sade, *The 120 Days of Sodom*, 253.
69 Sade, *The 120 Days of Sodom*, 254.

BIBLIOGRAPHY

Abnett, Dan. *Hereticus*. Nottingham, UK: Black Library, 2015.

———. *The Magos and the Definitive Casebook of Gregor Eisenhorn*. Nottingham, UK: Black Library, 2018.

———. *Malleus*. Nottingham, UK: Black Library, 2001.

———. *Xenos*. Nottingham, UK: Black Library, 2001.

ACLU. "Hunter v. Salem Public Library Board of Trustees." Press release. ACLU, January 3, 2012; http://www.aclu.org (accessed April 19, 2020).

Adler, Gilbert, dir. *Bordello of Blood*. Written by A. L. Katz and Gilbert Adler. Universal City Studios, 1996.

Alexander, Brooks. *Witchcraft Goes Mainstream*. Eugene, OR: Harvest House Publishers, 2004.

Alfrey, Mark, ed. *Sex and Horror: The Art of Alessandro Biffingnandi*. London: Korero Press, 2016.

———, ed. *Sex and Horror: The Art of Emanuele Taglietti*. London: Korero Press, 2015.

Allegro, John M. *The Sacred Mushroom and the Cross: A Study of the Nature and Origins of Christianity within the Fertility Cults of the Ancient Near East*. London: Hodder & Stoughton, 1970.

Altheide, David L. *Creating Fear: News and the Construction of Crisis*. New York: Aldine de Gruyter, 2002.

Amazon. "Bride of the Gorilla." Internet Movie Database; www.imdb.com (accessed June 20, 2019).

———. "The Secret War." Internet Movie Database; www.imdb.com (accessed July 5, 2019).

Amendola, David W. "The Secret War." In *SNAFU: Hunters*. Edited by Amanda J. Spedding and Geoff Brown. Bechworth, Australia: Cohesion Press. Kindle, 2017.

American Horror Story: Murder House. Season 1. Created by Ryan Murphy and Brad Falchuk. FX, 2011.

"Americans Escape from Tibet: Suffer Inhuman Cruelty." *Washington Post* (May 25, 1928): 3.

Anderson, Paul W. S., dir. *Resident Evil*. Written by Paul W. S. Anderson. Constantin Film, 2002.

"Apostate Priest Retracts Errors." *The Catholic* (October 16, 1930): 7.

Arakawa, Kaku, dir. *Never-Ending Man: Hayao Miyazaki*. Tokyo: NHK, 2016.

Ardrian, David L. "Toying Around: A Pagan Look at Sex Toys." *newWitch* 13 (September–November 2006): 13–15.

Arnold, Jack, dir. *Creature from the Black Lagoon*. Written by Harry Essex and Arthur Ross. Universal Pictures, 1954.

———, dir. *Revenge of the Creature*. Written by Martin Berkeley. Universal International Pictures, 1955.

Atran, Scott. *In Gods We Trust: The Evolutionary Landscape of Religion*. Oxford: Oxford University Press, 2002.

Badham, John, dir. *Dracula*. Written by W. D. Richter. The Mirisch Company, 1979.

Baigent, Michael, Richard Leigh, and Henry Lincoln. *Holy Blood, Holy Grail: The Secret History of Christ and the Shocking Legacy of the Grail*. New York: Bantam, 1983.

Baker, Roy Ward, dir. *The Vampire Lover*. Written by Tudor Gates. Hammer Films, 1970.

Baker, Tim. *Dewitched: What You Need to Know about the Dangers of Wicca and Witchcraft*. Nashville, TN: Transit Books, 2004.

Ball, Tom, and Abigail O'Leary. "Witch performs Pagan rituals while naked with her children—and claims stripping off helps them bond with nature." *Daily Mirror* (October 23, 2018); https://www.mirror.co.uk (accessed January 1, 2020).

Barker, Clive. *The Hellbound Heart*. New York: Harper Paperbacks, 1986.

———, dir. *Hellraiser*. Written by Clive Barker. Cinemarque Entertainment BV, 1987.

———. "Jacqueline Ess: Her Will and Testament." In *Books of Blood*, volumes 1–3, 2: 58–90. London: Warner Books, 1998.

———. *The Scarlet Gospels*. New York: St. Martin's, 2015.

Barker, Martin. *A Haunt of Fears: The Strange History of the British Horror Comics Campaign*. London: Pluto Press, 1984.

Barner-Barry, Carol. *Contemporary Paganism: Minority Religions in a Majoritarian America*. New York: Palgrave Macmillan, 2005.

Barrett, Justin L. *Why Would Anyone Believe in God?* Lanham, MD: AltaMira Press, 2004.

Barton, Bernadette. *The Pornification of America: How Raunch Culture Is Ruining Our Society*. New York: NYU Press, 2021.

Barton, Bernadette, and Constance L. Hardesty. "Spirituality and Stripping: Exotic Dancers Narrate the Body Ekstasis." *Symbolic Interaction* 33, no. 2 (2010): 280–96.

Barzun, Jacques. "The Art and Appeal of the Ghostly and Ghastly." In *The Penguin Encyclopedia of Horror and the Supernatural*. Edited by Jack Sullivan, xix–xxviii. New York: Viking, 1986.

Bataille, Georges. *Erotism: Death and Sensuality*. Translated by Mary Dalwood. 1962. San Francisco: City Lights Books, 1986.

———. *The Tears of Eros*. Translated by Peter Connor. 1961. San Francisco: City Lights Books. 1989.

Bate, David. *Photography and Surrealism: Sexuality, Colonialism, and Dissent*. London: I. B. Tauris, 2004.

Baudrillard, Jean. *The System of Objects*. Translated by James Benedict. London: Verso, 2005.

Bayona, J. A., dir. *Penny Dreadful*. "Night Work." Episode 1. Written by John Logan. Showtime Networks. May 11, 2014.

Beal, Timothy K. *Religion and Its Monsters*. New York: Routledge, 2002.

Bear, Greg. *Halo: Cryptum*. *The Forerunner Saga*, book 1. New York: Tor Books, 2010.

———. *Halo: Primordium*. *The Forerunner Saga*, book 2. New York: Tor Books, 2011.

———. *Halo: Silentium*. *The Forerunner Saga*, book 3. New York: Tor Books, 2013.

Bebergal, Peter. *Strange Frequencies: The Extraordinary Story of the Technological Quest for the Supernatural*. New York: Tarcher Perigee, 2018.

Beiser, Frederick C. *Weltschmerz: Pessimism in German Philosophy, 1860–1900*. New York: Oxford University Press, 2016.

Beit-Hallahmi, Benjamin. "'The Turn of the Screw' and 'The Exorcist': Demoniacal Possession and Childhood Purity." *America Imago* 33, no. 3 (1976): 296–303.

Ben-Atar, Doron S., and Richard D. Brown. *Taming Lust: Crimes Against Nature in the Early Republic*. Philadelphia: University of Pennsylvania Press, 2014.

Benshoff, Harry M. *Monsters in the Closet: Homosexuality and the Horror Film*. Manchester, UK: Manchester University Press, 1997.

Berger, Peter L. *The Sacred Canopy: Elements of a Sociological Theory of Religion*. 1967. Reprint. New York: Anchor Books, 1990.

Berger, Peter L., and Thomas Luckmann. *The Social Construction of Reality: A Treatise in the Sociology of Knowledge*. London: Penguin Books, 1966.

Bering, Jesse. *Perv: The Sexual Deviant in All of Us*. New York: Scientific American, 2013.

Berlant, Lauren, and Lisa Duggan, eds. *Our Monica, Ourselves: The Clinton Affair and the National Interest*. New York: NYU Press, 2001.

Bernstein, Matthew, and Gaylyn Studlar, eds. *Visions of the East: Orientalism in Film*. New Brunswick, NJ: Rutgers University Press, 1997.

Best, Joel, and Kathleen A. Bogle. *Kids Gone Wild: From Rainbow Parties to Sexting; Understanding the Hype Over Teen Sex*. New York: NYU Press, 2014.

Bhattacarya, Narendranath. *History of the Tantric Religion: A Historical, Ritualistic, and Philosophical Study*. New Delhi: Manohar, 1982.

Biale, David. *Eros and the Jews: From Biblical Israel to Contemporary America*. Berkeley: University of California Press, 1997.

Biller, Anna, dir. *The Love Witch*. Written by Anna Biller. Anna Biller Productions, 2016.

"Black Art in Tibet." *New York Times* (June 7, 1925): SM21.

"Black Bon Po Rites Rampant in Tibet." *New York Times* (August 22, 1928): 10.

Black, Candice, ed. *Lust for the Devil: The Erotic-Satanic Art of Félicien Rops*. New York: Wet Angel, 2013.

Black, Gregory D. *The Catholic Crusade Against the Movies, 1940–1975*. Cambridge: Cambridge University Press, 1997.

———. *Hollywood Censored: Morality Codes, Catholics, and the Movies*. Cambridge: Cambridge University Press, 1994.

Blacker, Ben. *Hex Wives*. Art by Mirka Andolfo. Burbank, CA: DC Comics, 2019.

Blackmore, Jen, ed. *Whispers in Darkness: Lovecraftian Erotica*. Cambridge, MA: Circlet Press, 2011.

Blanchard, David. "Magic and Religion: Toward a Hermeneutic of Popular Religiosity." *New Theology Review* 13, no. 2 (2000): 49–58.

Blanchard, Pascal, et al., eds. *Human Zoos: Science and Spectacle in the Age of Empire*. New York: Oxford University Press, 2009.

Blatty, William Peter. *The Exorcist*. New York: Book-of-the-Month Club, 1971.

———. "'The Exorcist's' Secret Message." Fox News, May 7, 2015; www.foxnews.com (accessed July 12, 2019).

Bloch, Ruth H. "Changing Conceptions of Sexuality and Romance in Eighteenth-Century America." *William and Mary Quarterly* 60, no. 1 (2003): 13–42.

Boccaccio. *Decameron*. Translated by J. G. Nichols. New York: Everyman's Library, 2008.

Bock, Darrell L. *Breaking the Da Vinci Code: Answers to the Questions Everyone's Asking*. Nashville, TN: Thomas Nelson, 2004.

Booth, James. "Human Sacrifice in Literature: The Case of Wole Soyinka." *Ariel: A Review of International English Literature* 23, no. 1 (1992): 8–24.

Booth, Rebecca, Valeska Griffiths, and Erin Thompson, eds. *Scared Sacred: Idolatry, Religion, and Worship in the Horror Film*. Belfast, Ireland: House of Leaves Publishing, 2020.

Boswell, John. *Christianity, Social Tolerance, and Homosexuality: Gay People in Western Europe from the Beginning of the Christian Era to the Fourteenth Century*. Chicago: University of Chicago Press, 1980.

Boyarin, Daniel. *Carnal Israel: Reading Sex in Talmudic Culture*. Berkeley: University of California Press, 1993.

Boyd, Brian. *On the Origin of Stories: Evolution, Cognition, and Fiction*. Cambridge, MA: Belknap Press, 2009.

Boyer, Pascal. *The Naturalness of Religious Ideas: A Cognitive Theory of Religion*. Berkeley: University of California Press, 1994.

———. *Religion Explained: The Evolutionary Origins of Religious Thought*. New York: Basic Books, 2001.

Boyle, Danny, dir. *28 Days Later*. Written by Alex Garland. DNA Films, 2002.

Brakke, David. *Demons and the Making of the Monk: Spiritual Combat in Early Christianity*. Cambridge, MA: Harvard University Press, 2006.

Brenner, Robin E. *Understanding Manga and Anime*. Westport, CT: Libraries Unlimited, 2007.

Bromley, David G., ed. *Falling from the Faith: Causes and Consequences of Religious Apostasy*. Newbury Park, CA: Sage, 1988.

———. *The Politics of Religious Apostasy: The Role of Apostates in the Transformation of Religious Movements*. Westport, CT: Praeger, 1998.

Bronstein, Carolyn. *Battling Pornography: The American Feminist Anti-Pornography Movement, 1976–1986*. Cambridge: Cambridge University Press, 2011.

Brown, Carter. *The Coven*. New York, Signet, 1971

Brown, Dan. *The Da Vinci Code*. New York: Doubleday, 2003.

Brown, Steven T. *Japanese Horror and the Transnational Cinema of Sensations*. New York: Palgrave Macmillan, 2018.

Browning, Tod, dir. *Dracula*. Written by Hamilton Deane and John L. Balderston. Universal Pictures, 1931.

Brownmiller, Susan. *Against Our Will: Men, Women, and Rape*. New York: Bantam Books, 1975.

Brunvand, Jan Harald. *The Vanishing Hitchhiker: American Urban Legends and Their Meanings*. New York: Norton, 1981.

Bullough, Vern L. *Sexual Variance in Society and History*. Chicago: University of Chicago Press, 1976.

Bullough, Vern L., and Bonnie Bullough. *Sexual Attitudes: Myths and Realities*. Amherst, NY: Prometheus Books, 1995.

Bunn, Cullen. *Harrow County*. Art by Tyler Crook. Milwaukie, OR: Dark Horse Books, 2015.

Burkert, Walter. *Homo Necans: The Anthropology of Ancient Greek Sacrificial Myth and Ritual*. Translated by Peter Bing. Berkeley: University of California Press, 1972.

Burleson, Donald R. "Desert Dreams." In *Black Wings of Cthulhu: Twenty-One Tales of Lovecraftian Horror*. Edited by S. T. Joshi, 47–60. London: Titan Books, 2012.

———. *Lovecraft: Disturbing the Universe*. Lexington: University Press of Kentucky, 1990.

Burton, Tim, dir. *Sleepy Hollow*. Written by Andrew Kevin Walker. Paramount Pictures, 1999.

Cabell, Craig. *James Herbert: Devil in the Dark*. London: Metro Publishing, 2003.

Cahn, Edward L., dir. *Invasion of the Saucer Men*. Written by Robert J. Gurney Jr. and Al Martin. Malibu Productions, 1957.

Callow, John. *Embracing the Darkness: A Cultural History of Witchcraft*. London: I. B. Tauris, 2018.

Cameron, James, dir. *Aliens*. Written by James Cameron, David Giler, and Walter Hill. Brandywine Productions, 1986.

Campbell, Jonny, dir. "The Rules of the Beast." *Dracula*. Episode 1. Written by Mark Gatiss and Steven Moffatt. Hartswood Films, 2020.

Campbell, Joseph. *The Hero with a Thousand Faces*. 2nd ed. Princeton, NJ: Princeton University Press, 1968.

Campbell, Ramsay. "The Correspondence of Cameron Thaddeus Nash." In *Black Wings of Cthulhu: Twenty-One New Tales of Lovecraftian Horror*. Edited by S. T. Joshi, 383–417. London: Titan Books, 2012.

Carpenter, John, dir. *The Fog*. Written by John Carpenter and Debra Hill. Debra Hill Productions, 1980.

——, dir. *Halloween*. Written by John Carpenter and Debra Hill. Compass International Pictures, 1978.

——, dir. *The Thing*. Written by Bill Lancaster. Universal Pictures, 1982.

——, dir. *Vampires*. Written by Don Jakoby. Largo Entertainment, 1998.

Carrasco, David. "Sacrifice/Human Sacrifice in Religious Traditions." In *The Oxford Handbook of Religion and Violence*. Edited by Michael Jerryson, Mark Juergensmeyer, and Margo Kitts. New York: Oxford University Press, 2013. https://doi.org/10.1093/oxforhb/9780199759996.013.001.

Carroll, Noël. *The Philosophy of Horror; or, Paradoxes of the Heart*. New York: Routledge, 1990.

Carroll, Stephen, dir. "Kama Sutra." Written by Stephen Carroll and Dan Oliver. *Lost Worlds*. Season 2, episode 2. Atlantic Productions, 2007.

Cartwright, Marc, dir. *Vexed*. Written by Baker Chase Powell. Glass Cabin Films, 2016.

Casapinta, Ferruccio, dir. *Satan's Doll* [*La Bambola di Satana*]. Written by Ferruccio Casapinta, Giorgio Cristallini, and Carlo M. Lori. Cinediorama, 1969.

Castiglia, Christopher. *Bound and Determined: Captivity, Culture-Crossing, and White Womanhood from Mary Rowlandson to Patty Hearst*. Chicago: University of Chicago Press, 1996.

Chaffey, Don, dir. *Jason and the Argonauts*. Written by Appolonios Rhodios. Morningside Productions, 1963.

Chateauvert, Melinda. *Sex Workers Unite: A History of the Movement from Stonewall to SlutWalk*. Boston: Beacon, 2013.

Cherry, Brigid. "The Wicca Woman: Gender, Sexuality, and Religion in *The Wicker Man*." In *The Quest for the Wicker Man: History, Folklore, and Pagan Perspectives*. Edited by Benjamin Franks et al., 111–25. Edinburgh: Luath Press, 2006.

Chesters, Timothy. *Ghost Stories in Late Renaissance France: Walking by Night*. Oxford: Oxford University Press, 2011.

Chiniquy, Charles. *Fifty Years in the Church of Rome*. New York: Fleming H. Revell, 1886.

——. *The Priest, The Woman, and The Confessional*. 43rd ed. New York: Fleming H. Revell, 1880.

Choi, Jinhee, and Mitsuyo Wada-Marciano. *Horror to the Extreme: Changing Boundaries in Asian Cinema*. Hong Kong: Hong Kong University Press, 2009.

Clark, Kenneth. *The Nude: A Study in Ideal Form*. Princeton, NJ: Princeton University Press, 1956.

Clasen, Mathias. *Why Horror Seduces*. New York: Oxford University Press, 2017.

Clover, Carol J. *Men, Women, and Chain Saws: Gender in the Modern Horror Film*. Princeton, NJ: Princeton University Press, 1992.

Cohen, Jeffrey Jerome, ed. *Monster Theory: Reading Culture*. Minneapolis: University of Minnesota Press, 1996.

Cohen, Larry, dir. *Q: The Winged Serpent*. Written by Larry Cohen. Arkoff International, 1982.

Colavito, Jason. *The Cult of Alien Gods: H. P. Lovecraft and Extraterrestrial Pop Culture*. Amherst, NY: Prometheus Books, 2005.

Considine, Austin. "Bored at Work? Try Creepypasta, or Web Scares." *New York Times* (November 12, 2010): ST 6.

Cooper, Merien C., and Edward B. Schoedsack, dirs. *King Kong*. Written by James Creelman and Ruth Rose. RKO Radio Pictures, 1933.

Corman, Roger, dir. *Attack of the Crab Monsters*. Written by Charles B. Griffith. Los Altos Productions, 1957.

———, dir. *Day the World Ended*. Written by Lou Rusoff. Golden State Productions, 1955.

———, dir. *It Conquered the World*. Written by Lou Rusoff. Sunset Productions, 1956.

———, dir. *Not of This Earth*. Written by Charles Griffith and Mark Hanna. Los Altos Productions, 1957.

———, dir. *Saga of the Viking Women and Their Voyage to the Waters of the Great Sea Serpent*. Written by Lawrence L. Goldman. Malibu Productions 1957.

———, dir. *She Gods of Shark Reef*. Written by Robert Hill and Victor Stoloff. Ludwig H. Gerber Productions, 1958.

———, dir. *The Undead*. Written by Charles Griffith and Mark Hanna. Roger Corman Productions, 1957.

Cowan, Douglas E. *America's Dark Theologian: The Religious Imagination of Stephen King*. New York: NYU Press, 2018.

———. *Bearing False Witness? An Introduction to the Christian Countercult*. Westport, CT: Praeger, 2003.

———. "Bearing False Witness: Propaganda, Reality-Maintenance, and Christian Anticult Apologetics." PhD diss. University of Calgary, 1999.

———. "Consider the Yattering: The Infernal Order and the Religious Imagination in Real Time." In *Theology and Horror: Explorations in the Dark Religious Imagination*. Edited by Brandon R. Grafius and John W. Morehead, 3–20. Lanham, MD: Lexington Books/Fortress Academic, 2021.

———. "The Crack in the World: New Thoughts on Religion and Horror." *Religious Studies Review* 41, no. 4 (2015): 133–39.

———. *Cyberhenge: Modern Pagans on the Internet*. New York: Routledge, 2005.

———. "Dealing a New Religion: Material Culture, Divination, and Hyper-Religious Innovation." In *Handbook of Hyper-Real Religions*. Edited by Adam Possamai, 247–65. Leiden: Brill, 2012.

———. *Magic, Monsters, and Make-Believe Heroes: How Myth and Religion Shape Fantasy Culture*. Berkeley: University of California Press, 2019.

———. "Pulp Evangelism and Narrative Structure in Evangelical Fiction." In *Border Crossings: Explorations of an Interdisciplinary Historian*. Edited by Ulrich van der Heyden and Andreas Feldtkeller, 31–41. Munich: Franz Steiner, 2008.

———. "Re-Iterations: On Tellings, Variants, and Why Monsters Always Come Back." In *Religion, Culture, and the Monstrous: Of Gods and Monsters!* Edited by Natasha L. Mikles and Joseph P. Laycock, 17–28. Lanham, MD: Lexington Press, 2021.

———. Review of *Science Fiction and the Imitation of the Sacred*. *Journal of Contemporary Religion* 34, no. 2 (2019): 386–88. https//doi.org/10.1080/13537903.2019.1628380.

———. *Sacred Space: The Quest for Transcendence in Science Fiction Film and Television*. Waco, TX: Baylor University Press, 2010.

———. *Sacred Terror: Religion and Horror on the Silver Screen*. Waco, TX: Baylor University Press, 2008.

———. "Seeing the Saviour in the Stars: Religion, Conformity, and *The Day the Earth Stood Still*." *Journal of Religion and Popular Culture* 21, no. 1 (2009). https://doi.org/10.3138/jrpc.21.1.003.

———. "'So we're just going to ignore the bear': Imagining Religion at *Midsommar*." *Journal of Gods and Monsters* 1, no. 1 (2020): 54–56.

Cowan, Douglas E., and David G. Bromley. *Cults and New Religions: A Brief History*. 2nd ed. Oxford: Wiley Blackwell, 2015.

Cowin, Roger, and James Ward Kirk, eds. *Lovecraft after Dark*. Indianapolis: James Ward Kirk, 2015.

Cox, Harvey. *Turning East: Why Americans Look to the Orient for Spirituality—And What That Search Can Mean to the West*. New York: Touchstone, 1977.

Craven, Wes, dir. *Scream*. Written by Kevin Williamson. Dimension Films, 1996.

Creed, Barbara. "Horror and the Monstrous-Feminine: An Imaginary Abjection." *Screen* 27, no. 1 (1986): 44–71.

———. *The Monstrous-Feminine: Film, Feminism, Psychoanalysis*. New York: Routledge, 1993.

Critelli, Joseph W., and Jenny M. Bivona. "Women's Erotic Rape Fantasies: An Evaluation of Theory and Research." *Journal of Sex Research* 45, no. 1 (2008): 57–70.

Cuinn, Catherine, ed. *Cthulhurotica*. Mercerville, NJ: Dagon Books, 2010.

Cushing, Nicole. "Diary of a Sane Man." In *Black Wings of Cthulhu 5: Twenty New Tales of Lovecraftian Horror*. Edited by S. T. Joshi, 37–56. London: Titan Books, 2018.

Daichmann, Graciela S. *Wayward Nuns in Medieval Literature*. Syracuse, NY: Syracuse University Press, 1986.

Dakan, Rick. "Correlated Discontents." In *Black Wings of Cthulhu 2: Eighteen Tales of Lovecraftian Horror*. Edited by S. T. Joshi, 291–315. London: Titan Books, 2014.

Daly, Mary. *The Church and the Second Sex*. 3rd ed. Boston: Beacon, 1985.

———. *Pure Lust: Elemental Feminist Philosophy*. New York: HarperSanFrancisco, 1984.

Datlow, Ellen, ed. *Lovecraft's Monsters*. San Francisco: Tachyon, 2014.

Davidsen, Markus Altena. "Fiction and Religion: How Narratives about the Supernatural Inspire Religious Belief; Introducing the Thematic Issue." *Religion* 46, no. 4 (2016): 489–99.

———. "The Religious Affordance of Fiction: A Semiotic Approach." *Religion* 46, no. 4 (2016): 521–49.

Davies, Alex. "*The Walking Dead*: How did the virus start? What created the Walkers?" *Daily Express* (September 16, 2019); www.express.co.uk (accessed October 2, 2019).

Davies, Owen. *Grimoires: A History of Magic Books*. Oxford: Oxford University Press, 2009.

Davis, Desmond, dir. *Clash of the Titans.* Written by Beverly Cross. Metro-Goldwyn-Mayer, 1981.

Davis, Hank, and Andrea Javor. "Religion, death, and horror movies: Some striking evolutionary parallels." *Evolution and Cognition* 10, no. 1 (2004): 11–18.

Davis, Wade. *The Serpent and the Rainbow.* New York: Touchstone, 1985.

Davisson, Zack. *Yūrei: The Japanese Ghost.* Seattle: Chin Music Press, 2015.

Deacy, Christopher. "Reflections on the Uncritical Appropriation of Cinematic Christ-Figures: Holy Other or Wholly Inadequate?" *Journal of Religion and Popular Culture* 13, no. 1 (2006). https://doi.org/10.3138/jrpc.13.1.001.

De Camp, L. Sprague. *H. P. Lovecraft: A Biography.* New York: Barnes & Noble Books, 1975.

Decker, Ronald, Thierry DePaulis, and Michael Dummett. *A Wicked Pack of Cards: The Origins of the Occult Tarot.* New York: St. Martin's, 1996.

Decker, Ronald, and Michael Dummett. *A History of the Occult Tarot, 1870–1970.* London: Duckworth, 2002.

Deeply Disturbed Old Witch. "*newWitch* too Goth?" Letter to the editor. *newWitch* 9 (May–July 2005): 5.

Deiss, Joseph Jay. *Herculaneum: Italy's Buried Treasure.* 2nd ed. Los Angeles: J. Paul Getty Museum, 1989.

Delving, Michael. *The Devil Finds Work.* New York: Leisure Books, 1969.

Demaree, Ben, dir. *Ouija House.* Written by Justin Hawkins and Jeff Miller. ITN Films, 2018.

"Demonology and Witchcraft Now Rule Tibetan Buddahism [*sic*]." *Atlanta Constitution* (July 15, 1928): 11A.

Demos, John. *Entertaining Satan: Witchcraft and the Culture of Early New England.* Rev. ed. New York: Oxford University Press, 2004.

Derie, Bobby. *Sex and the Cthulhu Mythos.* New York: Hippocampus Press, 2014.

Desai, Devangana. *Khajuraho: Monumental Legacy.* New Delhi: Oxford University Press, 2000.

Diderot, Denis. *The Nun.* 1780. Translated by Eileen B. Hennessy. Los Angeles: Holloway House, 1968.

Dijkstra, Bram. *Evil Sisters: The Threat of Female Sexuality in Twentieth-Century Culture.* New York: Owl Books, 1996.

———. *Idols of Perversity: Fantasies of Feminine Evil in Fin-de-Siècle Culture.* New York: Oxford University Press, 1986.

Dines, Gail. *Pornland: How Porn Has Hijacked Our Sexuality.* Boston: Beacon, 2010.

Disch, Thomas M. *The Sub: A Study in Witchcraft.* Minneapolis: University of Minnesota Press, 1999.

Donahoe, Patrick. *The Charlestown Convent: Its Destruction by a Mob, on the Night of August 11, 1834. With a History of the Excitement before the Burning, and the Strange and Exaggerated Reports relating Thereto; the Feelings of Regret and Indignation Afterwards; the Proceedings of Meetings, and Expression of the Contemporary Press.* Boston: Patrick Donohoe, 1870.

Doniger, Wendy. *Redeeming the Kama Sutra.* New York: Oxford University Press, 2016.

Donner, Richard, dir. *The Omen.* Written by David Seltzer. Twentieth Century Fox, 1976.

Douglas, Mary. *Purity and Danger: An Analysis of Pollution and Taboo.* London: Routledge, 1966.

Downey, Dara. *American Women's Ghost Stories in the Gilded Age.* New York: Palgrave Macmillan, 2014.

Dufty, David. *Losing the Head of Philip K. Dick: A Bizarre but True Tale of Androids, Kill Switches, and Left Luggage.* Oxford: Oneworld, 2012.

Duile, Timo. "Kuntilanak: Ghost Narratives and Malay Modernity in Pontianak, Indonesia." *Bijdragen tot de Taal-, Land-, en Volkenkunde* 176, no. 2/3 (2020): 279–303.

DuQuette, Lon Milo. *My Life with the Spirits: The Adventures of a Modern Magician.* Boston: Red Wheel/Weiser, 1999.

Durkheim, Émile. *The Elementary Forms of Religious Life.* 1912. Translated by Karen E. Fields. New York: Free Press, 1995.

Ebersole, Gary L. *Captured by Texts: Puritan to Post-Modern Images of Indian Captivity.* Charlottesville: University of Virginia Press, 1995.

Eckhardt, Jason C. "And the Sea Gave Up the Dead." In *Black Wings of Cthulhu 2: Eighteen Tales of Lovecraftian Horror.* Edited by S. T. Joshi, 195–212. London: Titan Books, 2014.

Editors. "Awful Disclosures." *Boston Recorder* (February 12, 1936): 28.

———. "Awful Disclosures of Maria Monk." *Christian Register and Boston Observer* (March 25, 1836): 50.

———. "Maria Monk's Awful Disclosures." *Niles' Weekly Register* (April 22, 1837): 125.

Eggers, Robert, dir. *The Witch.* Written by Robert Eggers. Parts and Labor Films, 2015.

Elliott, Dyan. *Fallen Bodies: Pollution, Sexuality, and Demonology in the Middle Ages.* Philadelphia: University of Pennsylvania Press, 1999.

Elliott-Smith, Darren. *Queer Horror Film and Television: Sexuality and Masculinity at the Margins.* London: I. B. Tauris, 2016.

Elliott-Smith, Darren, and John Edgar Browning, eds. *New Queer Horror Film and Television.* Cardiff: University of Wales Press, 2020.

Ellis, Bruce J., and Donald Symons. "Sex Differences in Sexual Fantasy: An Evolutionary Psychology Approach." *Journal of Sex Research* 27, no. 4 (1990): 527–55.

Ellul, Jacques. *Propaganda: The Formations of Men's Attitudes.* Translated by Konrad Kellen and Jean Lerner. New York: Borzoi Books, 1965.

Ephron, Nora, dir. *Bewitched.* Written by Nora Ephron and Delia Ephron. Columbia Pictures, 2005.

Evans-Pritchard, E. E. *Witchcraft, Oracles, and Magic among the Azande.* Oxford: Oxford University Press, 1962.

"Exorcist (1973) Crucifix *13+*, The." YouTube video, 0:55, posted by Cinema Cut. March 28, 2015; www.youtube.com/watch?v=gvPGkwmhIZO (accessed February 14, 2020).

Farmer, Philip José. *Blown.* 1969. Reprint. New York: Creation Books, 2001.

———. *Flesh.* 1974. Reprint. London: Titan Books, 2013.

———. *The Image of the Beast.* 1968. Reprint. New York: Creation Books, 2001.

Farrar, Janet, and Stewart Farrar. *The Witches' Way: Principles, Rituals, and Beliefs of Modern Witchcraft.* Custer, WA: Phoenix, 1984.

Faure, Bernard. *The Red Thread: Buddhist Approaches to Sexuality.* Princeton, NJ: Princeton University Press, 1998.

Feil, Ernst. "From the Classical *Religio* to the Modern *Religion*: Elements of a Transformation between 1550 and 1650." In *Religion in History: The Word, the Idea, the Reality.* Edited by Michel Despland and Gérard Vallée, 31–44. Waterloo, Ontario: Wilfrid Laurier University Press, 1992.

Felton, D. *Haunted Greece and Rome: Ghost Stories from Classical Antiquity.* Austin: University of Texas Press, 1999.

Fentone, Steve. *AntiCristo: The Bible of Nasty Nuns Sinema and Culture.* Godalming, UK: FAB Press, 2001.

Fessenden, Tracy, Nicholas F. Radel, and Magdalena J. Zaborowska, eds. *The Puritan Origins of American Sex: Religion, Sexuality, and National Identity in American Literature.* New York: Routledge, 2001.

Festinger, Leon, Henry W. Riecken, and Stanley Schachter. *When Prophecy Fails: A Social and Psychological Study of a Modern Group That Predicted the Destruction of the World.* 1956. Reprint. London: Pinter & Martin, 2009.

Filan, Kenaz. "The Magical, Mystical Phallus." *newWitch* 13 (September–November 2006): 51–53.

Fincher, David, dir. *Alien³.* Written by David Giler, Walter Hill, and Larry Ferguson. Brandywine Productions, 1992.

———, dir. *Se7en.* Written by Andrew Kevin Walker. Cecchi Gori Pictures, 1995.

Fisher, Terence, dir. *The Brides of Dracula.* Written by Jimmy Sangster, Peter Bryan, and Edward Percy. Hammer Films, 1960.

Fleming, Victor, dir. *The Wizard of Oz.* Written by Noel Langley, Florence Ryerson, and Edgar Allen Woolf. Metro-Goldwyn-Mayer, 1939.

Flood, Alison. "HP Lovecraft biographer rages against ditching of author as fantasy prize emblem." *Guardian* (November 11, 2015); https://www.theguardian.com (accessed August 14, 2020).

Flood, Gavin. *The Tantric Body: The Secret Tradition of Hindu Religion.* New York: I. B. Tauris, 2006.

Forbes, Bruce David, and Jeanne Halgren Kilde, eds. *Rapture, Revelation, and the End Times: Exploring the "Left Behind" Series.* New York: Palgrave Macmillan, 2004.

Foster, Lawrence. *Religion and Sexuality: Three Communal Experiments in the Nineteenth Century.* New York: Oxford University Press, 1981.

Foster, Michael Dylan. *The Book of Yōkai: Mysterious Creatures of Japanese Folklore.* Berkeley: University of California Press, 2015.

———. *Pandemonium and Parade: Japanese Monsters and the Culture of Yōkai.* Berkeley: University of California Press, 2009.

Franklin, Richard, dir. *Road Games.* Written by Everett De Roche. Essaness Pictures, 1981.

Freeland, Cynthia A. *The Naked and the Undead: Evil and the Appeal of Horror*. Boulder, CO: Westview, 2000.

French, Aaron J., ed. *The Gods of H. P. Lovecraft*. San Francisco: JournalStone, 2015.

Fresenborg, Bernard. *"Thirty Years in Hell"; or, "From Darkness to Light."* St. Louis, MO: North-American Book House, 1904.

Freud, Sigmund. *The Future of an Illusion*. 1927. Translated and edited by James Strachey. New York: Norton, 1961.

———. *Three Essays on the Theory of Sexuality*. 1905. Translated by James Strachey. London: Imago, 1949.

———. *Totem and Taboo: Resemblances between the Psychic Lives of Savages and Neurotics*. 1919. Translated by James Strachey. New York: Norton, 1990.

———. *The Uncanny*. 1919. Translated by David McLintock. New York: Penguin Classics, 2003.

Freund, Karl, dir. *The Mummy*. Written by John L. Balderston. Universal Pictures, 1932.

Friedkin, William, dir. *The Exorcist*. Written by William Peter Blatty. Warner Bros., 1973.

From One Who Knows. "Maria Monk and Her Awful Disclosures." *New York Evangelist* (April 9, 1936): 59.

Fry, Gary. "Sealed by the Moon." In *Black Wings of Cthulhu 4: Seventeen Tales of Lovecraftian Horror*. Edited by S. T. Joshi, 118–40. London: Titan Books, 2016.

Frykholm, Amy Johnson. *Rapture Culture: "Left Behind" in Evangelical America*. New York: Oxford University Press, 2004.

Fuest, Robert, dir. *The Devil's Rain*. Written by Gabe Essoe, James Ashton, and Gerald Hopman. Sandy Howard Productions, 1975.

Furedi, Frank. *Culture of Fear Revisited: Risk-Taking and the Morality of Low Expectation*. 4th ed. New York: Continuum, 2006.

Gafford, Sam. "Weltschmerz." In *Black Wings of Cthulhu 3: Seventeen Tales of Lovecraftian Horror*. Edited by S. T. Joshi, 313–36. London: Titan Books, 2015.

Gage, Matilda Joslyn. *Women, Church, and State*. 2nd ed. New York: Truth Seeker, 1893.

Gallup, Gordon G., Jr., and David A. Frederick. "The Science of Sex Appeal: An Evolutionary Perspective." *Review of General Psychology* 14, no. 3 (2010): 240–50.

Gammon, Vic. *Desire, Drink, and Death in English Folk and Vernacular Song, 1600–1900*. New York: Routledge, 2008.

Gerard, Jerry, dir. *Deep Throat*. Written by Jerry Gerard. Gerard Damiano Film Productions, 1972.

Gibbons, Jenny. "Recent Developments in the Study of the Great European Witch Hunt." *Pomegranate: The International Journal of Pagan Studies* 5 (1998): 2–16.

Gibson, Paul, dir. "The Mask of the Demon." *Father Brown*. Season 4, episode 1. Written by Jude Tindall. BBC Drama Productions, January 4, 2016.

Gilliam, Terry, and Terry Jones, dirs. *Monty Python and the Holy Grail*. Written by Graham Chapmen et al. Python (Monty) Pictures, 1975.

Gilmore, David D. *Monsters: Evil Beings, Mythical Beasts, and All Manner of Imaginary Terrors*. Philadelphia: University of Pennsylvania Press, 2003.

Girard, René. *The Scapegoat*. Translated by Yvonne Freccero. Baltimore, MD: Johns Hopkins University Press, 1986.

Gladwin, Stephen. "Witches, Spells, and Politics: The Horror Films of Indonesia." In *Fear Without Frontiers: Horror Cinema Around the Globe*. Edited by Steven Jay Schneider, 218–29. Godalming, UK: FAB Press, 2003.

Glassner, Barry. *The Culture of Fear: Why Americans Are Afraid of the Wrong Things*. New York: Basic Books, 1999.

Glitch. Created by Tony Ayres, Louise Fox, and Adam Hill. Matchbox Pictures, 2015–2019.

Goffman, Erving. *The Presentation of Self in Everyday Life*. New York: Anchor Books, 1959.

Goldberg, Ruth, and Steven Jay Schneider. "Sex and Death, Cuban Style: The Dark Vision of Jorge Molina." In *Fear Without Frontiers: Horror Cinema Across the Globe*. Edited by Steven Jay Schneider, 81–90. Godalming, UK: FAB Press, 2003.

Golden, Eve. *Vamp: The Rise and Fall of Theda Bara*. Vestal, NY: Emprise, 1996.

Goldstein, Diane E., Sylvia Ann Grider, and Jeannie Banks Thomas. *Haunting Experiences: Ghosts in Contemporary Folklore*. Logan: Utah State University Press, 2007.

Gordon, Joan, and Veronica Hollinger, eds. *Blood Read: The Vampire as Metaphor in Contemporary Culture*. Philadelphia: University of Pennsylvania Press, 1997.

Gordon, Stuart, dir. *Dagon*. Written by Dennis Paoli. Castelao Producciones, 2001.

Gottschall, Jonathan. *The Storytelling Animal: How Stories Make Us Human*. New York: Houghton Mifflin, 2012.

Grafius, Brandon. *The Witch*. Liverpool: Auteur, 2020.

Grant, Barry Keith, ed. *Planks of Reason: Essays on the Horror Film*. Lanham, MD: Scarecrow Press, 1996.

Gray, Beverly. *Roger Corman: An Unauthorized Biography of the Godfather of Indie Filmmaking*. Los Angeles: Renaissance Books, 2000.

Gray, Jonathan. *Show Sold Separately: Promos, Spoilers, and Other Media Paratexts*. New York: NYU Press, 2010.

Green, David Gordon, dir. *Halloween*. Written by Jeff Fradley, Danny McBride, and David Gordon Green. Blumhouse Productions, 2018.

Gresh, Lois H. *Sherlock Holmes vs Cthulhu: The Adventure of the Deadly Dimensions*. London: Titan Books, 2017.

———. *Sherlock Holmes vs Cthulhu: The Adventure of the Innsmouth Mutations*. London: Titan Books, 2019.

———. *Sherlock Holmes vs Cthulhu: The Adventure of the Neural Psychoses*. London: Titan Books, 2018.

Gribben, Crawford. *Writing the Rapture: Prophecy Fiction in Evangelical America*. Oxford: Oxford University Press, 2009.

Grieco, Sergio, dir. *The Sinful Nuns of St. Valentine*. Written by Sergio Grieco. Claudia Cinematografica, 1974.

Grigg, Richard. "God Is a Symbol for God: Paul Tillich and the Contours of Any Possible Radical Theology." In *Retrieving the Radical Tillich: His Legacy and Contem-*

porary Importance. Edited by Russell W. Manning, 47–64. New York: Palgrave Macmillan, 2015.

———. *Science Fiction and the Imitation of the Sacred.* London: Bloomsbury Academic, 2018.

Guillermin, John, dir. *King Kong.* Written by Lorenzo Semple Jr. Dino De Laurentis Corporation, 1976.

Guran, Paula, ed. *The Mammoth Book of Cthulhu: New Lovecraftian Horror.* London: Robinson, 2016.

Hadju, David. *The Ten-Cent Plague: The Great Comic-Book Scare and How It Changed America.* New York: Picador, 2008.

Haefele, John D. *A Look Behind the Derleth Mythos: Origins of the "Cthulhu Mythos."* Rev. ed. N.p.: Cimmerian Press, 2014.

Haggard, H. Rider. *She: A History of Adventure.* 1887. Reprint. New York: Modern Library, 2002.

Hahn, Jessica. "Jessica: A New Life." *Playboy* (September 1988): 158–62.

Hall, Melissa Mia. "The Ghost." In *Icons of Horror and the Supernatural: An Encyclopedia of Our Worst Nightmares.* Volume 1. Edited by S. T. Joshi, 215–42. Westport, CT: Greenwood, 2007.

Hallam, Lindsay Anne. *Screening the Marquis de Sade: Pleasure, Pain, and the Transgressive Body in Film.* Jefferson, NC: McFarland, 2012.

Halperin, Victor, dir. *White Zombie.* Written by Garnett Weston. Halperin Productions, 1932.

Hambling, David. "A Question of Blood." In *Black Wings of Cthulhu 5: Twenty New Tales of Lovecraftian Horror.* Edited by S. T. Joshi, 197–223. London: Titan Books, 2018.

Handley, Sasha. *Visions of an Unseen World: Ghost Beliefs and Ghost Stories in Eighteenth-Century England.* London: Routledge, 2007.

Hanegraaff, Wouter J., and Jeffrey J. Kripal, eds. *Hidden Intercourse: Eros and Sexuality in the History of Western Esotericism.* New York: Fordham University Press, 2011.

Hankiss, Elemér. *Fears and Symbols: An Introduction to the Study of Western Civilization.* Budapest: Central European University Press, 2001.

Hardacre, Helen. *Marketing the Menacing Fetus in Japan.* Berkeley: University of California Press, 1997.

Hardy, Robin, dir. *The Wicker Man.* Written by Anthony Shaffer. British Lion Film Corporation, 1973.

Harman, Graham. *Weird Realism: Lovecraft and Philosophy.* Winchester, UK: Zero Books, 2012.

Harms, Daniel. *The Cthulhu Mythos Encyclopedia.* 3rd ed. Lake Orion, MI: Elder Signs Press, 2008.

Harms, Daniel, and John Wisdom Gonce III. *The Necronomicon Files: The Truth Behind Lovecraft's Legend.* Rev. ed. Boston: Weiser Books, 2003.

Harner, Michael. "The Ecological Basis for Aztec Sacrifice." *American Ethnologist* 4, no. 1 (1977): 117–35.

———. *The Way of the Shaman*. 1980. 10th anniversary ed. New York: Harper & Row, 1990.

Hart, Mara Kirk, and S. T. Joshi, eds. *Lovecraft's New York Circle: The Kalem Club, 1924–1927*. New York: Hippocampus Press, 2006.

Hartwell, David G., ed. *The Dark Descent*. New York: Tom Doherty Associates, 1987.

———, ed. *Shadows of Fear: Foundations of Fear*, volume 1. New York: Tom Doherty Associates, 1992.

Haunting of Bly Manor, The. Created by Mike Flanagan. Intrepid Pictures, 2020.

Hawthorne, Nathaniel. *Tanglewood Tales*. 1853. Reprint. New York: Dover, 2017.

Hearn, Lafcadio. *Kwaidan: Stories and Studies of Strange Things*. 1904. Reprint. Rutland, VT: Charles E. Tuttle, 1971.

Heinlein, Robert. "They." 1941. Reprint. In *Shadows of Fear: Foundations of Fear*, volume 1. Edited by David G. Hartwell, 85–105. New York: TOR Books, 1992.

Hendershot, Cyndy. *I Was a Cold War Monster: Horror Films, Eroticism, and the Cold War Imagination*. Bowling Green, KY: Bowling Green State University Popular Press, 2001.

Hendrix, Grady. *Paperbacks from Hell: The Twisted History of '70s and '80s Horror Fiction*. Philadelphia: Quirk Books, 2017.

Herszenhorn, David M. "Witches Express Relief as Vexing Case Is Closed." *New York Times* (August 12, 2000): B5.

Hertz, Nathan, dir. *Attack of the 50-Foot Woman*. Written by Mark Hanna. Woolner Bros. Pictures, 1958.

Hickox, Antony, dir. *Hellraiser III: Hell on Earth*. Written by Peter Atkins. Fifth Avenue Entertainment, 1992.

Hill, Annette. *Paranormal Media: Audiences, Spirits, and Magic in Popular Culture*. London: Routledge, 2011.

Hillyer, Lambert, dir. *Dracula's Daughter*. Written by Garrett Fort. Universal Pictures, 1936.

Hogan, David J. *Dark Romance: Sexuality in the Horror Film*. Jefferson, NC: McFarland, 1986.

Honda, Ishirō, dir. *King Kong vs. Godzilla*. Written by Shinichi Sekizawa. Toho Studios, 1962.

Houellebecq, Michel. *H. P. Lovecraft: Against the World, Against Life*. Translated by Dorna Khazeni. London: Orion Books, 1991.

Howard, Robert E. "Black Hound of Death." *Weird Tales* 28, no. 4 (November 1936): 410–26.

———. "Red Nails." *Weird Tales* 28, no. 3 (October 1936): 334–53.

Howard, Ron, dir. *The Da Vinci Code*. Written by Akiva Goldsman. Imagine Entertainment, 2006.

Howe, Richard G. "Modern Witchcraft: It May Not Be What You Think." *Christian Research Journal* 28, no. 1 (2005); https://www.equip.org (accessed November 5, 2018).

Huddleston, Tom. "The 50 Best Monster Movies." Time Out, October 8, 2019; www.timeout.com (accessed February 20, 2020).

Huizinga, Johan. *Homo Ludens: A Study of the Play-Element in Culture.* 1950. Mansfield Center, CT: Martino, 2014.

Humphrey, Daniel. "Gender and Sexuality Haunt the Horror Film." In *A Companion to the Horror Film.* Edited by Harry Benshoff, 38–55. Oxford: Wiley-Blackwell, 2014.

Hutton, Ronald. *The Triumph of the Moon: A History of Modern Pagan Witchcraft.* Oxford: Oxford University Press, 1999.

———. *The Witch: A History of Fear, from Ancient Times to the Present.* New Haven, CT: Yale University Press, 2017.

Huxley, Aldous. *The Devils of Loudun.* 1952. Reprint. New York: HarperPerennial, 2009.

———. *The Doors of Perception.* 1954. New York: HarperPerennial Modern Classics, 2009.

Hyla [Jane Dunbar Chaplin]. *The Convent and the Manse.* Cleveland, OH: John P. Jewett, 1853.

Ingham, John M. "Human Sacrifice at Tenochtitlan." *Comparative Studies in Society and History* 26, no. 3 (1984): 379–400.

Irwin, Robert. *Dangerous Knowledge: Orientalism and Its Discontents.* New York: Overlook Press, 2006.

Jackson, Peter, dir. *King Kong.* Written by Fran Walsh, Philipa Boyens, and Peter Jackson. Wingnut Films, 2005.

Jackson, Shirley. *The Haunting of Hill House.* New York: Penguin Books, 1959.

James, M. R. "Ghosts—Treat Them Gently." In *The Haunted Doll's House and Other Ghost Stories.* Edited by S. T. Joshi, 260–64. New York: Penguin Books, 1999.

———. *The Haunted Doll's House and Other Ghost Stories.* Edited by S. T. Joshi. New York: Penguin Books, 1999.

———. "Some Remarks on Ghost Stories." In *The Haunted Doll's House and Other Ghost Stories.* Edited by S. T. Joshi, 253–60. New York: Penguin Books, 1999.

James, William. *The Varieties of Religious Experience.* 1902. Reprint. New York: Modern Library, 1999.

Jancovich, Mark. *Rational Fears: American Horror in the 1950s.* Manchester, UK: Manchester University Press, 1996.

Janus, G. H., ed. *Voluptuous Terrors: 120 Horror & Science Fiction Film Posters from Italy.* N.p.: Deicide Press, 2017.

———. *Voluptuous Terrors 2: 120 Horror & Science Fiction Film Posters from Italy.* N.p.: Deicide Press, 2018.

Jenkins, Henry. *Convergence Culture: Where Old and New Media Collide.* New York: NYU Press, 2006.

Jensen, Robert. *Getting Off: Pornography and the End of Masculinity.* Cambridge, MA: South End Press, 2007.

Johns, Catharine. *Sex or Symbol? Erotic Images of Greece and Rome.* New York: Routledge, 1982.

Johnson, Phillip E., and John Mark Reynolds. *Against All Gods: What's Right and Wrong about the New Atheism.* Downers Grove, IL: InterVarsity Press, 2010.

Joho, Jess. "*The Witch* isn't an empowerment narrative and that's why it's great." *Kill Screen* (February 23, 2016); www.killscreen.com (accessed December 2, 2018).

Jones, Mark Howard. "The Last Ones." In *The Madness of Cthulhu*, volume 2. Edited by S. T. Joshi, 151–70. London: Titan Books, 2015.

Jones, Robert Kenneth. *The Shudder Pulps: A History of the Weird Menace Magazines of the 1930s.* West Linn, OR: FAX Collector's Editions, 1975.

Jones, Stephen, ed. *Clive Barker's Shadows in Eden: The Books, Films, and Art of Clive Barker.* Lancaster, PA: Underwood-Miller, 1991.

———. *James Herbert: By Horror Haunted.* London: BCA, 1992.

———. *Shadows Over Innsmouth.* London: Titan Books, 2013.

Jordan, Mark D. *The Invention of Sodomy in Christian Theology.* Chicago: University of Chicago Press, 1997.

Joshi, S. T., ed. *Against Religion: The Atheist Writings of H. P. Lovecraft.* New York: Sporting Gentlemen, n.d.

———, ed. *Black Wings of Cthulhu: Twenty-One Tales of Lovecraftian Horror.* London: Titan Books, 2012.

———, ed. *Black Wings of Cthulhu 2: Eighteen Tales of Lovecraftian Horror.* London: Titan Books, 2014.

———, ed. *Black Wings of Cthulhu 3: Seventeen Tales of Lovecraftian Horror.* London: Titan Books, 2015.

———, ed. *Black Wings of Cthulhu 4: Seventeen Tales of Lovecraftian Horror.* London: Titan Books, 2016.

———, ed. *Black Wings of Cthulhu 5: Twenty New Tales of Lovecraftian Horror.* London: Titan Books, 2018.

———. *H. P. Lovecraft: A Life.* West Warwick, RI: Necronomicon Press, 1996.

———. "Introduction." In *Black Wings of Cthulhu 2: Eighteen Tales of Lovecraftian Horror.* Edited by S. T. Joshi, 7–10. London: Titan Books, 2014.

———. "Introduction." In *Black Wings of Cthulhu 3: Seventeen Tales of Lovecraftian Horror.* Edited by S. T. Joshi, 9–11. London: Titan Books, 2015.

———, ed. *The Madness of Cthulhu*, volume 1. London: Titan Books, 2014.

———, ed. *The Madness of Cthulhu*, volume 2. London: Titan Books, 2015.

———. *The Rise, Fall, and Rise of the Cthulhu Mythos.* 2nd ed. New York: Hippocampus Press, 2015.

Jowett, Garth, and Victoria O'Donnell. *Propaganda and Persuasion.* Newbury Park, CA: Sage, 1989.

Julliann, Philippe. *Dreamers of Decadence: Symbolist Painters of the 1890s.* Chicago: University of Chicago Press, 1971.

Juran, Nathan H., dir. *20 Million Miles to Earth.* Written by Charlott Knight and Ray Harryhausen. Morningside Productions, 1957.

Kalat, David. *J-Horror: The Definitive Guide to "The Ring," "The Grudge," and Beyond.* New York: Vertical, 2007.

Kane, Paul. *The "Hellraiser" Films and Their Legacy.* Jefferson, NC: McFarland, 2006.

Karlsen, Carol F. *The Devil in the Shape of a Woman: Witchcraft in Colonial New England*. New York: Norton, 1998.

Katz, Steven T. "Language, Epistemology, and Mysticism." In *Mysticism and Philosophical Analysis*. Edited by Steven T. Katz, 22–74. New York: Oxford University Press, 1978.

Kearney, Richard. *Strangers, Gods, and Monsters: Interpreting Otherness*. New York: Routledge, 2003.

Kelley, Brett, dir. *Attack of the Giant Leeches*. Written by Jeff O'Brien. Dudez Productions, 2008.

Kendrick, Walter. *The Secret Museum: Pornography in Modern Culture*. Berkeley: University of California Press, 1987.

———. *The Thrill of Fear: 250 Years of Scary Entertainment*. New York: Grove Press, 1991.

Kiernan, Caitlín. "Black Ships Seen South of Heaven." In *Black Wings of Cthulhu 4: Seventeen Tales of Lovecraftian Horror*. Edited by S. T. Joshi, 79–102. London: Titan Books, 2016.

———. "Houndwife." In *Black Wings of Cthulhu 2: Eighteen Tales of Lovecraftian Horror*. Edited by S. T. Joshi, 60–83. London: Titan Books, 2014.

———. "Houses Under the Sea." In *Lovecraft Unbound: Twenty Stories*. Edited by Eileen Datlow, 161–94. Milwaukie, OR: Dark Horse Books, 2009.

———. "Pickman's Other Model (1929)." In *Black Wings of Cthulhu: Twenty-One New Tales of Lovecraftian Horror*. Edited by S. T. Joshi, 15–46. London: Titan Books, 2012.

King, Stephen. *Carrie*. 1974. Reprint. New York: Anchor, 2002.

———. *Danse Macabre*. Rev. ed. New York: Gallery, 2010.

———. *The Dead Zone*. New York: Signet, 1979.

———. *Desperation*. New York: Viking, 1996.

———. *Different Seasons*. New York: Signet, 1982.

———. *Duma Key*. New York: Scribner's, 2008.

———. *Just After Sunset: Stories*. New York: Pocket Books, 2008.

———. *Needful Things*. New York: Signet, 1991.

———. *Night Shift*. New York: Doubleday, 1978.

———. *Nightmares and Dreamscapes*. New York: Pocket Books, 1993.

———. *Pet Sematary*. New York: Pocket Books, 1983.

———. "The Revelations of 'Becka Paulson." In *I Shudder at Your Touch: 22 Tales of Sex and Horror*. Edited by Michele Slung, 1–22. New York: ROC/Penguin, 1991.

———. *Revival*. New York: Gallery, 2014.

———. *Under the Dome*. New York: Gallery, 2009.

Kirkman, Robert. *The Walking Dead: Compendium One*. Berkeley: Image Comics, 2015.

Klein, Marty. *America's War on Sex: The Attack on Law, Lust, and Liberty*. Westport, CT: Praeger, 2006.

Koike, Mariko. *The Graveyard Apartment*. Translated by Deborah Bolivar Boehm. New York: Thomas Dunne Books, 1993.

Korshack, Stephen D., and J. David Spurlock. *The Alluring Art of Margaret Brundage: Queen of Pulp Pin-Up Art.* Coral Gables, FL: Vanguard Productions, 2013.

Kowalski, Bernard L., dir. *Attack of the Giant Leeches.* Written by Leo Gordon. Roger Corman Productions, 1959.

Kozlovic, Anton Karl. "The Structural Characteristics of the Cinematic Christ-Figure." *Journal of Religion and Popular Culture* 8, no. 1 (2004): https://doi.org/10.3138/jrpc.8.1.005.

Kramer, Heinrich, and James Sprenger. *The Malleus Maleficarum of Heinrich Kramer and James Sprenger.* 1486. Translated by Montague Summers. New York: Dover Publications, 1971.

Kristeva, Julia. *Powers of Horror: An Essay on Abjection.* Translated by Leon S. Roudiez. New York: Columbia University Press, 1982.

Kusumaryati, Veronica. "The Feminine Grotesque in Indonesian Horror Films." Cinema Poetica, March 15, 2016; www.cinemapoetica.com (accessed July 12, 2019).

Kyrou, Ado. *Le surréalisme au cinéma.* Paris: Le terrain vague, 1963.

LaBute, Neil, dir. *The Wicker Man.* Written by Neil LaBute. Alcon Entertainment, 2006.

LaHaye, Tim, and Jerry B. Jenkins. *Left Behind: A Novel of the Earth's Last Days.* Carol Stream, IL: Tyndale House, 1995.

Lal, Kanwar. *The Cult of Desire: An Interpretation of Erotic Sculpture of India.* 2nd ed. New Hyde Park, NY: University Books, 1967.

Lamarre, Thomas. "Platonic Sex: Perversion and Shôjo Anime (Part One)." *Animation* 1, no. 1 (2006): 45–59.

LaMartina, Chris, dir. *Call Girl of Cthulhu.* Written by Jimmy George and Chris La-Martina. Midnight Crew Studios, 2014.

Landis, John, dir. *Innocent Blood.* Written by Michael Wolk. Warner Bros., 1992.

Laquer, Walter. *Making Sex: Body and Gender from the Greeks to Freud.* Cambridge, MA: Harvard University Press, 1990.

———. *Solitary Sex: A Cultural History of Masturbation.* New York: Zone Books, 2004.

Larson, Bob. *Larson's Book of Spiritual Warfare.* Nashville, TN: Thomas Nelson, 1999.

———. *Larson's New Book of Cults.* Rev. ed. Wheaton, IL: Tyndale House, 1989.

Lau, Ricky, dir. *Mr. Vampire.* Written by Barry Wong. Golden Harvest, 1985.

Laven, Arnold, dir. *The Monster That Challenged the World.* Written by Pat Fielder. Gramercy Pictures, 1957.

Lee, Edward. *City Infernal.* 2001. Reprint. Orlando: Necro Publications, 2012.

———. *The Haunter of the Threshold.* Portland, OR: Deadite Press, 2010.

———. *House Infernal.* New York: Leisure Books, 2007.

———. *Incubi.* 1991. Reprint. Orlando, FL: Necro Publications, 2011.

———. *Infernal Angel.* New York: Leisure Books, 2004.

———. *The Innswich Horror.* Portland, OR: Deadite Press, 2010.

———. *Lucifer's Lottery.* Orlando, FL: Necro Publications, 2013.

———. *Messenger.* 2004. Reprint. Orlando, FL: Necro Publications, 2013.

———. *Succubi.* 1992. Reprint. Orlando, FL: Necro Publications, 2004.

———. *Trolley No. 1852*. Portland, OR: Deadite Press, 2010.

———. *Witch Water*. Orlando, FL: Necro Publications, 2012.

Lee, Edward, and Wrath James White. *Teratologist*. Hiram, GA: Overlook Connection Press, 2003.

Leeson, Peter T. "Human Sacrifice." *Review of Behavioral Economics* 1, nos. 1–2 (2014): 137–65.

Lévi-Strauss, Claude. *The Elementary Structures of Kinship*. Boston: Beacon, 1969.

———. *The Savage Mind*. Chicago: University of Chicago Press, 1966.

Levy, Ariel. *Female Chauvinist Pigs: Women and the Rise of Raunch Culture*. New York: Free Press, 2005.

Lewis, James R., and J. Gordon Melton, eds. *Sex, Slander, and Salvation: Investigating The Family/The Children of God*. Stanford, CA: Center for Academic Publication, 1994.

Lewis, Matthew. *The Monk*. 1796. Edited by Howard Anderson. Oxford: Oxford University Press, 1995.

Ley, David J. *The Myth of Sex Addiction*. Lanham, MD: Rowman & Littlefield, 2012.

Ligotti, Thomas. *The Conspiracy against the Human Race: A Contrivance of Horror*. New York: Penguin Books, 2010.

Linz, Daniel, and Edward Donnerstein. "Sex and Violence in Slasher Films: A Reinterpretation." *Journal of Broadcasting & Electronic Media* 38, no. 2 (1994): 243–46.

Lockhart, Ross E., ed. *Cthulhu Fhtagn!* Petaluma, CA: Word Horde, 2015.

Lovecraft, H. P. *The Annotated Supernatural Horror in Literature*. 1927. Edited by S. T. Joshi. New York: Hippocampus Press, 2000.

———. "The Call of Cthulhu." In *The Call of Cthulhu and Other Weird Stories*, by H. P. Lovecraft. 1928. Edited by S. T. Joshi, 139–69. New York: Penguin Books, 1999.

———. "The Cats of Ulthar." In *The Dreams in the Witch House and Other Weird Stories*, by H. P. Lovecraft. 1920. Edited by S. T. Joshi, 19–22. New York: Penguin Books, 2004.

———. "Celephaïs." In *The Call of Cthulhu and Other Weird Stories*, by H. P. Lovecraft. 1922. Edited by S. T. Joshi, 24–30. New York: Penguin Books, 1999.

———. "Cool Air." In *The Call of Cthulhu and Other Weird Stories*, by H. P. Lovecraft. 1928. Edited by S. T. Joshi, 130–38. New York: Penguin Books, 1999.

———. "Dagon." In *The Call of Cthulhu and Other Weird Stories*, by H. P. Lovecraft. 1919. Edited by S. T. Joshi, 1–6. New York: Penguin Books, 1999.

———. "The Dream-Quest of Unknown Kadath." In *The Dreams in the Witch House and Other Weird Stories*, by H. P. Lovecraft. 1934. Edited by S. T. Joshi, 155–251. New York: Penguin Books, 2004.

———. "The Dreams in the Witch House." In *The Dreams in the Witch House and Other Weird Stories*, by H. P. Lovecraft. 1933. Edited by S. T. Joshi, 300–334. New York: Penguin Books, 2004.

———. "The Dunwich Horror." In *The Thing on the Doorstep and Other Weird Stories*, by H. P. Lovecraft. 1929. Edited by S. T. Joshi, 206–45. New York: Penguin Books, 2001.

———. "From Beyond." In *The Dreams in the Witch House and Other Weird Stories*, by H. P. Lovecraft. 1934. Edited by S. T. Joshi, 23–29. New York: Penguin Books, 2004.

———. "The Haunter of the Dark." In *The Call of Cthulhu and Other Weird Stories*, by H. P. Lovecraft. 1936. Edited by S. T. Joshi, 336–60. New York: Penguin Books, 1999.

———. "The Horror at Red Hook." In *The Dreams in the Witch House and Other Weird Stories*, by H. P. Lovecraft. 1927. Edited by S. T. Joshi, 116–37. New York: Penguin Books, 2004.

———. "The Hound." In *The Call of Cthulhu and Other Weird Stories*, by H. P. Lovecraft. 1919. Edited by S. T. Joshi, 81–88. New York: Penguin Books, 1999.

———. "Pickman's Model." In *The Thing at the Doorstep and Other Weird Stories*, by H. P. Lovecraft. 1927. Edited by S. T. Joshi, 78–89. New York: Penguin Books, 2001.

———. "The Shadow over Innsmouth." In *The Call of Cthulhu and Other Weird Stories*, by H. P. Lovecraft. 1936. Edited by S. T. Joshi, 268–335. New York: Penguin Books, 1999.

Luhrmann, Tanya M. *Persuasions of the Witch's Craft: Ritual Magic in Contemporary England*. London: Picador, 1989.

Lupoff, Richard A. *The Doom That Came to Dunwich: Weird Mysteries of the Cthulhu Mythos*. N.p.: Venture Press, 2017.

Lussier, Patrick, dir. *Dracula 2000*. Written by Joel Soisson. Dimension Films, 2000.

Lutzer, Erwin W. *The Da Vinci Deception: Credible Answers to the Questions Millions Are Asking about Jesus, the Bible, and "The Da Vinci Code."* Wheaton, IL: Tyndale House, 2004.

Lynch, Paul, dir. *Prom Night*. Written by William Gray. Simcom Productions, 1980.

Lyons, Linda. "Paranormal Beliefs Come (Super)Naturally to Some." Gallup, November 1, 2005; https://news.gallup.com (accessed December 12, 2020).

Machen, Arthur. *The Three Imposters and Other Stories*. Edited by S. T. Joshi. Hayward, CA: Chaosium, 2007.

Magilow, Daniel H., Kristin T. Vander Lugt, and Elisabeth Bridges. *Nazisploitation: The Nazi Image in Low-Brow Cinema and Culture*. New York: Continuum, 2012.

Mallon, Jim, dir. "Attack of the Giant Leeches." *Mystery Science Theater 3000*. Season 5, Episode 6. Written by Michael J. Nelson and Trace Beaulieu. Best Brains, 1992.

Maltin, Leonard. *Leonard Maltin's Classic Movie Guide: From the Silent Era through 1965*. 3rd ed. New York: Plume, 2015.

Maltz, Wendy, and Larry Maltz. *The Porn Trap: The Essential Guide to Overcoming Problems Caused by Pornography*. New York: Harper, 2008.

Mama Roz. Letter to the editor. *newWitch* 8 (May–July 2005): 5.

Mannheim, Karl. *Ideology and Utopia: An Introduction to the Sociology of Knowledge*. 1936. Translated by Louis Wirth and Edward Shils. New York: Harvest Books, 1985.

Marcus, Steven. *The Other Victorians: A Study of Sexuality and Pornography in Mid-Nineteenth-Century England*. New York: Basic Books, 1966.

"Maria Monk Dead." *Southern Sentinel* (October 3, 1849): n.p.

Marshack, Philip, dir. *Dracula Sucks*. Written by David A. Marshak and Philip Marshak. Backstreet Productions, 1979.

Martino, Sergio, dir. *The Mountain of the Cannibal God*. Written by Cesare Frugoni and Sergio Martino. Dania Film, 1978.

Maseo, Higashi, ed. *Kaiki: Uncanny Tales from Japan*. 3 vols. Fukuoka: Kurodahan Press, 2009–2012.

Matheson, Richard. *I Am Legend*. New York: Gold Medal Books, 1954.

Mattei, Bruno, dir. *The Other Hell*. Written by Bruno Mattei. Cinemec Produzione, 1981.

McCabe, Bob. *The Exorcist: Out of the Shadows*. London: Omnibus Press, 1999.

McDaniel, June. "Death Visions of the Goddess Kali: The Bengali Shakta Corpse Ritual at the Burning Ground." In *Death, Dying, and Mysticism: The Ecstasy of the End*. Edited by Thomas Cattoi and Christopher M. Moreman, 189–202. New York: Palgrave Macmillan, 2015.

———. *Offering Flowers, Feeding Skulls: Popular Goddess Worship in West Bengal*. New York: Oxford University Press, 2004.

McDowell, John C. *The Gospel according to "Star Wars": Faith, Hope, and the Force*. 2nd ed. Louisville, KY: Westminster John Knox Press, 2017.

McGilligan, Patrick, ed. *Backstory 3: Interviews with Screenwriters of the 1960s*. Berkeley: University of California Press, 1997.

McGowan, Catherine. "Convent and Conspiracies: A Study of Convent Narratives in the United States, 1850–1870." PhD diss. University of Edinburgh, 2008.

McKenna, Terence. *Food of the Gods: The Search for the Original Tree of Knowledge*. New York: Random House, 1993.

McRoy, Jay. *Nightmare Japan: Contemporary Japanese Horror Cinema*. Amsterdam: Rodopi, 2008.

Meigs, Anna S. *Food, Sex, and Pollution: A New Guinea Religion*. New Brunswick, NJ: Rutgers University Press, 1991.

Melford, George, and Enrique Tovar Ávalos, dirs. *Drácula*. Written by Baltasar Fernández Cué. Universal Pictures, 1931.

Melton, J. Gordon. *The Vampire Book: The Encyclopedia of the Undead*. Rev. ed. Detroit: Visible Ink Press, 1999.

———. *Videohound's Vampires on Video*. Detroit: Visible Ink Press, 1997.

Mencken, H. L. "Memorial Service." 1922. Reprint. In *Prejudices: First, Second, and Third Series*, 434–37. New York: Library of America, 2010.

Merrick, Mollie. "Fifty-foot ape central figure in 'King Kong.'" *Atlanta Constitution* (January 22, 1933): 7B.

Migliore, Andrew, and John Strysik. *Lurker in the Lobby: A Guide to the Cinema of H. P. Lovecraft*. Rev. ed. Portland, OR: Night Shade Books, 2006.

Miles, Margaret. *Carnal Knowing: Female Nakedness and Religious Meaning in the Christian West*. New York: Vintage Books, 1989.

———. *A Complex Delight: The Secularization of the Breast, 1350–1750*. Berkeley: University of California Press, 2008.

Miller, Madeline. *Circe*. New York: Little, Brown, 2018.

Miller, Walter M., Jr. *A Canticle for Liebowitz*. New York: HarperCollins, 1959.

———. *Saint Liebowitz and the Wild Horse Woman*. New York: Bantam Books, 1997.

Milner, Dan, dir. *From Hell It Came*. Written by Richard Bernstein. Milner Brothers Productions, 1957.

Miner, Steve, dir. *Halloween H2o: 20 Years Later*. Written by Robert Zappia and Matt Greenberg. Nightfall Productions, 1998.

Molina, Jorge, dir. *Ferrozz: The Wild Red Riding Hood*. Written by Edgar Soberón Torchia. Candy Caramels Films, 2010.

———, dir. *Molina's Culpa*. Written by Alan Coronel and Jorge Molina. Escuela Internacional de Cine y Televisión, 1993.

Molitor, Fred, and Barry S. Sapolsky. "Sex, Violence, and Victimization in Slasher Films." *Journal of Broadcasting & Electronic Media* 37, no. 2 (1993): 233–42.

Monk, Maria [pseud.]. *Awful Disclosures of Maria Monk, As Exhibited in a Narrative of Her Sufferings During Her Residence of Five Years as a Novice and Two Years as a Black Nun in the Hotel Dieu Nunnery, at Montreal, Ont*. 1836. Rev. ed. New York: Truth Seeker Company, 1876.

———. *Further Disclosures of Maria Monk, Concerning the Hotel Dieu Nunnery of Montreal; also, Her Visit to Nun's Island and Disclosures Concerning That Secret Retreat*. Boston: Leavitt, Lord, 1837.

Moore, Alan, and Jacen Burrows. *Neonomicon*. Rantoul, IL: Avatar Press, 2017.

———. *Providence*. 3 vols. Rantoul, IL: Avatar Press, 2017.

Moore, David W. "Three in Four Americans Believe in Paranormal." Gallup, June 16, 2005; https://news.gallup.com/poll (accessed December 20, 2020).

Morgan, Edmund S. "The Puritans and Sex." *New England Quarterly* 15, no. 4 (1942): 591–607.

Murphy, Nick, dir. *The Awakening*. Written by Steven Volk and Nick Murphy. Studio Canal Features, 2015.

Murray, Margaret A. *The God of the Witches*. London: Oxford University Press, 1931.

———. *The Witch-Cult in Western Europe*. Oxford: Clarendon Press, 1921.

Myrick, Daniel, and Eduardo Sánchez, dirs. *The Blair Witch Project*. Written by Daniel Myrick and Eduardo Sánchez. Haxan Films, 1999.

Nakata, Hideo, dir. *Dark Water*. Written by Ken'ichi Suzuki and Yoshihiro Nakamura. Kadokawa Shoten, 2002.

———, dir. *Ringu*. Written by Hiroshi Takahashi. Basara Pictures, 1998.

Neal, Connie. *The Gospel according to Harry Potter: The Spiritual Journey of the World's Greatest Seeker*. Rev. ed. Louisville, KY: Westminster John Knox Press, 2008.

Neale, Steve. "'You Got to Be Fucking Kidding!' Knowledge, Belief, and Judgment in Science Fiction." In *Alien Zone: Cultural Theory and Contemporary Science Fiction Cinema*. Edited by Annette Kuhn, 160–68. London: Verso, 1990.

Neitz, Mary Jo, and Marion S. Goldman, eds. *Sex, Lies, and Sanctity: Religion and Deviance in Contemporary North America*. Greenwich, CT: JAI Press, 1995.

Newell, Adam. *The Art of the B-Movie Poster*. Berkeley: Gingko Press, 2016.

Newman, Kim. "Foreword." In *The Madness of Cthulhu*, volume 2. Edited by S. T. Joshi, 7–10. London: Titan Books, 2015.

Newport, Frank. "Americans More Likely to Believe in God Than the Devil." Gallup, June 13, 2007; news.gallup.com (accessed August 2, 2019).

———. "Most Americans Still Believe in God." Gallup, June 29, 2016; news.gallup.com (accessed August 2, 2019).

Newport, Frank, and Maura Strausberg. "Americans' Belief in Psychic and Paranormal Phenomena Is Up Over Last Decade." Gallup, June 8, 2001; https://news.gallup.com (accessed December 20, 2020).

Newton, Michael. "Written in Blood: A History of Human Sacrifice." *Journal of Psychohistory* 24, no. 2 (1996): 104–31.

Nietzsche, Friederich. *The Twilight of the Idols/The Anti-Christ*. 1895. Reprint. Translated by R. J. Hollingdale. London: Penguin Classics, 1990.

Niven, Anna Newkirk. "Ban nudity in *newWitch*?" *newWitch* 8 (December–February 2005): 14–15.

Noé, Ignacio, and Ricardo Barreiro. *The Convent of Hell*. Translated by Robert Legault. New York: Eurotica, 2015.

Nordstrom, Justin. *Danger on the Doorstep: Anti-Catholicism and American Print Culture in the Progressive Era*. Notre Dame, IN: University of Notre Dame Press, 2006.

Obeyesekere, Gananath. *Cannibal Talk: The Man-Eating Myth and Human Sacrifice in the South Seas*. Berkeley: University of California Press, 2005.

O'Bannon, Dan, dir. *The Return of the Living Dead*. Written by Dan O'Bannon. Hemdale Film Corporation, 1985.

O'Brien, Kevin L., ed. *Eldritch Blue: Love and Sex in the Cthulhu Mythos*. Aurora, CO: Lindisfarne Press, 2004.

Ogas, Ogi, and Sai Gaddam. *A Billion Wicked Thoughts: What the Internet Tells Us About Sexual Relationships*. New York: Penguin, 2011.

O'Gorman, Edith. *Convent Life Unveiled: Trials and Persecutions of Edith O'Gorman, Otherwise Sister Teresa de Chantal, of St. Joseph's Convent, Hudson, N.J.* Hartford: Connecticut Publishing, 1871.

Okorafor, Nnedi. "Lovecraft's racism and the World Fantasy Award statuette, with comments from China Miéville." *Nnedi's Wahala Zone*. December 14, 2011; http://nnedi.blogspot.com/2011/12/lovecrafts-racism-world-fantasy-award.html (accessed July 6, 2019).

———. *Who Fears Death*. New York: DAW Books, 2010.

Onoh, Nuzo. *The Sleepless*. Coventry, UK: Canaan-Star Publishing, 2016.

———. *Unhallowed Graves*. Coventry, UK: Canaan-Star Publishing, 2015.

Oplev, Niels Arden, dir. *Flatliners*. Written by Ben Ripley. Columbia Pictures, 2017.

Ortega, Kenny, dir. *Hocus Pocus*. Written by Mick Garris and Neil Cuthbert. Walt Disney Pictures, 1993.

Orwell, George. *1984*. 1949. Reprint. London: Penguin Books, 1987.

Ostling, Michael. "Babyfat and Belladonna: Witches' Ointment and the Contestation of Reality." *Magic, Ritual, and Witchcraft* 11, no. 1 (2016): 30–72.

Otto, Rudolf. *The Idea of the Holy*. 1923. Translated by John W. Harvey. London: Oxford University Press, 1950.

Ovid. *Metamorphoses*. Translated and annotated by Henry T. Riley. Overland Park, KS: DigiReads Publishing, 2017.

Packard, Rachel A. "Dancing along the Tightrope of Leisure: Puritans and Dance in Seventeenth-Century Massachusetts." MA thesis. University of New Mexico, 2012.

Pagels, Elaine. *Adam, Eve, and the Serpent*. New York: Random House, 1988.

Palmer, Susan J. *Aliens Adored: Raël's UFO Religion*. New Brunswick, NJ: Rutgers University Press, 2004.

———. *Moon Sisters, Krishna Mothers, Rajneesh Lovers: Women's Roles in New Religions*. Syracuse, NY: Syracuse University Press, 1994.

Partridge, Christopher. *High Culture: Drugs, Mysticism, and the Pursuit of Transcendence in the Modern World*. New York: Oxford University Press, 2018.

Paton, W. R., trans. *The Greek Anthology*, volume 1, books 1–5. Revised by Michael A. Tueller. Cambridge, MA: Harvard University Press, 2014.

Patrick, Robert. "Missouri library agrees not to block witch websites." *St. Louis Post-Dispatch* (March 6, 2013); https://www.stltoday.com (accessed December 21, 2020).

Paul, Pamela. *Pornified: How Pornography Is Transforming Our Lives, Our Relationships, and Our Families*. New York: Times Books, 2005.

Pavlacky, Jan, dir. *Haunted*. Netflix, 2018–2019.

Peele, Stanton. *Diseasing of America: How We Allowed Recovery Zealots and the Treatment Industry to Convince Us We Are Out of Control*. San Francisco: Jossey-Bass, 1995.

Penczak, Christopher. "Sex, Magic, and Healing." *newWitch* 7 (August–October 2004): 44–47.

Pendarves, G. G. "The Altar of Melek Taos." *Weird Tales* 20, no. 3 (September 1932): 292–315.

Pentangeli, Pep, ed. *Soft Brides for the Beast of Blood*. *Pulp Mayhem*, volume 3. N.p.: Deicide Press, 2014.

———. *Soft Flesh and Orgies of Death*. *Pulp Mayhem*, volume 1. N.p.: Deicide Press, 2014.

———. *Soft Nudes for the Devil's Butcher*. *Pulp Mayhem*, volume 2. N.p.: Deicide Press, 2014.

Petersen, Anders Klostergaard. "The Difference between Religious Narrative and Fictional Literature: A Matter of Degree Only." *Religion* 46, no. 4 (2016): 500–520.

Pheterson, Gail, ed. *A Vindication of the Rights of Whores*. Seattle: Seal Press, 1989.

Phillippe, Alexandre O., dir. *Leap of Faith: William Friedkin on "The Exorcist."* Written by Alexandre O. Phillippe. Exhibit A Pictures, 2019.

"Pierce on the Paranormal." *Zetetic Scholar* 1, no. 1 (1978): 31–33.

Pinker, Steven. *How the Mind Works*. New York: Norton, 2009.

Polanski, Roman, dir. *Rosemary's Baby*. Written by Roman Polanski. William Castle Productions, 1968.

Poole, W. Scott. *In the Mountains of Madness: The Life and Extraordinary Afterlife of H. P. Lovecraft*. Berkeley: Soft Skull Press, 2016.

Possamai, Adam. "Yoda Goes to Glastonbury: An Introduction to Hyper-Real Religions." In *Handbook of Hyper-Real Religions*. Edited by Adam Possamai, 1–21. Leiden: Brill, 2012.

Poutanen, Mary Anne. *Beyond Brutal Passions: Prostitution in Nineteenth-Century Montreal*. Montreal: McGill-Queen's University Press, 2015.

Price, Barbara J. "Demystification, Enriddlement, and Aztec Cannibalism: A Rejoinder to Michael Harner." *American Ethnologist* 5, no. 1 (1978): 98–115.

Price, Robert M. "Introduction." In *Acolytes of Cthulhu: Short Stories Inspired by H. P. Lovecraft*. Edited by Robert M. Price, 9–19. London: Titan Books, 2014.

———. *The Selma Horror and Others*. West Warwick, RI: Necronomicon Press, 2019.

"Production Code, The." In *Movies and Mass Culture*. Edited by John Belton, 135–49. New Brunswick, NJ: Rutgers University Press, 1996.

Prothero, Stephen. *Religious Literacy: What Every American Needs to Know—and Doesn't*. New York: HarperSanFrancisco, 2007.

Pyysïainen, Ilkka. *Supernatural Agents: Why We Believe in Souls, Gods, and Buddhas*. Oxford: Oxford University Press, 2009.

Quinn, Seabury. "The Hand of Glory." *Weird Tales* 22, no. 1 (November 1933): 3–25.

Qureshi, Sadiah. *People on Parade: Exhibitions, Empire, and Anthropology in Nineteenth-Century Britain*. Chicago: University of Chicago Press, 2011.

Rabinowitz, Paula. *American Pulp: How Paperbacks Brought Modernism to Main Street*. Princeton, NJ: Princeton University Press, 2014.

Ranke-Heinemann, Ute. *Eunuchs for the Kingdom of Heaven: Women, Sexuality, and the Roman Catholic Church*. Translated by Peter Heinegg. New York: Doubleday, 1980.

Raven. Letter to the editor. *newWitch* 9 (May–July 2005): 8–9.

Read, Donna, dir. *The Burning Times*. Written by Erna Buffie and Donna Read. National Film Board, 1990.

Reichert, Tom. *The Erotic History of Advertising*. Amherst, NY: Prometheus Books, 2003.

Reichert, Tom, Susan E. Heckler, and Sally Jackson. "The Effects of Sexual Social Marketing Appeals on Cognitive Processing and Persuasion." *Journal of Advertising* 30, no. 1 (2001): 13–27.

Reichert, Tom, and Jacqueline Lambiase, eds. *Sex in Consumer Culture: The Erotic Content of Media and Marketing*. New York: Routledge, 2006.

Reinl, Harald, dir. *Blood of the Virgins* [*La Tredicesima Vergine*; *Die Schlangengrube und das Pendel*]. Written by Manfred R. Köhler. Constantin Film, 1967.

Reis, Elizabeth. *Damned Women: Sinners and Witches in Puritan New England*. Ithaca, NY: Cornell University Press, 1997.

Reitman, Ivan, dir. *Ghostbusters*. Written by Dan Aykroyd and Harold Ramis. Columbia Pictures, 1984.

"Religious Lies." *Zion's Herald* (February 10, 1836): 22.

Rhodes, Ron. "Crash Goes the *Da Vinci Code*." Reasoning from the Scriptures Ministry, 2007; http://ronrhodes.org (accessed September 12, 2020).

Richter W. D., dir. *The Adventures of Buckaroo Banzai Across the 8th Dimension*. Written by Earl Mac Roach. Sherwood Productions, 1984.

Rives, J. "Human Sacrifice among Pagans and Christians." *Journal of Roman Studies* 85 (1995): 65–85.

Robison, Jennifer. "The Devil and the Demographic Details." Gallup, February 25, 2003; news.gallup.com (accessed August 2, 2019).

Rodriguez, Robert, dir. *From Dusk till Dawn*. Written by Quentin Tarantino. Dimension Films, 1996.

"Roerich Expedition Reaches Civilization after Perilous Trip: Suffered Five Months without Adequate Food or Fuel in High Reaches of Tibet—Nine White Persons in Party Are Safe." *Daily Boston Globe* (May 25, 1928): 14.

Rollin, Jean, dir. *The Nude Vampire*. Written by Jean Rollin. Les Films ABC, 1970.

———, dir. *Requiem for a Vampire*. Written by Jean Rollin. Les Films ABC, 1971.

"Roof of the World: Tibet a Kingdom of Filth and Depravity." *Washington Post* (May 29, 1904): E8.

Rosenthal, Rick, dir. *Halloween: Resurrection*. Written by Larry Brand and Sean Hood. Nightfall Productions, 2002.

———, dir. *Halloween II*. Written by John Carpenter and Debra Hill. Dino De Laurentis Corporation, 1981.

Ross, Catrien. *Japanese Ghost Stories: Spirits, Hauntings, and Paranormal Phenomena*. Tokyo: Tuttle Publishing, 2010.

Roy, Chase. "Maria Monk." Letter to the editor. *American* (March 1, 1895): 1.

Roy, Jessica. "Behind Creepypasta, the Internet Community That Allegedly Spread a Killer Meme." *Time* (June 3, 2014); https://time.com (accessed August 21, 2019).

Royal Collection Trust. *High Spirits: The Comic Art of Thomas Rowlandson*. 2015–2016; https://www.rct.uk (accessed September 1, 2019).

Russell, Ken, dir. *The Devils*. Written by Ken Russell. Russo Productions, 1971.

Russell, M. E. "A Scary Nonlinear Curse." *Oregonian* (August 20, 2004): Arts and Leisure, 33.

Ryan, Christopher, and Cacilda Jethá. *Sex at Dawn: The Prehistoric Origins of Modern Sexuality*. New York: Harper, 2010.

Sade, Marquis de. *Justine, Philosophy in the Bedroom, and Other Writings*. Translated by Richard Seaver and Austryn Wainhouse. New York: Grove Press, 1965.

———. *The 120 Days of Sodom and Other Writings*. Translated by Austryn Wainhouse and Richard Seaver. New York: Grove Press, 1966.

Said, Edward W. *Orientalism*. New York: Vintage Books, 1978.

Sales, R. H. "Human Sacrifice in Biblical Thought." *Journal of the American Academy of Religion* 25, no. 2 (1957): 112–17.

Salmonson, Jessica Amanda, and W. H. Pugmire. "Underneath an Arkham Moon." In *Black Wings of Cthulhu 3: Seventeen Tales of Lovecraftian Horror*. Edited by S. T. Joshi, 72–84. London: Titan Books, 2015.

Sanders, Don, and Susan Sanders. *The American Drive-In Movie*. New York: Crestline, 1997.

Sangster, Jimmy, dir. *Lust for a Vampire*. Written by Tudor Gates. Hammer Films, 1971.

Sapolsky, Robert M. "Dopamine Jackpot! Sapolsky on the Science of Pleasure." YouTube video, 4:59, posted by FORA.tv. March 2, 201; www.youtube.com/watch?v=axrywDP9Iio&t=124s (accessed March 14, 2021).

———. *Why Zebras Don't Get Ulcers*. 3rd ed. New York: Henry Holt, 2004.

Sapolsky, Burry S., Fred Molitor, and Sarah Luque. "Sex and Violence in Slasher Films: Re-Examining the Assumptions." *Journalism & Mass Communication Quarterly* 80, no. 1 (2003): 28–38.

Sarracino, Carmine, and Kevin M. Scott. *The Porning of America: The Rise of Porn Culture, What It Means, and Where We Go from Here*. Boston: Beacon, 2008.

Sasdy, Peter, dir. *Countess Dracula*. Written by Jeremy Paul. Hammer Films, 1971.

Savona, Leopoldo, dir. *Death Falls Softly* [*La Morte Scende Leggera*]. Written by Luigi Russo and Leopoldo Savona. Agata Film, 1972.

Scanlon, Noel. *Apparitions*. New York: Lorevan Publishing, 1984.

———. *Black Ashes*. New York: St. Martin's, 1985.

Schallert, Edwin. "'King Kong' stirring film." *Los Angeles Times* (March 27, 1933): A9.

Schlesinger, John, dir. *The Believers*. Written by Mark Frost. Orion Pictures, 1987.

Schreck, Nikolas. *The Satanic Screen: An Illustrated Guide to the Devil in Cinema, 1969–1999*. New York: Creation Books, 2000.

Schultz, Nancy Lusignan. *Fire and Roses: The Burning of the Charlestown Convent, 1834*. New York: Free Press, 2000.

Schumacher, Joel, dir. *Flatliners*. Written by Peter Filardi. Columbia Pictures, 1990.

Schweitzer, Darrell, and John Ashmead, eds. *Tales from the Miskatonic University Library*. Hornsea, UK: PS Publishing, 2017.

Scodel, Ruth. "Δόμων ἄγαλμα: Virgin Sacrifice and Aesthetic Object." *Transactions of the American Philological Society (1974–2014)* 126 (1996): 111–28.

Scooby-Doo, Where Are You? Created by Joe Ruby and Ken Spears. Hanna-Barbara Productions, 1969–1970.

Scott, John. "Fantastic film sets new pace: amazing processes used in making." *Los Angeles Times* (January 15, 1933): A1, A9.

Scott, Ridley, dir. *Alien*. Written by Dan O'Bannon. Brandywine Productions, 1979.

Scott, Tony, dir. *The Hunger*. Written by Ivan Davis and Michael Thomas. Metro-Goldwyn-Mayer, 1983.

Scruton, David L. "The Anthropology of an Emotion." In *Sociophobics: The Anthropology of Fear*. Edited by David L. Scruton, 7–49. Boulder, CO: Westview, 1986.

———, ed. *Sociophobics: The Anthropology of Fear*. Boulder, CO: Westview, 1986.

Searing, Helen. "B Movies." In *Penguin Encyclopedia of Horror and the Supernatural*. Edited by Jack Sullivan, 18–20. New York: Viking Penguin, 1986.

Sederholm, Carl H., and Jeffrey Andrew Weinstock, eds. *The Age of Lovecraft*. Minneapolis: University of Minnesota Press, 2016.

Shea, Michael. *Demiurge: The Complete Cthulhu Mythos Tales of Michael Shea*. Edited by S. T. Joshi. Sanford, NC: Dark Regions Press, 2018.

Shelley, Mary. *Frankenstein*. 1818. Reprint. Edited by Paul J. Hunter. 2nd ed. New York: Norton, 2012.

Shimizu, Takashi, dir. *The Grudge*. Written by Stephen Susco. Ghost House Pictures, 2004.

———, dir. *Ju-on*. Written by Takashi Shimizu. Pioneer LDC, 2002.

Sholem, Lee, dir. *Tobor the Great*. Written by Carl Dudley and Philip MacDonald. Dudley Pictures Corporation, 1954.

Shuck, Glenn W. *Marks of the Beast: The "Left Behind" Novels and the Struggle for Evangelical Identity*. New York: NYU Press, 2005.

Shyamalan, M. Night, dir. *The Sixth Sense*. Written by M. Night Shyamalan. Hollywood Pictures, 1999.

Sicart, Miguel. *Play Matters*. Cambridge, MA: MIT Press, 2014.

Siddique, Sophia, and Raphael Raphael, eds. *Transnational Horror Cinema: Bodies of Excess and the Global Grotesque*. London: Palgrave Macmillan, 2016.

Silver, Alain, and James Ursini. *Roger Corman: Metaphysics on a Shoestring*. Los Angeles: Silman-James Press, 2006.

Simmer-Brown, Judith. *Dakini's Warm Breath: The Feminine Principle in Tibetan Buddhism*. Boston: Shambhala Publications, 2002.

Simon. *The Gates of the Necronomicon*. New York: Avon Books, 2006.

———. *Necronomicon*. New York: Avon Books, 1977.

———. *Necronomicon Spellbook*. New York: Avon Books, 1998.

Siodmak, Curt, dir. *Bride of the Gorilla*. Written by Curt Siodmak. Jack Broder Productions, 1951.

Skal, David J. *Hollywood Gothic: The Tangled Web of "Dracula" from Novel to Stage to Screen*. New York: Norton, 1990.

———. *Screams of Reason: Mad Science and Modern Culture*. New York: Norton, 1998.

Slocum, J. J. *Confirmation of Maria Monk's Disclosures concerning the Hotel Dieu Nunnery of Montreal; Preceded by a Reply to the Priest's Book*. 3rd ed. London: James S. Hodson, 1839.

Slung, Michele, ed. *I Shudder at Your Touch: 22 Tales of Sex and Horror*. New York: ROC/Penguin, 1991.

Smith, Clark Ashton. "The Return of the Sorcerer." *Strange Tales* 1, no. 1 (September 1931): 99–109.

Smith, Jim Field, dir. "The Girl with All the Ghosts." *Truth Seekers*. Season 1, episode 3. Written by Nick Frost, Simon Pegg, Nat Saunders, and James Serafinowicz. Stolen Picture, 2020.

Smith, Jonathan Z. *Imagining Religion: From Babylon to Jonestown*. Chicago: University of Chicago Press, 1982.

———. *To Take Place: Toward Theory in Ritual*. Chicago: University of Chicago Press, 1987.

Smith, Wesley J. "The Exorcist Takes Christianity Seriously." *First Things* (October 28, 2016); www.firstthings.com (accessed September 20, 2019).

Smithee, Alan (Kevin Yagher), dir. *Hellraiser: Bloodline*. Written by Peter Atkins. Dimension Films, 1996.

Snyder, Scott. *Wytches*. Art by Jock. Portland, OR: Image Comics, 2017.

Sommers, Stephen, dir. *The Mummy*. Written by Stephen Sommers. Universal Pictures, 1999.

Songling, Pu. *Strange Tales from a Chinese Studio*. Translated and edited by John Minford. London: Penguin Books, 2006.

Soraya, Rocky, dir. *The 3rd Eye*. Written by Riheam Junianti and Fajar Umbara. Hitmaker Studios, 2017.

Sorrow, April Reese. "Magazine Trends Study Finds Increase in Advertisements Using Sex." *UGA Today* (June 5, 2012); https://news.uga.edu (accessed July 5, 2019).

Sperig Brothers, The, dirs. *Daybreakers*. Written by The Sperig Brothers. Lionsgate, 2009.

Spielberg, Steven, dir. *Indiana Jones and the Last Crusade*. Written by Jeffrey Boam. Lucasfilm, 1989.

Spottiswoode, Roger, dir. *Terror Train*. Written by T. Y. Drake. Sandy Howard Productions, 1980.

Stange, Mary Zeiss. "Jessica Hahn's Strange Odyssey from PTL to Playboy." *Journal of Feminist Studies in Religion* 6, no. 1 (1990): 105–16.

Starr, Summer. "Mother Ocean." *newWitch* 7 (August–October 2004): 38–43.

Steadman, John L. *H. P. Lovecraft and the Black Magickal Tradition: The Master of Horror's Influence on Modern Occultism*. San Francisco: Weiser Books, 2015.

Steele, Valerie. "Fashion, Fetish, Fantasy." In *Masquerade and Identities: Essays on Gender, Sexuality, and Marginality*. Edited by Efrat Tseëlon, 73–82. London: Routledge, 2001.

Stevenson, Robert, dir. *Bedknobs and Broomsticks*. Written by Bill Walsh and Don DaGradi. Walt Disney Productions, 1971.

Stoker, Bram. *Dracula*. 1897. Edited by Nina Auerbach and David J. Skal. New York: Norton, 1997.

Stone, Bryan. "The Sanctification of Fear: Images of the Religious in Horror Films." *Journal of Religion and Film* 5, no. 2 (2001); https://digitalcommons.unomaha.edu (accessed October 20, 2020).

Stone, Geoffrey R. *Sex and the Constitution: Sex, Religion, and Law from America's Origins to the Twenty-First Century*. New York: Liveright, 2017.

Stone, William Leete. *A Complete Refutation of Maria Monk's Atrocious Plot Concerning the Hotel Dieu Convent, in Montreal, Lower Canada*. Nottingham, UK: J. Shaw, 1837.

———. *Maria Monk and the Nunnery of the Hotel Dieu. Being an Account of a Visit to the Convents of Montreal, and Refutation of the "Awful Disclosures."* New York: Howard & Bates, 1836.

———. *Maria Monk's Show-up!!! or, The "Awful Disclosures," a Humbug*. New York: Go-Ahead-Press, 1836.

Strantzas, Simon. "Thistle's Find." In *Black Wings of Cthulhu 3: Seventeen Tales of Lovecraftian Horror*. Edited by S. T. Joshi, 336–54. London: Titan Books, 2015.

Strassman, Rick. *DMT: The Spirit Molecule*. Rochester, VT: Park Street Press, 2001.

Straub, Peter. "Blue Rose." In *Shadows of Fear. Foundations of Fear*, volume 1. Edited by David Hartwell, 335–401. New York: Tom Doherty Associates, 1992.

———. *Ghost Story*. New York: Berkeley Books, 1979.

Streiber, Whitley. *The Night Church*. New York: Pocket Books, 1983.

Strub, Whitney. *Perversion for Profit: The Politics of Pornography and the Rise of the New Right*. New York: Columbia University Press, 2011.

Struthers, William M. *Wired for Intimacy: How Pornography Hijacks the Male Brain*. Downers Grove, IL: IVP Books, 2009.

Sullivan, Margaret A. "The Witches of Dürer and Hans Baldung Grien." *Renaissance Quarterly* 53, no. 2 (2000): 333–401.

Sutton, Henry. *The Sacrifice*. New York: Charter Books, 1978.

Swallow, James. *Sisters of Battle: The Omnibus*. Nottingham, UK: Black Library, 2018.

Sylvain, Phillipe. "Monk, Maria." In *Dictionary of Canadian Biography*, vol. 7. Toronto: University of Toronto, 2003–; http://www.biographi.ca (accessed December 31, 2020).

Symons, Donald. *The Evolution of Human Sexuality*. New York: Oxford University Press, 1979.

Tal, Guy. "Demonic Possession in the Enlightenment: Goya's *Flying Witches*." *Magic, Ritual, and Witchcraft* 11, no. 2 (2016): 176–207.

Tambour, Anna. "Simply, Petrified." In *Lovecraft Unbound: Twenty Stories*. Edited by Ellen Datlow, 43–72. Milwaukie, OR: Dark Horse Books, 2009.

Tan, Kenneth Paul. "*Pontianaks*, Ghosts, and the Possessed: Female Monstrosity and National Anxiety in Singapore Cinema." *Asian Studies Review* 34, no. 2 (2010): 151–70.

Tatar, Maria. *Lustmord: Sexual Murder in Weimar Germany*. Princeton, NJ: Princeton University Press, 1995.

Taylor, Humphrey. "The Religious and Other Beliefs of Americans." Harris Poll, November 29, 2007; https://theharrispoll.com (accessed December 19, 2020).

Telotte, J. P. "The Doubles of Fantasy and the Space of Desire." In *Alien Zone: Cultural Theory and Contemporary Science Fiction Film*. Edited by Annette Kuhn, 152–59. London: Verso, 1990.

Thacker, Eugene. *In the Dust of This Planet. Horror of Philosophy*, volume 1. Winchester, UK: Zero Books, 2011.

———. *Starry Speculative Corpse. Horror of Philosophy*, volume 2. Winchester, UK: Zero Books, 2015.

———. *Tentacles Longer Than Night. Horror of Philosophy*, volume 3. Winchester, UK: Zero Books, 2015.

Thomas, Jonathan. "The King of Cat Swamp." In *Black Wings of Cthulhu 2: Eighteen New Tales of Lovecraftian Horror*. Edited by S. T. Joshi, 85–105. London: Titan Books, 2014.

Thomas, Keith. *Religion and the Decline of Magic: Studies in Popular Beliefs in Sixteenth- and Seventeenth-Century England*. New York: Penguin Books, 1971.

Thompson, Jason. *Manga: The Complete Guide*. New York: Del Rey Books, 2007.

Tillich, Paul. *Dynamics of Faith*. New York: Perennial Classics, 1957.

Tinee, Mae [pseud.]. "Monster ape in N.Y. Setting packs thrills in new talkie." *Chicago Daily Tribune* (April 23, 1933): SC1.

Tisdale, Sallie. "Talk Dirty to Me: A Woman's Taste for Pornography." *Harper's* (February 1992): 37–46.

Tovar, Lupita. "Introduction to the Spanish Version." Disc 4. *Dracula: Complete Legacy Collection*. DVD. Universal Pictures, 2004.

Tremelin, Todd. *Minds and Gods: The Cognitive Foundations of Religion*. Oxford: Oxford University Press, 2006.

Truzzi, Marcello. "Editorial." *Zetetic Scholar* 1, no. 1 (1978): 2, 34.

Tsutsui, William M. *Godzilla on My Mind: Fifty Years of the King of Monsters*. New York: Palgrave Macmillan, 2004.

———. *Japanese Popular Culture and Globalization*. Ann Arbor, MI: Association for Asian Studies, 2010.

Tsutsui, William M., and Michiko Ito, eds. *In Godzilla's Footsteps: Japanese Pop Culture Icons on the Global Stage*. New York: Palgrave Macmillan, 2006.

Tucker, Phil, dir. *Robot Monster*. Written by Wyatt Ordung. Three Dimension Pictures, 1953.

Tudor, Andrew. *Monsters and Mad Scientists: A Cultural History of the Horror Film*. London: Blackwell, 1989.

Turner, Victor. *Forest of Symbols: Aspects of Ndembu Ritual*. Ithaca, NY: Cornell University Press, 1967.

———. *The Ritual Process: Structure and Anti-Structure*. New York: Routledge, 1969.

Tutuolo, Amos. *My Life in the Bush of Ghosts*. 1954. Reprint. London: Faber & Faber, 2014.

Typewriter. Created and produced by Sujoy Ghosh. Sujoy Ghosh Studios, 2019.

Tyson, Donald. *Alhazred*. Woodbury, MN: Llewellyn Publications, 2005.

———. *The Dream World of H. P. Lovecraft: His Life, His Demons, His Universe*. Woodbury, MN: Llewellyn Publications, 2010.

———. *Grimoire of the Necronomicon*. Woodbury, MN: Llewellyn Publications, 2008.

———. "*The Necronomicon*: Shadow in the Mind." In *The Necronomicon Files: The Truth behind Lovecraft's Legend*, by Daniel Harms and John Wisdom Gonce III, ix–xiv. Rev. ed. Boston: Weiser Books, 2003.

———. *Necronomicon: Wanderings of Alhazred*. Woodbury, MN: Llewellyn Publications, 2004.

———. *Secrets of the Necronomicon*. Woodbury, MN: Llewellyn Publications, 2007.

———. "The Skinless Face." In *Black Wings of Cthulhu 2: Eighteen New Tales of Lovecraftian Horror*. Edited by S. T. Joshi, 317–51. London: Titan Books, 2014.

———. *The 13 Gates of the Necronomicon: A Workbook of Magic*. Woodbury, MN: Llewellyn Publications, 2010.

Tyson, Donald, and Anne Stokes. *Necronomicon Tarot*. Woodbury, MN: Llewellyn Publications, 2007.

Ulmer, Edgar G., dir. *Daughter of Dr. Jekyll*. Written by Jack Pollexfen. Film Ventures, 1957.

Urban, Hugh B. *Magia Sexualis: Sex, Magic, and Liberation in Western Esotericism*. Berkeley: University of California Press, 2006.

———. *Tantra: Sex, Secrecy, and Power in the Study of Religion*. Berkeley: University of California Press, 2003.

Vallée, Jacques. *Dimensions: A Casebook of Alien Contact*. New York: Ballantine Books, 1988.

———. *The Invisible College: What a Group of Scientists Has Discovered about UFO Influences on the Human Race*. New York: Dutton, 1975.

———. *Messengers of Deception: UFO Contact and Cults*. San Francisco: And/Or Press, 1979.

Vanderburgh, George A., and Robert E. Weinberg. "Introduction." In *The Horror on the Links: The Complete Tales of Jules de Grandin, Volume One*. Edited by George A. Vanderburgh, vii–xii. New York: Night Shade Books, 2017.

Van Hollander, James. 2010. "Susie." In *Black Wings of Cthulhu: Twenty-One New Tales of Lovecraftian Horror*. Edited by S. T. Joshi, 497–505. London: Titan Books, 2012.

Verbinski, Gore, dir. *The Ring*. Written by Ehren Kruger. MacDonald/Parkes Productions, 2002.

Verduin, Kathleen. "'Our Cursed Natures': Sexuality and the Puritan Conscience." *New England Quarterly* 56 no. 2 (1983): 220–37.

Vogel, Virgil, dir. *The Mole People*. Written by László Görög. Universal International Pictures, 1956.

Vogler, Christopher. *The Writer's Journey: Mythic Structure for Writers*. 3rd ed. Studio City, CA: Michael Wiese, 2007.

Vogt-Roberts, Jordan, dir. *Kong: Skull Island*. Written by Dan Gilroy, Max Borenstein, and Derek Connelly. Warner Bros., 2017.

Vout, Caroline. *Sex on Show: Seeing the Erotic in Greece and Rome*. Berkeley: University of California Press, 2013.

Waggner, George, dir. *Man-Made Monster*. Written by Joseph West. Universal Pictures, 1941.

———, dir. *The Wolf Man*. Written by Curt Siodmak. Universal Pictures, 1941.

Wainwright, Rupert, dir. *Stigmata*. Written by Tom Lazarus and Rick Ramage. FGM Entertainment, 1999.

Webb, Don. "The Megalith Plague." In *Black Wings of Cthulhu 3: Seventeen Tales of Lovecraftian Horror*. Edited by S. T. Joshi, 207–22. London: Titan Books, 2015.

Weinberg, Robert. *A Biographical Dictionary of Science Fiction and Fantasy Artists*. New York: Greenwood, 1988.

———. "Brundage, Margaret (1900–1976)." In *The Penguin Encyclopedia of Horror and the Supernatural*. Edited by Jack Sullivan, 61. New York: Viking, 1986.

———. "Illustration." In *The Penguin Encyclopedia of Horror and the Supernatural*. Edited by Jack Sullivan, 215–19. New York: Viking, 1986.

———. *The "Weird Tales" Story.* 1977. Reprint. Berkeley Heights, NJ: Wildside Press, 1999.

Weinberg, Steven. *Facing Up: Science and Its Cultural Adversaries.* Cambridge, MA: Harvard University Press, 2001.

Weitzer, Ronald. *Sex for Sale: Prostitution, Pornography, and the Sex Industry.* 2nd ed. New York: Routledge, 2010.

Welsh, Andrew. "On the Perils of Living Dangerously in the Slasher Horror Film: Gender Differences in the Association between Sexual Activity and Survival." *Sex Roles* 62, no. 11/12 (2010): 762–73.

———. "Sex and Violence in the Slasher Horror Film: A Content Analysis of Gender Differences in the Depiction of Violence." *Journal of Criminal Justice and Popular Culture* 16, no. 1 (2009): 1–25.

Westbrook, Bruce. "Retro Chill Factor: Japanese Film Takes the Boo out of a Twisted Monster Tale." *Houston Chronicle* (September 10, 2004): Star, 3.

Whale, James, dir. *Frankenstein.* Written by Garrett Fort and Francis James Faragoh. Universal Pictures, 1931.

———, dir. *The Invisible Man.* Written by R. C. Sherriff. Universal Pictures, 1933.

White, Wrath James. *Horrible Gods: The Little Book of Atheist Horror Stories.* Austin, TX: Sinister Grin Press, 2014.

Whitehouse, Harvey. "Terror." In *The Oxford Handbook of Religion and Emotion.* Edited by John Corrigan, 259–75. New York: Oxford University Press, 2008.

Whitney, Louisa Goddard. *The Burning of the Convent: A Narrative of the Destruction by a Mob of the Ursuline School on Mount Benedict, Charlestown, as Remembered by One of the Pupils.* Boston: A. R. Good, 1877.

Wilcox, Fred M., dir. *Forbidden Planet.* Written by Cyril Hume. Metro-Goldwyn-Mayer, 1956.

Williams, Kate, dir. *Pornography: A Secret History of Civilization.* "Road to Ruin: Antiquity." Channel 4 Television (UK). October 14, 1999.

Williams, Miriam. *Heaven's Harlots: My Fifteen Years as a Sacred Prostitute in the Children of God Cult.* New York: William Morrow, 1998.

Williams, Sara. "'The Power of Christ Compels You': Holy Water, Hysteria, and the Oedipal Psychodrama in *The Exorcist.*" *Literature Interpretation Theory* 22, no. 3 (2011): 218–38.

Wilson, Jeff. *Mourning the Unborn Dead: American Uses of Japanese Post-Abortion Rituals.* New York: Oxford University Press, 2008.

Wingrove, Nigel, dir. *Sacred Flesh.* Written by Nigel Wingrove. Heretic Films (II), 2000.

Winkelman, Michael. "Aztec Human Sacrifice: Cross-Cultural Assessments of the Ecological Hypothesis." *Ethnology* 37, no. 3 (1998): 285–98.

Winner, Lauren. *Real Sex: The Naked Truth about Chastity.* Grand Rapids, MI: Brazos Press, 2005.

Winter, Douglas E. *Faces of Fear: Encounters with the Creators of Modern Horror.* New York: Berkeley Books, 1985.

Wise, Robert, dir. *The Day the Earth Stood Still*. Written by Edmund H. North. Twentieth Century Fox, 1951.

Wiseman, Len, dir. *Underworld*. Written by Danny McBride. Lakeshore Entertainment, 2003.

Witherington, Ben, III. *The Gospel Code: Novel Claims about Jesus, Mary Magdalene, and Da Vinci*. Downers Grove, IL: InterVarsity Press, 2004.

Wood, Ghislaine. *Art Nouveau and the Erotic*. New York: Harry N. Abrams, 2000.

Wood, Ralph C. *The Gospel according to Tolkien: Visions of the Kingdom in Middle-Earth*. Louisville, KY: Westminster John Knox Press, 2003.

Wyndham, John. *The Chrysalids*. New York: Penguin Putnam, 1955.

Wynorski, Jim, dir. *Vampirella*. Written by Forrest J. Ackerman. Cinetel Films, 1996.

Zarchi, Meir, dir. *I Spit on Your Grave*. Written by Meir Zarchi. Cinemagic Pictures, 1978.

Zeller, Benjamin. *Heaven's Gate: America's UFO Religion*. New York: NYU Press, 2014.

Zika, Charles. "The Witch and Magician in European Art." In *The Oxford Illustrated History of Witchcraft and Magic*. Edited by Owen Davies, 134–66. Oxford: Oxford University Press, 2017.

Zillman, Dolf, and James B. Weaver III. "Gender-Socialization Theory of Reactions to Horror." In *Horror Films: Current Research on Audience Preferences and Reactions*. Edited by James B. Weaver III and Ron Tamborini, 81–101. Mahwah, NJ: Erlbaum, 1996.

Zipes, Jack. *Breaking the Magic Spell: Radical Theories of Folk and Fairy Tales*. Rev. ed. Lexington: University of Kentucky Press, 2002.

——. *Fairy Tales and the Art of Subversion*. 2nd ed. New York: Routledge, 2006.

——. *The Irresistible Fairy Tale: The Cultural and Social History of a Genre*. Princeton, NJ: Princeton University Press, 2012.

——. *Why Fairy Tales Stick: The Evolution and Relevance of a Genre*. New York: Routledge, 2006.

Zorkóczy, István, dir. *Love, Death, and Robots*. "The Secret War." Volume 1, episode 18. Written by Philip Gelatt. Netflix, March 15, 2019.

INDEX

Alexander, Brooks, 154

allegory, 7, 22, 30, 231, 260n117. *See also* enigma; metaphor; riddle

Alien (Scott), 2, 8

"Altar of Melek Taos, The" (Pendarves), 99–100, 102

ambiguity and ambivalence, 4, 15–17, 38, 41, 45, 47, 87, 94–95, 111, 139, 141, 166, 180, 186

Amendola, David, 79; "The Secret War," 79, 81

American Horror Story, 2, 32

Apparitions (Scanlon), 172–79; racism in, 175–76; sexism in, 174–75

apostasy, 10, 52, 227–28; apostate testimony, 125

Applewhite, Marshall Herff, 187

approbation bias, 52–52. *See also* good, moral, and decent fallacy

arousal and arousal cuing, 3, 8, 62–63, 73, 77, 111, 134, 168, 176, 245n87

Attack of the Crab Monsters (Corman), 54–55, 57, 58, 59, 63, 65–66

Attack of the Giant Leeches (Corman), 66–71, 177

Augustine, 9, 123, 134

availability heuristic, 13, 91, 248n52. *See also* source dissociation

Awakening, The (Murphy), 45

Awful Disclosures of Maria Monk (Monk), 129–34, 136–37; controversy over, 135–37; infanticide in, 130–31

Baker, Tim, 154

Baldung Grien, Hans, 139, 144–47; *The Witches*, 139, 145

Ballivet, Suzanne, 119

Bara, Theda, 46, 77, 241n82

Barker, Clive, 32, 42, 47, 53, 169; *Hellraiser*, 41–42, 43, 122, 170, 182; *The Hellbound Heart*, 32, 43; "Jacqueline Ess: Her Will and Testament," 24–25, 167–72; *The Scarlet Gospels*, 32

Barner-Barry, Carol, 155–56

Barreiro, Ricardo, 110, 119; *The Convent of Hell*, 110, 111–14

Barzun, Jacques, 44

Bataille, Georges, 119

Beal, Timothy, ix.

Bécat, Paul-Émile, 119

Beiser, Frederick, 206

Beit-Hallahmi, Benjamin, 29–30, 172

Bell, Book, and Candle (Quine), 150–51

Benshoff, Harry, 229

Berger, Peter, 60, 146, 191–92, 218

bias, 71, 125, 248n52; approbation, 51, 83; confirmation, 87; Western, 19–20. *See also* racism; colonialism

Black, Gregory D., 61, 244n30

"Black Ships Seen South of Heaven" (Kiernan), 197–99, 202, 220

Blair, Linda, 27–29. See also *The Exorcist* (Friedkin)

Blanchard, David, 165–66

Blatty, William Peter, 27–28, 43, 47. See also *The Exorcist* (Blatty)

305

ABOUT THE AUTHOR

Douglas E. Cowan is Professor of Religious Studies and Social Development Studies at Renison University College and author of *America's Dark Theologian: The Religious Imagination of Stephen King* and *Sacred Terror: Religion and Horror on the Silver Screen*. He lives in Waterloo, Ontario, Canada.